St Jarlath's College, Tuam
1800-2000

St Jarlath's College
Tuam
1800-2000

JOHN CUNNINGHAM

SJC Publications • Tuam

Published in Ireland by SJC Publications,
St Jarlath's College,
Tuam,
Co Galway

© John Cunningham, 1999

All rights reserved. No part of this publication may be reproduced, stored in a retrieval system, or transmitted in any form or by any means, without the prior permission of SJC Publications. Exceptions are allowed in respect of any fair dealing for the purpose of research, study, criticism or review.

*

The book is sold subject to the condition that it shall not, by way of trade or otherwise, be lent, re-sold, hired-out, or otherwise circulated, in any form of binding other than that in which it is published, without the permission of SJC Publishing

ISBN 0 9536978 0 0

Cover by Proactive Design, Mayoralty House, Galway

Printed for SJC Publications by
Colour Books, Unit 105, Baldoyle Industrial Estate, Dublin 13

Acknowledgements

I wish to thank those who helped in different ways during the two years that it has taken to write this book. Inevitably, some of their names will be omitted in the following. For that, I apologise.

First of all, I thank the members of the bicentenary committee of the Past Pupils Union, in particular the College President, Canon Oliver Hughes, and Michael Marren, for entrusting me with the project. Secondly, I thank the staff of St Jarlath's for their hospitality, their warmth and their active assistance during my many visits to the College archive.

Professor Gearóid Ó Tuathaigh was always generous with reassurance and with constructive advice. Alf MacLochlainn, too, gave valuable assistance at different times. Welcome suggestions regarding source material were received from Liam Bane, Tony Claffey, Padraig Ó Tuairisg, Fr Ciaran Waldron, Fr Seán Higgins, Professor Patrick Corish, Mary Clancy, Mary Kierce and Maurice Laheen. Fr Fintan Monahan, Charles Kelly and Fr Michael Molloy worked hard to assemble and select photographs, while information on football, on the opera and on PPU presidents for appendices was assembled by Fr Tod Nolan, Mr Joe Donoghue and Dónal Blake.

I am grateful too to the past students who agreed to be interviewed: John Fitzgerald, Padraig Folan, Conor Heaney, Tommy Heraty, Oliver Hughes, Jim Kearns, Liam Kitt, Paddy McMyler, Jack Mahon, Tod Nolan, Tommy Shannon and Paddy Williams.

I must also thank the directors and staff of the various archives and libraries where research was carried out. I am grateful to Dr Michael Neary for granting me access to the Tuam Diocesan Archives and to Fr Brendan Kilcoyne who facilitated my work there —and sometimes assisted with research. Thanks also to Mr Sheehy of the Dublin Diocesan Archive; to Mr Maye of the Galway Diocesan Archive; and to Fr Quinn who allowed me to consult the Tuam Parish records. The staffs of the both the James Hardiman Library at NUI, Galway, and of the Galway County Library at Island House, whom I have known for many years, were extremely helpful as they always have been. My gratitude also to staff at the Mayo County Library in Castlebar, at the National Library and at the National Archive.

Katie Cunningham and Liam Cunningham have asked that their co-operation be acknowledged. I acknowledge it. Finally, I would like to thank Mary Cunningham for her patience and affectionate support, especially during the last few busy months.

John Cunningham
26 October 1999

Introduction

In 1843 John Kells Ingram, in his poem *The Memory of the Dead*, asked the rhetorical question, 'Who fears to speak of Ninety-Eight?' In the years immediately following the bloody rebellion of 1798 there were many in Ireland who would have been reluctant, if not fearful, to speak of the rebellion which had resulted in the violent deaths of some 30,000 people. The respectable classes in general, including the Catholic bishops and the leaders of Catholic middle-class opinion, had been terrified not only by the violence of the rebellion itself and by the threat it seemed to pose to all established order and authority, but also by the ruthless violence with which it had been suppressed. Traumatised by the spectre of anarchy, the leaders of opinion in Ireland were now prepared to see the Irish parliament in Dublin abolished and Ireland joined with Britain by the Act of Union into a single constitutional and political entity.

On the face of it, these may not seem the most promising circumstances in which to establish a Catholic diocesan college which was to become, in various ways, a great national institution during the next two hundred years. Yet, despite the widespread sense of trauma and fear which prevailed in the aftermath of the 1798 rebellion, the general confidence of Catholics in Ireland had been growing in the second half of the eighteenth century. The gradual dismantling of the Penal Code of laws, which since the 1690s had comprehensively discriminated against Catholics, had begun in the middle decades of the eighteenth century and had been gathering momentum from the late 1770s. Catholics were re-emerging into the civil and political life of the country. They were gradually being permitted to secure land and to enter the higher professions. Catholic educational institutions were being founded in the closing decade of the eighteenth century. Indeed, such was the political excitement of the early 1790s, with Britain at war with revolutionary France, that the British government of the day deemed it expedient to found a major Catholic seminary at Maynooth, in a bid to placate middle-class Catholic opinion in Ireland, the Catholic bishops in particular.

Thus, the founding of St Jarlath's College may be seen as a milestone in the emergence of Irish Catholics from the shadow of discrimination and exclusion, and as a promise of the remarkable expansion of the institutional framework of Irish Catholicism during the nineteenth and early twentieth centuries. New religious and charitable foundations; new religious orders and lay societies; and an impressive record of overseas missionary activity: these were key features of the expansionist role of Irish Catholicism from the early nineteenth century to the 1950s. The large diocesan colleges were the corner-stones of the institutional structure which sustained this remarkable growth in the influence and authority of the Catholic Church in Ireland from the early nineteenth century.

As educational institutions, the Irish diocesan colleges reflected the values and the ideas (about education itself, discipline, social roles, political sentiment) of the largely farming and country-town communities whose sons provided both the students and the staff of the colleges. St Jarlath's, as John Cunningham's excellent study now demonstrates, has been a major force in the educational, social and cultural life of Connacht, and indeed of Ireland as a whole, during the past two centuries. It has played a pivotal educational role in the west, a province noted for the difficult economic and social challenges it has faced in many periods during the past two centuries, but noted also for the inspiring and sometimes controversial leadership it has provided in ecclesiastical as well as in political organisations.

This study brings to life the human story, as well as all the key institutional developments, of St.Jarlath's. The cultural and sporting reputation of the college, together with its academic record, are carefully and affectionately chronicled and analysed. In particular, the constant challenge of change, particularly in recent decades, is a key theme in this rich and absorbing account of a great educational institution which has served its pupils, its province and its country well during the past two centuries.

Professor Gearóid Ó Tuathaigh.

Table of contents

Introduction	by Professor Gearóid Ó Tuathaigh	
Chapter 1	"…boys educated along the best possible lines."	1
Chapter 2	"…a fit and proper person."	7
Chapter 3	"… respectable appearance and remarkable propriety."	28
Chapter 4	"…with suitable breadth and proportion."	51
Chapter 5	"A cheerful aspect to proceedings…"	70
Chapter 6	"Another roar from St Jarlath's."	88
Chapter 7	"In those Intermediate times…"	128
Chapter 8	"…an exemplary boy, but he cannot live on air."	147
Chapter 9	"…uniform observance of rule."	165
Chapter 10	"…four was normal, six was considered a bit much…"	181
Chapter 11	"…football is life…"	202
Chapter 12	"…a tendency to make the best of our life here."	232
Appendices		265
Bibliography		274
Index		288

1. "...boys educated along the best possible lines."

> *We, sons of fathers, who through ages grim*
> *Held bleeding on to hope, now see their dreams*
> *Fulfilled, and may, tho' Europe's lamp grows dim*
> *Pursue the flame of learning where it gleams*
> *As once before, when Jarlath's wheel was broke,*
> *Bright gleamed our Age of Gold, though all abroad*
> *The Roman eagle sank 'mid havoc's smoke*
> *And bloodstained Vandal prowled the Caesars' road*
> *'Mid howling waste, once more our peace is willed,*
> *God's mighty wheel its cycle has fulfilled.*[1]

Bicentenary histories sometimes begin by reflecting on the circumstances surrounding the centenary commemorations. To what extent had the institution consolidated itself after one hundred years? Was it still fulfilling its original mission?

But there was no stocktaking in St Jarlath's in 1900, as the College's patron, Dr John MacEvilly, entered his eighty-fifth year and his seventy-second year of close association with the College, during which he had been student, professor, president and ultimately archbishop and patron.

And, notwithstanding the intimate involvement of one with a personal perspective on the College's early history, there was no discernible awareness that a significant milestone had been reached. It is true that anniversaries were not as readily or as thoroughly celebrated one hundred years ago as they are today, but there were two well-marked centenaries in the closing years of the nineteenth century which might have inspired imitation in Tuam — these were the Maynooth centenary of 1895 and the '98 commemorations three years later.

The fact was that 1800 was not then regarded as the College's founding date. Most of those who thought about the matter at all dated the modern College's origins to the moment when it first occupied the building known as the 'Old College', the former Ffrench's Bank premises in Bishop Street. This occurred early in 1817, so centenary celebrations might have been anticipated for 1917.

---

1. From 'A Sonnet' dedicated to the Leaving Certificate Class of 1941 (*Iarlaith*, 1957, p111).

Such a comparatively modern vintage was not at all to the taste of antiquarians. One such, Richard J. Kelly — owner of the *Herald*, a founder member of the Galway Archaeological and Historical Society and an expert on the history of North Galway — was the author of the 1896 work on the history of St Jarlath's which was probably considered definitive in 1900. He went back much further in time in search of the College's origins, to the earliest Christian foundation in Tuam. After recounting the legendary advice given by St Brendan to St Jarlath — to set out on a journey eastwards and to establish a monastery at the location where his carriage-wheel broke — he continued: 'This was the foundation of the College of Tuam, sometime about the early part of the sixth century, as Jarlath is believed to have died about the year AD 540 at the advanced age of 90 years.' Then, according to Kelly, the College was 're-established in 1814 after the long dark night of persecution and proscription had passed away.'[1] One senses that this version of the story would have appealed to the romantically nationalistic Archbishop John MacHale, patron from 1834 to 1881 and the dominant figure in the College's nineteenth century history.

It was 1906 before the date now accepted for the foundation of the College was first widely mooted. This was in the first substantial history of the College, written by lay professor, Frank Guy, and published over eight issues in the *Irish Catholic* during the winter of 1906 and the spring of 1907. Guy's account of the founding of St Jarlath's was as follows:

> In the year 1800 then Dr Dillon [the then archbishop] sent the Rev. Oliver Kelly to the Protestant archbishop of Tuam, Dr Beresford, for the requisite permission to open in Tuam a preparatory school for Maynooth... The humble institution he opened on the Mall, Tuam, soon merged into another and more commodious one, which has gone on with the passing years, lengthening its bonds and strengthening its stakes...'[2]

1. *Tuam Herald*, 24 October 1896.
2. ibid., 24 November 1906. The *Irish Catholic* articles were reprinted in the *Herald* and the *Western People:* they will be cited as Guy's History, pt.i - pt.viii. Guy drew on unpublished research in the Feeney papers which were held in the College. His series ended abruptly, indicating that he may have inadvertently caused offence. This was easily done: in 1896 Richard J. Kelly felt obliged to subsequently publish an addendum to his history: "In our account of St Jarlath's College, we forgot to mention the munificence of our present Archbishop... He has established seven free places in St Jarlath's College for ecclesiastical students... Dr Kelly may have founded St Jarlath's College, but Dr MacEvilly has secured it." (*Tuam Herald*, 7 November 1896).

Subsequent versions of the College's history have accepted 1800 as the founding date. Influential in copper-fastening the orthodoxy on the matter was an article prepared by 'A.P.N.' in 1933 — with the acknowledged and active assistance of the then president, Monsignor Joseph Walsh — which was reprinted at least once.[1] Two decades later, in an article prepared for the first issue of the Past Pupil's Union journal, Rev. P.V. O'Brien tentatively suggested that there might have been a diocesan college in Tuam in the late 1790s, before allowing that 'the first official College of St Jarlath' was founded in 1800.[2]

If the College's centenary passed by unnoticed, this was not permitted to happen with the 150th anniversary, when the patron was former president, Joseph Walsh. In October 1947, well in advance of the sesquicentenary, he addressed a special pastoral letter to the people of his diocese, assessing the contribution of the College before seeking financial contributions towards the building of an extension which would mark the anniversary.

> May I point out a fact which can be easily forgotten? The Diocesan College is very closely bound up with Catholic life and culture of the whole diocese. It was established to give the best possible education to boys of every class, and that aim has never been overlooked. Even those parents who are not blessed with great means can take advantage of the College burses and scholarships and in that way have their boys educated along the best possible lines. One can safely say that no college in Ireland can point to a history more interesting or honourable than St Jarlath's. Hundreds of her students have gone forth as priests: they have dared and suffered everything for the love of Christ. In spite of oceans and deserts they are to be found everywhere — amid the sands of Africa, in the rice-fields of China, in the cities and hinder-lands of America and Australia, always keeping up the highest standards of the Catholic priesthood, always bringing honour to their own College

---

1. A.P.N. 'Notes on the School of St Jarlath' in *Connacht Tribune*, 18 February 1933; SJC, Correspondence between Joseph S. Walsh and Louis B. Roche, National Library, 31 May, 8 June 1932. The article was reprinted in 1939 in the Souvenir Programme for Jubilee Celebrations of the Pioneer Total Abstinence Association, held in Tuam (pp.30-37).
2. Rev. Patrick V. O'Brien, 'Pages from the history of St Jarlath's College' in *Iarlaith*, 1955, pp.83-91.

Not less honourable nor less religious are their class-fellows who chose a secular career. They too are to be found in many different places, in diverse walks of life: and everywhere their material success, their fine Catholic spirit testify to the excellence of the training they have received. So we can claim that the College has always maintained the ideals of its founder, and has exercised a big influence in forming the character and shaping the destinies of our people.[1]

The substantial response to the appeal from parishes throughout the diocese indicates that Dr Walsh's positive assessment of the College's contribution was widely shared. There was support too from a more impartial source for his assertions about the quality of education in St Jarlath's. In the period before the publication of the pastoral, the reports of Department of Education Inspectors were uniformly positive in tone, with evidence that suggestions for minor improvements were immediately embraced by the College authorities. Such was the background to the reference to the purchase of maps in the following report by the far-from-acerbic Mr Bithery:

Latin, Greek and English are taught by a strong staff of highly qualified and energetic teachers. The appointment of an additional teacher has made it possible to grade the senior pupils more finely and the results of this are certain to be highly satisfactory. Two new tennis courts have been constructed for all the year use, and a number of new pictures and maps have been hung in the halls and corridors at very considerable expense but to the very great advantage of teachers and students.

A splendid spirit prevails throughout the College and the prospects for the success of the school year 1933-34 are very bright indeed.[2]

However, there were some dissenters. One was a former student of the College, living in London, who was provoked into putting pen to paper by an appeal for greater state-funding for Catholic

---

1. Tuam Diocesan archive, *Pastoral letter to the clergy and laity of the archdiocese of Tuam, to be read Sunday, 13 October 1946.*
2. SJC, Inspectors' Reports file, report for head of school on classes inspected by Mr J. Bithery.

Colleges issued by Archbishop Walsh in 1951. Under the pen-name 'Justitia' he sent a long letter to the editor of the *Connacht Tribune* criticising the education he received in the College and making some more general points about the clerically-dominated secondary education system in Ireland. Before the letter could be published, however, it was intercepted by a zealous staff member at the *Tribune* and passed on to the College authorities. The writer clearly had a chip on his shoulder — perhaps he had a grudge against Dr Walsh. Moreover, he had a rose-tinted view of the British educational system and a somewhat out-of-date impression of the situation in Ireland in general, and in Tuam in particular. Nevertheless his remarks are worth quoting for a contrary view:

> I have read the press report of the recent appeal by the Archbishop of Tuam for further state-aid for his "College" and as an Old Boy of St Jarlath's, who sampled all the intellectual fare served out by its "professors", I was somewhat amused by His Grace's reference to the sons of "poor" parents receiving education of the "highest class" in his seminary, where, as is common knowledge, only children of well-to-do farmers, teachers, and merchants are boarders. The sons of poor parents in the archdiocese save those within easy reach of a few secondary schools in some of the towns have to be content with primary education. In Great Britain, on the other hand, free secondary education coupled with concessions as regards meals and transport is available for all pupils.
>
> ...The archbishop's allusion to the "highest class" of education provided in St Jarlath's College sounds very piquant to me who went through that mill. I never saw a play or opera staged by or for the students. There was no instruction whatever in botany, art, metalwork, woodwork, physical training, French, German, Honours Mathematics. The ancient classics (in which St Jarlath's stood supreme) were considered as the peak of learning and a more than adequate compensation for the neglected subjects. About 18% of the candidates of the entire country offered Greek at the public examinations: exhibitions were easy to win — and so the admiration of an undiscriminating public — by means of the ancient classics!
>
> ...The truth is that the curriculum of the "college" was

arranged to suit the minority of "students" who intended to proceed to Holy Orders, though of course the parents in general paid the cost.[1]

If the roughly contemporaneous statements of 'Justitia' and of Dr Walsh appear to contradict one another, the differences can be explained in terms of the contrasting perspectives of the two men. 'Justitia' (was he conscious of the irony in drawing his pen-name from the classics?) was evidently a confirmed secularist and modernist. Consequently, he remembered only the hours wasted in what for him was the pointless study of Latin and Greek. But for Dr Walsh, these languages did indeed represent 'the peak of learning'.

Nor would the archbishop have disputed that St Jarlath's was 'arranged' to suit clerical students. His sesquicentenary appeal, after all, emphasised that the College had been established to educate boys for the priesthood and that it was still successfully pursuing this objective. And, as for the education of 'poor' boys, Dr Walsh knew that, in an underfunded educational system, between a quarter and a third of St Jarlath' students were being supported, to a greater or a lesser degree, by various foundations associated with the College. Such subsidies, no doubt, appeared inadequate, uneven and arbitrary from the vantage point of the British post-war welfare state, but they had enabled many 'bright' west of Ireland boys who couldn't otherwise have afforded it, to receive a secondary education.

---

1. Tuam Diocesan archives, Letter of 'Past student', 11 February 1952.

2. "... a fit and proper person."

No vicar superior e'er flourished in Rome,
So boundless his virtue, so spotless his mind,
That he as a right takes the lead in our church
And straightway may leave the dull Dean in the lurch.[1]

In 1800, shortly after leaving the Irish College at Salamanca and soon after ordination, twenty-three year old Oliver Kelly returned to his native diocese of Tuam. During his absence in Spain, the world had been shaken by the fallout from the French revolution. And not least among the institutions rocked by the political storms of the 1790s was the Catholic Church in Ireland.

That Kelly showed academic promise in Salamanca is indicated by his having spent a while teaching philosophy in the Irish College before his return. Evidently, his reputation preceded him and, on arrival in Tuam, the young priest was assigned two important duties by Archbishop Edward Dillon: he was given responsibility for Tuam parish and was charged with establishing a new educational institution in the town, described as 'a preparatory school for the Royal College of St Patrick, Maynooth.' This latter appointment was confirmed on 17 October 1800 by Tuam's Protestant archbishop, Dr Beresford, who stated that the young priest was 'a fit and proper person to keep a preparatory school.' The permit to operate the school came with the condition that 'you continue to behave yourself well, and to discharge your duty with propriety..., having first taken the oath of allegiance...'[2] Thus was St Jarlath's College founded.

The involvement of the protestant archbishop in the establishment of a Roman Catholic seminary was due to a provision of the Relief Bill passed by the Irish parliament in 1782. This legislation had eased penal restrictions, enabling Catholics to legally send their children abroad for education and allowing the establishment of Catholic schools at home — but under certain

---

1. Pat O'Kelly, from *The Eudoxologist or an Ethnographical Study of the western parts of Ireland*, 1812. The 'vicar superior' was the poet's namesake, Oliver Kelly, the 'dull Dean' was Boetius Egan.
2. SJC, Feeney papers, Beresford letter; M. Coen, 'The choosing of Oliver Kelly for the See of Tuam,' JGAHS 36, p.18; P. Ó Tuairisg, 'Faisnéis faoi Oilibhéar Ó Ceallaigh,' *Galvia* 12, pp.46-47.

conditions. One of these conditions was that Catholic schoolmasters should function under licence from local Church of Ireland bishops who, as senior officials of the state church, historically had responsibility for education in their dioceses. There was a degree of uncertainty as to whether this requirement remained in force following the further relaxation of 1792, but legislation of 1799 offered partial exemption from window tax on school buildings used by licensed schoolmasters.[1] The financial saving involved would have probably been incentive enough to comply with the formalities, but for Dr Dillon the need to demonstrate the loyalty of Connacht Catholics in the fraught aftermath of 'The Year of the French' would also have been an important consideration.

The establishment of a diocesan college in Tuam had been considered for some time, probably since the Relief Act of 1782. Soon after that date, a college was opened in Kilkenny[2] and, in 1789, the first diocesan college in the Province of Tuam, when Athlone's new Canal School announced that it was 'under the immediate inspection' of the Catholic bishop of Elphin. The decision to open the Athlone seminary had been taken a few years earlier at a meeting of the bishops of the Tuam province.[3] By St Patrick's Day 1791, according to the surviving correspondence of a prominent priest of the diocese, it was 'in contemplation to establish a Roman Catholic diocesan school in Tuam.' That the preparations were well advanced is indicated in a letter sent a few months earlier by the then archbishop of Tuam,

---

1. Peter Birch, *St Kieran's College, Kilkenny*, 1951, pp.7-8.
2. Incidentally, Dr Beresford, who issued the licence for St Jarlath's, was bishop of Ossory when 'the earliest Catholic College in the Kingdom' was established there at Kilkenny in 1782 (Birch pp.22-23). He succeeded to Tuam and Ardagh in 1794 and was created Baron Decies in 1812. Following his death in 1819 the Church of Ireland archdiocese of Tuam was reduced to a diocese and was separated from the diocese of Ardagh. Beresford was buried at Curraghmore, Co Waterford, his family's seat.
3. John Brady, *Catholics and Catholicism in the eighteenth century press,,* 1965, pp.247, 264-65. A few years later a newspaper observed: 'The establishment of the Roman Catholic seminary at Athlone has been attended with very beneficial consequences to society; here many youths have acquired a liberal and virtuous education, who must otherwise have remained in a state of uncultivated ignorance, from the incapacity of their parents to defray the necessary expenses of a foreign education —and the impossibility of procuring it elsewhere in this Kingdom, upon that enlarged scale which has been so happily introduced into this newly instituted seminary' (ibid., pp.281-82).

Boetius Egan, to his Dublin counterpart inquiring whether 'the clause obliging Roman Catholics to obtain a licence from the Protestant bishop to teach public schools has been repealed last session.'[1]

Two years later, a meeting of Irish bishops resolved that

> diocesan schools... be promoted in each diocese; that thence the students may be sent to provincial seminaries; and that those who are most distinguished... to be sent... to the National House hereafter to be established.[2]

The meeting considered in detail how these plans might be financed, before deciding that donations should be sought from 'the most opulent of the laity' to augment the income from levies of 'at least one guinea' a year on each parish priest and ten guineas on each bishop — 'if he can afford it.'[3]

In planning for a national network of colleges and seminaries, the Irish bishops were very belatedly setting out to implement an important decree of the Council of Trent. That Council, which was called by Pope Paul III and sat between 1545 and 1563, put in place significant doctrinal and disciplinary reforms in the Catholic Church, enabling it to face the challenge of the Reformation. The calibre of their clergy — the front-line troops of the Counter-Reformation — was among the principal concerns of the assembled ecclesiastics and it was recognised that this could not be improved without improving the quality of the education available to students for the priesthood. Accordingly, it was decided that a seminary, or cathedral school, should be established in each diocese under the direction of the local bishop. But because of the political situation in the country, in particular the restrictions on Catholic education, more than two centuries would pass before the implementation of this decree could be realistically considered in Ireland.[4]

In the meantime, candidates for the Irish priesthood received their education illegally: elementary education in so-called

---

1. Galway Diocesan archives, Wardenship papers: letter from Revd John Keaghry, 17 March 1791; Dublin Diocesan archives, Troy papers, AB2/116/5/18, Egan to Troy, 4 December 1790.
2. Troy papers, AB2/116/5/143.
3. ibid. See William J. Waldron, 'The Catholic Church in the Archdiocese of Tuam,' unpublished thesis, 1993, pp.7-25.
4. Patrick Corish, *Maynooth College: 1795-1995*, 1995, pp.1-6.

The Palace, Tuam
17 October, A.D. 1800

William by Divine Providence Lord Archbishop of Tuam by Divine permission Bishop of Ardagh, Primate and Metropolitan of the Province of Connaught, to our beloved in Christ, the Rev. Oliver Kelly, of Tuam aforesaid, greeting:

Whereas the Most Rev. Edward Dillon, Roman Catholic Archbishop of the Diocese of Tuam, and Roman Catholic Primate of Connaught, hath by his nomination in writing, bearing date 13th day of October, in the year of our Lord 1800, appointed and recommended unto us you, the said Oliver Kelly, as a fit and proper person to keep a preparatory school for the Royal College of St. Patrick, Maynooth, to be by him holden in the town of Tuam aforesaid; and we, therefore, being satisfied as to your abilities and due qualifications in discharging your duties therein, and having, therefore, accepted of such, the appointment of the said Rev. Edward Dillon, do by these presents, grant and confirm unto you the office or employment of schoolmaster of the said preparatory school for Maynooth as aforesaid, with all the rights, profits and emoluments to the same belonging, or in any wise appertaining, so long as you shall continue to behave yourself well, and to discharge your duty with propriety in the said office of schoolmaster of said preparatory school, you, the said Oliver Kelly, having first taken the oath of allegiance as by law required. In testimony whereof we have caused our archiepiscopal seal to be therefore affixed to this, the aforesaid 17th of October, A.D. 1800.

*WILLIAM TUAM,
*CHARLES DAVIES
(Not. Pub. D. Registrar.)

Text of permit issued by William Beresford, Protestant Archbishop of Tuam, to Rev. Oliver Kelly allowing him to open a 'preparatory school for Maynooth' in Tuam.

hedge-schools (or from private tutors for those who could afford them); preparatory education in 'classical' or 'latin' schools; theological training in the Catholic countries of Europe. It was usual that poorer clerical students were ordained at home — first having acquired an understanding of Latin — before entering one of the European Irish Colleges. In this way they were enabled to support themselves on Mass stipends while studying abroad. Those from wealthier backgrounds generally went to the Irish Colleges at a younger age and were ordained when their studies were completed. It was this more rigorously-educated and politically-connected group that provided the leadership of the Catholic Church in Ireland.[1]

For a number of reasons, however, this system of Catholic education was utterly transformed in the last two decades of the eighteenth century. Firstly, the need to placate Irish Catholics in the face of the American revolution and the challenge from the Volunteer movement at home persuaded the British government that Penal Laws should be liberalised.[2] The liberalisation made it possible to establish an alternative system for the education of the clergy at home, but there are indications that the old system was already decaying in parts of the country. In particular it became difficult for candidate clergymen to acquaint themselves with the classics. Archbishop Mark Skerret of Tuam wrote in 1760:

> In these parts, there is nowhere else for teaching boys the Roman language except in those schools kept by non-Catholics in the cities, where boys called by the Holy Spirit to sacred orders cannot easily support themselves.[3]

Almost three decades later but in similar vein, Archbishop Boetius Egan of Tuam wrote to a colleague:

> The point will be then for us to... keep the spark that remains alive... Latin schools are totally on the decline in this province, and so much so that in some time hence, we shall hardly get proper candidates for ordination.[4]

---

1. Liam Swords, *A Hidden Church: the Diocese of Achonry*, 1998, pp.197-218.
2. Thomas Bartlett, *The fall and rise of the Irish nation: the Catholic Question, 1690-1830*, 1992, pp.82-103.
3. Cited by Swords in *A Hidden Church*, p.186.
4. Troy papers, AB2/116/66.

If the American revolution encouraged the British government to make provision for Catholic education, then the French revolution compelled the Catholic hierarchy to urgently embrace the offer. For reasons which will be discussed later, the French colleges which had educated the Irish clergy were associated with the *ancien regime* and, consequently, revolutionaries acted to suppress them. Some colleges remained open and others re-opened, but the bishops were wary of continuing to expose their seminarians to the enlightenment ideas, the anti-authoritarian attitudes and the republican politics then prevailing in educational institutions throughout Europe.[1] Like their French colleagues, some of the younger Irish priests had already been affected by their contact with radicalism, something which led — in the words of one Archbishop of Tuam — to the 'intemperate loquacity and rash conduct of several of our clergy all over the kingdom.'[2] One manifestation of 'rash conduct' led to the excommunication of Tuam priest Fr Robert McEvoy who, having got married in Dublin, justified his action on the grounds that 'the French National Assembly had released all priests from their vow of celibacy.'[3] If such Jacobin attitudes and behaviour was the result of a foreign education, then, as far as the Irish bishops were concerned, it was better that students be quarantined in Ireland. And in this much at least, the British administration agreed with their lordships.

In less than two decades, therefore, it became both possible and necessary to establish an autonomous system for clerical education in Ireland. Maynooth — founded in 1795 with government assistance — was at the centre of this new system, and by the end of the eighteenth century there was already a small network of minor seminaries throughout the island. Oliver Kelly's 'preparatory school' in Tuam became part of this network.

Like other Irish diocesan colleges, however, the early St Jarlath's fell somewhat short of the prevailing ideal for *petits seminaires*. Because of the relative poverty of the Irish Catholic Church and of the Irish Catholic people, it was not possible to establish institutions which confined themselves to the education of candidates for the priesthood. The College, therefore, admitted both lay and clerical students.

---

1. Corish, *Maynooth*, pp.5-13.
2. Troy papers, AB2/116/7/72
3. ibid., AB2/116/5/83-96.

At the outset, the College building was modest enough. Located in the Mall and improvised from two adjacent houses, it had a thatched roof like most of the ecclesiastical buildings in the diocese at the time. Otherwise information is scant. Almost a century ago, when Frank Guy was researching his history of the College, he admitted that he could discover but 'little about the Mall school.' So, in presenting his morsel about the premises, he had to depend on speculation as much as on ascertainable fact:

> Though probably only a day school, it was no doubt attended by students from a distance who found board and sleeping accommodation in the town. A plain and unostentatious building at its best, it had about twenty-five years ago [about 1880?] become an unsightly ruin and so was levelled to the ground and now almost nought remains.[1]

Oliver Kelly remained in charge for six years, until he was transferred to the parish of Kilmeena (Westport) in 1806. There, despite being remote from Tuam, he remained Archbishop Dillon's key lieutenant, holding the post of vicar-general of the archdiocese. He was succeeded as superior of St Jarlath's by Paul McGreal, a native of Westport. McGreal served until 1816 when he was succeeded by Professor James McKeal (later MacHale).[2]

Other staff members at the Mall included Caherlistrane man, Fr John Mulloy, who taught in the College from 1800 to 1812, Fr Michael Waldron who arrived in 1810 and, apparently, died soon afterwards and Fr John Hughes of whom there is little definite information. Of all the early professors, Fr Thomas Kielty (c.1773-1861) generated the most folklore, both because he was somewhat eccentric and because he was probably the

---

1. Guy's History, pt.i.
2. McKeal served as President of the College until 1821. According to his obituarist (*Tuam Herald*, 29 March 1856), he was the first student to embark on postgraduate studies at Maynooth's Dunboyne establishment in 1806. Later, according to the same source, he was cherished in Tuam for his 'courteous, urbane and dignified deportment.' McKeal spent twenty-six years as parish priest of Kilcommon and Robeen, whence he transferred to Castlebar in 1847. He was archdeacon of the diocese when he died in 1856. Another admirer summed him up as follows: 'He was the model of an old Irish priest and Catholic gentleman: courteous without servility; frank without coarseness; hospitable without ostentation'.

longest serving professor in the College's history — his career straddled the Mall, the Old College in Bishop Street and the New College of 1858. 'Daddy' Kielty, as he was known in the College, was born in Castlebar and was reputed to have acted as an interpreter for French forces following the 'Races of Castlebar'. His vocation to the priesthood, apparently, came relatively late in life. Later students remembered Kielty as a figure from another age, a 'quaint little man, with a dry humour of his own, wearing knee breeches and top boots and frequently astride a spirited steed...' Evidently, he refused the presidency on several occasions, preferring to teach than to take on the responsibility of administering the institution. One legend about him which has been retailed by historians of the College concerned the attempted collection of a debt due by Kielty to a local horse-trainer. In order to prove that he had successfully completed the task for which he was engaged, the trainer rode Kielty's horse as far as the College, continued on horseback through the front door and up the stairs as far as the priest's door. After he recovered from the shock, 'Daddy' promptly paid the amount due.[1]

If details about the early St Jarlath's are scant, and many of them unverifiable, it can at least be stated that the College filled a significant gap in the educational requirements of the Catholic Church in the archdiocese of Tuam and indeed in the province as a whole. To more fully appreciate the context in which the College emerged, it is necessary to examine in more detail the situation of the Church and its adherents during the previous century.

If the Catholic church in eighteenth century Connacht had distinctive features, this was due to earlier developments, to the Cromwellian banishment of Catholic landowners in particular. Not alone was Catholicism more dominant demographically — by 1800 all Protestant denominations made up only 4% of the population of Connacht — but it had a different social profile in the west: there were more affluent Catholics.

Among these were the merchant families of Galway town, but there was also a Catholic landed element — some of it descended from the Galway merchant community. And even though penal legislation through the eighteenth century thinned the ranks of the Catholic landlords of Connacht, there remained a consider-

---

1. Guy's History, pt.i; A.P.N., 'Notes on the School of St Jarlath', pp.35-36.

able number of them. Moreover, many who conformed to Protestantism to protect estates remained favourably disposed towards Catholicism. Such converts sometimes colluded with their Catholic connections to evade penal laws and were available to politically represent the interests of excluded Catholics.[1]

Because the social climate — and relative isolation — offered a certain immunity from anti-clerical legislation, the west of Ireland was well supplied with clergy during the early eighteenth century. But, due to clerical recruitment procedures which took little account of the pastoral and spiritual potential of candidates, many priests were of indifferent quality. The Gaelic tradition, whereby certain families provided clergymen just as others had provided bards and jurists, lingered on, while Catholic 'noble' or 'gentry' families still claimed the right to nominate favourites to clerical vacancies in their own parishes. Moreover, Catholic landed families, of both Gaelic and Anglo-Norman origins, sought to avoid the sub-division of their estates under the penal law of gavelkind by placing younger sons in holy orders. Such practices were not very discriminating, and some of the bishops who came through the system were not very discriminating either. Some, allegedly, regarded their faculties as a source of income, and were prepared to ordain anybody provided the requisite fee was paid. This lack of scrupulousness — and concern in Ireland that there were more priests than could be decently supported by the Catholic population — led to the Propaganda Fide order of 1741 limiting each bishop to ordaining twelve priests during his episcopacy.[2]

Thus, just as the Irish population was about to enter a period of extraordinarily rapid increase, the number of priests stabilised. The growth in population was most rapid in Connacht, and quickest of all in dioceses like Tuam and Killala which, in terms of natural resources, were least well equipped to handle the increase. By the early nineteenth century, with less than one priest per 4,000 Catholics, the archdiocese of Tuam had the worst ratio in the country.[3] This had implications for religious practice in the area.

---

1. John Solan, 'Religion and Society in the ecclesiastical province of Tuam before the Famine', unpublished thesis, 1989, pp.68-99. See also J.G. Simms 'Connacht in the eighteenth century'. in *I.H.S.* vol.xi, no.42, pp.116-133.
2. Swords, *A Hidden Church*, pp.295-6; Hugh Fenning, 'Clerical recruitment, 1753-1783', in *Archivium Hibernicum* 30 (1972), pp.1-2.
3. Solan's 'Religion', Ch.4, pp.100-169.

One important consequence of the high laity/clergy ratio was that the religion of the people became relatively independent of the clergy. Practices which could proceed without the participation of a priest and which were later designated 'traditional' — such as pilgrimages, 'pattern' days and wakes — loomed large in the devotional lives of the majority of the people, while attendance at formal worship was poor.[1] Studies have indicated that by the early nineteenth century weekly mass attendances were low throughout the west in general, but lowest of all in the archdiocese of Tuam. The relatively small number of priests was one reason, the breakdown in ecclesiastical authority as a result of Penal legislation was another, while an inadequate infrastructure, the inattention to duty of some priests and the geographical isolation of some congregations did not help matters either.[2]

Isolation also contributed to the comparatively low level of educational attainment in the archdiocese of Tuam. Surviving evidence indicates that literacy levels in the late eighteenth/early nineteenth century were among the lowest in the country, something which was very directly linked to the fact that the majority of the people spoke only Irish, a language in which it was virtually impossible to be literate at that point in history.[3] Moreover, the education system, such as it was, was uneven and arbitrary.

The established church was charged by law with maintaining a system of education. But, since that church was stretched to maintain even a religious infrastructure throughout the country, it was hardly in a position to fulfil its educational responsibilities. Even where it did, Catholics were reluctant to attend Protestant schools. A Protestant diocesan school in Tuam had operated intermittently for several centuries, but an early nineteenth century visitor was not convinced of its usefulness or of its suitability. A master was paid £70 a year to supervise 'no

---

1. S.J. Connolly, *Priests and People in pre-Famine Ireland: 1780-1845*, 1982, pp.135-48; D.W. Miller, 'Irish Catholicism and the Great Famine', *Jnl of Social History*, ix, 1, 1975, pp.88-89.
2. Connolly, *Priests and People*, pp.88-90; Emmet Larkin, 'The devotional revolution in Ireland, 1850-75' in *The Historical Dimensions of Irish Catholicism*, Washington 1976, pp.57-89.
3. Garrett Fitzgerald, 'Estimates for baronies of minimum level of Irish-speaking among successive decennial cohorts', Dublin 1984; Mary E. Daly 'Language and literacy change in the late nineteenth and early twentieth centuries' in *The origins of popular literacy in Ireland*, 1990, pp.153-166.

boarders and very few day scholars'; the schoolhouse was large but 'nearly in ruins' with the 'roof on one side quite open and exposed to the weather.'[1]

Catholics of middling and small resources patronised pay-schools or hedge-schools, which were conducted semi-clandestinely until the 1780s, but survived until the spread of the national system. Such schools were often superintended by the local parish priest, but they could only operate in communities that could afford to support a teacher. Moreover, teachers were not always available, and when they were, they were not necessarily worth supporting. Classes were held in improvised settings, in barns, in cottages and, sometimes in parish chapels.[2] A French traveller was shown around one such rudimentarily-housed school in the Tuam district by the parish priest during the 1830s:

> What most distinguished it was a certain number of small windows, or rather holes of different shapes, which had been cut in the earthen walls and in which the fragments of window panes had been placed. Some peasants were seated at the door, and inside I noticed the heads of several children. This is our school, the priest said to me... We entered the house, or rather the room, for the entire house formed only a room, [which] contained about thirty children. The space was too narrow to enable one to be seated there, and besides, the school did not have any seats. At one end stood the teacher. He was a man of middle age, barefooted, who taught scholars in rags.[3]

Conditions in the generality of 'Latin' or 'classical' schools of the diocese, presumably, were somewhat less primitive than that. There was little luxury, however, if Thady Connellan's establishment, a 'miserable cabin' at Templeboy in the diocese of Killala, was in any way typical:

> The interior of Thady's cabin perfectly corresponded with its external aspect. It was divided into two apartments

---

1. Cited by John A. Claffey, 'The Tuam Diocesan School' in his *Glimpses of Tuam since the Famine*, 1997, pp.89-97.
2. Connolly, *Priests and People*, pp.82-83.
3. *Alexis de Tocqueville's journey in Ireland, July-August 1835*, translated and edited by Emmet Larkin, pp.118-19.

which boasted no other furniture than an old deal table covered with copybooks and slates, and a few boards placed on stones which served as seats to the young students.[1]

A number of Latin schools in the archdiocese can be identified from the biographies and obituaries of priests. John MacHale studied under Patrick Staunton in Castlebar, William Flannelly at Ballinrobe under a Mr Rooney, Thomas Feeney at Ballindine under Michael Garry, who — in common with many of his colleagues — was 'considered the best Latin grammarian in Europe.' For his part, Oliver Kelly attended the renowned school kept by Laurence Kelly at Kilthomas, near Peterswell, in the diocese of Kilmacduagh.[2]

After the Boyne and Aughrim, Irish Catholics continued to identify with the defeated Stuart dynasty. This identification was strongest in the west, where the institutional church was, in some respects, part of the Jacobite court in exile. Landed Catholic families which had officered the Jacobite forces in the late seventeenth century maintained their military connections with the exiled Stuarts and their royal allies on the continent. In a number of cities in Europe, there were significant Irish Catholic communities, comprising the younger sons of gentry, the representatives of merchant families — notably of the so-called Galway 'tribes' — as well as the staff and students of the Irish colleges. The largest of these colleges was in Paris, where 180 students and priests were housed in 1787. The College in Paris and several of the others were financially supported by the Stuarts, who continued to feel a responsibility towards their Irish subjects, and by the Stuarts' main patrons, the French monarchy. The College at Salamanca which educated Oliver Kelly was supported by the Spanish monarchy and permitted to call itself 'The Royal College of Irish Nobles'.[3]

James II and his son — the *soi-disant* James III who was known as the 'Old Pretender' — were recognised during their

---

1. Lady Morgan's description is cited by Swords in his *A Hidden Church*, p.189.
2. Nuala Costello, *John MacHale: Archbishop of Tuam*, 1939, pp.15-16; Waldron's *Archdiocese of Tuam*, p.11; SJC, Feeney papers, p.25; J. Fahey, *The History and Antiquities of the Diocese of Kilmacduagh*, 1893, p.390.
3. The Irish Colleges in Europe are discussed by Cathaldus Giblin, 'Irish exiles in Catholic Europe' in vol.iv, of Patrick Corish's *History of Irish Catholicism*. 1971, pp.3-26.

lifetimes by successive popes as the legitimate rulers of Britain and Ireland. And like other Catholic monarchs, they nominated the bishops who were to serve in their own kingdoms. The formal arrangement came to an end, when Clement XIII refused to recognise the succession of the 'Young Pretender' otherwise 'Bonnie Prince Charlie', in 1766. But Stuart nominees — for example, Philip Philips, appointed bishop of Killala in 1760 and archbishop of Tuam in 1785 — remained in episcopal office in Ireland until the late eighteenth century. Such high level connections between the Catholic Church and Stuart claimants to the British throne fuelled establishment suspicion of Catholics. Indeed in some minds it was a justification for the penal laws.[1]

A large proportion of senior church appointments in Connacht during the eighteenth century went to members of the 'Tribes of Galway', a tightly organised network of inter-connected merchant and landed families of Norman origin.[2] To secure their influence, these so-called 'Tribes' maintained an underground Jacobite corporation in the town of Galway until the early nineteenth century. Since local authority functions were carried out by the official corporation, the sole overt function of the shadowy Tribal body was to elect the Catholic Warden of Galway, an official of episcopal rank who had historically administered the Church in the town of Galway and vicinity. The Tribes' influence extended further than Galway town, however, and its corporation — together with connections at home and abroad — operated a kind of freemasonry which enabled members to significantly influence church administration throughout Ireland.[3]

The French revolution had a profound effect on Irish ecclesiastical politics. Since the Stuarts settled in their Parisian exile, the French court had been an important arena as far as church affairs in Ireland were concerned. The breaking up of that court and the execution of Louis XVI was seen by senior Irish ecclesiastics as a treasonous assault on temporal authority but, because of the different attitude of many lay people, it was not easy to be forthright on the matter. Bishops could 'heartily disapprove of the civil and religious doctrines of the French

---

1. See Brady & Corish 'The Church under the Penal Code' in ibid., pp.47-56.
2. The 'Tribes' bore the following surnames: Athy, Blake, Bodkin, Browne, d'Arcy, Dean, Ffont, Ffrench, Joyce, Lynch, Kirwan, Martin, Morris, Skerrett.
3. Rev. Fr. Martin Coen, *The Wardenship of Galway*, 1984, pp.21-32.

National Assembly,' but yet agree that 'it may not be prudent to denounce them publicly as yet.'[1] But when symptoms of 'the French disease' unambiguously manifested themselves in Ireland in 1798, it was time to cast prudence aside and to rally to legitimate authority. And such authority, it was by now unequivocally accepted by the bishops, resided in London. An address from the Irish hierarchy to King George III, dated 30 May 1798, stressed

> the necessity of laying aside all considerations of religious distinctions and joining in our common effort for the preservation of our constitution and of social order, and of the Christian religion, against a nation [France] whose avowed principles aim at the destruction of them all.'[2]

Even so, when Dr Edward Dillon, who succeeded Boetius Egan as archbishop of Tuam in 1798, issued a pastoral announcing the excommunication both of those who administered the United Irishman oath and those who continued to adhere to such oaths, he was opposed by 'more than one of the episcopal order in the province of Tuam.'[3] But the archbishop was not deflected. He was equally resolute in opposing the wave of agrarian unrest which followed the Rising, when he instructed his clergy to refuse absolution to those who had been 'guilty of the infamous crime of houghing cattle, or have been active agents of the Prince of Darkness by leading their fellow creatures into destructive plots and conspiracies.'[4] During the very months that he was founding the College, the archbishop was actively supporting the Act of Union, which came into effect in January 1801. Like his fellow bishops, he was convinced that Union would secure and guarantee equal rights for Catholics. But, for his attempts to 'bring back the people to a sense of their duty', Dr Dillon complained to a colleague, he got little thanks. Promoters of unrest in his diocese got their own back 'by styling me an Orange bishop, the tool of government, well paid for my services, &c.'[5]

---

1. Troy papers, AB2/116/5/94, Dr Bray to Dr Troy.
2. Cited by Oliver J.Burke in *The History of the Catholic Archbishops of Tuam*, 1882, pp.199-206.
3. Troy papers, AB2/116/7/72
4. ibid., AB2, 116/7/130.
5. C. Vane, *Memoirs and Correspondence of Viscount Castlereagh*, vol.iv, p.347-8.

Dr Dillon died on 20 August 1809, having asked that Oliver Kelly be appointed his coadjutor. And within days of the archbishop's funeral, the canons of the Tuam archdiocese met and elected Kelly Vicar-Capitular — the official who administered a diocese between episcopacies. Moreover, the diocesan clergy wrote collectively to Rome, stating that Kelly was the preferred choice of the late archbishop, and that the priests and the Catholic people of Tuam were keen to see him succeed to the episcopacy. They pointed out that he was diligent, that he was eloquent in both Irish and English and that, as a former professor of theology at Salamanca, he was academically qualified to fill the vacancy. Similar sentiments were expressed in a letter from the archbishops of Armagh and Dublin.

There was a limit to the emerging consensus. however, and the surviving bishops of the Tuam province were as opposed to Kelly's elevation as they were in favour of the appointment of one of themselves. Nor were they slow to express their opposition. Following an irregularly-convened provincial synod at Moylough, the bishops of Kilmacduagh and Kilfenora, of Killala, of Elphin and of Clonfert, together with the Catholic warden of Galway, protested to Rome that Kelly was 'an inexperienced, ambitious, imprudent young man' and should not be chosen.[1]

International politics intervened to transform what might otherwise have been a nine days' wonder into a six-year-long scandal. Because he was imprisoned by Napoleon, Pope Pius VII was not in a position to resolve the emerging discord in Tuam by making an appointment. There could be no final resolution until he did.

The roots of the dispute went back decades and involved several stubborn and awkward personalities. Essentially, what was at stake was control of the Catholic Church in the west of Ireland. The other bishops belonged to, or identified with, the beleaguered Catholic nobility of Connacht. And while individuals among them, notably Dr Bellew of Killala, were personally hopeful of being translated to Tuam, they were united by the more important consideration that Oliver Kelly — the son of a tenant farmer, albeit one with some pretensions — was not socially equipped to be a bishop, let alone to be their metropolitan.

---

1. Martin Coen's 'The Choosing of Oliver Kelly for the See of Tuam, 1809-1815' in *JGAHS*,xxxvi, 1977-78, pp.19-20.

The western bishops had a few allies among the more patrician priests of Tuam. One of them was Dean Boetius Egan, nephew of Archbishop Dillon's predecessor. Egan had boycotted the meeting of the Tuam clergy which elected the Vicar Capitular and, on the basis that he was absent, protested to Dr Bellew that the meeting was invalid. Bellew agreed and, as the senior suffragan of the province, appointed Egan as Vicar Capitular.

The existence of two rival claimants to this important office led to fears of schism, prompting the intervention of the primate, Dr O'Reilly of Armagh. His right to intervene, however, was not accepted by the western bishops, especially since he seemed to share the archbishop of Dublin's opinions on 'the crazy Dean Egan' and the 'absolutely detested' Dr Bellew.

Solid episcopal support outside of Connacht, together with the deaths of half of the remaining Connacht bishops, wore down the opposition to Kelly and only Bishop Archdeacon of Kilmacduagh and Kilfenora and Boetius Egan were actively hostile to him by 1813. By then, Dr Troy of Dublin had been formally delegated by Rome to investigate the conflict and to make a decision. There was no doubt about the outcome and Kelly was confirmed as Vicar Capitular.

The pope was released in March 1814 and in September he appointed the thirty-seven year old Kelly as archbishop. The consecration took place in Tuam on Passion Sunday, 12 March 1815. Bishop Archdeacon declined to attend and persisted in his refusal to recognise Kelly's appointment, which he said, was 'fraudulently' obtained.[1]

The episode emphasised the archaic and idiosyncratic nature of some of the conventions and practices of the church in the west of Ireland. Accordingly, the new archbishop moved quickly to initiate reform and to restore order. In 1817, the Synod of Tuam examined all aspects of religious life in the province and made relevant decrees. Among them were regulations enforcing clerical discipline and orthodoxy in devotional practice. Significantly, other decrees forbade canvassing for church offices and insisted that Catholic landlords had no particular influence in the selection of their local parish priest.[2]

The formal decrees of the Synod reflected the dawn of a new era in the life of the archdiocese. The lifting of Penal laws, the

---

1. ibid., pp.20-28.
2. Waldron's *Archdiocese of Tuam*, p.59.

Parishes of the archdiocese of Tuam, 1998. [From Mícheál MacGréil, *Quo Vadimus* Tuam 1998]

The 'Old College', formerly Ffrench's Bank, occupied continuously since 1817 by St Jarlath's College.

Oliver Kelly, founding superior of St Jarlath's College, later archbishop of Tuam and patron of the College (*From an original portrait, reproduced courtesy of Mrs Joan Barrows*)

Boetius Egan, archbishop of Tuam, 1787-1798, who made plans for the establishment of a diocesan seminary in Tuam.

Dr Thomas Feeney, professor and president of St Jarlath's College, 1817-1831; later bishop of Killala.

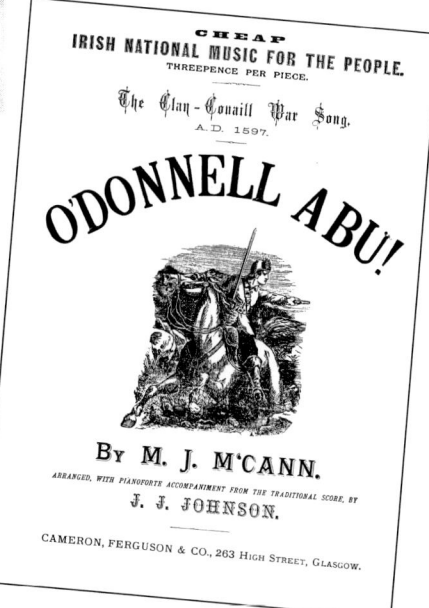

Sheet music for 'O'Donnell Abu!', composed by St Jarlath's professor, M.J. McCann.

Banknote for one Irish guinea issued by Ffrench's Bank.

President Ulick J. Bourke with students, outside the 'New College' of 1858 and new wings completed in early 1870s.

The 'New College' with addition of c.1905 on the left. The ambulatory in the left foreground was added in 1920.

foundation of Maynooth, the sundering of the religious ties with pre-Revolutionary Europe, combined to create an entirely new religious climate. Anachronistic deference could be abandoned; indeed, it had to be abandoned. The Synod and Oliver Kelly's episcopacy also ushered in an era of infrastructural improvement in the archdiocese, which culminated in the building of Tuam cathedral, between 1827 and 1836. At the same time parish churches replaced Mass-houses and residences were built for the clergy.

One of the most inadequately housed institutions was the diocesan seminary so when the Ffrench's Bank building in Bishop Street became available during 1816, Kelly moved quickly to acquire it.

The building itself was comparatively new, although it had a rather complex legal history. The site, comprising a house formerly occupied by John Proven and a piece of ground known as Derham's plot — and also known as the Bullock Yard and Haggard — was owned ultimately by the Church of Ireland archdiocese of Tuam. It was leased in 1785 for a term of forty years from Sir John Hort of Lisbon, Portugal by John Davis of Tuam. Sir John was a relative of Josiah Hort, Protestant archbishop of Tuam until 1751, who, evidently, had granted a long lease to himself and his heirs. The sub-lease descended to Charles Davis, who, in 1797, sold his interest to John Bermingham of Dalgan. Bermingham built the large stone house which eventually became the 'Old College', but following his death it was sold in chancery in 1809 to meet debts. John Browne of Dublin was the purchaser for £500.

Two years later, Browne sold his interest to the Honourable Thomas Ffrench of Ffrench's Bank. The bank, with offices in Tuam, Galway and Dublin, was set up in 1803 and established itself as the leading financial institution in the west of Ireland during the agricultural boom of the Napoleonic war. The economic down-turn at the end of the war caused problems for the bank, but it was the loose financial management of the directors which caused its bankruptcy in December 1815. This was a severe financial blow to the many depositors throughout Connacht.

Disgrace — and the loss of £40,000 — led to the suicide of Lord Ffrench and the tidying up of his affairs transferred ownership of the bank building to Catherine Whitehead, a sister of his lordship's and the mother of Reverend Robert ffrench

Whitehead (1807-79) who served as vice-President of St Patrick's, Maynooth between 1845 and 1872. Charles, the new Lord Ffrench, administered his aunt's property and it was he who negotiated with Archbishop Oliver Kelly regarding the renting of the building. A complication arose in 1818 when the original ground interest reverted to the Protestant archdiocese. Dr Beresford, however, came to the rescue and restored the lease for a term of forty years to the original lessees. In September 1819, an agreement on a twenty-one year lease was concluded between Catherine Whitehead and Dr Kelly at £80 a year, payable in instalments, as was customary, on 25 March and 25 September. In a separate transaction, the lodge and garden attached to the main building, which had remained in the possession of the Bermingham family, were leased to the College at £20 per annum.[1]

The acquisition of the building was a start, but the undertaking had to be financed. Thus, the public meeting chaired by John Bodkin (later an M.P. for County Galway) held in Tuam on 10 January 1817. Among the resolutions passed was one amounting to a mission statement which declared the object of the institution to be 'the education of the community at large and particularly to facilitate the education of zealous, enlightened missionaries.'

The public meeting went on to elect a large school board, consisting of nineteen clergymen and sixteen laymen. President of the board was Dr Kelly while other clerical members included several professors and eminent clergymen of the diocese, notably Dean Boetius Egan, the archbishop's recent rival. The lay members were drawn from the Catholic gentry of the diocese. At the top of the list was Lord Ffrench, as the senior nobleman, followed by Christopher Bellew, a substantial landowner, whose family gave its name to the towns of Mountbellew and Newtownbellew (now Moylough village).[2] Also included was Matthias McDonnell of Castlebar, brother of Eneas McDonnell, the London 'ambassador' of the Irish bishops. Remarkably, seven of the sixteen laymen had the surname Blake, and thirteen of them bore surnames of the ancient 'tribes' of Galway. By

---

1. Tuam Diocesan archives: Deed of conveyance, 23 December 1809; lease of house and premises, 21 September 1819; deed of assignment, 17 April 1828; SJC, receipts book 1838-67,'Additional brief' pp.114-16; Daithí Ó Murchú, 'Ffrench's Bank' in *Tuam*, 1971; 'Local family and place history' in *Tuam Herald*, 6 October 1917.
2. For the Bellews, see Karen J. Harvey's *The Bellews of Mountbellew*, 1998.

At a meeting of the Roman Catholic inhabitants of Tuam, held on the tenth day of January, 1817, for the purpose of establishing a seminary for the education of the community at large and particularly to facilitate the education of zealous, enlightened missionaries, John Bodkin, Esquire, in the chair, the following resolutions were entered into:

Resolved, that the following gentlemen do constitute a board for the management and direction of this seminary

Most Rev. Doctor O. Kelly	Right Hon. Lord Ffrench
Rev. Malachy O'Kelly	Christopher Bellew, Esq
Rev. Dean Egan	John Bodkin, Esq
Rev. Peter Burke	James Blake
Rev. Peter Heffernan	Martin J. Blake, Esq., Ballinafad
Rev. Paul McGreal	Isodore Blake
Rev Laurence Waldron	Charles Blake, Esq
Rev Bartholomew Fitzpatrick	Maurice Blake, Esq., Ballinafad
Rev Bernard Burke	Henry E. Lynch, Esq.
Rev. John Loftus	Maurice Blake, Esq., Tower Hill
Rev Redmond Hardigan, Snr	Francis Lynch, Esq.
Rev Thomas Kean	Robert Kirwan, Esq.
Rev John Burke	John Browne, Esq.
Rev Patrick Nolan	Matthew McDonnell, Esq.
Rev Peter Griffin	John Egan., Esq.
Rev Patrick Gibbons	John Blake, Esq.
Rev M. Green	
Rev John Mulloy	
Rev Pat Mullin	

Resolved, that eleven of the above members do constitute a board.

Resolved that Most Reverend Dr O. Kelly be requested to act as President of the institution, John Blake, Treasurer, and Reverend Bartholemew Fitzpatrick as secretary to the institution

Resolved, that subscriptions be immediately be entered into to raise a fund for the support of the institution, that each member of the board do exert himself in procuring subscriptions in his neighbourhood

Resolved, that we request the president to use his influence with the clergy of the diocese to procure subscriptions in their respective parishes

Resolved, that the next meeting of the Board be held on 25 February.

John Bodkin, having left the chair and Charles Blake having been called thereto, the thanks of the meeting were given to John Bodkin for his proper conduct in the chair.

contrast, not a single tribal name was to be found among the nineteen clergymen.

In forming the board, Archbishop Kelly's approach was consistent with the hierarchy's 1793 blueprint on the financing of Catholic further education, which anticipated that diocesan colleges would have to be subsidised by 'opulent members of the laity' as well as by priests and bishops. Indeed, the only formal responsibility of the ordinary members of the St Jarlath's board was that each 'exert himself in procuring subscriptions in his neighbourhood.' For his part, the archbishop undertook to 'use his influence' with the diocesan clergy to raise subscriptions.

If the lay gentlemen did not overly exert themselves in fundraising, it was expected that they would at least make substantial personal contributions. But even this modest expectation was not realised. £451.0.3 was subscribed to an appeal, but only ten of the eighty-three subscribers were lay people, while only three of these ten were board members. And the average contribution from these 'opulent members of the laity', at £6.13.9, was not significantly greater than the average of £6.3.8 contributed by 73 clergymen. Moreover, the lay average would have been significantly lower but for the £20 given by Lord Ffrench who, arguably, had a vested interest in the success of the institution.[1]

In explanation, it should be pointed out that the timing of the appeal was not auspicious. The post-Napoleonic war depression was beginning to eat into agricultural incomes and most of the Catholic gentry of the archdiocese were dependent on rural prosperity — whether as landlords, as agents, or as owners of livestock themselves. In addition, many of them lost considerable sums in the crash of Ffrench's Bank. But the timing of the appeal was inauspicious in another respect also. Oliver Kelly's very succession was seen as an encroachment on the traditional prerogatives of the Catholic gentry of Connacht. And, later in 1817, the Synod of Tuam would further clip their wings. So, by making so many of them governors of his seminary, Oliver Kelly was seeking to placate this alienated segment of his flock. That they were not so easily placated is indicated by their paltry financial contribution to the College.

Archbishop Kelly used his 'influence' effectively to raise money from his clergy. A levy of five guineas was placed on

---

1. SJC, Account book, 1817-35.

each parish priest of the diocese; some curates contributed as much, while others parted with one, two or three guineas. The number of contributors from outside the diocese was negligible, but one name on the list catches the eye: 'Rev. Jno. McKeal, Maynooth.' This was John MacHale, who would later make his mark on the College as its patron for almost fifty years.

Evidently, the new building was already occupied when the account book was opened on 17 January 1817. At any rate, the alterations necessary to transform the bank into a residential college were already under way. In February, Professor Thomas Kielty, presented a bill for £1.17.7 made up of the following: 'two boards for a press, 7s 7d; making a shelf for same, 5s 0d; repairing a grate, 5s 0d; for painting his room £1.0.0.' Professor Bartholemew Fitzpatrick paid £3.9.2 for 'repairs and painting his room,' while President McKeal claimed for a 'large, polished gridiron — 6s 6d;' for 'a pair of pot-hooks — 1s 7d;' for 'twenty-six stair-rods at four pence each — 8s 8d;' and 'for making a garden &c, &c — £10.' On 31 May 1817, McKeal sought £14.12.0 for 'expenses incurred by building the ball court' which, incidentally, is the earliest surviving reference to sport at St Jarlath's.[1]

---

1. ibid.

3. "...respectable appearance and remarkable propriety."

Sacred the cause that Clan-Conaill's defending,
The altars we kneel at, the homes of our sires;
Ruthless the ruin the foe is extending
Midnight is red with the plunderers' fires!
On with O'Donnell then,
Fight the old fight again,
Sons of Tir Conaill, all valiant and true!
Make the false Saxons feel
Erin's avenging steel!
Strike for your country! — O'Donnell Abu.[1]

As might be expected, given his prominent part in the foundation and consolidation of the institution, Dr Kelly remained keenly concerned about every aspect of life in the College. He was as interested in the progress of individual students as he was in the disposition of professors, and he was closely involved in the recruitment of staff — domestic as well as academic.

His approach is illustrated by his overture in 1818 to Thomas Feeney, then finishing his studies at St Patrick's, Maynooth. Dr Kelly wrote to Feeney, seeking to meet him in the town of Maynooth to discuss the vacant professorship in philosophy at St Jarlath's — if such an encounter was not 'a violation of rule' for interns of the national seminary. Equal attention to detail is indicated a decade later in another letter from Kelly to Feeney, by which time the younger man had become president of the College. Writing from Dublin about a vacancy in St Jarlath's for a housekeeper, the archbishop referred enigmatically to the recent 'disappointment of Mr Ward,' before instructing that the unfortunate man's wife — 'a genteel, respectable woman' left behind in Tuam — be engaged at a salary of £10 a year, 'besides an allowance of two guineas for tea.'[2]

If Dr Kelly was meticulous in choosing the staff of the

---

1. From 'The Clanconnell War Song' better known as 'O'Donnell Abu', composed by Michael J. McCann, a former student of the St Jarlath's, who returned as professor of mathematics. The ballad was published in the *Nation* on 28 January 1843, while the writer was on the College staff.
2. SJC, Feeney papers, pp. 34, 51.

College, his surviving letters to President Feeney show that he also exercised great care in selecting the next generation of clergy from among the students there. Even during the periods he spent away from his diocese — mostly because of ill-health — he was careful that those to whom he delegated responsibility acted in accordance with his wishes. While recuperating at Leamington Spa during the summer of 1827, for example, he wrote in fairly specific terms to President Feeney:

> I presume that your examinations are over by this time and that the relative merit of each student has been ascertained. I have not exactly in my recollection who the candidates are for Maynooth but my mind is made up that your brother and Butler are to fill two places. The other two vacancies are to be offered to the four most meritorious, who are to pay half pension, with the understanding that they will be appointed to the next vacancies as they occur. If four should not be found to accept the places on these terms, you will offer them to three, if three cannot be found, then you will offer them to two, leaving you free to make the choice from among the theologians, philosophers, or the humanities class, as you may think fit.[1]

Two years later, on the same topic, the archbishop wrote from Rome in similar terms:

> I therefore request that you, in conjunction with Mr Kielty, will make such a selection as will appear most creditable to the Establishment over which you preside... I cannot, however, refrain from warmly recommending the friend and relative of Mr Lyons of Erris, Dean of Killala, who has been for some time at the Seminary and who has, I hope, been conducting himself in a manner to deserve your approbation. Should he be found duly qualified, it is my particular wish that he be sent to the first vacancy at Maynooth... I do not now recollect the name of the young man in question, but from this description I give, I believe you will not mistake who I mean.[2]

The letter left President Feeney in no doubt as to how he should

---

1. ibid., pp.70-1, 19 July 1827.
2. ibid., pp.78-9, letter from +Oliver to Thomas Feeney, 16 July 1829.

act and he promptly wrote as follows to a colleague on the College staff: 'The archbishop himself has so strongly recommended Mr Lyons that I consider him appointed by the Bishop. I therefore request that you write to Mr L and tell him from me to prepare for Maynooth.' And in filling the two other available free places in Maynooth that year, Feeney and Kielty chose well: their nominees, Anthony O'Regan and William Cullinane, both later became presidents of the College.[1]

Dr Kelly also interested himself in the mundane task of rule-making and a document entitled 'College Statutes' appeared over his name, dated 18 February 1819.[2] His statutes indicate that the archbishop considered it desirable to severely regulate the daily life of students in all its aspects — educational, spiritual and recreational. Study should be strictly supervised; religious observance should be 'closely watched'; time spent in private quarters should be restricted. But transgressions were not to be too drastically punished, a slender rod being 'the only instrument' permitted. And, as far as the professorial staff were concerned, community life was encouraged among them.

From the glimpses into devotional routine presented by the statutes, it would appear that mass was celebrated daily in the College — probably in the morning — and that boys attended at public worship in Chapel Lane on Sundays and on holy days of obligation. The Rosary, evidently, was recited nightly during Lent.

And, since it indicates that the College authorities were anxious about the matter, it is noteworthy that the relationship between students and College servants was mentioned twice in such a short document. Were the domestic staff being persuaded to introduce contraband at that time? Or was there concern that romantic entanglements might develop if contact between the boys and the young female servants was not restricted?

But the statutes did no more than set boundaries; far more detailed guidelines were required if St Jarlath's was to be run effectively. This task was not neglected by the College's patron and, during February 1821, he wrote: 'For the last three weeks, I've given my undivided care and attention to the concerns of the Establishment [St Jarlath's] and its plan of studies.' Resulting from this he formulated a plan for the 'distribution of time' which he 'reduced to writing and pasted up on the walls of the Halls.'[3] But

---

1. ibid., pp.80-1, letter from Pres. Feeney to Prof. Hosty.
2. ibid., 'College statutes'
3. ibid., misc. loose leaves at end of volume.

his efforts were directed only at streamlining and refining a system that he regarded as already quite satisfactory:

> In forming the plan of studies and distribution of time, I am singularly indebted to the zealous and indefatigable exertions of the professors. To enforce the observance of discipline, to forward the literary improvement of their pupils and strictly to adhere to the rules and regulations of the seminary (so far as they have been communicated to them) are objects that have been most sedulously and most successfully attended to by each of the professors.[1]

Five weeks later, Kelly reiterated what he had previously written:

> I have very frequently visited the Seminary during the last month and have always been delighted in observing the unabated zeal and unanimity of the Professors… I have also witnessed with pleasure the literary proficiency of the students and their general good conduct.[2]

On occasion, the archbishop may have involved himself rather too closely in the daily life of the establishment. That, at any rate, would account for an undated resolution of the board of governors stating that the system of reward and punishment in the College was entirely in the hands of the president and insisting that 'even His Grace the Archbishop as well as the Professors of the House shall not interfere with the tenor and practical effects of this resolution.' That the president felt that some infringement of his prerogative had occurred can be inferred from the codicil to the resolution: 'The secretary of the Board is hereby requested to communicate in the most respectful manner to His Grace and the Professors, a copy of the above.'[3]

Dr Kelly's impression that his seminary was functioning satisfactorily was shared by at least one visitor to Tuam during the early 1820s:

> There is also in Tuam the College of St Jarlath, for the education of Roman Catholics, under the superintendence of

---

1. ibid.
2. ibid.
3. ibid., p.39.

COLLEGE STATUTES DEVISED BY ARCHBISHOP OLIVER KELLY, 1819

1. The students never to be allowed to go upstairs during study hours. Each of the boarders to leave his linen marked and numbered on his bed each Monday morning between 9 and 10 o'clock to be taken to the wash and to be returned at the hour appointed. Notice of this regulation to be given to the servants, and the hours so regulated as to preclude the necessity of any intercourse between students and servants.

2. The professors to attend the morning studies and the classes, precisely at 10 o'clock, and to say Mass, day and week about in turn; and when a Professor sits in one hall, the door of the adjacent hall is to be left open in order that attention to studies and silence may be observed. The monitors appointed to teach the under classes to make a written report each day to one of the Professors of the conduct of the students committed to their care.

3. Any scholar who shall be detected in conversation with or in the company of a servant is to be punished.

4. A slender rod the only instrument to be used in inflicting punishment.

5. The conduct of boarders on Sundays and holy days at chapel to be closely watched. They are each of them to read a prayerbook during Mass, and they are to kneel inside the rails, and no other boys will be allowed to occupy that space; and instead of going to chapel at night during Lent, the Rosary is to be recited after supper in the College, at which all the inmates are to assist.

6. The Professors are earnestly recommended to commune frequently and familiarly with each other as to the best mode of enforcing the observance of the statutes, and no vacant days and nights are to be given.

the Roman Catholic archbishop of Tuam. Many young men are educated here for the priesthood and are sent to Maynooth previous to their taking orders. I am well informed that it is admirably conducted, and every person who has been often to Tuam must bear testimony to the respectable appearance and remarkable propriety of the students at such periods as are devoted to study.[1]

Their 'respectable appearance' and 'remarkable propriety' aside, there is little enough information about the students during Oliver Kelly's heyday. Clearly, some of them were well-to-do, with the likes of Master Nicholas Ffrench, Master Edward Browne and Masters John and Martin Blake, who were all on the rolls in 1817-18, coming from gentry backgrounds. Certain snippets in letters from parents and guardians to President Feeney provide clues about the social background and expectations of others: 'His uncle, Major Staunton, will be able to procure his appointment as soon as he can attain a sufficient degree of education'; 'A dignitary of our church, the Right Hon. Andrew O'Regan of Marmesa has requested & empowered me to apply to Yr Grace on behalf of two of his nephews... — Ffrench, Castleffrench'; 'the boy is to be educated for the mercantile profession, such was the father's.'[2]

As far as the educational life of the College was concerned, several things can be established — or at least inferred — from Dr Kelly's statutes and from other sources. The first class of the day, it would appear, did not start until 10 a.m., and it was preceded by an hour of recreation. Before that again, there was a period of study supervised by one of the professors.

There was a regular professorial staff of only four — including the president — during most of Oliver Kelly's episcopacy, but their efforts were supplemented by those of others. Entries in the accounts book like 'Michael Connaughton, Prof. Mathematics, for one months attendance commencing 16 April' and 'James Dorcan for two months writing in the College, due 14 April', show that part-time or temporary lay staff were employed when required.[3] And the College statutes show that the monitorial system, widely used in early nineteenth century education, was employed in St Jarlath's. In this instance, it was

---

1. Hely Dutton, *Statistical and agricultural survey of Co. Galway*, 1824, p.409.
2. SJC, Feeney papers, pp.15, 77, 83.
3. SJC, Account book 1817-35.

decreed that the senior students nominated to give lessons to the junior classes were obliged to give a 'written report each day to one of the Professors of the conduct of the students committed to their care. By the mid-1830s, according to one source, the College was

> under the superintendence of three ecclesiastical and two lay professors and has a very extensive library: the premises being inadequate to accommodate the number of students are about to be rebuilt.[1]

The results of house examinations give occasional glimpses of the curriculum. Lists of prizewinners were published annually in local newspapers in order to draw attention to the College's capabilities, and a few editions of these newspapers from the the pre-Famine period have survived. The earliest such results discovered were for an examination held in the College 'on the 3rd, 4th, 5th and 6th of July, and on the 20th and 21st August 1817' which were placed in the Galway-based *Connaught Journal*. Thirty-three individuals were awarded prizes in thirteen different subject areas: Philosophy, Greek, Latin, French, English Grammar, Elocution, Spelling, Writing, History, Geography, Use of Globes and Book-keeping. The next such list from 1830 shows considerable change. Arithmetic had been added, History had been divided into two — Profane History and History of the Bible, while Philosophy had been sub-divided into Logic and Metaphysics, Theology (Dogmatic and Moral) and Sacred Scripture. What had occurred, in fact, was that that St Jarlath's College had grown from 'a preparatory school for the Royal College of St. Patrick, Maynooth' in the early 1800s, into an ecclesiastical seminary in its own right. This development was forced upon the College authorities because of a shortage of places in Maynooth. During the 1820s, the 1830s and the early 1840s, therefore, candidates for the priesthood were ordained directly from St Jarlath's, without having attended another seminary. According tor the Commissioners of Education Report of 1827:

> The College of Maynooth supplies at present about 50 candidates for holy orders. It is stated to us that 80 or 90 are annually required by the different parishes throughout

---

1. Samuel Lewis, *A Topographical Dictionary of Ireland*, 1837, vol.ii, p.648.

Ireland. Besides the priests educated in Maynooth we are informed that about 120 students are in the course of education in other Seminaries in Ireland. The greatest of these are in Carlow; others are at Kilkenny, Tuam, Waterford and Wexford.[1]

Incidentally, the placing of the 1830 examination results in the Dublin-based *Freeman's Journal* provoked an interesting piece of correspondence. Henry J. Prendergast, an employee of the newspaper who had been an 'ecclesiastical boarder' in St Jarlath's during the early 1820s,[2] wrote to President Feeney to explain that the advertisement could not be inserted on the date requested:

> I've just received your communication addressed to Mr Lavelle who left for Killarney ten days past. I must scarcely add how pleasing a duty has devolved upon me of noticing the progress of an institution, the recollection of which is so intertwined with my boyhood days. Time may destroy the finest and firmest fabrics of the best artistes, but it cannot efface schoolboy reminiscences. I am sorry that your communication did not reach me on time for our publication of this day — if it had your advertisement would have had a timely insertion. On Monday, however, I shall order it into the Daily Freeman's Journal, accompanied by a few remarks from myself, which I hope will be of no disservice at least — with regards to Mr Kielty and sincere wishes for the welfare of St Jarlath's.[3]

Prendergast was as good as his word, and he drew attention to the advertisement in an editorial column in the following terms:

> By an advertisement of the order in which the students of the Seminary of Tuam distinguished themselves at the last Summer examination, which will be found in another column, it will be seen how fine an opportunity country gentlemen have of giving their sons an extensive and extraordinarily cheap theological, philosophical and classical

---

1. House of Commons, *Irish Education Inquiry: Second Report of the Commissioners*, 1826-7, vol.xii.
2. SJC, Accounts, 1817-1835, January 16 1821.
3. SJC, Feeney papers, p.85.

education. It is really astonishing how much the mode of instruction is in the present day improved, and with what facility a young gentleman may now become schooled in all the essentials of a polished and useful education. The efforts of the Catholic archbishop of Tuam to diffuse useful knowledge throughout the province of which he is metropolitan are amazing...

From a thorough and intimate acquaintance with that unrivalled establishment, its rules, regulations and management, under as amiable a clergyman as lives, we are justified in recommending St Jerlath's Seminary as a place admirably adapted to the wants and circumstances of the youth of the present time.

Twenty-five guineas a year for, to our knowledge, excellent boarding and a liberal and able instruction... Can the moderation of this charge be equalled? In Ireland it is not — and in England it certainly cannot be equalled. The house, a magnificent building, is salubriously situated and the attention which is invariably paid to the students by the talented and worthy principal and other professors, we had ourselves abundant opportunity of witnessing and appreciating during three years sojourn in the institution. We will venture to affirm that the 'march of intellect' has been more accelerated by this Seminary than by all the chartered and endowed schools, whether pretendedly liberal or avowedly prejudiced, which government has established in Ireland.[1]

Prendergast, clearly, was well satisfied with his education in the College and considered that 'a theological, philosophical and classical education' was as appropriate to a lay career as to a clerical one.

Unlike theology and the classics, there is no solid evidence regarding the place of the Irish language on the curriculum in the period before the MacHale episcopacy. There are, however, indications of an interest in the language among staff and some students of the College. Such interest had a strongly practical aspect, given the necessity of catechizing in the language that the ordinary people spoke, which, over most of the diocese, was Irish in the pre-Famine period. One indication of this, was the publication around 1830 of an edition of Kirwan's catechism,

---

1. *Freeman's Journal*, 24 August 1830.

which was prepared by Tuam parish clerk, Thomas Hughes, and acknowledged the input of Rev. James Ronan, professor of logic and future president of the College. Another priest of the diocese, Rev. Martin Loftus, professor of Irish at Maynooth between 1820 and 1828, had returned to Tuam by this time. Ronan and Loftus were later described by archbishop MacHale, as 'good Irish scholars'. Loftus's successor as professor of Irish at Maynooth, James Tully, was also from the diocese and was a former student of the College. He remained in that position at Maynooth for almost fifty years, until his death in 1876. Tully, however, has not been considered a particularly distinguished holder of his office, and he was criticised by, among others, Ulick Bourke, a Maynooth student in the 1850s who was a learned revivalist and a long-serving president of St Jarlath's. But, to his credit, it has been acknowledged that Tully was 'generous to the poor and a sought after confessor'.[1]

Student numbers varied. During the academic year 1817-18, seventy-five students paid fees, either as boarders or as day attenders. Some of these enrolled rather late in the year, so it is likely that average attendance was considerably lower than that. It would appear that about half the students during this period were day attenders, most of them from the town of Tuam. But when it was practical, because space was limited, some students from further afield resided with relatives during their junior years. As far as boarders were concerned, the expenditure records show that, some time after the move to Bishop Street, they were divided between an 'ecclesiastical house' and a 'lay house'.[2]

In 1826-27, according to the Commissioners of Irish Education, there were fifty students, forty-nine Roman Catholics and one member of the Established Church. The Commissioners further noted that the College (which they rendered, fairly exotically, 'St Terlagth's seminary, Bishop-street') was in 'an excellent house with an adjoining piece of ground'; that its system of education was 'the same as Maynooth'; and that its running costs were subsidised to the tune of £10 per annum by Dr Kelly and

---

1. William J. Mahon, ed., *Doctor Kirwan's Irish catechism by Thomas Hughes*, n.d., pp.xiii-xxxvi; 'The late Dean Lyons, PP' in *Tuam Herald*, 16 November 1912; Corish's *Maynooth*, pp.74-75; Proinsias Ó Maolmhuaidh, *Athair na hAthbheochana*, 1981, pp.35-36.
2. SJC, Account Book, 1817-35; Rev. Thomas Brett, *Life of Dr Duggan*, 1921, pp.8-9.

by 'every R.C. clergyman in the diocese from £1.2.9 to £5, according to means.'[1]

By the academic year 1839-40, student enrolment had risen to ninety-five. Of these, sixty were from the archdiocese, ten were from the diocese of Elphin, six were from Meath; six from Kilmore, three from Ardagh; three from Kilmacduagh; two from each of Clogher and Achonry and one from each of Killala, Kilrush and Dublin.[2]

What of that universal source of complaint in boarding institutions, the diet in the College? Evidence of grievance has not survived from the pre-Famine period, but certain facts can be established from the records of expenditure. These do not give a complete picture, however, since much of the food consumed at that time was raised on the College farm. Regular sales of by-products like hides, tallow and sheepskins, even 'kitchen stuff', suggest a thrifty self-sufficiency. And the necessity of economy caused the president, Thomas Feeney, to take a strong interest in the potato market in 1823 and to notice the low price of hay in Westport during the summer vacation of 1829.[3]

Unsurprisingly, there were different diets: professors, students and servants ate from separate boards but there were also differences within the student body, the fare of the parlour boarders being superior to that given to ecclesiastical boarders.[4] Expenditure on 1 March 1838 of 7s 4d on 22lbs. of salmon and 10d on 'herrings for the servants' shows not everybody was feeding from the same trough, but the purchase of a dozen codfish for 11s (55p) and 400 herrings for 19s (95p.) in February 1839 indicates that herrings were considered good enough for at least some of the students on occasion.[5]

A detailed examination of expenditure during one month — November 1844 — will fill out the picture further. Fish was purchased once a week — presumably for consumption on Friday — and total spending on this item during the month was 10s 10d (54p). Beef, it would seem, was very much a staple, if expenditure of £8.15.3 during the same month is any indication. A bill of £1.11.2, together with £2.4.6 paid for 'a fat pig.' shows that bacon too was often on the menu, while mutton

---

1. *Irish Education Inquiry:* Appendix to Second Report of Commissioners, pp.130-31.
2. SJC, Receipts Book 1838-67.
3. SJC, Feeney Papers, pp.50, 80-81.
4. ibid., p.47.
5. SJC, Expenditure Book, 1837-56.

was purchased twice in the course of the month. The abundance of eggs is established by the considerable bill of £2.12.9, but the small amounts expended on fowl, fruit and scallops would suggest that these were luxuries for the professors — or perhaps supplementary fare for delicate boys. Assuming that vegetables from the College's fields were added to the list, there would seem to have been a fairly varied diet.[1] Beer, incidentally, was part of the regular menu during the 1820s and 1830s, but the change in attitudes wrought by the temperance movement from the late 1830s saw it removed.

The late 1820s and early 1830s saw a number of changes in St Jarlath's, notably the purchase of the College building from the Ffrench family, the building of the metropolitan Cathedral on what had been the College grounds, and the death of Archbishop Oliver Kelly, who had been so intimately connected with the establishment since its foundation.

The purchase of the Ffrench interest in the Old College was not an initiative of the College authorities and indeed the transaction took place at a difficult moment as far as diocesan finances were concerned. Lord Ffrench wrote in October 1827 asking whether the archbishop was 'disposed to purchase the interest of the Lease which you hold of the College House',[2] and offering the premises at the valuation which would put on them by a notary. It was not an opportunity to be missed, but Ffrench was in a far greater hurry to conclude the affair than the archbishop and, by March 1828, matters had come to a head:

> I request that urgent circumstances will not permit me to postpone the sale of the College House at Tuam longer than about the middle of the month. May I therefore request you to acquaint me whether Your Lordship will become the purchaser thereof at the sum lately proposed.[3]

Ffrench stated that he would accept a promissory note redeemable in ninety-one days if it was received before 16 March 1828 and that — if luck money would expedite the sale — he was 'willing to allow £50 to be applied to the erection of the Cathedral.' These terms proved acceptable, but there were no funds to meet the promissory note, so Kelly and Feeney had

---

1. ibid.
2. SJC, Feeney papers, p.71.
3. ibid., p.87.

to quickly borrow money from whoever was willing to lend. The largest sums — a hundred pounds each — were lent by two of the original 1817 trustees who had remained closely involved in the College, Matthias McDonnell of Westport, a lay trustee elected in 1817 and Bernard Burke, parish priest of Westport and dean of Tuam.[1] Unfortunately, however, the title purchased was not freehold, something which would give rise to difficulties a few decades later.

The financial strain referred to was occasioned by the building of the Cathedral. This was an enormous project which, because it was adjacent, had a significant effect on life in the College in the decade between the laying of the foundation stone by Oliver Kelly in April 1827 and the dedication ceremony conducted by John MacHale in August 1836. To raise more than £14,000 for a project in the poverty-stricken west of Ireland was going to be a difficult task and there were several interruptions in the work because of financial shortfalls. Indeed, the original architect, Dominick Madden, resigned after it was decided to reduce the scale of the apse to save money, something he regarded as almost sacrilegious from the architectural point of view. Significant debts were incurred by the committee in the course of construction, some of which were still being serviced as late as 1928.[2] But, if the expenditure was a headache for Dr Kelly and his committee, it was a boon to the many Tuam families who were able to look forward to a regular pay packet over several years. Preference was given to workers from the parish and, indeed, this social consequence of the project was repeatedly stressed by the fundraising committee. In their report of February 1832, for example, the members of the committee looked forward 'to a continuance of the support they have hitherto experienced' which enabled them

> during the disastrous period of last summer to give constant employment to upwards of one hundred distressed labourers and thereby prevented them from being a burden upon the public charities. This circumstance, along with having for their object the raising of a temple to the Living God will, it is hoped, secure a prompt and efficient response to this last appeal.[3]

---

1. ibid., p.86.
2. Tuam presbytery, typed notes on the construction of the Cathedral; Monsignor E.A. D'Alton *History of the Archdiocese of Tuam*, 1928, vol.i, 357-60.
3. SJC, *Tuam Metropolitan Cathedral: Report for the year ending 1st February 1832*.

In the same spirit, with the notable exception of the altar, most of the materials, fixtures and fittings were sourced locally.

The altar was purchased in Rome by Dr Kelly, but the archbishop was not destined to see it installed in his new Cathedral. Before he could return home, he died at Albano on 18 April 1834, aged only 57. He was buried at the Church of Propaganda Fide in Rome.

His successor was appointed according to procedures introduced by the Pope in 1823. A consultative vote was held among the diocesan parish priests and the names of the three with the highest votes — the *dignissimus*, the *dignior* and the *dignus*— were sent for consideration to Rome. The favourite of the diocesan clergy was Bernard Burke of Westport, dean of the diocese, but on 21 July 1834 Propaganda Fide chose the *dignior*, the controversial bishop of Killala, John MacHale. Three months later, MacHale travelled to his See in 'an elegant Swiss carriage' presented to him by the people of Killala. A few miles from Tuam, he was met by the students of the College, and escorted by them through the vast crowds that had gathered in the town to greet the new archbishop.[1]

St Jarlath's had a new patron, one who would be at least as influential in its affairs as Oliver Kelly had been. MacHale's fame drew national attention to his diocesan seminary, while his strongly-expounded opinions affected all within it — in one way or another. From the administrative point of view, MacHale appointed a total of nine presidents over the next forty-seven years. The choices he made had important implications, both for the daily lives of the inmates and for the general direction of the institution. Long-serving presidents might leave a mark on the College which would take decades to fade. A short presidency, by contrast, might make no obvious impression at all.

During the first half of MacHale's episcopacy, presidential terms were quite short — the first six presidents he appointed averaged a little over three years in office. Such a pattern would tend to strengthen the importance of the patron and to diminish the role of the president in College administration. This was not necessarily a matter of choice — one presidency was brought to an end by the incumbent's death. But there is compelling evidence that presidents found it difficult to work with MacHale (or, perhaps, he with them). The abrupt departure of

---

1. Ulick Bourke, *The life and times of the Most Rev. Dr MacHale, Archbishop of Tuam*, 1882, pp.118-21; Costello's *MacHale*, p.40-1.

two presidents for missions in the United States surely suggests that such differences blighted some career prospects in the archdiocese. And it is unquestionable that two presidents who remained in Ireland, John MacEvilly and Peter Reynolds, became sworn enemies of MacHale.

According to an historian who spoke to people who remembered them, these early presidents were 'not without their faults.' Such faults, however,

> were almost invariably the fruit of mistaken zeal and not the outcome of positive malevolence. One had perhaps a proud and arrogant head with his colleagues, another an unsympathetic heart with his pupils in the classroom, and a third a grudging hand with both in the refectory, some were tart and impetuous, others were vehement and ambitious; but taking them all in all, they... were heartily devoted to the welfare of those whose training had been committed to their care.[1]

One thing which early nineteenth century presidents had in common was their relative youth. Oliver Kelly, we have seen, took over directly after ordination, while the usual age, on appointment, of presidents of the 'Old College' seems to have been about thirty. Many went on to greater things and, of the eight presidents who served between the mid-1820s and the mid-1850s, three became bishops. The following short sketches trace the presidential succession during that period.

Thomas Feeney, who later became Bishop of Killala, replaced James McKeal as president, probably in 1821. His presidency is among the best documented because he had a relative who admired him enough to transcribe his papers and to do some preparatory work on a biography. Feeney was a native of Crossboyne, Co. Mayo, the son of a merchant and prosperous farmer. He was appointed to St Jarlath's directly from Maynooth in 1817, shortly after the move to the Ffrench's Bank premises. Within a few years, he was president, a post he held for ten years. Although severe and cranky, he was regarded as a good administrator and he guided the College through a few difficult years. According to one source, he persuaded Dr Kelly not to close down St Jarlath's during one financial crisis. From the College, he took over the parish of Kiltulla in Co. Roscommon where he oversaw a number of building projects. Dr MacHale

---

1. Guy's History, pt.viii.

pleaded with him to resume the presidency in 1838, while still retaining his parish and, in the following year, he was appointed bishop of the strife-ridden diocese of Killala, a post he held until his death in 1873.[1]

Feeney was succeeded by Martin Browne (1800-1872), who was born in the parish of Annaghdown. He attended St Jarlath's before going to Maynooth where he was ordained in 1824. He returned as a professor to his alma mater — possibly after a short period as a curate in his native parish — and became a close confidant of Archbishop Kelly. A 'distinguished divine and a refined scholar' he served as president for six and a half years, before taking charge of the parish of Balla in 1837. On his departure from Tuam, an early issue of the *Herald* commented on his 'suavity of manners, deep erudition, unostentatious charity and excellence as a preacher.'[2] He ended his life as archdeacon of the diocese and pastor of Aglish.

James Ronan, a native of Bekan, was a professor in the College for three years before becoming president in 1837. He was the first president appointed by Archbishop MacHale who, incidentally, had served as coadjutor to Ronan's uncle, Dr Peter Waldron, in the diocese of Killala. Ronan died a few months into his presidency, still evidently on good terms with the archbishop who remembered him with great affection.

William Cullinane became president in 1839. He was a past student of the College, who went on to Maynooth in 1829 and returned as Professor of Theology and Belles Lettres in 1836. A decade after leaving the College, he had become its president, but he only served for a short time, before departing for the diocese of Albany in the United States in 1842.

John Flannelly, ordained at Maynooth in 1838, was a few years a professor before being appointed to the presidency of the College in 1842. He served until 1844, when he succeeded to the parish of Ballintubber.

Anthony O'Regan was born in the parish of Kiltulla, Co. Roscommon in 1809. His career path followed closely that of William Cullinane. They were class-fellows at St Jarlath's and Maynooth, and both returned directly from Maynooth to the staff of the College. O'Regan had to wait until 1844, however, to be appointed president. He served until 1849, at which point he departed for the United States to take over the diocesan seminary

---

1. Feeney papers, passim.
2. *Tuam Herald*, 27 May 1837.

of St Louis, on the invitation of Bishop Kendrick, another classfellow at Maynooth. O'Regan was appointed bishop of Chicago in 1854, but his tactlessness caused difficulties in his diocese, which difficulties in turn exacerbated his ill-health, and he retired to Brompton, London, where he died in 1866.[1]

O'Regan was succeeded in 1849 by another native of the parish of Kiltulla, Peter Reynolds. Reynolds was ordained at Maynooth in 1838, and served a few years in Kilcolman before being posted to Tuam as administrator, where he was also attached to the College. He achieved prominence in the town and had served as chairman of the town commissioners shortly before he took on the presidency. From the College he returned to Kilcolman and he was Chancellor of the diocese when he died there in 1875. He has been identified as the author of a pamphlet entitled *Facts and circumstances illustrative of the MacHale method of managing a diocese,* published anonymously under the by-line 'A priest of the Archdiocese of Tuam' in 1849.[2] John MacEvilly, a noted scripture scholar, took over from Reynolds in 1852 and remained until he was appointed Bishop of Galway in 1857. According to one of his students, MacEvilly was 'deeply impressed' by those biblical texts 'which tell us that folly is bound up in the heart of the child, and that the rod of correction shall drive it away.'[3]

The short duration of presidencies and the small teaching staff meant that many of the professors succeeded to the presidency. Thomas Kielty, exceptionally, did not hold the senior post but that, apparently, was his own choice. One individual who served on the staff but could not, as a layman, ever have become president was Michael J. McCann, 'a notable English scholar' who was professor of Mathematics during the 1830s and 1840s. While in the College, he wrote the 'Clanconnell War Song' (better known as 'O'Donnell Abu'), first published in the *Nation* in 1843. Forty years later, McCann died in London, where he had edited a number of newspapers directed at the Irish emigrant community.[4]

---

1. SJC, 'Bishop O'Regan' — photocopied chapter from unidentified history of the Chicago Archdiocese.
2. See D'Alton, vol.ii, pp. 272, 360, and James Mitchell, 'The appointment of Revd J.W. Kirwan' in *JGAHS*, vol.li, 1999, pp.17, 22.
3. Cited by T.P. Boland in *Thomas Carr: Archbishop of Melbourne*, 1997, p.12.
4. Unless otherwise indicated, details on presidents and professors were gleaned from 'Sacerdotes Tuamensis' (photocopied manuscript in SJC), Feeney papers and Guy's History.

An insight into staffing arrangements during the 1830s was provided by President Martin Browne in a letter to Archbishop Kelly:

> I have employed Mr Stack a celebrated declaimer — who had been occasionally for the last three years in Maynooth — to give lectures in Elocution during the next three weeks at our Seminary. I regret to say that the Rev. Mr Ronayne is latterly very delicate and I fear that the symptoms of his illness are indicative of consumption. Since your departure from Ireland, two tutors have been engaged by me, one of them highly recommended to us by Rev Misters Tully and Furlong of Maynooth College, and yet strange to say, both of them after giving them a short trial have been judged utterly incompetent for the classical department in this House. As the character of the College is advancing in public estimation I would be very anxious to secure it by getting some lay teachers of high literary attainment. Mr Matt[hias?] McDonnell had been here on Holy Thursday and appeared quite pleased with the progress made by his children and their general appearance. I consulted him on the propriety and necessity of getting some competent person and he told me he would speak to Dean Burke on the subject. I trust that they will succeed in making a proper selection and very speedily, otherwise it may prove ruinous to this establishment.[1]

Incidentally, as well as the staffing worries, President Browne had concerns about competition from another educational establishment, the recently-opened Killala diocesan seminary. His letter continued: 'Doctor MacHale is about establishing — once more — a Diocesan Seminary. For the life of me I cannot divine his reason. I suppose it will be a counter college to throw us all in the shade.'[2]

Teaching staff aside, the College provided significant employment of a non-academic character. Sundry tradesmen, shopkeepers and farmers catered to the needs of the institution; their names and minimal details of the transactions they

---

1. Browne to Kelly, 1 April 1834, in Padraic Ó Tuairisg, *Ábhar a bhaineann le Ard-dheoise Thuama sa 19ú aois i gcartlann Choláiste na nGael sa Róimh*, unpublished thesis, 1982, pp.123-24.
2. ibid.

engaged in survive in account books. If the frequency in the record of his name is any indication, the busiest of these was the glazier, Mr Stockwell, indicating the exuberant extent of window-breaking during the 1830s and 1840s. Stockwell, according to tradition in his family, was an Englishman and a Protestant who came to Tuam to carry out specialist work on the new cathedral. After this work was completed, he remained in the town, converted to its dominant religion and married. The association of successive painting and glazing generations of Stockwells with the College, incidentally, continues to the present day.[1]

Other contractors included Bridget Murphy and Mrs Heneghan, who provided milk and butter; Mrs Fahy, who supplied eggs; and the butcher, Mr Cullinane, who purveyed his own meat or killed College animals as required.

The College farm provided direct employment, both full-time and casual. Regular workers like Darby Niland, Bartley Collins, James Roche and James Burke were mentioned by name in the accounts; seasonal labourers were denied this recognition. The extent of seasonal employment, moreover, was considerable; the payment of £3.10.6 in August 1838 to 'labourers for saving hay' would have paid for more than 100 man-days at the prevailing rate. The prevailing rate, incidentally, was eightpence a day, which may have been supplemented by generous rations. Some casual employees, in any case, were able to negotiate significant perks for themselves: car-men engaged to transport sea-weed to fertilize the College farm were paid 2s 1d (10.5p) 'for filling the sea-weed' but also 3s 6d (17.5p) 'for drink ...(as) per agreement.' Another, identified in the accounts as 'the man watching the field,' was employed because of a territorial dispute with Le Poer Trench, the Anglican Archbishop. He was paid 2s 6d for ensuring that the College cattle did not trespass further on his Lordship's patience or property, and was supplied with tobacco, gratis, during his lonely vigil.

There is scarcely more information about the domestic staff. Archbishop Kelly's statutes of 1819 show that he was concerned to restrict friendships between servants and students. One writer has suggested that this is indicative of the extent of elitism in the College at the time,[2] but there may have been a more mundane explanation.

---

1. Conversation with Mr F. Stockwell, Nov. 1997.
2. Waldron's 'Archdiocese of Tuam', p.15.

The payment of four shillings to 'Costello, tailor', in January 1838 'for making College liveries for servants' indicates that a distinctive uniform was worn in the early nineteenth century. Certain things — but only rarely their surnames — can be ascertained about the wearers. Wages, which were additional to full board and lodgings, varied widely according to responsibility and experience: 'Cook' received £18 a year; Judy, house maid, £6; Andrew, parlour servant, £5; Michael, kitchen boy, £1.10.0; Carroll, the students' servant, £2. Certain domestic tasks, apparently, were performed by casual workers. Mary Kelly was paid small sums on several occasions during 1837 and 1838 for 'mopping' and for 'washing.' But several years later she had constant employment as a kitchen maid, and her former occasional duties were being carried out by one 'Biddy.'

During the 1830s, the College had been bursting at the seams. From the mid-1840s, however, there were changes in the broader circumstances which served to reduce the pressure on space. The first of these was the Maynooth Bill, the second was the Great Famine.

The passage of the Maynooth bill introduced by Peel's Tory government in 1845 brought an end to a period of political acrimony and controversy, although the debate it provoked revealed the substantial extent of latent anti-Catholicism in England. The bill's provisions secured the future of the national seminary, provided funding for proper staffing, allowing 300 additional students to be admitted.[1]

By agreement between the bishops, fifty of the additional places were allocated to the Tuam province. This had significant implications for St Jarlath's. In August 1844, President O'Regan, announced that in view of the anticipated endowment of Maynooth, the study of Logic, Metaphysics and Divinity would cease in Tuam, to be resumed, however, 'should the freedom of religious instruction, or any other necessity, require their resumption.'[2] Instead there would be more extensive and elaborate courses of Classics, Rhetoric, Geometry and Mathematical science, together with the other branches of useful and practical learning, calculated to fit the young students either for entrance into the College of Maynooth, if destined for the church, or to

---

1. Corish, *Maynooth*, pp.97-105 and Donal A. Kerr, *Peel, priests and politics: Sir Robert Peel's administration and the Roman Catholic Church in Ireland, 1841-1846*, 1982, pp.226-289.
2. *Tuam Herald*, 9 August 1844.

graduate in any of the Universities, if intended for the learned and secular professions.¹

President O'Regan was as good as his word. It would appear that he himself had a particular interest in scientific work and had kept in contact with his mathematics professor at Maynooth, the eminent scientist, Nicholas Callan. When a new laboratory was fitted out late in November 1845, the equipment — on which, according to the College accounts, £20 was expended — was personally selected by Callan, and was deemed by an awestruck *Herald* columnist to reflect well on the reverend gentleman's 'judgement and taste.' The instruments were 'new, richly finished and of the best materials,' and made provision not only for illustrating the abstruse principles of science; but also for exciting the attention of the youthful pupil by the many amusing and interesting experiments which will accompany each lecture.²

The amusement was not restricted to the students of the College and, in December, O'Regan gave a two hour public lecture in his laboratory, one of a series, on 'The science of electricity' — also the specialism, incidentally, of his mentor, Callan. Again the *Herald* was impressed, this time by 'a series of the most interesting experiments which we ever had the happiness to witness:'

> The electric fluid was presented to all the senses in every variety of form that could amuse, awe, or terrify the beholder, now playing in every fanciful mood that the mind could imagine — now dazzling with the most varied but brilliant lights — again equalling in its velocity the rapid speed of lightning, with which terrific agent it was shown to be identical.³

Meanwhile, outside the College, most scientific attention was being directed at discovering the cause of and the cure for *phytophthora infestans*, the potato blight which had reached Ireland in September 1845 and which was noticed locally during October. There is little information about conditions in the College during the famine period which followed. The impression is that the number of students declined sharply to the

---

1. ibid.
2. ibid., 8, 15 November 1845.
3. ibid, 13 December 1845.

extent that the institution was barely ticking over. According to Frank Guy, who spoke to two 'survivors' of that period — Rev. Laurence Ansbro, P.P. Annaghdown, and Canon Patrick Flatley of Aughagower — the student body 'dwindled in numbers, until at one time, there were only sixteen or seventeen students left.'[1] Incidentally, Guy's informants are not contradicted by the College accounts. One of the sixteen or seventeen was future president Ulick Bourke who was later troubled by one vivid memory:

> In April 1847, he beheld a boy of about nine years reduced to the appearance of a skeleton. He came to the College, Tuam, where the writer was a student, to beg a crust of the ecclesiastical students, who were themselves almost as starved as the poor child. The hair of his head stood on end, his eyes were glaring and sunken in their sockets, which appeared overshadowed by prominent eyebrows and arched forehead — hair fully a half inch long, a false growth caused by decay, brought on by hunger, covered his bare skinny arms and cheeks.[2]

Such harrowing poverty, endemic in the streets of the town, was the major concern of the College staff in the late 1840s. Tuam was in a particularly dire position, not least because relief supplies coming from Galway were almost invariably pillaged or otherwise appropriated before they reached the town.[3] Among those most directly involved in seeking to address the problem was Peter Reynolds, who served as chairman of the Tuam Town Commissioners during most of 'Black Forty-seven'. Other professors were also involved in the relief effort.[4] One of these was John MacEvilly, who was given to recounting the following story during his anecdotage[5]:

> O'Regan was president and he had, as they say, a niggard

---

1. Guy's History, pt. vii.
2. Burke's *MacHale*, pp.145-6.
3. J. Cunningham, *Galway*, Ch.4 forthcoming.
4. Guy's History, pt.vii; Liam Bane, *The Bishop in Politics: Life and Career of John MacEvilly*, 1993, pp.7-8.
5. According to Monsignor D'Alton, MacEvilly was 'as alert at the age of eighty-two as he had been at thirty.' However he 'had acquired to the full the garrulity of old age. And while he told the same old stories in the same old way, the priests at table were bound to be attentive or pretend to be.' (*Archdiocese of Tuam*, p.112-3).

hand, even for famine times, and the professors — not to talk of the students — were growing visibly thin. How were they to get one decent dinner? A light broke in upon their brain. It was the inspired thought of quietly slaying at dead of night one of the College sheep, in the hope that when the carcass was found by the president in the morning he would see no alternative but to serve it up in due course at their table in the refectory. Lots were cast, the hungry but learned butcher fixed upon, and Macbeth-like to his task he went; the bloody deed was accomplished but parbleu! when the shocked president learned of the sheep's unaccountable misadventure, he did see an alternative to wasting the blessed mutton on the professors; what! he would offer it for sale to the highest bidder in the open market. Ultimately, however, at the earnest appeal of of his colleagues (no doubt with tears in their eyes) he consented to retain the dead sheep in the College, and leave it to them as a treasure-trove, and so there was compartively luxurious feasting by the staff for weeks, or it may be months after.[1]

The contrasting memories of Bourke and MacEvilly reflect different attitudes towards the famine. Bourke, at a more impressionable age, was profoundly affected and was attracted by John Mitchell's uncompromisingly nationalist analysis of the catastrophe.[2] The political outlook of MacEvilly and his peers was already formed by the mid-1840s and, moreover, they were the people who had to address the complex realities of the tragedy on the ground. Having made mistakes themselves and witnessed the exploitation or neglect of the needy by their neighbours, they were less inclined to place all of the blame for the famine on 'perfidious Albion.'

---

1. Guy's History, pt. viii.
2. Ó Maolmhuaidh, *Athair na hAthbheochana*, pp.31-32.

4. "...with suitable breadth and proportion."

Who could have thought that since you witnessed last
Our mimic sports; an eventful year has passed.
What vast changes through the wide world since then appear,
What a glorious transformation even here;
Long live the builder's art — the genius of Goban Saor.[1]

The Ffrench's bank building was an improvement on the improvised College at the Mall. Indeed, until the building of the Cathedral, it was among the most imposing buildings in Tuam. Hely Dutton wrote in 1824: 'The Roman Catholic Archbishop has lately erected a handsome house which, with the Catholic college of St Jarlath, adds much to the appearance of the town.'[2] And evidently, some attention was paid to the general surroundings for, during the summer vacation of 1829, President Thomas Feeney wrote to Professor Hosty as follows: 'I need not tell you to take care of the premises... I know the garden will be neat and free from weeds on my return — do not forget the flower-knot.[3]

Dutton also provided a more general description of Tuam. Almost opposite the College and the Catholic archbishop's house was the Protestant archbishop's palace which he said was 'highly ornamented by a handsome and extensive demesne,' but itself lacking in 'much architectural beauty.' The agriculturalist's summary of Tuam was generally favourable, although it concentrated on facilities and amenities rather than on the town's physical aspect. But in praising the markets, the dispensary, the 'two newspapers well-edited', 'the two good inns at which the mail and canal coaches stop', while avoiding commentary on the streets and lanes, one senses that Dutton was being diplomatic.[4] After all, if two suburban houses could add 'much' to its appearance, the town as a whole was hardly very impressive.

Other commentators were less circumspect. Mr and Mrs Samuel Carter Hall, who passed through in 1840, advised their

---

1. Excerpt from prologue to pre-Christmas entertainment in the College, 1871 (*Tuam News*, 15 December 1871).
2. Hely Dutton's *Survey*, p.327.
3. SJC, Feeney papers, pp.80-81.
4. Hely Dutton's *Survey*, p.327.

readers that it would be 'no great loss' to avoid Tuam altogether, although they allowed that 'if approached from the east' the view of the town was picturesque. And while the new Cathedral impressed them, they considered that it was 'sadly out of harmony with the dull and dingy habitations upon which it looks down.' All in all, they contended that Tuam was 'a dirty and ruinous looking place.'[1] At the time of the Halls' visit, Tuam had a population of 6034 people with 1208 families occupying 1158 houses. Of these, more than three quarters lived in utterly abominable conditions with 555 families living in fourth class houses and 368 in third class houses. It was the occupants of these third and fourth class houses who were, to a large extent, the casualties of famine later in the decade. By 1851, in the aftermath of that famine and notwithstanding some migration from its hinterland, the population of Tuam had fallen to 4940. The decline continued for the rest of the century: 4223 people remained in 1871; 3012 in 1891; 2896 in 1901.[2]

There was some physical improvement in the post-Famine period. New houses were erected, gas lighting was provided and footpaths were paved, while the railway arrived in 1860. The impressions of visitors did not change much, however, and Henry Coulter who visited the town in the New Year of 1862 detected 'a want of neatness and cleanliness... in many directions.' As far as he was concerned, the only building in the town with the 'slightest merit' architecturally was the Catholic cathedral. His description continued:

> Tuam is remarkable for the extent of its suburbs, which are larger in proportion than any other place I have visited, and I regret to say that much poverty exists among the people who inhabit them. Rows of mud cabins extend in various directions, some to a distance of fully one mile from the town, and the aspect they present is miserable in the extreme. Occasionally we meet one that has a good thatch, whitewashed walls and decent windows, contrasting vividly with the squalor, dirt and discomfort of the adjoining hovels, but these exceptional cases are very few. The mass — I may say the whole of the cottages constituting the extensive suburbs of Tuam — are neither water-

---

1. Mr & Mrs Samuel Carter Hall, *Hall's Ireland*, 1984 edn, vol.ii, p.408.
2. Census for 1841, 1851, 1871, 1911.

tight nor air-tight and are unfit for the habitation of human beings... The back lanes and streets within the town are occupied by artisans and labourers of the poorest class; the houses are of the most inferior description and in many of them two or three families are congregated together where they 'suffer in foulest rags and dire disease', and drain the bitter cup of poverty to its dregs.[1]

The same 'suburbs' continued to attract attention and, in 1912, one commentator took a closer look. The inhabitants of places like Barrack Street, the Tierboy road and the Cloonthoo road, he observed, had to spend their days in the open air because the stench inside their houses 'prevents the regular living-in system.' Having invited himself inside, he noted that 'in several of these hovels, large families were occupying a single room' while 'old sacks fastened on cross-bars served the purpose of partitioning off a small corner, in which a bed stretched on the cold damp floor was the only family resting place.'[2]

In general, visitors were struck by the contrast between the substantial ecclesiastical buildings and the fragile and makeshift appearance of the rest of the town. In 1839, a visitor who admitted that his impression was coloured by 'imaginative prejudice' described the place as having a 'Romish look — that indolent, un-business-like, "ne'er do weel" look — which belongs to most towns all over the world where priests enjoy too much power.' He went on: 'Here is a town, ...an archiepiscopal see, the residence of two most reverend lords, ...and yet there is no public walk, no library, either circulating or stationary.'[3] Later visitors put it more more pithily: for one, Tuam was 'a poor town, of which the staple trade is religion'; for another, it was a town with 'two cathedrals and no barber.'[4]

Until the mid-1840s, the quality and availability of houses in the town was of very practical relevance to the College authorities. Because, impressive and all as the French's Bank building might have appeared to Hely Dutton, it did not have the capacity to meet the demands placed upon it and, soon after the move to

---

1. See 'Tuam in 1862' in Claffey's *Glimpses of Tuam*, pp.33-34.
2. *Connacht Tribune*, 29 June 1912.
3. Caesar Otway, A *tour in Connaught, comprising sketches of Clonmacnoise, Joyce Country, and Achill,* 1839, pp.178, 185.
4. Noel O'Donoghue, *Proud and upright men,* n.d., p.8; *Tuam Herald,* 25 October 1902.

Bishop Street, some students had to find 'digs' in the town and vicinity.[1]

And the College authorities had to find additional buildings in the town on such leases as were available. In 1834, President Browne informed Oliver Kelly that he had acquired 'Doctor Clarke's large house for the accommodation of the students' and that he had taken this step 'for the purpose of arresting disease more readily should it again visit our establishment' (A scarlatina epidemic had recently passed through the College). The rent of the house, at £40 a year, was high, but the president agreed to that amount in exchange for the power to surrender the building whenever he wished. In the same letter, he informed the archbishop that 'the Long Ballroom which was occasionally converted into a Lesson House is to be repaired.'[2]

According to tradition, premises occupied by the College during these years included the house subsequently owned by Dr Costello on Bishop Street, a house across the road in Bishop St adjoining the entrance gate to the Presentation Convent, and Cornfield House on the Dublin Rd owned by the Handcock family which later became the core of the Mercy Convent.[3] But suitable premises were scarce in Tuam and, for one reason or another, some buildings were used for only a short time. A notice in the recently-established *Tuam Herald* in 1837, for example, offered for letting 'a large house with spacious offices and lock-up yard', adding that his Bishop Street house had been 'lately occupied as a College.'[4] Clearly, the accommodation problems which resulted from the loss of this building proved difficult to solve. And the difficulty, it would be reasonable to presume, was exacerbated by the problem of finding a suitable successor for President Ronan who died soon after his appointment in 1838. In that year, in any case, the College was forced to extend the summer vacation by three weeks. Students were informed by means of an advertisement in local papers: 'In consequence of new arrangements that are taking place regarding some of the houses and premises that formed portion of the

---

1. Brett's *Duggan*, pp.8-9. One who provided 'digs' for students was a well-known Tuam figure John 'the Minor' Gannon (see *Tuam Herald*, 30 March, 29 June 1918).
2. Browne to Kelly, 1 April 1834; Kielty to Kelly, 6 April 1834, in Ó Tuairisg's *Abhar...*, p.123-25.
3. Guy's History, pt.vi.
4. *Tuam Herald*, 28 October 1837.

Early twentieth century view of the College, including ball alley on the right.

Aerial view of the modern College.

The College Refectory, post-1930.

The swimming pool, post-1930.

The oratory, post-1950.

Dormitory, post-1930.

Anthony O'Regan, president 1844-49, later bishop of Chicago.

Mark Ryan, an active Fenian while a student in the College and subsequently.

Archbishop John MacHale, the most influential figure in the College's nineteenth century history.

Cardinal Paul Cullen, who disagreed with MacHale on Church affairs.

Martin A. O'Brennan: student and teacher in the College; Gaelic enthusiast and newspaper proprietor.

Controversial past pupil: Fr Patrick Lavelle, at Cong Abbey.

Students of the College during the 1870s.

Rev. Ulick J. Bourke, College president 1865-1878, early Gaelic revivalist and fenian sympathiser. *(courtesy of P.Ó Maolmhuaidh)*

Jeremiah O'Donovan Rossa: sent three sons to St Jarlath's.

establishment, the College will not open this year until 3 September.'¹ Some reassurance was offered a month later, however, in the editorial columns of the *Herald* :

> We are glad to be able to state that the inconvenience to which the College had been subjected by the surrender of Mr Handcock's houses was merely temporary. With the aid of the lodge, a very comfortable building within the premises of the old establishment (which is now being repaired) it is found that St Jarlath's will be able to accommodate as many students on this as on any former year. The College has been open for the last eight or ten days for their reception.²

The problems were not entirely resolved, however. Notices in the local press summoning students back in January 1839, admitted that 'owing to circumstances, the precise day for the termination of the Christmas recess had not been fixed on...'³

Developments in the 1840s eased the accommodation problems. The expansion of Maynooth meant that more clerical students could be accommodated in the National House, while famine-related emigration played its part in thinning the ranks of potential students.

During the following decade, a few legal difficulties emerged concerning title to the 'Old College' building. One of these — the interest acquired by Celia Kelly as an inheritance from her brother, Archbishop Oliver Kelly — was easily dealt with, and she assigned her rights to the College trustees. The other claim — on behalf of two sisters who inherited the Hort interest purchased by their father on the bankruptcy of Tuam banker, Michael Morris — could not be resolved without conflict.⁴

Increasing demand for places in the 1850s, arising out of a perceived 'increasing thirst for education which is fast spreading amongst all classes', provided the spur for a major extension of the College and the foundation stone of the 'New College' was laid in 'an imposing ceremony on 4 February 1858, shortly after

---

1. ibid., 18 August 1838; SJC, Feeney papers, p.35-36.
2. *Tuam Herald*, 22 September 1838.
3. ibid., 29 December 1838.
4. Tuam Archdiocesan Archive, deed of conveyance, 1855; SJC. 'Additional notes on behalf of plaintiffs' transcribed into Receipt book 1838-67, pp.114-115.

the appointment of Patrick J. O'Brien as president'. Presiding was Dr MacHale, who was assisted by 'a numerous body of the clergy of the surrounding parishes.'[1]

The representative of the *Herald*, in noting 'the large concourse of the people of the town' who were in attendance on the occasion, took the opportunity to reflect on the work of the College, an institution, he said, which had 'during more than half a century' succeeded in imparting 'a sound secular and religious education, not only to aspirants for the sacred ministry but to hundreds who have risen to eminence in the professional and mercantile walks of life'[2] The building work was carried out under the direction of noted local architect and contractor, Andrew Egan, who had previously built the Town Hall, the Cathedral bell-tower and, according to his obituarist, 'almost all of the churches and public buildings within twenty miles of Tuam.'[3]

The new building would become the core of the modern college. A contemporary described the plans:

> The building will exceed a hundred feet in length, and will be three storeys high, with suitable breadth and proportion. It will contain a corridor, dormitories and rooms for deans and professors. In conjunction with the old College, it will afford a great amount of accommodation.'[4]

In July 1859, the *Herald* was able to tell its readers that the 'towering and splendid structure' was 'completely finished and conveniently fitted up' for the coming term and that the College was now able to accommodate sixty students 'at the very least.' That the expanded establishment would soon be able 'to boast of its full complement of youthful inmates' the journalist was in no doubt and he continued in hyperbolic vein:

---

1. *Tuam Herald*, 6 February 1858.
2. ibid. The following was the inscription placed beneath the foundation: Fundamentum Collegii huiusce novi in honorem Sancti Jarlathi, diaecescos Patroni posuit illustrassimus Archiepiscopus Joannes MacHale, die quarto Februarii, anno 1858, anno Pontificatus Pio Noni, feliciter regnantis duodecimo, et Regno Victoriae reginae anno vigesimo secundo; assistente frequentissimo numero tum cleri, tum alumenorum Collegii, necnon et populi, qui ad lœtam ceremoniam conspiciendam turmatim convenerant. +JOANNES Archiepiscopus Tuamensis
3. *Connaught Patriot*, 24 October 1863.
4. *Tuam Herald*, 6 February 1858.

> Apart from the singularly interesting and swaying motive which attaches to its very name — a name fondly endeared to every Irishman by the apostolic virtues, lofty patriotism, and unrivalled eloquence of the present great successor of St Jarlath; this College enjoys the invaluable advantages of a most eligible site and of recreation grounds unequalled, perhaps, in Europe or in the world for extent and healthfulness. The annual pension for "Ecclesiastical Students" alike and "Lay Boarders" — as may be seen from the Prospectus — is beyond all question extremely moderate. Its immediate, auspicious and fostering patron is "John, Archbishop of Tuam." The "creature comforts" — as we ourselves can testify — are well and abundantly supplied by the worthy President; whilst the literary department in all its varied and important branches is committed by His Grace to the careful and conscientious charge of an eminent staff of learned, pious, and painstaking clergymen.[1]

If the New College was the core of the modern institution, its site and construction was also an important landmark in the development of Tuam. It was built on the extensive Keighrey Park property purchased in 1856 by Dr MacHale from J.S. Handcock. The acquisition allowed the development of an 'ecclesiastical quarter' in the town, located in the belt between Bishop Street and Dublin Road.[2] There are indications, too, that even if the precise geographical term had not yet been coined, contemporaries were conscious that they were witnessing the formation of such a quarter.[3] One was the *Herald* writer in 1849 who, prompted by the 'large and massive and majestic form' of the new Presentation convent, remarked on its position 'immediately near' the Cathedral, the Old College, other convents and archbishop's palace. Taken together, he wrote,

> the buildings constituted the most beautiful collection of religious structures that ever stood so closely and judiciously grouped, on a site where air and light and cleanli-

---

1. ibid., 16 July 1859.
2. Keighrey's Park also provided the grounds for the Christian Brothers' Schools, for the Mercy Convent and, early in the 20th century, the site for the Archbishop's House.
3. Mairín Doddy, 'Tuam Architectural Survey Report,' n.d., p..90; Kevin Whelan, 'The regional impact of Irish Catholicism, 1700-1850' in Smyth & Whelan's *Common Ground: essays on the historical geography of Ireland*, 1988, pp..252-277.

ness combine with a rich extensive prospect to unite the loveliest blessings of nature with the most beautiful forms of religion.¹

And fourteen year later, on a similar theme, The *Connaught Patriot* was positively triumphalist:

> ...there will be presented to the view of the traveller as he enters our city on the Dublin Road a coup d'oeil not to be surpassed — if equalled — in Ireland. First in order, his eye will light upon the Christian Brothers grand establishment; next that of the Sisters of Mercy; then the lofty Cathedral with its lofty tower and spires looking towards Heaven; the new College; the old St Jarlath's, the veteran nursery of candidates for the priesthood; the palace of our illustrious archbishop, Ireland's hope and religion's brightest pillar; and then the spacious concerns of the pious Sisterhood.²

Keighrey Park was also a fine amenity for students, and one the College authorities were not slow to boast about. An 1865 prospectus claimed that because of 'its geographical elevation, the situation of the College and playground, in all some ten acres, is exceedingly healthful.' Moreover, the old and new College formed ' a portion of a semi-circular group of ecclesiastical buildings which are considered not only picturesque but beautiful.'³

This advertisement, placed by Ulick Bourke on his appointment as president, presaged further development. Bourke, as shall be shown in a later chapter, immediately set about increasing the number of students. His success necessitated further expansion a few years later. But if the O'Brien expansion of the late 1850s had been accomplished discreetly enough, Ulick Bourke was incapable of attempting any project without a fanfare, and his appeal for contributions from Irish Catholics at home and abroad was as much an attempt to add to the fame and prestige of his College as it was a fund-raising exercise. He later admitted that a hundred pounds was spent in publicising his appeal, a substantial sum in 1870.⁴

---

1. *Tuam Herald*, 17 February 1849.
2. *Connaught Patriot*, 11 February 1863.
3. SJC, History file, 1865 prospectus.
4. *Tuam News*, 27 September 1872.

It would appear that Bourke's decision to extend the College was taken suddenly and that it was his decision alone. His announcement of 8 December 1869 — less than six weeks after the Archbishop's departure for the Vatican Council in Rome — did not claim that the extension was initiated by MacHale, but rather that it was 'a duty of the superiors' to the students of the College and, ingenuously, that it was 'a duty sanctioned by the encouraging approbation of the Archbishop'. MacHale's subsequent letter to Bourke shows that he first learnt of the development while in Rome: 'Your account of the increasing number of the students at S. Jarlath's is so encouraging that I am not surprised at your having so promptly undertaken to enlarge the building.'[1]

Bourke's appeal is an interesting and lengthy document, in which he considered the role of the seminary in Catholic education and the words on the subject of St Alphonso Liguori. He argued, moreover, that in the absence of 'a government really and fully enlightened,' the diocesan colleges had also provided a secular education and were, 'for the vast majority of the Catholics of Ireland, the only substitute for a University.' For its part, 'St Jarlath's College had not been the least useful, nor the least Catholic and national, in tone and language.' He was appealing chiefly to people in the Tuam diocese who had 'a practical interest' in the fortunes of the College. But no 'itinerant collectors' would be sent forth; those 'kindly disposed' were exhorted to have a whip-around for the building fund among their friends.

The possibility of failure to raise the necessary sum was not even entertained, since the work had 'actually commenced', both because of the need to accommodate extra students and the desirability of improving 'the present edifice, in keeping with the architectural elegance of the religious institutions with which it is surrounded.'[2]

During 1870, Bourke published reports on the progress of the work and the fundraising in letters to the editor of the *Tuam Herald* and other publications. By May, over £400 had been raised, but the president advised the 'priests and people of Ireland and those in England, America or Australia' that much more was required. 'A thousand and more' he estimated, 'will

---
1. *The Tablet*, 5 March 1870.
2. ibid. Liguori's example was important to Bourke insofar as it provided a precedent for proceeding with the construction of a seminary before considering how the building costs might be paid.

not suffice to defray the entire costs of both wings.'[1] In November 1870, Ulick Bourke established a newspaper, the *Tuam News*, under the editorship of his nephew, John MacPhilbin. The content of the paper would reflect its owner's preoccupations, including his interest to the Irish language, but during its first year, an inordinate amount of space was devoted to the progress of the College building. A regular message from the proprietor listed the latest contributors while the more poignant covering letters were printed in part or in full. On 16 June 1871, for example, two letters were published. One came from Eugene Griffin of Innislacken Island, Roundstone. Griffin described himself as 'poor' and apologised that he was only able to send thirty stamps — 'I am sorry and I moan that my contribution is so very small.' The other came from Philadelphia, from Patrick Ruane, formerly of Woodpark, Annaghdown:

> Dear Father Bourke, — Enclosed please find a cheque for £10 sterling, collected by me amongst a few friends, in response to your eloquent appeal... I would have been enabled to send you a sum much more worthy of the good cause which you represent, but I am sending now a similar sum to the patriotic Father Lavelle, towards his new church in Cong. Although your appeal was addressed only to Galway men and Mayo men, the four provinces are represented by the above mite, and justly so, for in my opinion, the cause for which you appeal is not a diocesan, but a provincial and a national cause. For I consider Irishmen in general indebted to St Jarlath's, and to the illustrious names connected with it, especially and above all, to his Grace the Archbishop, and to you for your great efforts and success in restoring and reviving our almost obsolete mother tongue.[2]

Over the following two years, money dribbled in slowly. On St Patrick' Day 1871, President Bourke issued a fresh appeal, in which he increased his target from 'a thousand and more' to a total 'say of two thousand pounds.' When the fund closed in September 1872, however, only £765 had been contributed by 337 donors, most of them from the diocese and many of them

1. *Tuam Herald*, 28 May 1870.
2. *Tuam News*, 16 June 1871.

priests. The majority had given modest enough amounts: 142 gave £1 each; 61 gave less than £1; 117 gave between £2 and £5; 16 gave more than £5.[1] The larger donors included a number of dignitaries: Baron O'Hagan, the Lord Chancellor; Under Secretary Thomas Burke — later assassinated by 'Invincibles'; Mitchell Henry, M.P., of Kylemore; Captain John Philip Nolan — later a controversial Home Rule and Parnellite M.P. for North Galway; Rev. Robert French Whitehead, vice-President of Maynooth and grand-son of Lord French. The names of donors, large and small, were to be 'written on parchment and elegantly illuminated and framed,' and 'in the College halls handed down to encourage the youth of the coming generations to "go do likewise"' Those who had promised to contribute but had not yet done so were offered a grace period of six months, if they wished their names to be entered on the parchment. The opportunity was availed of only to the extent of twenty pounds.[2]

To the cost of the new building and other improvements over the previous few years, the College itself had managed to contribute a little from current income. There were substantial borrowings, and in addition to these, the sum of £400 was owed to builders and suppliers; this had to be paid by the end of 1872. Bourke was not discouraged, however, and he immediately launched another appeal, this time for a library. The 'splendid collection' of a former president, Bishop O'Regan of Chicago, he insisted, would have been given to the College but for the want of accommodation. During the recent work, a special room had been set aside and fitted out, but was as yet bereft of books. Money therefore, or donations of suitable books, would be most welcome.

Bourke was nothing if not enthusiastic and, adverting to his belief that even small towns in Britain, France and Germany had public libraries, he insisted that there should be at least one decent library in Connacht. St Jarlath's College could become 'the seat of a grand public library for the western province' where the needs of all those 'pretending to scholarly acquirements' would be satisfied.[3] Evidently, the library was soon stocked but Bourke was not finished yet. In February 1873, he announced that he was 'completing and fitting out' a chapel in the College. As was usual with Bourke, the work was begun

1. ibid., 27 September 1872.
2. ibid.; Some financial questions answered' (draft by Ulick Bourke) in SJC, Receipt Book 1837-68.
3. *Tuam News*, 27 September 1872.

before its cost was considered but the president was certain that members of the public would once again come to his rescue. And his faith was rewarded with donations of £46 from forty-two individuals over the following eight weeks.

For the previous forty years, students had attended services in the Cathedral, but this was no longer practical. According to the president:

> As the number of students is being daily increased, their presence in the Cathedrals on Sundays and holidays necessarily demands a larger amount of space than that which, in days past, had been allotted to them. On that account, and for their own better accommodation, and for the convenience, too, of the Catholic flock who attend in their thousands at the celebrations of the divine mysteries on feast days and Sundays, it is deemed the better way to have a domestic chapel in connexion with the College.[1]

In the fifteen years between 1858 and 1873, therefore, there were two major infrastructural developments and, in the form of the oratory, a minor addition. Three decades would pass before it became necessary to embark on any further extensions. Moreover, such was the financial confusion left in Ulick Bourke's wake when he became pastor of Claremorris in 1878, that no fresh expenditure could have been contemplated for a period. While president, Bourke spent £3614 on 'improvements'. And when the dust had settled on these, there were debts of £600 to a priest of the diocese, of £700 to the nuns of the Convent of Mercy in Ballinrobe, and of £300 to a bank. The president's appeals through the newsapers raised only £816 — a little over 20% of what he spent — and even a belatedly-authorised special church gate collection throughout the diocese added only another £875.[2]

John MacEvilly's episcopacy (1881-1902) did not pass without some developments. The College property was added to in 1884 with the purchase of a 'very large two storey high house' in Bishop St. This acquisition must have given the archbishop some satisfaction because the premises were formerly the offices of the *Connaught Patriot* — a 'malicious Garribaldian rag' according to MacEvilly — which was edited by Martin O'Brennan between 1859 and 1865.[3]

---

1. ibid., 28 February 1873.
2. SJC, 'Some finacial questions answered'.
3. *Tuam Herald*, 5 April 1884.

The installation of central heating by President John Fallon[1] in 1897 was a major landmark as far as the comfort of both professors and students was concerned. The contractors, Messrs Musgrave & Co. Ltd. of Belfast and London, undertook to fit their 'patent small pipe hot water apparatus' in the study hall, the class halls, the oratory, the dormitories and the corridors. The level of detail, including technical detail, in the *Herald's* account indicates that institutional heating was very much a novelty in the west of Ireland at the time. It describes how the various rooms in the College were to be

> filled up with hot water pipes, the length of pipe used being in proportion to the size of each apartment. A temperature of 60°F. will be obtained in the College when the outside temperature is at 32°F. This will be sufficient to keep it warm and comfortable throughout the coldest days in winter, and what is equally important, it will keep the students' clothes in their rooms perfectly dry and safe at all times even during the dampest weather. The boilers will be so constructed so that the temperatures can be raised or lowered at will, and also that a slow fire can be kept burning all night in the furnace, so that an equable temperature can be maintained in the College during the winter. The heating apparatus requires about 3610 feet of wrought iron hydraulic tube, the same as fitted in Maynooth College last year by the same firm.[2]

The necessity for a further extension was recognised by the turn of the century during the presidency of Michael McHugh.[3] Before plans reached fruition, however, Archbishop MacEvilly

---

1. A native of Dunmore, John Fallon was ordained at Maynooth in 1882. He served in Annagh until 1884, when he became a professor in St Jarlath's. He served in Ballinrobe from 1890 to 1893, when he returned to the College as president. He went on to serve in Knock (1898-1909) Moylough (1909-1918) and Castlebar, where he died, as archdeacon, in 1946 at the age of 89. According to his obituary, he was 'a strong advocate of the gaelic ideal', was 'fond of outdoor sport' and 'in his day was a noted horseman'.
2. ibid., 24 July 1897.
3. Michael J. McHugh was a native of Dunmore. He attended Maynooth before before being ordained in Tuam Cathedral in 1883. He was appointed to Spiddal, Kilconly, Bekan and the parish of Tuam, before serving as College president between 1898 and 1903. His subsequent career took him to Crossboyne, Annagh and Kilcolman, where he died as parish priest and canon in 1942 at the age of 83.

died on 26 November 1902. He was succeeded by the bishop of Clonfert, John Healy.[1] On appointment, Healy set about leaving his mark on the College. He appointed a new president, created three new professorial positions, announced additional scholarships which intensified the 'very keen competition among the boys,' and proceeded with the improvements.[2] President Higgins's[3] first annual report was fulsome in its praise of his superior's efforts:

> you have furnished a new study hall that is second to none, and that has won the admiration of superintendents who presided over examinations there, and not to speak of various other equipments you have provided to bring us up to date in every respect. In a short time you will have provided us with a sadly-needed extension to our buildings which, I presume to say, will make our College one of the finest Diocesan Colleges, I shall not say in Connaught, but in Ireland.[4]

Tenders for the 'sadly-needed extension' were sought in February 1904; by April 1905, the 'spacious study hall of the new wing' was ready for a public entertainment consisting of *Robert Emmett*, — 'a history play by Mangan'; *The Lad from Largymore*, a farce by Séamus MacManus; and a 'brief but select concert.'[5] As a result of the improvements, the enrolment increased from 97 boarders 'accommodated only at great inconvenience' in 1904-5 to 107 — 'the largest number... that was ever in the College' — two years later.[6]

Shortly after the completion of the College extension,

---

1. Rev. P.J. Joyce, *John Healy: Archbishop of Tuam*, 1931, p.258.
2. SJC, President's Report Book, 1903-1936, report for 1903-04.
3. According to one who knew him, Castlebar-born Dr Michael Higgins was 'a man of great prudence and humility and a theologian remarkable for the practical accuracy of his knowledge rather than for its unpractical depth. Not a footnote escaped his attention' After ordination in Tuam in 1888, he served in Kilcommon, Aughawell, Aglish, St. Jarlath's College (1891-94), Annaghdown and Dunmore. He served as College president from 1903 to 1910, when he became parish priest of Cummer. Shortly afterwards, he was appointed auxiliary bishop of Tuam. During the remainder of his life, he resided in Castlebar, but he died in 1918 at the age of 56. Higgins's death took place on the eve of Dr Healy's month's mind , so he did not become archbishop.
4. President's report for 1903-04.
5. *Tuam Herald*, 6 February 1904, 29 April, 6 May 1905.
6. President's reports for 1904-05 and 1906-07.

fundraising began for a new palace for the archbishop — 'a suitable residence that will be worthy of the metropolitan city of Tuam.' The project was completed in the spring of 1906, aided by a successful 'St Jarlath's Bazaar', held during August 1905 in the College grounds, and other events organised by the national teachers of the archdiocese.[1] Significantly, although Dr Healy moved only a few hundred yards, he moved from the periphery of Tuam's 'ecclesiastical quarter' to its centre. He was no further from St Jarlath's, but he was much closer to the other religious-run services of the town. This tended towards an equalisation in the status of the various institution and may have resulted in a greater degree of formality in relations between the College and the archbishop. The institution by Dr Healy of an 'annual visit' to the students in the study hall, would indicate that the casual visits of the MacHale days were a thing of the past.[2]

Meanwhile, more low-key refurbishment continued in the College. In December 1906, for example, £61 was paid to one Blake for 'putting in urinals', while £42.10.0 was expended on 'renewing old oil paintings in refectory and getting new frames, also new paintings.' In 1919, an ambulatory or cloister was constructed for the use of professors and students in inclement weather.[3]

Another stage in the development of the College came with the provision of electricity in 1920 after the establishment of a Tuam Electric Power and Light Company. The College, indeed, was to the fore in the formation of the Company and remained a major shareholder. At the meeting to establish the Power Company in March 1919, the principal speaker was President Eaton who proposed the engineer's report. Progress was slow enough, possibly due to the political climate, but during the following year a 'power house' was built on the Dublin Road on land purchased from the archbishop and the town and college were wired.[4] Light was the main goal of electrification, but in its aftermath, other labour saving devices were embraced. Among

1. *Tuam Herald*, 13 May, 12 August 1905; Joyce's *Healy*, pp..272-73.
2. Joyce's *Healy*. p.259.
3. SJC, Expenditure Book 1903-70, 31 December 1906.
4. *Tuam Herald*, 8 March 1919, 24 July 1920. Alexander Eaton, a native of Bekan and the brother of Dean Malachy Eaton of Maynooth and Rev. Bernard Eaton, was ordained in 1895 and almost immediately joined the College staff. Regarded as a good teacher of the classics, he remained on the staff, being appointed president in 1915. According to his obituarist, Eaton took a 'lively interest' in 'anything pertaining to the progress and advancement of the town of Tuam'. He died in a Dublin hospital on 31 May 1923, the first president to die in office since James Ronan in 1838.

these was a vacuum cleaner, purchased from the Electrolux Company in 1925 at a cost of £16.3.6. The Tuam Electricity Company, incidentally, remained in existence until 1936. Shareholders protested in 1929 when their investment appeared to be threatened by the Shannon scheme, but when the company was taken over by the Electricity Supply Board in 1936, shareholders, including the College, were richly compensated.[1]

In 1923, a past pupil, Canon Patrick Colgan, parish priest of Kilkerrin, suggested that a monument to the College's patron saint should be erected. When the Canon backed up his suggestion with a cheque for £200, it was eagerly adopted and a statue was commissioned from a Dublin sculptor, Mr Shortall. The president, Canon Ryder, announced that it would be placed in a 'niche' over the front door, promising that it would be 'an artistic piece of work, and true to the time in which St Jarlath lived.'[2]

The College was in remarkably good financial shape a few years later when President Ryder drew up plans for a major extension. The new state had changed the funding mechanism for second-level education from a performance-based system to a capitation system, but public subsidy of Colleges continued. St Jarlath's, meanwhile continued to attract large numbers of students and the operation of the farm meant that they could be supported economically enough. It would appear also that College investments were earning significant dividends. In the half year January to July 1927, remarkably, income exceeded expenditure by almost a thousand pounds. And President Ryder reported in June 1927 that in the four years since he took office, he had been able to lodge £3000 in a Building Fund account. This money had come from current income and there was also a balance of some thousands in a current account. Because of the buoyant financial position, the president thought that improvements might be undertaken without any appeal to the public, although if a diocesan library was included in the plans, he understood that a number of priests would be 'anxious' to contribute. Money could be borrowed on a short-term basis, if this was necessary to complete the work.

Already the president had ascertained that Thomas Flately was willing to sell a plot of land at the rear of the College which was both 'suitable and ample' for a new wing 'in extension of the present oratory, and a one storey hall and room for shower

---

1. *Connacht Tribune*, 25 May 1929; SJC, Expenditure Book 1903-70, June 1936.
2. SJC, Various reports of Presidents, financial report, 10 January 1924.

or needle baths.'¹ The wing should include 'a diocesan library and two class rooms on the ground floor, dormitories on first floor and an infirmary and room on the top floor together with suitable lavatories… all heated by hot water pipes.'[1]

By the following summer, the plans were somewhat firmer: a Dublin-based architect, Thomas J. Cullen, had produced drawings, a clerk of works had been employed and contractors were waiting to begin. James Stewart of Galway was the main contractor; Mullally of Mullingar secured the contract for plumbing. The likely total costs at this point were estimated at £12,000.[2]

In the course of the work, improvements to the original plan were suggested. Great attention was paid to the oratory, which would have to accommodate a larger number of students. Advice was sought and considered, as architect and client tried to reconcile the practical with the aesthetic. One correspondent stressed the importance of ventilating the oratory where 'so many boys must be for so long a time'. Another stressed, that for reasons of discipline, there should not be more than one entrance to the oratory for students.[3]

In response to a query, the architect recommended that the gymnasium and the boot room be kept separate because, if they were combined in one room, it wouldn't be possible to 'keep it as clean and free of dust as a gym floor should be.' Also regarding a gym, Cullen suggested that it should be designed for adaptation as a theatre or cinema when needed. 'Many colleges', he argued, 'shew pictures weekly at present, and they are certain to be used more in the future both for amusement and education.' This advice was not taken.[4]

---

1. ibid., report dated 11 July 1927. Denis Ryder was born in Dunmore and educated at St Jarlath's and Maynooth, where he was ordained in 1897. After a year of post-graduate studies at the Dunboyne establishment, he was appointed professor at St Jarlath's College in 1898, becoming vice-president in 1915. He succeeded Alexander Eaton as president in 1923, when he also became Canon Penitentiary of the diocese. After leaving the College, he was parish priest of Ballindine (1929-38) and of Balla (1938-42). He died shortly after transferring to Ballinrobe in 1942. According to his friend, Dr Joseph Walsh, he was noted for his 'devotion to his work and his clearness of exposition. Consequently, 'his power of imparting knowledge to even weak students was remarkable, and in science and mathematics his students gained the highest places in Ireland'.
2. ibid., report dated 9 July 1928.
3. SJC, building correspondence file, McDonald to Walsh, 27 September 1929, undated note from (ex-President) M.J. McHugh.
4. ibid., Cullen to Ryder, 3 January 1928.

A significant addition to the plans was the construction of a swimming pool which was carried out by Verso Brothers of Drumcondra, Dublin. A friend of the new president, Joseph Walsh, wrote in November 1929 that a resident of the Westport area who had recently visited the College had been 'telling the people here about the magnitude and wonders of St Jarlath's. Everything he saw appealed to him, but the swimming pond most of all.[1]

If the scale of the plans had grown since the first proposals, then so also had the expense. In January 1930, President Walsh reported that £16,084 had already been spent, but that most of the work would be finished within six weeks. At that point he would have to consider the 'other necessary work' and the painting and decorating of the entire establishment. The president further noted that the number of students was 178 and that 'in addition there were two day boys' This was 'thirty more than the highest number that had ever been reached in the history of the College.' Within a short period of time, the president went on, it would be possible 'to state without any exaggeration that our College, while eschewing all snobbishness, will be more comfortable and up to date than any College in Ireland.' A few years later, the number of boarders would exceed two hundred for the first time.[2]

St Jarlath's loomed larger than ever in the town of Tuam. By the mid-1930s, between students and professors, almost 10% of the ordinary population of the town resided in the College. And although the St Jarlath's community was largely self-contained and relatively self-sufficient, it had a significant impact on the economic life of the town. Some direct employment was provided — of lay teachers, farm labourers and ancillary staff — but the indirect effects were greater. The account books show the extent of commercial relationships between the College and local traders. Not shown are the sums spent by the students themselves or, more particularly, by the many visitors that they attracted to the town.

At the annual prizeday ceremony in December 1930, Dr Gilmartin commented on the changes since his last address.

---

1. ibid., C.G. Verso to Walsh, 24 April 1930; M. McDonald to Walsh, 15 November 1929. According to tradition, the decision to build the swimming pool was taken following the accidental drowning of a student who went for a swim in the Ballygaddy river.
2. SJC, Various reports of Presidents, 13 January 1930, 5 January 1934.

While the 'essential work' of the institution had not been interrupted, he nevertheless felt that he was in a 'new college' such was the extent of developments. He proceeded to catalogue the improvements:

> A splendid swimming bath, shower and foot bath, dressing rooms and games rooms, not to speak of an additional wing, including a new study hall and an up-to-date infirmary, gave a transformed appearance to that old institution. Outside, the grounds were converted into a smiling garden on one side; on the other side were the foundations of three tennis courts, while on a third side, there were several courts for handball. At the back was erected machinery for renewing and heating the swimming bath. A new and artistic railing now cuts off those immediate surroundings from the extensive grounds which provide pitches for hurling and football. In all Ireland there is not a college better equipped materially for the well-being of its staff and students.[1]

---

1. SJC, President's Report Book, 20 December 1930. From Castlebar, Thomas Gilmartin was educated in St Jarlath's and Maynooth. He was ordained in Tuam in 1884 and was a professor in St Jarlath's until appointed to Maynooth in 1891. He became Bishop of Clonfert in 1910 and Archbishop of Tuam in 1918. He died, at 78, in 1939.

5. "A cheerful aspect to proceedings..."

No joys so sweet as those are found,
When festive nights do come around,
And kindly faces gather here
To smile upon our festive cheer.
Your Grace, who greets us day by day,
To you first, welcome to our play;
The welcome written on the wall
May seem our welcome to you all
But no skill can show in arts
The welcome written in our hearts.[1]

St Jarlath's Day, the 6th of June, was always a holiday. According to Martin O'Brennan — a student in the 1820s, a teacher in the 1830s, and a frequent visitor in the 1860s — the feast-day had 'been kept since the foundation of that establishment with great solemnity.' On what was also an occasion of 'special devotion in the town, the students took a prominent place at High Mass in the Cathedral. But it was not all solemnity. By custom, the students, the staff and their guests came together for a celebratory dinner which, by all accounts, was a jovial affair. A description of the 1867 gathering shows it to have concluded with a number of toasts, the last one to Dr MacHale being drunk 'with expression of joy and delight by the Superiors of the College, by the students, who were present at the same board, and by the guests.'[2] As we shall see, when sports days were organised, the free afternoon of the St Jarlath's holiday was deemed to be the logical time to hold them.

If St Jarlath's Day came once a year, other significant events came by with less regularity during most of the nineteenth century. It was only a small minority of students who could look back on great occasions like the dedication of the Cathedral or the MacHale funeral or, indeed, the laying of the foundation stone of the new College buildings in 1858. More would

---

1. Excerpt from prologue to entertainment presented by the students of the College, December 1888.
2. *Connaught Patriot*, 8 June 1867; see also *Tuam Herald*, 17 June 1865 and *Tuam News*, 7 June 1872.

remember the departure of a president, something which happened, on average, approximately every five years. The changing of the guardian, an important event in the life of any boarding school, was marked by the presentation of a valedictory address from the students, read by one of their number before the entire house and invited notables, followed by a reply from the guest of honour himself. The format of the ceremony did not change much, nor did the tenor of the sentiments expressed in successive tributes. In 1837, students acknowledged that the departing Martin Browne had 'enforced the rules of the house, but with so much sweetness and urbanity of manners, that they seemed a counsel on your part rather than a command.' Fifty-one years later, it was Patrick Kilkenny's turn to be told that his 'bearing towards us on all occasions united the tenderness and condescensions of a parent with the firmness and dignity of a superior'.[1]

As the century progressed, the academic year was punctuated by more extra-curricular activities, with a consequent improvement in the quality of student life. This chapter will trace involvement in such activities: in drama, in sport and in the annual student excursion. As his biographer pointed out, much innovation in these areas is traceable to the presidency of Ulick Bourke (1865-1878), who consciously set out to broaden the scope of the education offered in the College.[2] The greater variety in the annual programme may be regarded as one element in the significant expansion of the College which occurred during his stewardship. However, one should bear in mind before damning his predecessors, that Bourke was the owner of a newspaper, the *Tuam News*, which gave extensive coverage to his preoccupations and his activities. Consequently, more is known of his presidency than of any other in the nineteenth century.

Drama and performance
In many respects, annual summer 'exhibitions' and prize-giving ceremonies in the College were public performances. The four-day examination of 1840, which began on Tuesday, 23 June, was a case in point. Attending with the archbishop were 'a large number of clergymen, ...the most distinguished scholars of the archdiocese' and a representative of the *Tuam Herald*. The latter was impressed by 'the decidedly cleverest answering we ever

---

1. *Tuam Herald*, 8 July 1837; *Tuam News*, 24 February 1888.
2. Ó Maolmhuaidh, *Uilleog de Búrca* , pp.85-90.

had the pleasure to witness.'[1] On such occasions, students declaimed and recited from classical authors, read their own compositions, and responded to interrogation. More informally, examiners and visitors were entertained by students at the dinner which traditionally marked the examinations' end. This provided an opportunity for flattering Dr MacHale with a rendition of one of the popular songs which he had translated into Irish.[2]

The difficulty in drawing a clear line between academic exercise and dramatic performance is further illustrated by the elocution syllabus of the 1830s. Mr Stack, who had previously been employed in moderating the idioms of Scotland, was engaged as an elocution teacher. For so endeavouring to enhance the preaching skills of the coming generation of clergy, the College authorities were praised by the *Connaught Telegraph*. In support of its attitude the newspaper insisted that there was nothing 'more calculated to create a prepossession in our favour than a graceful and gentlemanlike address' and that there was 'no country in the world' where this accomplishment was needed more. Evidently, Mr Stack's approach stressed the practical, for he organised public 'readings' in the lecture rooms of the College at which his pupils were put through their paces. It is perhaps a reflection on the social life of Tuam at the time that these readings were attended 'not only by many of the parents and guardians of the students, but by a large proportion of the respectable inhabitants of Tuam and its vicinage.'[3]

Other arts also found a space on the curriculum in the 1830s. During the presidency of Martin Browne, parents of would-be-students were advised that 'Music, Dancing and Washing are an extra charge.' It may have been Browne's encouragement of elocution and music that caused students to pay cryptic tribute, on his departure from the College for the parish of Balla in 1837, to his 'attention to the improvement, not only of the more advanced portion of our community, but even to the minor departments.'[4]

At some point, the occasional display of accomplishments before visitors grew into a fully-fledged and rehearsed entertainment. There is no reason to presume that the presentation by the students in 1859 of *William Tell*, recalled thirteen years

---

1. *Tuam Herald*, 4 July 1840.
2. ibid., 3 July 1869; Dr Mark F. Ryan, *Fenian Memories*, 1945, p.27. MacHale's translation of a selection of Moore's 'melodies' was published in Dublin in 1842.
3. SJC, Feeney Papers, pp.146-47.
4. *Connaught Telegraph*, 20 August 1836; *Tuam Herald*, 3 August 1837.

later by John MacPhilpin, was the first full dramatic production in the College.[1]

One reason why an annual play became part of the pre-Chrismas routine was that rehearsals served to occupy the long winter evenings. A student actor admitted as much when introducing the 1872 entertainment thus:

> As dark December glooms the day,
> And takes our sylvan sports away
> We've met to tell of a time gone by…[2]

It was not until 1870, during the presidency of Ulick Bourke, that the student drama became a great public spectacle, an event on the social calendar of counties Galway and Mayo. The new hall provided the necessary accommodation, while the robustly patriotic nature of the material chosen at that period served to communicate the tone of St Jarlath's to the world outside.[3] Commenting on the December 1870 production of *Robert Emmet*, the *Nation* newspaper enthused: 'We say that the example of St Jarlath's, if it were taken as it might be, would cause incalculable good in Ireland.' The songs chosen to round off the evening, he went on, 'were songs of the right sort for Irishmen.' These included several of the 'best and sweetest of our national melodies …in the original words' as well as *God Save Ireland* and the archbishop's translations into Irish of *The Harp that Once* and *The Last Rose of Summer*.[4]

Possibly the greatest success during this period was the 1871 production, *Lord Edward Fitzgerald*, arguably an ironic choice of material, given the contemporary hostility of the College's founder, Dr Dillon, towards Lord Edward's comrades in the United Irishmen. Any such irony did not inhibit the large cast or the director, Professor Thomas Carr.[5]

1. *Tuam News*, 13 December 1872. In the 1820s, according to the *Connaught Journal* (13 September 1824), clergy of 'both denominations' were opposed to theatre.
2. *Tuam News*, 13 December 1872.
3. The strongly nationalist political atmosphere in the College will be considered in detail in the following chapter.
4. *The Nation*, 24 December 1870.
5. Thomas Carr was born into a minor gentry family at Moylough in 1839. He attended St Jarlath's and Maynooth, where he was ordained in 1866. He served briefly at Oughawell and Tuam, before joining the St Jarlath's staff in 1870. From 1872, he was a professor at Maynooth and in 1883 he was appointed Bishop of Galway. He was Archbishop of Melbourne from 1887 until his death in 1917.

Proceedings began, as usual, with the recitation of a specially-written prologue, in the course of which the ongoing structural developments in the College were referred to. There was also some philosophical reflection:

> 'Tis only when some landmark meets the travellers's eye,
> He notes how swiftly time and distance go gliding by;
> So on life's journey does some festive scene appear
> To recall its past and remind us of the new year...
> The old have grown older, little boys become big men,
> As for myself, I don't think I was that height then.
> Another landmark, tonight, we mean to raise,
> You fixed it by your presence, now crown it by your praise
> We'll tell you but the truth, we'll give you day and date,
> Lord Edward is our hero — the time is '98.[1]

The well-publicised inclusion in the cast of John and Jeremiah Jnr., sons of the exiled O'Donovan Rossa, reinforced the nationalist statement already inherent in the choice of dramatic material.

Given its ownership, the *Tuam News* was not going to be critical of the play, and it duly praised the acting, the scenery, the costumes and the production. Singling out a few actors for particular mention, the reporter remarked that Simon Conway 'acted the Frenchman with the greatest Sang Froid' and rendered the *Marseillaise* in a most 'soul-stirring' manner. He deemed John Hogan's impersonation of Lord Edward to have been 'even, dignified and noble', but reserved the highest praise for John O'Connor Power:

> who even now may rank as a finished elocutionist, and whose distinct and powerful utterance, joined to the grace and fitness of his gesture, marks him as one who can essay and achieve the highest flights of oratory.[2]

The evening continued on a lighter note with the cockney farce, *Box and Cox*, a long-standing staple of amateur theatricals, written by the Birr-born founder of *Punch*, Joseph Stirling Coyle

---

14. *Tuam News*, 15 December 1871.
15. ibid. This remark showed some perceptiveness: Power became a noted public speaker and later wrote a manual on eloquence, *The making of an orator*, 1906.

(1803-1868). Several songs, including the comic *Pat Murphy is my name*, the patriotic *Green Flag* and the melodramatic Minstrel number *Massa's in de cold ground* brought proceedings to the finale, which as usual, was St Jarlath's own anthem, *O'Donnell Abu*.[1] The dramatic fare — a tragedy, followed by farce, and concluding with songs and recitations — was much the same as that put on in other Irish Colleges of the period.[2] What was different was the overtly political content of the material on offer in St Jarlath's.

Professor Carr's promotion to Maynooth during the year notwithstanding, the College was again able to put on a show in December 1872 — a revival of William Tell. Two hundred and nineteen members of the audience were named in the *Tuam News*. They included the archbishop, priests of the diocese, gentry, professionals and traders. Not named were the non-participating students and an unspecified number of 'ladies of the Academy'. John O'Connor Power was the bowman in Sheridan Knowles' play about Switzerland's legendary fourteenth century liberator, a hero with a resonance equal to that of the would-be liberators commemorated in the previous two years. For this production, the hall was elaborately decorated with coats of arms, 'quaint devices' and 'scrolls executed in Irish and English grotesque character.' In front of the stage was the same striking drop scene used in the previous few years. Depicting 'the grand Gothic Cathedral of Tuam and the religious edifices which are grouped around it as a centre,' it had been painted by artist, Mr O'Malley.[3]

If the *Tuam News* could always be relied upon to find something positive to say about a performance, the *Herald* was sometimes alert to shortcomings. On one occasion, the paper pointedly observed that the 'audience, though not particularly numerous, was well conducted;' Did the writer expect less than exemplary behaviour from the clergy of the archdiocese and the shopocracy of Tuam? The following year, the *Herald* commented on the actors' 'youthful indiscretion as displayed in occasional flashes of puerile prudishness together with a want of real appreciation of the trying incidents of the situation.'[4] Whether

---

1. ibid.
2. G.K. White, *A history of St Columba's College*, 1980, p.105; T. Cunningham & D. Gallogly's *St Patrick's College, [Cavan]: a centenary history*, 1974, p.31.
3. *Tuam News*, 13 December, 1872.
4. *Tuam Herald*, 6 November 1875, 4 November 1876.

such tetchiness arose out of genuine critical misgivings or out of jealousy provoked by the *Herald's* loss of circulation and advertising revenue to Ulick Bourke's *News*, it is difficult to judge at this distance.

Other late nineteenth century productions included *Sarsfield* in 1876 and *Robert Emmet* in 1875 and 1888. The topical reference in the prologue on the latter occasion was to the exam pressure occasioned by the introduction of the Intermediate Examination. The complaint was greatly appreciated by the students in the audience and the grievance was reiterated a year later when the performance was of Richard Brinsley Sheridan's adaptation of Kotzebue's *Pizarro*. Like *William Tell* — and notwithstanding its exotic setting or the fact that it is regarded as Sheridan's poorest effort — this play was a great favourite with nineteenth century Irish nationalist audiences. Indeed it had been produced a few years earlier by amateurs in the town of Tuam. At that time, the *Herald* commented that the play's 'appeal to patriotism and the generous instincts of humanity make it a fit proper subject for youthful study and reproduction'.[1]

Ulick Bourke's innovation, then, survived his departure to Claremorris in 1878. The annual school concert which he transformed into a public pageant continued to be a regular feature of Tuam's cultural scene. And he brought colour, or at least hyperbole, to other occasions in the annual calendar. Under his stewardship, the routine end-of-year examination became a 'Midsummer Exhibition' while the traditional post-exam dinner for students and examiners grew into a 'choice dejeuner' in 1868, becoming a 'splendid dejeuner' a year later, and ending up as a 'banquet' in 1871.[2]

Bourke also encouraged music. As we have seen, music lessons were available as an 'extra' during the 1830s, while expenditure on sheet music and a 'music board' in 1869 suggests that this was still the case three decades later. In 1875, however, a school band was formed, which gave its first halting public performance during the interval in that year's annual play This band, apparently, had gone out of existence by 1888 when it was necessary to bring the Industrial School band from Galway to

---

1. *Tuam News*, 6 December 1889; *Tuam Herald*, 17 October 1885. For *Pizarro* see Fintan O'Toole's *The Traitor's Kiss: The life of R.B. Sheridan*, 1997, pp.342-48.
2. *Connaught Patriot*, 4 July 1868; *Tuam Herald*, 3 July 1869; *Tuam News*, 16 June 1871.

provide instrumental entertainment. Another school might have opted to invite an army regimental band, but in St Jarlath's that was not an option that would have been considered. A minor resurgence of music in the school during the following year is indicated by the compliment paid to students for their 'skilful rendering of several pieces of music' during the annual entertainment of 1889.[1]

Occasional diversion on winter evenings during the late nineteenth century was provided by 'magic lantern' displays. The college purchased a lantern and several dozen slides in 1867. Later, it became possible to rent sets of slides from a company in Dublin. The pattern of expenditure would indicate that there was an annual lantern show during the last decade of the century.[2]

Travelling troubadours visiting Tuam were sometimes invited to give matinee performances in the College. In 1892, four guineas was paid to visiting bell-ringers for 'entertainment' while in the following year, the Belvedere Musical Society put on a special performance.[3] One such entertainer was the anonymous 'Cinematograph performer' who was paid the sum of £1.10.0 on 23 March 1898, just a little over two years after the Lumiere brothers' pioneering display in Paris. The account book tells no more than that about the arrival of cinema in St Jarlath's. It can be assumed, however, that the performance was not dissimilar to an exhibition given by Monsieur Le Clair in Galway's Racquet Court Theatre some months earlier which showed 'the departure of employees from a Manchester factory, followed by a picturesque view of Galway Bay.' [4]

Excursions
At 9 a.m. on the feast of St Gregory, 26 March 1868, 'the president, professors, prefects and students' — sixty-four people altogether — mounted 'carriages, vans and vehicles of every description' which had gathered outside the College gates. The motley cavalcade passed through the streets of Tuam, through Belclare and Donaghpatrick, reaching Headford within two

---

1. SJC, Expenditure book, 1867-1902, December 1869; *Tuam News*, 9 November 1888, 6 December 1889.
2. ibid., 16 December 1867, 30 February 1896, 30 December 1897, 23 March, 19 November 1898, 13 October 1899.
3. SJC Expenditure Book 1867-1902, 7 May 1892; *Tuam News*, 14 February 1893.
4. *Galway Observer*, 24 April 1897.

hours. There, Peter Conway[1], the parish priest, welcomed his guests and guided them around his new church, dubbed the 'Irish-American church' because of the source of the funds which had built it. Next on the itinerary were visits to the three schools of the town, in each of which President Bourke examined the children in geography, arithmetic and catechism.

Back in the open air, the students spent a while chasing hares in a field, before going to see the ruins of the nearby Abbey of Ross Errily. From there, it was a half-hour journey to Fr Conway's newly-renovated residence, located beside the other Church of the parish, at Claran. Finally, at three o'clock, along with 'the local clergy and gentry', the excursionists sat down to a hearty dinner around Fr Conway's table.

Afterwards, a toast to the reigning Pope Pius IX wished him 'many happy years, and a glorious defeat to his enemies. The toast to Dr MacHale expressed similar sentiments.

Standing to thank the host, the president introduced fourteen year-old Stephen Lavan, from Savannah, Georgia, representing the students and those 'Irishmen in America' who had contributed to the building of the Headford church. The boy paid tribute to Fr Conway, for his hospitality and for his 'labours in the cause of the good old faith.' The magnificent new church, he went on, proved that 'the pious spirit which raised the walls of Ross Abbey is not yet extinct.'

Fr Conway was obviously moved by the words of the young Irish-American and, after praising the regime of the College which, he said, recognised that the acquisition of learning and spirituality were dependent on 'good bodily health', he referred to the great generosity, hospitality and strength of character he had himself encountered while collecting funds in the United States. Such qualities, evidently, were being nurtured in St Jarlath's, for the priest remarked on his impression that there was 'so much of American manners, independence and honesty

---

1. Peter Conway (1819-1872) was born in the parish of Kilmeena. After attending St Jarlath's and Maynooth, he was ordained in 1841. He served in Carna, Partry and Ballinrobe and was appointed P.P. of Killursa (Headford) in 1858. According to his obituarist his life was spent 'doing good for the poor of his parish, erecting schoolhouses for the purpose of education, building chapels, fighting for the poor with the officials who administered the poor laws in Ireland...' He was a fiercely committed nationalist and, immediately before his death, was accused by Judge Keogh of intimidating electors in the Nolan/Trench by-election. It was the opinion of his friends that 'Fr Peter was not the same man after that foul and fatal harangue'. (*Tuam Herald*, 28 June 1872; 'Sacerdotes Tuamensis').

of purpose amongst them.' Concluding in the same vein, and echoing the prevailing 'advanced' nationalist approval of American (as opposed to English) qualities, Fr Conway declared himself 'proud' of Master Lavan who, he said, embodied the 'noble trait in the present body of students.'[1]

A reference to the outing as 'the Gregory of 1868' indicates that the saint's day was marked in some such way during these years. Would it be fanciful to deduce that it was an occasion of pilgrimage by St Jarlath's students to one of the many new churches springing up within a few hours distance of Tuam?

The favourite secular destination for outings was Castlehackett, located about half way between Tuam and Headford. This demesne was the seat of the Kirwans who, as the leading landed family in the vicinity of Tuam, played an active role in the life of the town. Although protestant since the eighteenth century, they maintained good relations with the Catholic community. They were regarded by their tenants as 'good landlords', an opinion which was buttressed by the energetic commitment of one of the dynasty — Sir Denis — to agricultural reform, and also by their early and amicable transfer of most of the estate to its tenants in 1898. Castlehackett itself lies in the shadow of the hill of *Cnoc Ma* which, despite rising only a modest 550 feet, featured largely in the folklore of the region, probably because of its eminence in the otherwise flat landscape of North Galway and South Mayo.[2]

Castlehackett was a popular picnic spot with Tuam people generally. Accounts of other excursions, including one by the 'children and choirboys of the Tuam Protestant cathedral', testify to this.[3] The reasons why it was favoured are suggested by the following extract, contributed anonymously to the *Herald* by 'One of the Students' who participated in the St Jarlath's outing of 5 May 1870.

> ...We started about eleven o'clock for Castlehackett, a place long renowned in the west for its romantic site and

---

1. *Tuam Herald*, 28 March 1868. For nationalist approval of American influence see Paul Bew's *Land and the national question in Ireland, 1858-82*, pp.31-32.
2. Éibhlín Bean Mhic Choistealbha, *Amhráin Mhuighe Seóla*, 1923, p.iii; Michael J. Hughes, *History & Folklore of the Barony of Clare (Co. Galway)*, n.d., p.87, 173-79; The Knight of Glin, 'Castle Hackett' in Christie's Castlehackett catalogue, vol.ii, London 1986, pp.7-9; *Tuam Herald*, 14 May 1898.
3. *Tuam News*, 2 August 1889; *Tuam Herald*, 1 November 1902.

for being the resort of those who find pleasure in admiring the works of nature's hand. For a considerable distance of the way thither from Tuam, the country presents to the eye no interesting features. The only objects which absorbed my attention were the ruins of once humble but happy homesteads — those traces which so frequently in this country testify to the perverse will of man. As we approached Castlehackett, the comparatively barren landscape merges into rich and fertile land. At an abrupt turn of the road the hill itself suddenly appears with its steep side densely clad with trees, which were fast clothing themselves with the verdant foliage of spring. At the distance of a couple of hundred yards from the base of the hill, the chimneyed roof of Mr Kirwan's mansion is seen peeping from the beautiful trees by which it is environed. We begin to climb the hill. We tread the intricate serpentine paths that lead up to the steep ascent, and emerge from the trees on the craggy summit. Here, indeed, a magnificent panorama is revealed to the enraptured gaze of the spectator. Far south west were dimly visible the distant hills of Clare, frowning across Galway Bay on the ancient "Citie of the Tribes." To the west lay Lough Corrib, studded with countless isles and stretching onward its low-lying waters to the many-peaked mountains of Connemara.. Northward, loomed the colossal sides of Croagh Patrick, through the bluish mist, by which it was almost obscured... Bordering the nude, sloping hillside on the west, the land was neatly parcelled out with almost geometrical accuracy into figures of different shapes and sizes... After fully enjoying the intellectual delight, which nature unfolded to the eye, we ascended to the base of the well-wooded declivity to take luncheon, for which spartan exercise and a bracing air had had duly prepared us. Here reclined on the verdant carpeting, near the ruins of the ancient castle, from which the hill derives its name, we take refreshment with a keen appetite. The ancient castle is in a dilapidated state and is mantled with ivy... Our warmest expressions of gratitude are due to Mr Kirwan, for the kindness he evinced in showing us the many beauties that surround his favoured home. It is one of the signs of the times, clearly proving the kindly feeling that is beginning to exist between Irishmen of all creeds, and evidencing the downfall of the odious barrier of sectarian animosity.[1]

The same ambiance and the same hospitality were experienced by the following generations of students who joined the 'fete champetres' at Castlehackett on May Day 1873 and again on May Day 1876. Thereafter, the hill continued to be the destination of occasional outings but, during the first world war and its aftermath, the Castlehackett excursion became an annual event.[2] In latter years, according to one former student, the boys walked the six-odd miles in each direction accompanied by a horse and dray, so that the weaker boys might take an occasional rest. The annual outing of 1923 was cancelled due to the sudden death of the president, Canon Eaton. It may have been that the use of Castlehackett House by Free State forces and its consequent destruction by republicans would, in any case, have broken the connection with the College.[3]

The arrival of the railway in 1860 greatly expanded the scope of a day trip from Tuam and the annual excursionists, occasionally, at least, availed of the new facility. The few surviving descriptions show that the organisers sought to maximise the educational benefits of these outings, while the same descriptions reveal a persistent preoccupation with food on the part of the boys. The St Jarlath's Day outing of 1871 took the students, via Athenry, to Galway. Little time was wasted during a day which took in the Claddagh, the docks, the 'neatly-fitted' Catholic churches, St Nicholas's, the Railway Hotel, the Queen's College and Blackrock. There, 'the heat of the day and the fatigue of the walk induced many to have a plunge into the briny deep, after which we all did ample justice to the abundance of good things which had been sent with us from the college.'[4]

Even more ambitious was the 1890 Sunday outing to Killaloe and Lough Derg on the Shannon. Accompanying the students on this occasion, 'by kind permission of the president', were the

---

1. *Tuam Herald*, 21 May 1870.
2. SJC, Expenditure Book 1903-70, 17 June 1904, 14 June 1905, 2 May 1914, 12 June 1916, 20 June 1917, 20 June 1918, 29 June 1919, 2 June 1920.
3. Interview with Canon Heaney, 29 July 1997; Hughes, *Barony of Clare*, p.66.
4. *Tuam News*, 18 June 1871. Indispensable on all outings and other special occasions during the late nineteenth and early twentieth centuries were the services of Tuam's leading confectioner, Mr John Cunningham of the Square, (see SJC, Expenditure Book, 1903-70, 28 February 1903, 10 June 1904, 20 June 1905, 18 December 1906).

members of the Tuam Catholic Temperance Society. After attending the special 6.30 a.m. mass in the Cathedral, the excursionists made their way to the station for their 8 a.m. departure, where they were welcomed by Stationmaster Egan who had undertaken to lead the party. A brief stop in Ennis broke the three hour journey to Limerick. There, the short wait on the platform was filled with the proficient cornet-playing of one P. Reddington. Another delay was called for, however, because

> by this time the inner man demanded attention, so an excellent place was selected for luncheon on the opposite side of the river to Kincora, where stood the palace of Brian Boroimhe, and ample justice was done to the viands and other good things provided for the occasion.[1]

From a cruiser on the Shannon, the travellers were guided past ancient ecclesiastical and military sites, geographical features and the houses of notables. And before returning home, due to the influence of Stationmaster Egan who was able to delay the train, they had time to examine 'different objects of interest' in the city of Limerick itself.[2]

There is another description of a trip to Killaloe from around the same period — it may be the same trip. It was written by Thomas Gilmartin, future archbishop of Tuam, possibly while he was a senior student in the College in the late 1870s, but more probably during his period as a professor in the years before 1891. A few excerpts will give a flavour:

> On last Sunday, the students of St Jarlath's, accompanied by the president and professors had their annual excursion. A special train was engaged to take them to Killaloe where the Shannon expands into Lough Derg and the steam launch, the "Ida" was chartered to take the party for a four hour's sail up the lough. I was one of those who had the privilege of joining the excursion...
>
> The engine was put on the other end of the train and after a short delay we headed off for Killaloe where we arrived after a half hour's drive through an interesting country. It was a very short walk (5 minutes) from the station at Ballina to the Shannon bridge which connects Ballina with Killaloe. As you walk across the bridge,

---

1. *Tuam News*, 23 May 1890.
2. ibid.

Killaloe rises up before you, as if it was built in a mountain gallery, conveying a view of the beautiful scenes around. A Hotel occupies a front (seat?) and a fine female did for a moment grace the Hotel entrance. After some enquiry, we recrossed the bridge, turned left and walked towards what was there called the jetty, where our steamer was supposed to be waiting. It was now about 12.30 and, after some discussion, it was agreed to have luncheon before going on board. Everybody was doing everything during luncheon, carving, opening bottles, attending to every-other-body; until in less than three-quarters of an hour, we were all on board, happy in the anticipation of pleasure. There was no snorting or mighty puffing or shouting of sailors but, as if in continuation of rest, she glided to the brow supreme of Lough Derg.[1]

In 1896, the expenses of an excursion to Limerick were again shared with a local group, while other outings brought the student body to Sligo in 1898; to Cong in 1899; to Gort in 1900; to Cong again in 1903; to Lough Cutra, near Gort, in 1906, to Ballinasloe in 1907.[2] At that point, excursions by train were discontinued although, as we have seen, the less expensive outings to Castlehackett continued until the early 1920s. Then, after more than half a century, the annual St Jarlath's excursion became extinct.

Games and physical activity

Only the occasional tantalising snippet regarding sport and games survives in the record of the first ninety years of College life. The business-like nature of the records themselves partly explains this, but the general attitude to sport in society at large until the closing decades of the nineteenth century is a more significant factor in the explanation. Sport was regarded as play and, as such, too commonplace to be worthy of comment unless, of course, it was an occasion of rule-breaking. When President Thomas Feeney 'drastically punished' the future Canon Peter Geraghty for playing marbles, one presumes that he was expressing disapproval of play in the study hall rather

---

1. Tuam Diocesan Archives, T. Gilmartin notebooks.
2. SJC, Expenditure Book 1867-1912, 5 April 1896, 13 April 1898, 23 May 1899, 26 May 1900; Expenditure 1903-70, 30 June 1903, 13 June 1906, 1 April 1907.

than disapproval of marbles.[1] Not so, however, when two students, Noel and John Egan, were found to have attended a duel — arguably an ancestor of the modern athletic contest. The church strongly disapproved of duelling and Feeney, evidently, sought the advice of Archbishop Kelly as to how this disapproval might best be communicated. In any case, the two transgressors were required to 'ask God's pardon in the presence 'of all the scholars.' This done, Feeney was empowered to 'raise the Excommunication which they have incurred.'[2]

Handball has a strong claim to be regarded as the quintessential St Jarlath's sport. References to the playing of the game are few but there can be no doubt but that it was given a high priority from the earliest days. In 1817, soon after the acquisition of the French's Bank building, the sum of £14.10.0 was spent by President James McKeal in building a ball-court. There are indications that the game was widely played in Irish boarding schools of the period.[3]

Many years later, Ulick Bourke's 1867 horarium includes a reference to the ball-court, indicating that it was the scene of one of the principal spare-time activities. The document gives the first clear picture of the daily regime in the College and it shows that students spent a considerable part of each day out of doors. Week-day free periods — 9.15 to 10am; 12.30 to 1pm; 4pm to 5.30 — were to be spent in 'the parks or ball court'; if it was raining students were to play in the corridors. In order, presumably, to facilitate easy supervision, the student body was not permitted to divide itself. All stayed indoors, or all went out.

Decades before organised sport became important in the College, the authorities were enthusiastic about the benefits of exercise and fresh air. The 1867 timetable set aside an hour and a half for a Sunday afternoon walk and short daily walks were taken in the grounds by students and professors alike. Contemporary advertisements stressed the 'salubrity' of the site and the opportunity it offered for regular exercise:

> Not in Ireland or perhaps in any other country are there recreation grounds that combine more of the healthiness and extent than those of the College of St Jarlath, comprising about twelve acres of ground near the summit of the

---

1. Brett's *Life of Duggan*, p.11.
2. Feeney papers, p.49, undated letter from +Oliver.
3. SJC, Account book 1817-35, 31 May 1817; Tom McElligot, *The story of handball: the game, the players, the history*, 1984, pp.16-17.

province and surrounding on all sides the magnificent Cathedral.[1]

The occasional necessity of replacing somebody's cricket cap — expressed in correspondence and accounts — indicates that this too was a popular game for a time. The game was played by all social classes in Tuam in the period immediately before Gaelic football took root in the town.[2] Its heyday had passed by 1893 when the College purchased the Tuam cricket ground which adjoined its own property.

The earliest surviving account of a match involving St Jarlath's is of a cricket game between the College and the Tuam Cricket club. The contest, a return match, was played in the College grounds on Ascension Thursday 1886, under 'very favourable' weather conditions. According to a newspaper report, the match was 'spiritedly contested' but, thanks to 'the bowling of Mr Greally and the steady batting of Mr Kelly,' the victory went to the College side. The result was accepted with bad grace by the Tuam men who 'objected to' and 'condemned' two decisions of the umpire.[3]

Some years earlier, the fashion for athletics meetings had begun to manifest itself in the College. In June 1879, a well organised sportsday was attended, according to one newspaper, by 'a great number of the clergy and the aristocracy of the town and neighbourhood.' It would appear that senior students were the organisers, but they had been rendered 'every facility' by President Kilkenny. A total of fifteen events were run off over three and a half hours of the afternoon, the last two being junior and senior consolation races 'in which defeated champions got an opportunity of retrieving their lost honour.' Remarkably, for an event that had been organised by the students themselves, the prizes were substantial: they included clocks, a concertina, a writing desk, a set of gold studs, fishing rods, volumes of verse and 'a fancy ink bottle.'[4]

After this rather auspicious beginning, the sportsday seems to have lapsed for some years. It was revived, however, on St

---

1. *Catholic Register* 1843, p.318.
2. O'Donoghue, *Proud and upright men,* pp.22-26. Among the Tuam cricket clubs was one composed of workers in the Curragh match factory (*Tuam Herald*, 10 July 1886).
3. *Tuam Herald*, 5 June 1886.
4. *Galway Vindicator*, 18 June 1879.

Jarlath's Day 1888, with the promise that it would become 'an annual occasion.' Again, the managing committee was composed of senior students and the prizes were valuable. There were twenty-one events which, as well as the usual track and field events, included a donkey derby that 'afforded a fund of mirth', and a tug-of war competition that pitted boarders against day-boys. A Hungarian band lent 'a cheerful aspect to proceedings' that were overshadowed by dark clouds and occasional showers. On 6 June 1889, a German band provided entertainment between the several 'closely contested events.' Later, another musical interlude from 'an amateur band composed of some of the students passed the time before the evening fireworks display.[1]

On the same day of the following year the 'large and distinguished' attendance included the archbishop, whose arrival and departure was 'enthusiastically cheered by the students.' Arrangements, according to the *Tuam News*, were creditable to both the organising students and the College, which received praise for aiming 'not only at developing the minds but also in their due measure the sinews and the muscles of the young students.' Track events in the programme included, 100 yards, 300 yards, 450 yards, a half mile race, 300 yards hurdles as well as a 'juvenile race' and a 'consolation race'; the field events were high jump, pole jump, long jump, 'hop, step and jump' and 'putting the 28lb'; the novelty events were egg and spoon race, 'Siamese twin race' and sack race. Two members of the committee, Vincent Smyth of Claremorris and James Vahey of Manulla, Co. Mayo, between them took most of the medals for the senior events. Again, the day ended with a fireworks display which attracted hundreds of townspeople to the Cathedral grounds.[2]

The incorporation of a sportsday into the annual calendar was just one example of the gradually growing status of games and physical activity in the last decade or so of the nineteenth century. In his description of the College in 1896, *Herald* proprietor Richard J. Kelly remarked upon the 'fine expanse of field covering several acres with a gravelled walk all around.' He noted that there was also 'a ball-alley, a gymnasium and ample accomodation for healthy sport.' The furnishing of the said gymnasium is confirmed by expenditure on a 'horizontal bar' in 1890 and 'swings for gymnasium' in 1899, while money was

---

1. *Tuam News*, 8 June 1888, 14 June 1889.
2. ibid.,, 13 June 1890.

spent on tennis nets in 1897.[1] For those of a less physical disposition, billiard tables were purchased in 1891 and 1892; outgoings on billiards and a table cover in 1900 show that the game remained popular.[2]

---

1. *Tuam Herald*, 24 October 1896; SJC Expenditure Book 1867-1902, 21 November 1890, 5 June 1897, 10 May 1899.
2. SJC Expenditure Book 1867-1902, 24 January, 7, 12 February 1891, 23 September 1892, 9 April 1900.

6. "Another roar from St Jarlath's."

A pastor true and fond is he, beloved by rich and poor,
A patriot spirit bold and free to do or to endure;
No traitor's wile, no force or guile, with them can e'er prevail
Whose watch and ward, whose guide and guard, is noble John MacHale.[1]

St Jarlath's College was established in the shadow of the Penal laws, under licence from the established church. Consequently — and reflecting the prevailing disposition within Irish Catholicism — those associated with the institution in its early days preferred to avoid public controversy. And in this respect, Thomas Feeney, Professor and president between 1817 and 1831, was typical enough. Addressing the 'patriotic inhabitants of Tuam' many years later, he recalled that 'during the period of fourteen years during which I had the pleasure of residing amongst you, I had not been called upon to address a public meeting assembled for politics'.[2]

During Feeney's presidency, nevertheless, things were beginning to change, as Catholics realised that restraint alone would not secure the concessions promised them at the time of the Act of Union. The O'Connell-led movement for Catholic emancipation drew the parish clergy into politics as collectors of the Catholic rent in the mid-1820s. But already some of the younger Maynooth-trained priests had become impatient with the political pusillanimity of their elders. The most outspoken was *Heirophilos* — nom de plume of John MacHale, Mayo-born Professor of Dogma at Maynooth.

MacHale was appointed to Killala in 1825, the first entirely Irish-educated bishop since the sixteenth century. In 1834, despite British lobbying to block the advancement of such a resolute nationalist, he became archbishop of Tuam, a post he would hold for forty-seven years.[3]

As patron for almost half a century at a formative stage in

---

1. From 'John MacHale, Archbishop of Tuam,' a ballad by T.D. Sullivan, M.P.
2. SJC, Feeney papers, p.41.
3. Corish, *Maynooth College*, pp.56-63 and Ó Tuathaigh 'Seán Mac hÉil, Ardeaspag agus Conspóidí: Athbhreithniú' in Áine ní Cheannain *Leon an Iarthair*, Dublin 1983, pp.73-74.

the College's development, MacHale was the single most influential figure in its history. Even the modern spelling of its name is his — up to 1835, it was rendered St *Jerlath's*.[1] During his time in Tuam, he lived next door to the College in Bishop Street, attending frequently at meal-times. He appointed College staff, including nine presidents, but his influence was also felt in day-to-day matters. It was hardly a coincidence, for example, that students were examined in 'History of Ireland' in 1835, in the first annual examinations over which he presided.[2]

The College was inevitably associated with the views of its patron, and not only because they had the same postal address. As a diocesan seminary, the institution was part of the archiepiscopal court, so that when the archbishop was involved in political or ecclesiastical controversy, the president and staff of the College were almost invariably implicated to a greater or lesser extent. Moreover, the attitudes and convictions of the directors of the establishment determined its tone and, in influencing the formation of the next generation of diocesan clergy, affected both their social and spiritual outlooks. Networks of contemporaries, and their mentors, took these influences into the wider world. This chapter will trace the involvement of St Jarlath's College in Irish public life — political and ecclesiastical — from the 1860s to the aftermath of the Civil War. By and large, the public careers of past-pupils will not be considered, except insofar as they directly related to the College itself. Rather, it is the involvement of serving presidents and professors which will be examined, with due attention being paid to those pre-occupations of patrons which impacted upon the lives of students and staff. The examination will necessarily be wide-ranging, since the national and regional contexts of certain episodes will have to be sketched. Throughout, it is the intention to give a vivid impression of how the world looked from the vantage point of St Jarlath's College during the half-century or so when the modern Irish state was being forged.

There is no doubt that it was during the episcopacy of Dr John MacHale that the public profile of St Jarlath's was at its highest. This was in no small measure due to that archbishop's attested tendency 'to equate religious and political issues,' According to one authority, MacHale saw the fortunes of Irish

---

1. For St *Jerlath's*, see *Connaught Journal*, 4 September 1817, *Freemans' Journal*, 23 August 1830, *Connaught Telegraph*, 22 July 1835; for St *Jarlath's* see *Connaught Telegraph*, 20 July 1836.
2. *The Telegraph*, (Castlebar), 22 July 1835.

Catholicism as being completely intertwined with those of Irish nationality and, therefore, he was 'prepared to commit himself, his clergy, and inasmuch as he was able, the Irish Church, to that sacred cause.'[1] This was no more than the Irish Catholic people expected and his unequivocal espousal of their interests made him both the best-known and the most popular of the bishops. MacHale was a firm ally of Daniel O'Connell but also a recognised leader of Irish nationalism in his own right. And neither age nor preferment blunted the firmness of his opinions, the feistiness of his temperament, or the pugnacity of his language. These were the qualities that prompted the *Times* of London to print one of his many letters to its editor under the headline: 'Another roar from St Jarlath's.'[2]

Under MacHale, presidents could no longer avoid public affairs to the extent that Thomas Feeney had during the 1820s. Indeed, in ecclesiastical terms, according to one scholar, the presidency became one of 'the three most influential positions in the Catholic Church in Galway.'[3] Presidents spoke on behalf of the archbishop when he was absent, but also when protocol or prudence precluded his direct intervention in controversy. And when the president did speak, it was understood that he was speaking with the authority of the archbishop. Likewise, his attendance at functions signified archiepiscopal approval for their promoters' efforts.

If presidents were public figures, some professors too achieved this status. As men of above average education and intellect, their pronouncements were respected and reported. As we have seen, lay professor Michael J. McCann won modest fame when his composition, 'O'Donnell Abu' was published in 1843 in *The Nation*, newspaper of the Young Ireland movement. Before becoming professor of mathematics, McCann had been a student in St Jarlath's, so it is probable that the robustly nationalistic views expressed in the song were formed in the College. The rousing ballad became an Irish nationalist anthem, but it was also regarded as a St Jarlath's anthem and it continued to be performed in subsequent decades at College concerts and social functions.[4]

---

1. Emmet Larkin, *The Consolidation of the Roman Catholic Church in Ireland, 1860-1870*, 1987, p.61.
2. *Catholic Registry*, 1882, MacHale obituary, pp.237-42.
3. William Nolan, 'Introduction' to Gerard Moran, ed., *Galway: History & Society*, 1996, p.xxi.
4. For McCann, see Guy's History, pt.x; 'O'D. Aboo', *Tuam News*, 15 December 1871.

In mid-century, ample opportunity for priests to engage in controversy was offered by the proselytising missionaries of the Second Reformation, who selected the Tuam archdiocese as their principal field of operations. Widely publicised was an 1852 contretemps between the renowned preacher, Professor — later President — Patrick J. O'Brien, and the Earl of Mayo who had dropped into the Cathedral during an O'Brien sermon. Six months later, at an evangelical meeting in Dublin, the earl referred to his visit, saying 'he did not hear a word of the Gospel or Divinity …merely a tirade against landlords and the government.' O'Brien's reply was a masterpiece of invective which, in denying the Earl's specific charges, revealed something of what had upset the nobleman in the first place:

> Imagine not… that I write this letter to apologise… for the few words of complaint which have, it seems, so terribly shocked your right honourable nerves… I shall not remain dumb in the fold of Israel while the flock is being unmercifully devoured by ravening wolves; and although it may not appear either 'gospel or divinity' to your Lordship, the priest you heard in Tuam shall, nevertheless, according to his humble powers, continue to imitate the inspired pensman, and whenever it comes within the sphere of his duty, fearlessly rebuke 'those who sit in the high places' and 'whose tabernacles prosper,' should they, like their heaven-accursed prototypes of old, inhumanly persist in 'grinding the faces of the poor.'[1]

Shortly afterwards, O'Brien helped to convert several prominent local Protestants, successes which were in the circumstances gleefully publicised in the pro-Catholic press.[2] Also in 1852, President Peter Reynolds captured the headlines when he led local clerical criticism of the M.P. for County Galway, Anthony O'Flaherty, an 'Irish Brigade' associate of Sadlier and Keogh. On this occasion, Reynolds took exception to the accusation that his views did not coincide with those of Dr MacHale.[3]

---

1. *Tuam Herald*, 1 May 1852. A native of Athenry, (Canon) Patrick J. O'Brien joined the college staff in 1846 shortly after his ordination. He succeeded John MacEvilly as president in 1857, remaining in the position until 1865. He subsequently served in the parishes of Boyaunagh (1865-79) and Athenry, where he died in 1883 at the age of sixty-three.
2. ibid, 30 October, 18 December 1852.
3. ibid., 10, 17 April, 1, 8 May 1852. But Reynolds, evidently, was a closet critic of MacHale (see Chapter 3 above).

MacHale's vigorous espousal of nationalism, together with his indulgent attitude towards those of his priests who followed his example, was distasteful to some within the Irish church. The Irish priesthood's vociferous and unrestrained political engagement might be understandable after the enforced silence of the Penal days, but was it wise? One who felt strongly that his subordinates should remain politically aloof was Paul Cullen, who was appointed archbishop of Armagh in 1849 after almost thirty years in Rome, latterly as agent of the Irish bishops and rector of the Irish College there. Cullen's long sojourn in the eternal city, and his experience as a functionary, had naturally affected his outlook on church government. He had acquired a Roman perspective and a centralising disposition — as well as some influential friends in the Vatican.

On most issues, Cullen's views were diametrically opposed to MacHale's and, given their temperaments, conflict between the two was inevitable. Over three decades, until Cullen's death in 1878, a long battle was fought about the direction of the Irish church, a battle that has been characterised as constituting the Irish manifestation of the general struggle within the nineteenth century church between the forces of ultramontanism and gallicanism. While such a characterisation slightly over-simplifies their respective positions, MacHale has been regarded as representing the gallican position — favouring devolution of authority to national and diocesan level — with Cullen representing the ultramontane — advocating greater powers for the pope. Cullen held the high ground in the conflict and time, generally speaking, was on his side. For one thing, his Roman contemporaries were coming into more influential positions, while MacHale's contacts were expiring. And thus bolstered, Cullen was enabled to translate to the See of Dublin in 1852 and to become Ireland's first cardinal in 1866. More importantly, he was able to secure the appointment of like-minded men to vacant bishoprics, thereby, altering the balance of forces within the hierarchy to MacHale's detriment.[1] Ultimately, then, the 'roar from St Jarlath's' proved more impressive than the bite, but it was not silenced until life departed the Lion of the West.

A constant reminder of MacHale's declining influence within the hierarchy was his immediate episcopal neighbour, John MacEvilly of Galway. MacEvilly was a former protégé of the

---

1. Larkin's *The making of the Roman Catholic Church in Ireland, 1850-1860*, 1980; and *Consolidation*, passim.

archbishop, who was appointed professor of Scripture and Hebrew in St Jarlath's in 1842 and president in 1852. At some point after this, relations between the two Mayomen became strained, and MacEvilly found his way into Cullen's good books. The estrangement was complete in 1857 when MacEvilly was chosen by Cullen as his instrument for thwarting MacHale's ambition to gain the Galway diocese for his nephew, Dr Thomas MacHale. Thereafter, in the ongoing battle for the heart of the Irish church between MacHale and Cullen, MacEvilly was firmly in the Cullen camp. Moreover, as a suffragen bishop in the province, and one with excellent personal contacts in the Tuam archdiocese, he was something of a trojan horse in MacHale's territory.[1]

As far as the culture of the College was concerned, the effects of MacHale's proximity were profound. His influence permeated all aspects of the institution's life and was visible particularly, as shall be seen later, at prize-days and other public functions. In his dealings with students, it would appear that the archbishop was frank, and averse to glossing over the fault-lines of controversy for their benefit. Instead he sought to persuade them of his own outlook. His address to staff and students on the eve of his departure for Rome for the First Vatican Council — where, incidentally, he was one of the minority of bishops to oppose the promulgation of the doctrine of papal infallibility — was a case in point:

> The people of Ireland... clung during the long night of suffering and of sorrow to the priests of their church — who at the peril of life... administered the saving sacraments of the Holy Church to the persecuted children of the ancient faith. It is only right that this intercommunion between priests and people, which was then cemented so strongly, should still continue... I trust that it will never be said by the enemies of both that the priests abandoned the cause of the people (Loud cheers). No! the cause of the priests of the Catholic Church in Ireland and of the faithful of that Church are the same. Let no one say that the priests ought to keep aloof from defending the cause of the people (Hear). They are one in faith, one in hope, one in the bonds that bind them in seeking for national amelioration (Cheers). Politics and religion are so entwined in

---

1. Bane's *MacEvilly*, pp.40-41.

Ireland, that politics in fact cannot be abstracted from religion, nor religion set free from politics, by the most astute logical reasoners… It may do very well to theorise on abstract forms, but men of the world, men seeking for their rights have to deal with realities. (Hear.) The cause of the people of Ireland and the religion of Ireland are handmaids of the same Lord of Truth.[1]

It would be unsurprising if exposure to such uncompromising rhetoric encouraged some students to go a step further politically, strictly speaking, than the archbishop could have recommended. Some alumni, in any case, were early members of the Fenians. Shortly before the Fenian rebellion of 1867, Professor James O'Leary of St Colman's College, Fermoy, met a group of twelve men in Queenstown. All were 'colonels and captains,' veterans of the American Civil War who had returned to lead the Irish people into battle against England. Of the twelve, according to O'Leary, 'four of them were educated in Tuam Seminary as aspirants to the Church and three had brothers priests in America.'[2]

The political outlook of the these peripatetic colonels and captains may have been forged in St Jarlath's, but they could not have become actively engaged until they left the College. Within the institution, public affairs were, generally speaking, the preserve of the patron, of the president, of some professors. The intensely political atmosphere, reflected in an untypically strong emphasis on Irish language and culture in the curriculum, left its mark, but except for a period in the late 1860s and early 1870s, when Fenianism penetrated the College walls, the students were passive politically. And during the exceptional period, the very fact of Fenian infiltration indicated that the ordinary discipline of St Jarlath's was under strain.

Fenianism was already part of the battle-ground in the broader MacHale-Cullen conflict. Cullen, a neophyte as far as the nuances of Irish politics were concerned, often acted on the basis of simplistic analogies with the Italian situation. Fenians, therefore, as *soi-disant* revolutionaries, were the local equivalent of Garribaldians and, equally with them, the irreconcilable enemies of religion. For his part, MacHale expressed disapproval of Fenianism, especially insofar as it was secret and oathbound,

---

1. *The Tablet*, 13 November 1869.
2. Cited in Larkin's *Consolidation*, p.407.

but he was prepared to fudge the issue in order to avoid a split between a substantial section of the Irish Catholic people and their church.

It was the disputatious parish priest of Partry, Fr. Patrick Lavelle, who forced the Fenian issue to centre-stage. Lavelle, a Jarlath's-educated priest of the Tuam archdiocese and the former professor of Philosophy at the Irish College in Paris, made his reputation as a fighter against both landlordism and proselytism during the notorious Partry evictions case. But as vice-president of the Brotherhood of St Patrick — a Fenian front organisation — and as one who defended putative Fenian violence from a theological perspective, Lavelle put himself at odds with the majority tendency within the church. Open conflict became unavoidable when the so-called 'patriot priest of Partry' became involved in arrangements for the Fenian-organised funeral of Young Irelander Terence Bellew MacManus, a funeral which Cullen forbade the priests of Dublin from attending. Not only did Lavelle publicly attack Cullen for his attitude, but he associated with his rebuke other Tuam priests — including Professor Ulick Bourke of St Jarlath's — and then, to add provocation to insult, he travelled to Cullen's diocese to deliver the graveside oration.[1]

Cullen had no choice but to raise the matter at a meeting of the hierarchy, and he secured passage of a resolution demanding that Lavelle apologise and that he resign from the Brotherhood of St Patrick. Lavelle would not comply and MacHale was ordered by Rome to discipline him. The matter remained contentious for most of the 1860s, with MacHale protecting his priest insofar as he could, with Cullen continuing to insist on compliance, and with Lavelle persistently fighting his corner, mostly in the pages of the paper described by John MacEvilly as 'a malicious Garribaldian rag' — the Tuam-based and church-backed *Connaught Patriot*,.[2]

The 'Garribaldian rag' in question was established in 1859 by Martin A. O'Brennan of Ballyhaunis, a distinguished former student of St. Jarlath's. In the 1830s, O'Brennan had gained experience as a 'public professor, historiographer and lecturer' in the College before moving to Dublin, where he established his own so-called 'Collegiate Seminary', a grinding establishment which prepared young men for examinations. Although he dabbled in

1. Gerard Moran, *A radical priest in Mayo*, 1994, passim; Tomás Ó Fiach, '"The patriot Priest of Partry': Patrick Lavelle, 1825-1866' in *JGAHS*, vol.xxxv, 1976, pp.137-45.
2. ibid.; Bane, *MacEvilly*, pp.41-44.

Young Ireland politics in the 1840s, his principal interest was in the Irish language and Irish antiquities and, by the time he returned to Tuam, he had established a reputation as an authority on matters 'Celtic.' O'Brennan's newspaper reflected these interests and, more importantly, promoted his political outlook, which was intensely nationalist and avowedly Catholic. But neither his nationalism or his Catholicism were accepted as being quite orthodox. Despite his advocacy of their front organisation, Fenians regarded him as a not-always-amiable eccentric and, at best, a useful dupe; because of his advocacy of the Brotherhood, Cardinal Cullen regarded him as a dangerous revolutionary.

But O'Brennan was welcome enough in Tuam. For his publication, which he placed 'under the patronage of the Blessed Virgin', he claimed the 'sanction of the venerated prelate and the revered clergy of Connaught.' The paper certainly benefited from more than its share of advertising from institutions and organisations connected to the Church. Nor did the notoriety of its editor, who served a prison sentence for encouraging Fenianism, prevent the 'venerated prelate,' John MacHale, from recommending the *Connaught Patriot* as an 'organ of Catholicity', or from rescuing it financially on at least one occasion.'[1]

Thus, two St Jarlath's alumni were engaged in a long-term public controversy with the acknowledged leader of the Catholic Church in Ireland — and evidently with the tacit support of MacHale. The fact hardly went unremarked in the College, where O'Brennan was a frequent visitor. Moreover, O'Brennan's passionate cultural nationalism was shared by one of the College professors, Ulick Bourke.

Ulick Bourke — whose mother was a first cousin of John MacHale's — was born at Laherdane, Castlebar in 1829. He attended St Jarlath's College and Maynooth, before being ordained by his cousin in Tuam Cathedral in 1858. As a clerical student, Bourke was critical of the neglect of Irish in Maynooth where, despite the existence of a professorship in Irish, he insisted that the language was 'treated as the language of the Hebrew race, as something foreign, not the language of thought of the country, of life, of business.' He was conscious also that Irish was being strangled elsewhere in the educational system and, in

---

1. Marie Louise Legg, 'Martin A. O'Brennan and the Connaught Patriot' in Claffey's *Glimpses of Tuam,* pp.67-72; Patrick Diskin, 'Irish scholars and language workers in the West, 1800-1900 in *Iarlaith,* 1961, pp.88-92.

an attempt to provide the tools to resist this process, he published his *College Irish Grammar* in 1856, two years before his ordination. And for some years, he contributed a regular column 'Easy lessons or self-instruction in Irish' to the *Nation* newspaper. On ordination, Bourke was appointed professor of Irish in the College. He also acted as secretary to the archbishop, who liked to surround himself with relatives. With respect to Bourke, his dependability as a relative was complemented by his expert knowledge of Irish, which made him a useful editor for MacHale's catechetical works in that language.

Bourke's principal interest was in cultural rather than political affairs but, inevitably, many of those who shared his interests or admired his pioneering work were as 'advanced' in nationalist political terms as they were in their espousal of Irish. His biographer considers that Bourke was personally sympathetic to Fenianism, although a long way from being as militant in this respect as his friend Lavelle. Another writer has argued that Bourke was 'one of those most influential on the intellectual development of Fenians in the last quarter of the century because he had taught them in their youth.'[1]

Bourke took over as president from P.J. O'Brien in October 1865. Although only thirty-five, he was firmly established as one of the leading Gaelic scholars of the day. And, personally ambitions and energetic, he was keen to place his talents at the disposal of the College and enhance its status among the colleges of Ireland. Unlike several of his predecessors, he was trusted by John MacHale who seems to have given him free rein to manage the College as he wished.[2]

The position of St Jarlath's could not be advanced without increasing student numbers. Although the infrastructure had been extended during O'Brien's tenure with the building of the new College, enrolment had remained low for several reasons. Firstly, the expansion of Maynooth in the mid-1840s removed senior seminarians from the rolls; then, famine emigration had taken away other potential pupils. Emigration, moreover, persisted in the post-Famine period: almost 12% of Co. Galway's population, for example, and 8% of Mayo's, left the island between 1851 and 1855. In an ever-diminishing pool, meanwhile, a growing number of Catholic post-primary schools were competing for pupils.

1. Ó Maolmhuaidh, *Uilleog de Búrca;* pp.88-90; Marie Louise Legg, *Newspapers and nationalism: the Irish provincial press, 1850-1892*, 1999, pp.93-108.
2. ibid., Ó Maolmhuaidh, *Uilleog de Búrca,* passim..

Bourke was not content to fish in restricted waters and he looked to the world outside of the archdiocese of Tuam to provide the students who would secure the finances and enhance the status of the College. His extensive cultural contacts throughout Ireland offered certain possibilities in this respect. And if emigration was one cause of two decades of stagnation, the new president concluded that it might also offer a solution — in the shape of the sons of prospering but nostalgic emigrants.

Accordingly, on his appointment, Bourke placed a notice in several publications, announcing the fact and seeking pupils. In emphasising the quality and range of the education provided and in stressing the College's other virtues — salubrity, piety, probity and benign authority — it followed the conventions for such advertisements. But there was an important short addendum:

> In consequence of some fathers and friends in America and in the Colonies, having expressed a wish to have their sons or relatives trained in an Irish College, the President is happy to announce that he can now receive from those countries any number who may wish to study at St Jarlath's.[1]

The mere announcement, however, would not sufficiently boost the profile of St Jarlath's, so Bourke followed with what amounted to an intensive advertising campaign. In common with other educational institutions, it had been customary to keep the College's name before the public by publishing the results of the annual internal examinations in local papers like the *Herald* and Castlebar's *Telegraph*. Now these began to appear regularly in Dublin papers like the *Nation* and the pro-Fenian *Irishman*, regional papers like the *Waterford Citizen* and the *Ulster Examiner*, and publications whose readership included Irish emigrants such as the English Catholic *Tablet,* Glasgow's *Catholic Banner*, the *Liverpool Times* and the *Boston Pilot*.[2]

Advertising could only achieve so much; equally important was Bourke's own reputation as a Gaelic scholar. This enhanced the credibility of his College among 'advanced' nationalists of all stripes, including sworn Fenians. Such people were well disposed towards St Jarlath's in any case. It was after all the

---
1. SJC, 1865 prospectus.
2. SJC, Expenditure book, 1867-1902: 29 June 1868; 17 February, 29 April, 1 July 1869; 23 August - 25 September 1870.

diocesan college of John MacHale, the most nationalist of the bishops and the enemy of the Fenians' enemy, Cardinal Cullen.

Bourke's efforts at expansion were quite successful. There had been less than sixty on the rolls in 1867-68; by 1870-71 there was seventy-eight. Numbers continued to increase thereafter, with students drawn from all over the Anglophone world so that Galway and Mayo accents were no longer dominant in the corridors. The enrolment of youngsters like Terence Tobin, a 'freshman from Waterford' and P. Doyle, 'boarder, Kingstown, Co. Dublin' testify to the efficacy of advertisements but they were not the most exotic student specimens. That honour — probably — was shared between William Oliver Anselm Ewart from Liverpool, whose father 'was a Protestant but had the happiness of being received into the Catholic Church before his death' and Master Thomas Carr 'freshman boarder of Keighley, Yorks — a convert who wishes to be a priest on the English mission.' The diaspora was represented by such as 'Joseph MacLaughlin, freshman from Glasgow, by 'Patrick Canavan from Australia, South,' by 'Master E.F. Dunne, Peoria, Illinois, America,' by 'Master MacMahon of Savannah, Georgia,' by 'John MacCosker of Mobile, Alabama' and by 'Patk McCorry, New York.'[1]

One notable student was Patrick Larkin, son of Michael Larkin, one of the 'Manchester martyrs' whose sentencing and execution in November 1867 had mobilised nationalist Ireland and, at the same time, divided the Catholic priesthood between those who were wary of the slightest association with Fenianism and those who were concerned to keep in touch with popular sentiment. Indeed, Archbishop MacHale had broken ranks on this issue by allowing the use of his Cathedral for a High Mass in the martyrs' memory. His example was widely followed and the episode was remembered when the time came to choose a College for young Larkin. That his family could afford to send him, incidentally, was due to the benevolence of the Marchioness of Queensbury, who paid all bills from the College.[2]

More notorious than the Manchester martyrs, as far as most members of the Catholic hierarchy were concerned, was the

---

1. SJC, Receipt Book, 1867-81: 3 October, 1 November 1867; 18 March 1868; 9 November 1869; 28, 31 August, 21 September 1870.
2. ibid, 3 January, 10 June, 15 July 1870; Ryan's *Memories*, p.26; Larkin's *Consolidation*, p.431-32. The Marchioness had written as follows to Michael Larkin before his execution: 'Yet we will remember your souls constantly at the altar of God after your departure, as well as those whom you leave in life'(Paul Rose, *The Manchester Martyrs: a fenian tragedy*, 1970, pp.90-91.

Fenian leader, Jeremiah O'Donovan Rossa. From a prison cell, he had unexpectedly defeated the clergy's favourite in the Tipperary by-election of 1869.[1] Released soon afterwards, he went to live in the United States but, before his departure, Rossa made arrangements for a College education for three of his nineteen children. He was no better able to afford this than Mrs Larkin, so Jeremiah junior, John and Con O'Donovan were sent to St Jarlath's on foot of an unusual agreement between their father and the disreputable owner of the ostensibly-Fenian *Irishman* newspaper, Richard Pigott. Pigott — later infamous as the author of the Parnell forgeries in the *Times* — undertook to pay the boys' fees, if their father contributed a regular column to his newspaper. That Ulick Bourke approved the arrangement is shown by his comment in the receipt book:

> Pigott inserts a condition in his letter that if the children's father, Rossa, now in America, does not continue to write in Irishman and for Irishman and if any untoward event should happen, Pigott will not be bound but O'Donovan himself must pay. I accepted the sum on those conditions.[2]

Although Larkin and the O'Donovans were sons of notorious fathers, there was nothing particularly remarkable about their receiving an education in a Catholic diocesan college. Elsewhere though, their equivalents would not have been regarded as trophies; nor would their presence have been advertised in publicity surrounding plays and exhibitions.

There were two students at St Jarlath's in the late 1860s and early 1870s, however, who would not have been accepted, under any conceivable circumstances, in any other college in Ireland. As seasoned revolutionaries, indeed, it is doubtful whether Mark Ryan or John O'Connor Power would have been allowed, even as visitors, inside the walls of most ecclesiastical foundations.

That they received an education in St Jarlath's demonstrates ambivalence, at the very least, in Ulick Bourke's attitude towards Fenianism. However, it also reflects the president's ambition to develop the College — no student should be turned away; if a young man needed a higher education, then the College should provide it. And circumstances at the time favoured his efforts to

---

1. Larkin's *Consolidation*, pp.651-52.
2. Ryan, p.26, Receipt Book, 21 October 1871.

develop a third-level enclave within St Jarlath's. The College's status as a seminary had been restored when theological education was resumed in the late 1860s after a gap of more than two decades. Clerical students, therefore, could remain on for a period after they completed their second-level education. It was a logical step then to slightly expand the third-level provision and to offer advanced courses to lay students. And if this put the College in competition with the ailing Catholic University in Dublin, that was no great problem, since Archbishop MacHale had long been less than enthusiastic about that institution, regarding it as a bastion of West Britonism and Cullenism.[1]

The admission of adults who could not easily be made amenable to clerical discipline inevitably brought with it certain difficulties. Such difficulties were going to be all the greater in the case of extraordinary individuals like John O'Connor Power and Mark Ryan.

Mark Ryan was born at Kilconly in 1844. In 1860, his family was evicted and moved to Lancashire, where the young man was sworn into the Fenian movement by Michael Davitt. Having participated in engagements in the North of England, he returned with a sawn-off rifle to Tuam in 1867 to join in the planned rebellion. Disappointed with the failure to mobilise in the area, he nevertheless remained to 'start building up the Fenian movement again.' He also decided to 'improve a defective education' and enrolled in St Jarlath's. For some reason, he left after one term and attended the Christian Brothers' school for a year. Ryan's mother came to believe he had a vocation, so she persuaded him to go back to St Jarlath's in 1868 where he paid the reduced fees of an ecclesiastical student. There is no indication that young Mark ever shared his mother's ambition but President Bourke evidently did, since he had him appointed sacristan of the Cathedral. During his three years in the College, Ryan was an outspoken Fenian but also a particular favourite of the president because of his fluent interest in the Irish language.[2]

John O'Connor Power came from even greater poverty than

---

1. Emmet Larkin, *Consolidation*, pp.173-74 and *The Roman Catholic Church and the Emergence of the Modern Irish political system, 1874-1878*, 1996, pp.152, 159.
2. Ryan's *Memories*, pp. 1-30; SJC, Receipt Book, 1867-81, 13 June 1869. Ryan's later recalled having spent two and a half years with the Christian Brothers. The St Jarlath's record, however, shows him to have paid in June 1869 'his entrance fee since last year,' indicating that he spent about a year in the Brothers' school.

Ryan. Born in Ballinasloe, he spent part of his childhood in the workhouse, before joining relatives in Lancashire, taking up their trade of housepainting, becoming acquainted with Michael Davitt and embracing Fenianism. His energy, talent and zeal won him prominence in the revolutionary movement and he was involved in several important operations in Britain. Although still only twenty-one, he was chosen to go the United States to join in discussions about Fenian reorganisation after the fiasco of 1867, but his work as the delegate of the American organisation was interrupted on his return in early 1868 by a five-month jail term. On his release, he carried out his mandate to create new structures including a representative body, the Supreme Council, of which he himself became a key member. In that capacity he was involved in gun-running, but he also promoted co-operation between Fenians and constitutional politicians. Then in January 1871, at the age of twenty-four, John O'Connor Power entered St Jarlath's College to acquire a formal education. His fees and other expenses over the next three years were paid from the proceeds of lectures organised for the purpose in both Ireland and Britain.[1]

Power was not about to take a sabbatical from intrigue, however, and despite being closely watched — his police file of the period noted that he was 'clever in composition and recitation' and that his appearance was 'smart'[2] — he remained on the IRB Supreme Council and continued to supervise its traffic in arms. Like Ryan, Power became a favourite of the president and his talents were fully utilised in College theatricals and public exhibitions. On one remarkable occasion, in the presence of the archbishop and several dozen of the diocesan clergy, he 'brought the broadside of his arguments and the power of his elocation to bear' in a debate entitled 'Was the Inquisition justified in condemning Gallileo?' The *Tuam News* was impressed by both the honesty and quality of the discussion:

> And here let us remark that in nothing did the character of St Jarlath's as a model of educational establishments stand out so clearly marked as in this debate. There was no sickly palliation of the acts of what is often called an ecclesiastical tribunal; there was no glossing over

---

1. T.W. Moody's *Davitt and the Irish Revolution*, 1981, pp.47-50; Donald Jordan, 'John O'Connor Power, Charles Stewart Parnell and the centralisation of popular politics in Ireland ' in *Irish Historical Studies*, vol.xxx, 1986, pp.47-48.
2. National Archives, FP 391.

inquisitorial misdeeds by command, or no intentionally weakened defence of [Gallileo].[1]

The cause of the Manchester martyrs and that of the remaining Fenian prisoners mobilised popular sympathy for Fenianism after 1867, even among those who disapproved of its methods. Ambivalence was evident even among the clergy, although few priests went as far as Father Lavelle of Partry in publicly disputing Cardinal Cullen's proscription of the movement. But, while the Irish bishops were in Rome for the first Vatican Council, one half of their clergy signed a petition demanding an amnesty for Fenian prisoners, forcing the issue to the top of the hierarchy's agenda. Although Cardinal Cullen had previously failed to secure an outright condemnation of Fenianism from the pope, he knew that if the request came from the Irish bishops as a body he would succeed. Only MacHale and Derry of Clonfert dissented from the request, so an official and authoritative condemnation of Fenianism was issued by the Pope in January 1870. News of the development reached St Jarlath's in a letter from the archbishop to Bourke — 'a Fenian at heart' according to Mark Ryan — who passed on the news to his Fenian student.

MacHale's attitude ensured that the papal rescript was not zealously enforced in the archdiocese of Tuam and Ryan continued for another eighteen months in the College. Then, according to his own account, he was summoned to the president's room in the summer of 1871, when the following conversation took place:

Bourke: You are known to be carrying on the Fenian movement. You know I am not against the Fenians.

Ryan: I know that you are not.

Bourke: I told you about the archbishop's letter and what took place at the Vatican Council. Whatever you do, if you are here, let it be done as quietly as possible. Your activities are interfering with the discipline of the College

Ryan: All right, I have arranged to leave the College when the summer holidays begin.

Bourke: Oh, very well, but remember I am not asking you to leave.

Ryan: I know that you are not.[2]

---

1. *Tuam News*, 28 June 1872
2. Ryan's *Memories*, pp.28-29

Mark Ryan went on to the Queen's College in Galway to study medicine and then back to England to complete his training and to work as a doctor. Nevertheless, his connection with St Jarlath's continued for several years, as he kept up his Fenian contacts there. In England, Ryan's maladroit attempts to make contact with arms-dealers attracted the notice of the police. Thereafter, his activities were closely watched, and his mail opened. Among Ryan's correspondents were two in the College, John Delaney — identified by the police as O'Connor Power — and M.R. Biggins. In one letter, Biggins' announced that he had persuaded forty students in the College to become Home Rulers, but Ryan was unimpressed. Writing that he had 'not much faith in the [Home Rule] movement.' he remarked that Biggins would have been better occupied if he had 'got the forty to cross the Rubicon, when they could do greater services to Ireland.'[1]

Seemingly, some few students were persuaded to make that journey, given Biggins's subsequent assertion that 'the organisation is working well.' There might have been more, but 'one thing discourages them, they have no small arms.' Thus the request to Ryan — 'bring some revolvers with you when you are coming.' In another exchange about Fenian business, Ryan urged Biggins to 'leave your land-marks on the College before you leave it' and reassured him following police raids on houses in Tuam that 'the bobbies... will not attempt to go into the College.'[2]

The political excitement of the period found an electoral outlet. Between 1868 and 1872, the political power of landlords in the archdiocese was broken. Staff and students of St Jarlath's played their part in this critical development.

The national context was coloured by the determination of the Catholic hierarchy to ensure that constituencies returned 'reliable' representatives, who could be depended upon to support moves to disestablish Anglicanism. All Catholic factions were in agreement on this. One incidental effect was to create a coincidence of interest between Fenians and the clergy in certain areas. In Mayo, the popular candidate for the 1868 general election was the radical Catholic landlord, George Moore of Moore Hall. Moore was a friend of Patrick Lavelle and a Fenian sympathiser himself. He was backed by MacHale and the Mayo

---

1. National Archives, Fenian papers, A files, A567, Box 4, Biggins to Ryan, 14 March 1874, Ryan to Biggins, 13 April 1874.
2. ibid., Ryan to Biggins, 10 April 1874.

clergy, who declared that Catholics should support only candidates that stood for 'tenant right, ...Catholic denominational education, the disestablishment and disendowment of the Protestant Church,' and Repeal of the Union.[1]

Implicit in this appeal was a threat to politically disengage Catholic tenants from their landlords. The threat was successful to the extent that the landlord interest withdrew rather than face turbulence. This outcome was not achieved without an intensive canvassing campaign. Mark Ryan recalled that President Bourke 'got about a dozen of the students, myself included, to write out a number of appeals to prominent and influential electors on behalf of Moore.[2]

No longer a St Jarlath's student, Mark Ryan was involved in the Galway election of 1872. Again, the popular candidate, John Phillip Nolan of Ballinderry, Tuam, was a Catholic landlord, whose candidature was promoted by Lavelle and supported by MacHale. MacHale's episcopal colleagues in the county were less enthusiastic — they feared Nolan's candidacy would 'divide the rich Catholics from the poor' — but popular sentiment forced them to support him. Again, Fenians were to be found canvassing alongside Catholic clergymen, some of whom took up the cause rather too enthusiastically. The result was a landslide victory for Nolan but, on appeal, the seat was awarded to the Conservative candidate, William le Poer Trench, by Judge Keogh on the grounds that Nolan's vote was achieved through 'undue influence' by the clergy. Among those who influenced the outcome were the College staff but past pupils, Fr Lavelle and Fr Peter Conway, were considered worthy of special mention by the judge. Trench's victory proved to be a Pyrrhic one, however, which enraged the tenantry and served to stiffen anti-landlord politics in the constituency.[3]

Meanwhile, John O'Connor Power remained as a fee-paying student until 1874. Since several sources described him as 'a teacher at St Jarlath's' during his final year, it is possible that he had begun to give some classes. If so, the work was very much secondary to politics, in which arena his stature continued to grow. In several respects his efforts during the period were remarkable, especially insofar as they appear to anticipate the

---

1. Larkin, *Consolidation*, pp.600-04.
2. Moran's *Radical priest*, 96-99; Larkin's *Consolidation*, p.599-604; Ryan's *Memories*, p.41.
3. Moran's *Radical priest*, pp.136-42; Emmet Larkin, *The Roman Catholic Church and the Home Rule movement in Ireland, 1870-1874*, 1990, pp.123-35.

so-called 'New Departure' negotiated at the end of the decade. Having been among those who persuaded the Fenian movement to give critical support to parliamentary home rulers, he made a remarkable speech to the home rule conference of November 1873, a speech which in giving voice to the aspirations of the rank and file supporters of constitutionalism, utterly radicalised the tone of their gathering.[1] If Power was 'ahead of his time,' however, this was no guarantee that he would not be found to be out of step with the prevailing tempo when it mattered most.

But that was in the future. In early 1874 Power's star was ascendant and he knew it. Nevertheless, his announcement that he was going to contest the Mayo constituency in the 1874 general election met with considerable surprise and some resistance. Anticipating this, he had discussed the matter in advance with Ulick Bourke and had secured his support. In the chaotic politics of the period such support was important. The absence of any party infrastructure worthy of the name ensured that the influence of the clergy — who were organised — was critical. Nor was this influence wielded discretely. The priests of a constituency customarily met prior to selection conventions to consider the merits of prospective candidates and to make recommendations. And such recommendations had carried great weight in Mayo politics.[2]

In return for Bourke's support, and through him that of the archbishop, Power had promised that he would withdraw from the contest if he was not supported at the meeting of the Mayo clergy, an outcome he must, in the circumstances, have considered unlikely. But there emerged substantial opposition to his candidacy, some of it from predictable quarters. The most emphatic opposition, however, came from the previously pro-Fenian Fr Lavelle, who, motivated by personal dislike more than political difference, was diligent in persuading his colleagues that Power was an opportunist and an interloper.

The Castlebar meeting and its aftermath was described by one of the participants:

> Please observe that the Archbishop came from Tuam accompanied by his cousin, Rev. U. Bourke, to promote the candidature of madman Power, the Fenian. But thanks

---

1. Jordan's 'Power, pp.46-51; Moran's *Radical priest*, pp.146-47; Fenian papers, A567, memo 7 May 1874.
2. Jordan's 'Power', pp.48-51.

> to the stand made by Dr Conway & all of the priests of the county here, he was obliged to set him aside. He could not conceal his humiliation, by his embarrassed manner, nervous and choking voice. The roughs & all the Phalanxes of Fenians paraded the town, round & round with banners, fife & drum, shouting and hurraing for Power. Father Lavelle was mobbed & hooted, priests & Bishops denounced as traitors... The mob passed backwards and forwards where the Archbishop was, hooting & shouting & groaning and so, on Thursday morning... he fled to Tuam amidst the reproaches and hootings of the mob. Grand times, grand results of Fenian lectures & the coming down of our St Jarlath pupils who daily associate with young candidates for the priesthood &c.[1]

The decision of the meeting was not binding on the candidates, but in deference to Bourke and MacHale, O'Connor Power withdrew. The two candidates approved by the clergy, George Browne and Thomas Tighe, took the constituency's two seats as Home Rulers. For technical reasons which had nothing to do with the controversy, however, the result of the general election in the constituency was found to be invalid and a by-election was called for May. O'Connor Power resolved to stand and explained his position thus:

> When I last addressed you as a parliamentary candidate, I was bound by a pledge, which made my candidature conditional on my adoption by his grace the archbishop of Tuam and the bishops and clergy of Mayo... Before, however, my committee accepted my resignation, they, in the name of the nationalists of Mayo, extracted a promise from me that I would again become a candidate for the county if, at any ensuing election they should be dissatisfied with the candidates then in the field. Sooner, many years sooner than I could have anticipated, I am now called upon by a numerously signed requisition of the electors... I kept my word on the last occasion, I am determined not to break it on this...[2]

Influenced, probably, by the snub he received in February, MacHale did not call a meeting of the clergy on this occasion. This in no way diminished the clerical opposition to his

---

1. Cited in Larkin's *Home Rule*, pp.253-54.
2. Cited in Jordan's 'Power', p.51.

favourite in the constituency, which was vigorous and desperate. Power's campaign, managed by outsiders such as Mark Ryan, drew on the Fenian network in the county and appealed particularly to the impoverished, a section of the community greatly under-represented on the list of voters. The contest was followed with great interest and partisanship all over Ireland. Dr MacEvilly kept Cardinal Cullen briefed: 'O'C.P is a Fenian and swore in as Fenians some alumni of the College he was in, among them a brother of a P.P. in the diocese of T. It would be most humiliating if he was returned.'[1] But returned he was, with forty votes to spare.

To the disappointment of his most enthusiastic supporters, Power proved to be a moderate public representative. His advocacy of federalism, in particular, strengthened the argument of those 'irreconcilables' in the Fenians who wanted no truck with parliamentarianism, and within three years of his election Power was removed from the supreme council and anathemised by the Fenian movement.

The moderating of O'Connor Power's politics occurred in St Jarlath's; whether it was effected *by* St Jarlath's is open to question. He acknowledged himself that his 'college years' marked an important phase in his life, so it could be argued that he absorbed more from the atmosphere than knowledge of the classics and the techniques of composition and exposition. Arguably therefore, the admissions policy of MacHale and Bourke was wiser than their opponents allowed. By domesticating 'the madman Power' and several of his comrades, they kept open imperilled communication lines. Fenians alienated by the unsympathetic 'Roman' Catholicism of Cullen and his followers were not pushed into becoming openly anti-clerical. They could register their protest by sending their sons to St Jarlath's

Power's later career, however, was not the high-flying one that the mentors of his college years anticipated. And in part, this was because the watering down of his politics turned out to be somewhat premature. When co-operation between revolutionaries and parliamentarians resumed at the end of the 1870s — heralding the Land League — the Fenian element was adamant that Power have no role in their 'New Departure.' Despite this, his popularity among the men of little or no property in his constituency, together with his early involvement in the burgeoning land agitation of the period, meant that Power

---

1. Cited in Larkin's *Home Rule*, p.255.

could not be easily side-lined, and he was regarded as a possible leader of the new national movement. It was Parnell — incidentally, the other M.P. for Mayo from 1880 — who proved the more politically astute, however, and John O'Connor Power's political career was finished by 1885.[1]

*

John MacHale celebrated the golden jubilee of his consecration as bishop on 5 June 1875. In his eighty-fifth year, he was still 'vigorous' and 'quite active,' according to one source, capable of celebrating daily mass in the Cathedral and of preaching at the nine o'clock mass each Sunday. Nevertheless, the jubilee forced him into the realisation that he could not expect to remain archbishop of Tuam forever. Accordingly, in July 1875, he requested that Rome appoint a coadjutor bishop, someone to assist him in his declining years and to succeed him when he died. Rather than leaving matters to chance following his death or incapacity, the archbishop sought to safeguard his legacy by securing the appointment of a like-minded individual. The O'Connor Power affair showed that his influence among the clergy was waning; they might well select an unworthy successor for want of guidance from himself.

Unwisely — and not only because such suggestions were considered the prerogative of the diocesan clergy — the archbishop asked that Thomas MacHale be appointed. The old man, moreover, was not alone in believing that his nephew was a chip off the old block. Cardinal Cullen, when he was informed of the development, warned Cardinal Franchi, the head of Propaganda Fide in Rome that Thomas was '...of restless character, much disposed to opposition, ... similar to his uncle.'[2]

If John MacHale was determined that his nephew be coadjutor, Cardinal Cullen was equally determined that he should not. Cullen's candidate was his close ally and confidant, John MacEvilly, who was eager for promotion from Galway to Tuam. Between them, the two men were able to control the tempo of events relating to the succession, delaying or expediting proceedings to suit their shared purpose. In this respect, Cullen's high-level contacts in the Vatican and MacEvilly's connections throughout the archdiocese of Tuam were equally useful.

When Rome eventually consented to a coadjutorship, MacHale was not given the successor of his choice. Instead, he was instructed to hold the usual consultative vote among the

1. Jordan's 'Power', p.p.54-66.
2. Larkin's *Emergence*, pp.71-74.

senior diocesan clergy to select a *terna* — three names for consideration by the Pope. The announcement that a meeting for this purpose would be held on 17 August 1876 brought to a climax a period of intensive canvassing and lobbying among the clergy of Tuam, during which the College staff had been energetic on the MacHale side.[1]

When the senior clergy gathered to vote, there was an air of unreality surrounding the proceedings. As well as uncertainty regarding the composition of the electorate, there were question marks about the candidacies of the principal contenders. On the first, the archbishop bowed to precedent and agreed to confine the vote to parish priests; on the second, the ambiguity persisted. The archbishop advised that MacEvilly — as an existing bishop and as one he could not work with — was ineligible for the coadjutorship. On the grounds that he had previously 'been not accepted' by Rome, he also announced the withdrawal of his nephew.[2] This last move was interpreted as a tactical device: if, despite his withdrawal, Thomas MacHale polled reasonably, there would be a good case for appointing him.

When the votes were counted, MacEvilly led the field with sixteen votes to Thomas MacHale's twelve, while Professor Thomas Carr of Maynooth had nine. The other candidates were also-rans: Canon James Ronayne had three votes; Ulick Bourke had two; the bishops of Achonry and Clonfert had one each.

The result was disappointing to both factions. MacEvilly had expected a clear majority, he received barely a third of the total cast. MacHale's expectations had been somewhat lower, but after forty years in the archdiocese, he was taken aback to discover that he commanded the loyalty of only a quarter of his parish priests.

The archbishop continued to press for the appointment of his nephew, although no longer seeming to believe that this object was possible. Indeed, he indicated that he might be prepared to sacrifice Thomas's prospects if he was guaranteed that MacEvilly would not succeed. His objections to the Bishop of Galway were powerfully felt and had already been forcefully

---

1. ibid., pp.75-78, 82-85.
2. The archbishop announced the withdrawal of his nephew as follows: Since it happened that the Rev. Thomas MacHale, Doctor in Theology and Philosophy, was two or three times put forward as one worthy to fill the position of bishop and has not been by the Holy See accepted, it can of him be fairly said: "Him the Lord has not chosen." He has for that reason very earnestly expressed a wish that his name should not at all be introduced at the election about to be held (Ó Tuairisg, *Ábhar…*, N.K., B.4, 4 August 1874).

presented to the diocesan clergy.[1] Arguing that it was vital for the Church that there be 'peace and charity' among its members, the archbishop warned that

> the practice of these virtues would be difficult in a situation where an assistant-bishop is appointed in opposition to the wishes of the prelate to be assisted. The reason becomes stronger still, when there is a question of appointing a bishop already accustomed, in a diocese of his own, to the exercise of unrestrained power, to become coadjutor to an aged prelate.
>
> But more dangerous still to peace and harmony would be the result in case the alienated feeling of the coadjutor had become a matter of public notoriety.[2]

Both parties continued to promote their cases. MacHale despatched his nephew to Rome and intimated that he would sooner have no coadjutor at all than have MacEvilly. It was to no avail. On 2 February 1877, the Pope approved the appointment of MacEvilly, recommending that the announcement be postponed.

Having won the battle, Cullen and MacEvilly were keen to wrap up the matter. They continued to send complaints to Rome, detailing the poor state of religion in the archdiocese of Tuam. Proselytisers, they insisted, were winning the struggle for souls in Conamara, discipline was lax among the parish clergy; Fenianism was rife in the diocesan seminary, St Jarlath's.[3]

---

1. Larkin's *Emergence*, p.85-89.
2. Cited ibid., p.88.
3. Many of the letters of complaint were gossipy in tone and implausible in content. The following example is an excerpt of a communication from Cardinal Cullen to his friend Nicholas Kirby, rector of the Irish College in Rome: '...the greatest excesses are committed in the diocese of Tuam in the way of drinking and... within the last twenty years at least six and twenty priests have died there (generally suddenly) from drinking. The Archbishop does not exercise the least influence over them on this head, and he cannot, as he drinks a great deal himself, tho' he does not get drunk. At present, the drunken priests are very numerous, they are generally opposed to Dr MacEvilly, as they think he would be severe upon drunkenness. In Tuam they have kept up the old system of stations. The priests dine at them in miserable houses where they learn to drink whiskey as the poor people give nothing else. This horrid state of things will be kept up if the archbishop wishes be carried out or his nephew appointed. ...Dr Thomas MacHale drinks very freely but... he does not get drunk. However, it is clear that if such be the case that he could not do good (Ó Tuairisg, *Ábhar...*, N.K, B.4, 23 January 1877).

MacHale was kept in the dark for some months. Eventually, towards the end of 1877, Cardinal Franchi decided it was time to break the news and Fr. Tom Burke, the celebrated Galway-born Dominican preacher and a friend of the archbishop's, was the medium chosen to deliver the tidings. On St St Stephen's Day 1877, Burke arrived in Tuam, delivered Franchi's letter, and tried to convince his lordship to submit to the wishes of the Holy See. He was not so successful. Some days later, the archbishop wrote to Cardinal Manning of London, seeking his intervention on the grounds that

> ...of all the ecclesiastics of the province, there is none more obnoxious to me as he [MacEvilly] has uniformly showed himself to be my most inveterate personal enemy. I cannot by any means consent to have him...[1]

Having appointed MacEvilly to Tuam, Rome was uncertain whether its wishes could be put into effect. Consequently, the coadjutor retained his existing responsibilities in the neighbouring dioceses and the income that went with these responsibilities. Evidently, it was not expected that any immediate provision would be made for him in Tuam.

In May 1878, MacHale was instructed to confer the necessary faculties to govern the diocese upon MacEvilly within one month. If he failed to act, the Pope himself would intervene to make the appointment effective. After first ignoring the order, MacHale threatened to resign and at the same time bring the reasons for this unusual step before the Irish public. The threat caused some alarm. Archbishop MacHale's popularity among Irish people, at home and abroad, was such that few members of the hierarchy had any confidence that they would emerge with much credit from the controversy which would inevitably follow such an abdication. Thomas MacHale, meanwhile, was appointed Vicar General of the archdiocese, further emphasising his uncle's determination to get by without a coadjutor. This appointment, in the opinion of the archbishop of Dublin, meant that 'Dr Thomas MacHale is really the archbishop.'

The sudden death of Cardinal Cullen in October 1878 delayed a final resolution of the issue. Thereafter, a consensus began to emerge that it would be preferable to allow time, and the assuredly imminent death of John MacHale, to solve the problem.[2]

1. Larkin's *Emergence*, p.119.
2. ibid, pp.118-30.

But MacEvilly and his supporters were becoming impatient and they continued to bombard Rome with alarmist communications, in which the allegedly deplorable state of St Jarlath's College featured prominently. MacEvilly wrote early in 1878 that the college had been 'a nest of Fenianism and many students sworn in as Fenians.' In March, he wrote: 'In the very College some of the students received revolvers.'[1] It would appear that the bishop was referring to the state of affairs of several years previously, but this would not be immediately clear to a reader of the letters. Archbishop McCabe, Cullen's successor in Dublin and a supporter of MacEvilly, also took an interest in the College's affairs. In a letter to Kirby, he observed as follows:

> In reference to the financial condition of the College of St Jarlath's [it] is not so easy to form an opinion. The present Superior of the College [Patrick Kilkenny] charges in the public press the late president, Canon Bourke, with leaving the College £1800 in debt. The friends of the latter denied the charges pretty vigorously and, as you may suppose, no great edification follows. Strange stories are told… If they were true it was a nursery of Fenianism. But I have no proof of this… It is stated but I could not prove it that the property of the diocesan college will rest in the hands of Dr Thomas MacHale on the occasion of the Archbishop's death. Dr MacHale is, I am sure, a very good man but no one man, no matter how good he may be, should hold public property.[2]

The financial difficulties of the College were also raised by MacEvilly. He, however, attributed these to expenditure by Richard MacHale, a nephew of the archbishop and a professor in the College from 1866 to 1875.[3] Neither man mentioned that St Jarlath's had expanded enormously, both in student numbers and physical size, during the Bourke presidency and that, in the circumstances, a certain indebtedness might be excusable.

It was the recurring complaints from the MacEvilly camp about the pervasiveness of proselytism in the archdiocese, however, which eventually led to some movement and, in September 1879, more than four years after the beginning of the

---

1. Ó Tuairisg, *Ábhar…*, K78/20, 14 January 1878; NK B.4, 17 March 1878.
2. Ó Tuairisg, *Ábhar…*, K/79/322, 8 August 1879.
3. ibid., K/79/374, 2 September 1879.

process, John MacEvilly arrived in Tuam, intending to stay and bearing a strongly worded letter from Propaganda Fide. Archbishop MacHale refused to see him then, or indeed at any other time during the two years which elapsed before his death. Whenever he requested a meeting, MacEvilly was able to see Dr Thomas MacHale — 'de facto the Archbishop,' according to the would-be-coadjutor — but received little satisfaction from such encounters. Without full faculties, it was an extremely frustrating period for the bishop.[1] He complained in January 1880 that 'not a single suggestion of mine in any single instance was attended to since I came here'. The frustration extended to his accommodation, which was in St Jarlath's:

> I have apartments in the College. I am obliged to get stairs built at my own expense and other articles of furniture for the refectory, to consult with decency. The President can do nothing as the College is very deeply in debt.[2]

According to Emmet Larkin, the arrangement whereby two bishops had jurisdiction over the same diocese, independently of each other, was unique in the history of the Church. In fact, MacEvilly did not seriously attempt to exercise authority during these two years. In his room in the College, he waited for the old man to die, wary that any decisive move on his part might result in unwelcome controversy.

John MacHale died on Monday, 7 November 1881, aged ninety, surrounded by clerical friends and relatives. Uniquely, he had been a public figure during eight decades since he took up his first post as lecturer in Dogma at Maynooth in 1812-13. As far as many in the Irish Church were concerned, however, he had outstayed his welcome. MacEvilly wrote in relief to Kirby:

> It is all over now and Heaven knows I suffered in silence to prevent scandal and exposure which was threatened. Since the poor man's death I have acted as if he were my greatest friend and mean to do so until after the month's mind.[3]

The remains of the archbishop were laid out in an improvised mortuary in St Jarlath's College, where over several days crowds

---

1. Larkin's *Emergence*, pp.122-29.
2. Ó Tuairisg, *Abhar...*, K79/469, 20 October 1879, K80/22, 15 January 1880.
3. Bane's *MacEvilly*, p.58.

thronged 'from morning till night,' according to the *Freeman's Journal*, 'kissing for the last time the hand that was so often raised in loving benediction over them.' On Sunday, at 2 p.m., the remains were removed from the College to the Cathedral. From an early hour 'schools, sodalities, societies and other bodies,' lined up in the College fields to take their places behind the cavalcade. Prominent in the procession through Bishop St., the Square, Dublin Road and the Mercy Convent grounds were the students of the College wearing 'armlets of crape.'

The funeral, on Tuesday 15 November, was one of the great occasions of the nineteenth century in Tuam, although one senses it might have been an even greater occasion had it occurred a decade or two earlier. (Arguably, the funeral was anticipated by the archbishop's Golden Jubilee celebrations of June 1875. That occasion witnessed a great gathering of ecclesiastics and politicians and the erection of a white marble statue of MacHale.)

Chief celebrant of the Requiem Mass was John MacEvilly, one of the ten bishops, headed by McGettigan of Armagh, who were present. Other dignitaries included the President of Maynooth and the mitred abbot of Mount Melleray; public figures who travelled to Tuam included Edmund Dwyer Gray M.P., proprietor of the *Freeman's Journal,* and A.M. Sullivan M.P., of *The Nation*. Professor Thomas Carr, Maynooth and ex-Jarlath's, was the master of ceremonies; he was assisted by the College President, Patrick Kilkenny. The College students acted as acolytes during the service.[1]

For the coterie that had surrounded John MacHale, the atmosphere in Tuam proved uncongenial after the death of the great patriarch. Thomas MacHale returned to the Irish College in Paris while several found missions in the United States. One of these, Bernard O'Reilly, wrote a hagiographical biography of his hero, while others were equally ardent in protecting the dead man's reputation.[2]

---

1. *Freeman's Journal,* 11, 14, 15. 16 November 1881. A ballad described some of the funeral scenes: 'Each shop that was in the town of Tuam put up their shuts that day / And from the window of each house a black flag did display / And in the centre was a cross which was of lily white / To remind us of the sorrow the town was in that night. The men of Tuam and women too most lovingly they came / With evergreen and laurel for the honour of his name; / Young children with downcast eyes and brow most full of care / In grandeur decorated the stone cross at the square (Nuala Costello's, *MacHale,* p.147-48).
2. Bane's *MacEvilly,* pp.58-59.

MacEvilly's strongest public rebuke to his predecessor was his de facto renunciation of long-standing educational policy in the diocese, for which he won the praise of the Commissioners for National Education. Sixty-eight national schools, according to the Commissioners, were established in the archdiocese of Tuam during 1884 alone. In fact, most of them were existing schools which were newly vested in the Board. The *Tuam Herald* took up the theme, castigating the dead archbishop as one who had 'held not alone the diocese but the greater part of the province under intellectual darkness.' This provoked John MacHale — grand-nephew and former St Jarlath's professor, but now curate of far-away Newport — into an angry protest 'against the attempt to extol one man at the expense of the reputation of another.'[1]

In fact the opposite also occurred, and MacHale's memory was regularly invoked by the disgruntled as a reproach to his successor, to the latter's irritation. Evidently MacEvilly regarded the MacHale scholarships and the MacHale Irish prizes at the College as something of a reproach also, as he introduced a substantial scheme of scholarships of his own in St Jarlath's: seven free places for ecclesiastical students, paid for from his personal resources.[2]

MacEvilly's innate conservatism was somewhat out of step with the prevailing politics during his early years in Tuam. His arrival in the archdiocese coincided with the birth there of the Land League, a development which, uncharacteristically, had been opposed by the MacHales, mainly because they felt that they had been disregarded by the founders. MacEvilly was instinctively suspicious of the movement but, almost echoing MacHale on Fenianism, he was anxious that it not be condemned by the Pope lest its supporters become alienated from the Church. His efforts on the ground, meanwhile, were directed at curbing the radicalism of the younger priests, while encouraging conservative and older clergymen to maintain a profile in the land movement. The bishop's biographer maintains that MacEvilly later became more sympathetic towards the militant tenantry, citing his apparent ambivalence about the illegal tactics of the Plan of Campaign, of which Parnell disapproved.[3]

---

1. See *Tuam Herald*, 22 May 1886 and *Tuam News*, 11 June 1886.
2. *Tuam Herald*, 7 November 1896, 9 September 1899.
3. Bane's *MacEvilly*, pp.99-114.

The 1880s in Ireland, according to historian Emmet Larkin, saw the consolidation of 'a clerical-nationalist alliance,' constituting, in effect, an embryo Irish state. Parnell was the leader of this de facto state, but the Catholic bishops reserved the right to determine policy in areas of particular interest to themselves, notably education. The split in the Irish party following the O'Shea divorce case of November 1890 threatened this arrangement, but Parnell's stature was such that the immediate reaction among Irish nationalists to his implication in scandal was one of shocked immobility. It was otherwise with British non-conformists.

Embarrassed at having been outflanked on a moral question by English Protestants, and by then confident that they could prevail, the Irish bishops condemned Parnell on 3 December 1890. Their statement, coming more than two weeks after the scandal broke, was intended to boost those M.Ps seeking the leader's resignation and, in the event, the party divided sixty-forty against Parnell. But, although the bishops won a majority among parliamentarians, they were less successful with grass-roots activists, and most of the party's damaged machinery was retained by the Parnellites.

Nowhere was this more evident than in Tuam, centre of the North Galway constituency represented by Colonel Nolan of Ballinderry. One of Parnell's firmest supporters, Nolan retained the backing of local bodies and institutions, including the *Herald*. As elsewhere, the demoralisation of lay anti-Parnellites forced the Church into an active role in building alternative political structures. But, in deference to the strength of Parnellite feeling in Tuam, MacEvilly's public statements on the issue were considerably milder than his private feelings. And while he gave free rein to the diocesan clergy, his own interventions could be rather oblique, as when he used his Lenten Pastoral on 'evil literature' to castigate the pro-Parnellite *Freemans Journal* — and by implication the *Herald* — for 'making light of, nay, ostentatiously parading, as a matter of comparative indifference, a revolting public scandal' and thereby blunting 'the moral sense of the public in regard to the shocking crime of adultery.'[1]

Such was the atmosphere of mutual antipathy that it was impossible for the local minority, the anti-Parnellites, to hold meetings in the town and, when one was arranged on Sunday, 1 March 1891, the organisers deemed it wise to seek sanctuary in the private grounds of St Jarlath's. Members of the College staff

---

1. *Tuam News*, 13 February 1891.

were prominent at the meeting, particularly the president, Michael O'Connell, who was the principal speaker and, de facto, the archbishop's deputy on the occasion. Attendance was poor, 'inconsequential' according to a biased *Herald* which insisted that: 'Without the students of St Jarlath's College and ladies, it would not have been a meeting at all.'[1] For his part, Fr. O'Connell claimed that people had been deterred by intimidation from attending. The tone of the president's address was militant, employing rhetoric which was designed to claim the mantle of the Land League for Parnell's opponents.:

> Comrades of the old vanguard... for three years, I have been leading a quiet, humdrum sort of life, without giving a blow or getting one. And I feel so bluemoulded now that I would almost sooner get a thrashing than have no fight at all (laughter). I am glad to see the old familiar faces before me once again, to see the men who not merely spoke bravely, but acted bravely, the men who not only were in the midst of the fight, but in the very foremost van. . I see here the men who staked their all... I see here... Mr MacPhilpin... the editor of the Tuam News, who faced the prison cell and lay down to rest on the plank bed.[2]

Even if the meeting was disappointing to the organisers, it mobilised local anti-Parnellites and, shortly afterwards, a branch of the National Federation was established at a meeting in the Town Hall.

The death of Parnell in November 1891 did not ease rancour and, shortly afterwards, the first nation-wide test of opinion on the controversy, the general election of June 1892 was fought amidst high excitement. North Galway was one of only nine nationalist constituencies which returned a Parnellite, when Colonel Nolan easily defeated the clerically-championed

---

1. O'Donoghue's *Men*, pp.127-30.
2. *Tuam News*, 6 March 1891. Michael O'Connell was born in the parish of Moore and educated at St Jarlath's and Maynooth, where he was ordained in 1868. He served in Islandeady, Castlebar and Ballinakill before being appointed Administrator of Tuam in 1882. He succeeded Patrick Kilkenny as president of St Jarlath's in 1888. According to his obituarist, he was 'extremely popular in Tuam and took a prominent and useful part in the great work of education'. In 1893, he was transferred to the parish of Burriscarra where he remained until his death in 1920.

The Patrons of St Jarlath's College, archbisops of Tuam, 1815 - 1999:

Oliver Kelly John MacHale John MacEvilly

John Healy Thomas Gilmartin Joseph Walsh

Joseph Cunnane Joseph Cassidy Michael Neary.

Football team, 1905-1906. *Front row*: M. Dwyer (Dunmore), P. McHugh (Islandeady), J. Morgan (Cloonascragh), T.F. O'Donnell, J.J. Kelly (Ballinlough). *Middle row*: T. Gunnigan (Aughamore), E. Whelan (Cross), J.J. Sheehy (Tuam), P. Ruane (Menlough), J. Gibbons (Louisburgh), A. Moran (Newport). *Back row*: M.Grogan (Bekan), D. Morley (Bekan), M. Lyons (Dunmore), J. Lyons (Ballyhaunis), T. Garvey (Headford), D. Corcoran (Tuam).

Football team, 1907-1908. *Front row*: W. McHugh, J. Sheridan, M. McHale, A. Moran (capt.), P. O'Loughlin, B. Laurence, D. Corcoran. *Middle row*: F. Hession, A Heaney, P. Ruane, M. Lyons, T. Dwyer, T. Gunnigan, Fr. J.A. Morgan. *Back row*: G. Delaney, M. Goaley, M. Monaghan, J.F. McDermott, M. Finnegan.

Football team, 1909-1910. *Front row*: P. Delaney, C. Cunningham, J. Tarpey. *Middle row*: M. Heaney, P. Mullins, T.P. Flanagan, T. Garrett, D. MacEvilly, F. Egan. *Back row*: T. Fitzmaurice, G. Corr, T. Ó Máoláin, P. King.

Football team, 1920-1921. *Front row*: (Dr) Mattie Moran, (Dr) Tommy Molloy, (Fr) James Mulrennan, Paul Colleran. *Middle row*: (Fr) John Berry, (Fr) Mick Godwin, Paddy McGrail, (Fr) John Concannon, (Dr) Michael Joe Duffy. *Back row*: Fr M. King, (Fr) Pa Carty, (Fr) Tommy Carty, Tommy Connolly, (Fr) Mick Moran, (Mons.) Walter Burke, Willie Hegarty, (Fr) W. Nohilly.

Examination Certificates issued to St Jarlath's students by Intermediate Education Board in 1922 and by new Department of Education in 1925.

Junior A class, 1929-1930. *Front row*: Tommy Keyes, Michael Kitt, Michael Garvey, Michael O'Callaghan, Patrick J. McEllin, Louis Berry, Michael Gallagher, Martin Hannon. *Second row*: James Hynes, Joseph Cunnane, Martin Noone, Michael Lyons, John Davis, Thomas Murphy, Michael McKeon. *Third row*: James Higgins, James Greaney, Patrick Diskin, Michael J. Foley, Michael Mooney. *Back row*: Francis McMenamin, Malachy Eaton, Patrick Prendergast. *Photo courtesy of M. Gallagher*

Protestant physician, Charles Tanner. During the campaign, members of the College staff were active. President Michael O'Connell was particularly busy, accompanying Tanner on his canvass and speaking at meetings throughout the constituency. In the fraught atmosphere, the most notorious local episode was the recapture of the anti-Parnellite election platform in the Market Square. The leaders of the attack included the candidate and several priests, notably Father Mark Eagleton, curate of Cummer. President O'Connell was also prominent among those who risked 'giving a blow or getting one.' It took the intervention of magistrate and police and the reading of the riot act to restore order.

The *Tuam News* was unabashedly partisan in its report. The local Parnellites, the paper insisted, were 'fiends in human form,' and went on:

> The right those priest-blood-spillers exercised was the right of brute force. The gang of ruffians, however were well licked by the Tannerites, and had to clear the platform. If during the political campaign, those worse than Garribaldian Red-shirts again attempt to attack the priests, they must be taught a lesson with their own weapons that they will not easily forget... Only for the forbearance shown by the priests and those who sided with them, a shred of those wretched fellows could nowhere be found.[1]

Tempers had cooled somewhat by the next general election, held in 1895. Then, Nolan's lack-lustre campaign, a product of over-confidence in his camp, allowed Kilbride, the anti-Parnellite candidate, to take the seat, a result attributable to the effectively channelled energy of the diocesan clergy. During the campaign, a local paper reported that 'Rev. Martin Healy, Professor, St Jarlath's College, accompanied Mr Pinkerton to canvass Killererin.' Their first call was to the parish priest who assured them that the electors were 'sound solid for Mr Kilbride'. In 1900, having made his peace with MacEvilly, Nolan was the agreed candidate of the reunited Parliamentary Party.[2]

The healing of the major rift within nationalism reduced the necessity for clerical intervention in public life, but priests were

---
1. ibid., 1 July 1892.
2. ibid, 26 July 1895; *Tuam Herald,* 23 June 1900.

still regarded as natural leaders of their communities and they were expected to bestow legitimacy on local events by patronising them. If that priest was a professor, or even a president, additional gravitas and import attached itself to otherwise routine proceedings. And staff of the College were often able to oblige the promoters of meetings with their presence, not least because they had more free time than the parish clergy. An examination of the record in the few years after the reunification of the parliamentary party indicates that the professors had a wide and varied involvement in public affairs. For example: during 1902, President McHugh and Professor Tuffy participated in the United Irish League's selection conventions for county council, district council and urban council elections; the same two men were prominent at a lecture on the Irish industrial movement in the Town Hall in October 1903; the College Vice-President, Professor Macken chaired a public meeting of the Gaelic League in October 1904. More intriguingly, the new President, Michael Higgins, accompanied by Professors Macken and Ryder, travelled to Belclare in the following month to attend a meeting of tenant farmers concerned about the purchase of their holdings. The invitation of such a high-powered delegation suggests that parish priest Fr. Mark Eagleton was not confident of getting his own way at the meeting.[1]

Vice-President Macken was appointed administrator of Tuam in 1905, in which capacity he maintained his public profile. He continued to be prominently involved in the Gaelic League, an involvement which brought him national notice in 1907, when he opposed the nomination of Canon Hannay, Church of Ireland rector of Westport, as a member of the organising committee of the League's *Feis Chonnacht* and argued that the reverend gentleman should be removed from the national committee of the language revival movement. Hannay had just been unmasked as the author of the humorous novels, published under the pen-name George A. Birmingham, in which local figures and institutions had been lampooned. Given the time and place, these inevitably included Catholic religious, notably the Sisters of Charity who managed the woollen industry at Foxford and Fr McDonnell of Westport, a friend of Macken's. The episode became notorious as an indicator of the extent of intolerance in the revival movement. Possibly the incident, and especially the publicity which surrounded it, discouraged some Protestants from joining the Gaelic League, but

---

1. *Tuam Herald,* 26 April 1902; 21 February 1903; 15 October, 3 December 1904,

Macken was adamant that he was not acting out of sectarian motives but purely out of a sense of justice, since Hannay had been 'grossly unjust to a well-known and estimable community of nuns, clearly conveying that they were hypocrites and liars, and, ...particularly offensive, not merely to individuals, but to the general body of priests.'[1]

At the end of the decade, the most publicly prominent member of the College staff was lay professor, Frank Guy. A native of Sligo, he had arrived in Tuam as secretary to his cousin, Archbishop Healy. Immediately, he took a great interest in St Jarlath's and its traditions. He was first to propose the establishment of a past pupils' union and he wrote a detailed history of the College, which was serialised over eight weeks in the *Irish Catholic*. Guy also became prominent in the public life of Tuam and its vicinity and, as an 'advanced nationalist of considerable talent and ability' according the *Herald*, he announced his candidacy for the 1911 North Galway by-election. He withdrew, however, when Richard Hazelton, the constituency's former M.P., entered the race. His death in 1916, a few years after he took up a post as Inspector under the new National Insurance scheme, brought a premature end to Guy's career.[2]

Frank Guy's identification was with the established politics of the period. However, an alternative politics arose in the town in the early years of the new century. The Gaelic League was one manifestation of this, but a vibrant branch of Sinn Fein also attracted notice following its establishment in October 1906. Sinn Fein fizzled out after a few years, but erstwhile members of the branch were prominent when the Irish Volunteers were established in the town some time later. And, echoing the position in Tuam during the Parnell controversy, the local branch of the Volunteers was among the few which broke with John Redmond after he declared his support for the British war effort in 1914. Subsequently, the Tuam Volunteers were active in anti-recruitment activity. These developments were observed by the students, sometimes at fairly close quarters. They were present, for instance, at a celebrated Sunday afternoon public meeting addressed by Seán MacDiarmada and Liam Mellows during May 1915. Apparently, the boys were on their weekly walk, under the care of Professor Joseph Walsh who permitted them to listen to the

---

1. Brian Taylor, *The Life and Writings of James Owen Hannay, (George A. Birmingham) 1865-1950,* 1991, pp.61-68
2. Joyce's *Healy*, pp.x-xii *Tuam Herald,* 14 January, 14 October 1911; 13 January 1912; 21 October 1916.

speeches. According to one jaundiced source, the students formed a large proportion of the crowd on this occasion, but they made no protest when MacDiarmada was dragged away by the police.[1]

Indeed, Liam Mellows visited Tuam regularly during those years on behalf of the I.R.B, priming the local Irish Volunteers to participate in the forthcoming rebellion. However, circumstances determined that the Mellows-led insurrection in the west, which was centred in the Athenry area, was a much smaller affair than anticipated. And in the confusion of order and countermand at Easter 1916, the 'humdrum little town of Tuam' remained quiet. Locally, one piece of distressing news in the weeks following Easter was that the printinghouse of Thomas & Sealy Bryers in Dublin had been destroyed in a 'rebellion fire' and that 'all the unsold copies of the several editions of the learned and thoughtful works' of the late Dr MacEvilly had been lost. Since the plates had also been destroyed, it was considered unlikely that the archbishop's scriptural commentaries would ever be republished.[2]

A year after the rising, a branch of the revivified Sinn Fein organisation emerged in Tuam. Christened the Dr John MacHale Club, its first activity was to celebrate De Valera's important East Clare by-election victory. Thereafter, the youthful exuberance of the Tuam Sinn Feiners was reflected in their efforts to organise the hinterland, most colourfully in a Sunday recruitment expedition to Belclare, Caherlistrane and Headford by fifty cyclists behind a tricolour-bedecked motor.[3] In the early part of 1918, the St Jarlath's priests became involved in opposition to conscription, an issue of immediate relevance to many of their senior students and recent graduates.[4] The anti-conscription campaign was ostensibly a cross party movement, but Sinn Fein, generally speaking, approached the question more energetically. Moreover, Redmond's party lacked credibility on the issue because of its earlier involvement in promoting recruitment to the British forces. De Valera's party duly harvested the rewards for its commitment in the November 1918 election.

Involvement by the clergy in the 1918 general election was minimal enough. Parish priests generally turned out to back

1. J. Cunningham, *Labour in the West of Ireland, 1890-1914*, 1995, pp.140-43; W.J.V. Comerford's 'Recollections of Tuam, 1912-16' (p.186) and John J. Waldron's 'Tuam and the Irish Volunteers, 1914-15' (pp.192-202) in Claffey's *Glimpses of Tuam*.
2. *Tuam Herald*, 17 June 1916.
3. ibid., 23 June, 14, 28 July 1917, 14 December 1918.
4. ibid., 20, 27 April 1918.

Redmond's party's nominees, although it was already clear that the tide was against them. A prisoner, Bryan Cusack, took the North Galway seat for Sinn Fein. On his release in mid-March 1919, Cusack was welcomed to his constituency by supporters and local notables but, significantly, there were no clergy among them. Nor was there a clerical presence at a Sinn Fein meeting in the Square on St Patrick's Day. St Jarlath's, however, was represented on that occasion by a lay professor, J.B. Whelehan, who took a prominent role in the local Sinn Fein movement.[1] Professor Whelehan, indeed, would soon be nationally known as the originator of the so-called 'Belfast boycott.'

The 'Belfast boycott' was conceived originally as strategy to convince — or coerce — the pragmatic men of business in Ulster to drop their support for partition. It was first advocated by Professor Whelehan at a meeting of the traders of Tuam on 2 December 1919, and backed a few days later at a further meeting attended by the Tuam branches of the Gaelic League, Sinn Fein, Ancient Order of Hibernians, Irish Transport and General Workers' Union, National Foresters, GAA, United Irish League, Grocers' Assistants Association and Drapers' Assistants Association. Whelehan's argument was straightforward: Belfast traders were dependent on the rest of the country; their travellers were the mainstay of inns and hotels in even the smallest towns; therefore a boycott by nationalist Ireland would bring them to their knees and their senses.

Whelehan's proposal was widely reported, attracting the attention, even, of the London *Times*. George Bernard Shaw was moved to oppose the idea, arguing forcefully, on the grounds that such an action would exacerbate rather than heal divisions, that 'nothing so stupid could be conceived.' Initial support for the boycott was modest enough, being confined to a few centres in the west of Ireland. Ballinrobe District Council, for example, called on traders in its district — the home of boycotting — to stop dealing with Belfast firms 'unless and until the latter declared themselves anti-partitionist.'[2]

1. ibid., 22, 29 March 1919.
2. *Tuam Herald*, 13, 20 27 December 1919; 3, 10, 31 January, 7, 14 February 1920; D.S. Johnson, 'The Belfast Boycott, 1920-1922' in Goldstrom & Clarkson (eds), *Irish Population, Economy, and Society: Essays in honour of the late K.H. Connell*, 1981, pp.287-307. Incidentally, Johnson does not credit (or blame) Whelehan for originating the boycott, but remarks in a footnote that '[P.S.] O'Hegarty suggests that the boycott started in Tuam in the early 1920s.' The contemporary west of Ireland newspapers were in no doubt but that Whelehan was the inventor of the boycott.

The sectarian disturbances in the north-east during the summer of 1920, especially the 'pogrom' directed at Catholics employed in the Belfast engineering industry, revived the tactic. Belfast republican councillors petitioned the Dáil to enforce the commercial boycott, but their request was turned down. When the pogrom worsened, however, the Cabinet agreed to support a limited boycott, which would be overseen by local authorities. This was widely, if somewhat unevenly, observed, and provoked a counter-boycott by northern Unionists. Thus revived, the 'Belfast boycott' was effective insofar as it reduced commercial traffic between North and South but, according to one contemporary, 'it was an utter failure inasmuch as it did not secure the reinstatement of a single expelled nationalist, nor the conversion of a single Unionist.'[1] Indeed, by curtailing commercial contact between Belfast and the South in the longer term, the boycott was one of the factors which served to copperfasten partition.

Professor Whelehan was also involved in other aspects of the struggle, especially in organising the Republican courts. He presided over the first public sitting of the Tuam court, held in the Town Hall during July 1920. This was taken as a provocative challenge to their authority by the British forces and, few days afterwards, during the so-called 'sack of Tuam,' particular attention was paid to people and places connected with the illegal court. The Town Hall was burnt and there was an attempt on the life of one Casey who had acted as court clerk.[2]

Whelehan's employer, Archbishop Gilmartin, was believed to be hostile to the Republican courts, but he denied that he had prohibited his clergy from attending, insisting that he had 'left it to the discretion of each priest.' However, Gilmartin was outspoken in opposing other aspects of the struggle. His Lenten Pastoral of 1920 warned that those seeking to change their system of government were obliged to 'keep within the moral law as expressed in the ten commandments.' Some months later, he returned to the theme, invoking 'just war' doctrine to argue that 'in the present circumstances' armed rebellion against 'the existing government' was contrary to moral law, 'firstly, because there is no chance of success and, secondly, the evils of such a course would be much greater than the evils it would try to remedy.'[3]

---

1. Johnson, op.cit.
2. *Tuam Herald*, 17, 24 July 1920.
3. ibid., 21 February 1920, 1 January 1921.

It would appear that the internal life of the College was not unduly affected by the political climate of the period, although Professor Whelehan's high profile drew the searchlight on his workplace and it was one of the premises raided by troops during May 1921.[1] Otherwise, students travelling to and from home at vacation times incurred certain risks. One story, apocryphal maybe, describes an encounter between a group of senior boys and a party of Black and Tans at the railway station. On discovering Greek texts in the students' luggage, the Englishmen assumed them to be secret republican codes and would have taken the boys away, but for the intervention of an officer acquainted with Greek character.[2]

Professor Whelehan won a seat in the second Dáil in May 1921. He was re-elected in June 1922 when, as a pro-Treaty T.D., he found common ground with Dr Gilmartin. The Treaty, indeed, and the subsequent election, brought the clergy, including the staff of the College, back onto political platforms to a degree not witnessed since the early 1890s. At one public meeting in Tuam in March 1923, addressed by Whelehan, the platform party included the president of the College, Alexander Eaton, and Professors Kelly and Moran, as well as the Administrator and the Catholic dean of Tuam. The message to this gathering from Dr Gilmartin was non-directive, but pro-Treatyite in tone. The archbishop's other pronouncements during and after the civil war were equally partisan, but carefully phrased so as not to unduly annoy the substantial republican segment of his flock. In advance of the 1923 election, he refrained from 'committing [himself] to an approval of all the existing government has done' but, on the grounds that the 'country has been restored from a state of anarchy and lawlessness' he thought that 'of all the parties before the country at present they are the best qualified to govern.'[3]

Gilmartin's attitude accurately reflected the political position of the Church in the immediate post-Treaty period. But its patron's views did not win automatic acceptance within the walls of the College. One student of the period recalled that his contemporaries tended to reflect the views of their families, so that both sides in the Civil War had their partisans in the student body.[4] Suspicion of the anti-Treatyites lingered, even following

1. ibid., 21 May 1921.
2. Williams interview.
3. *Tuam Herald*. 25 August 1923.
4. Heaney interview

de Valera into Fianna Fail, and it was not unusual to find priests on Cumann na nGaedheal platforms in the decade following the Civil War. President Joseph Walsh, indeed, appeared on a government platform during the election campaign of 1932. His presence on that occasion, however, was probably due as much to his desire to support the local candidate, solicitor and longtime friend of the church in Tuam, Fred McDonagh, as to his wish to endorse any party.

After Fianna Fáil took office in 1932, and when the party showed that it was not about to turn the world upside down, most of the remaining clerical suspicion was allayed. Thereafter, members of the clergy, by and large, refrained from identifying themselves too publicly with either of the main parties. Subsequent political pronouncements from this source were of a non-partisan nature, warning about dangers to morality — such as socialism, English Sunday newspapers, cinema and jazz — or urging the Irish people to adopt a practical patriotism. The following exhortation from Dr Gilmartin was typical enough:

> Now is the time for us all, young and old, to build up a real Irish Ireland. Irish land must be made more productive, Irish people should use and buy Irish goods. Irish boys and their sisters ought to see that all their new clothes are going to be of Irish manufacture. Let us cultivate our own games, our own amusements, our own language, and our own music.[1]

But the disengagement of the clergy from formal politics did not terminate St Jarlath's long tradition of public service and occasional agitation. The careers of land warriors like Patrick Lavelle and John O'Connor Power found a contemporary echo in the late 1930s when it became clear that native government — of whatever hue — was not going to satisfactorily tackle the particular problems of West of Ireland farmers. The realisation prompted the establishment of a remarkable political party — Clann na Talmhan — which sought to win redress for farmer grievances. To the fore in the movement were St Jarlath's past pupils. Both leaders of the party — Michael Donnellan and Joe Blowick — were College alumni, as was the party's most important organiser, Paul Colleran of Moylough. Clann na Talmhan's

---

1. *Irish Catholic Directory,* 1931. I am grateful to Mary T. Kierce for this reference.

greatest success was achieved in North Galway and Mayo — the constituencies of the archdiocese of Tuam. No doubt the College connections, which reached into every parish of the archdiocese, were useful in spreading its influence. In an important sense, therefore, St Jarlath's can claim a share of the credit for Clann na Talmhan's achievements — notably for promoting drainage in the west — during a bleak period of the region's economic history.[1]

---

1. For an account of Clann na Talmhan in County Galway, see Tony Varley's 'Farmers against nationalists' in Moran's *Galway: History & Society*, pp.589-622.

7. "In those Intermediate times..."

> *Lawyers find their woes in peace,*
> *And hope disputes will never cease.*
> *Doctors find their woes in health,*
> *We hear there're even woes in wealth,*
> *We find our night of tribulation*
> *In Intermediate Education.*[1]

The single most sensitive issue in nineteenth century Ireland was education. Proposals for innovation or improvement almost invariably foundered in the choppy and capricious political atmosphere. Each generation faced the same conundrum: how to reconcile the Irish Catholic hierarchy's implacable insistence on denominational education with the equally firm opposition to the endowment of Catholic institutions from influential English opinion. Any workable proposal had to have at its core either a mechanism for fudging this contradiction, or some means of disguising the actual effects of its implementation.

Unlike both primary and university sectors, post-primary — or intermediate — education excited relatively little controversy for most of the century. And when the sector finally became conspicuous in the 1870s, its salience was due more to political expediency than to any great public demand. Dealing with the post-primary situation allowed functionaries to appear busy and innovative, while they postponed the grief attendant upon efforts to solve the university question. Nevertheless, given the intractability of both primary and third level problems, it is remarkable that the intermediate question was solved to the approximate satisfaction of the parties involved within a few years of its first being raised. This relative ease and speed was partly attributable to the political situation, which had echoes of that pertaining seven or eight decades earlier. With Fenianism apparently rampant, British statesmen were sensitive to the concerns of the Catholic hierarchy who seemed to be the best available bulwark against political radicalism.[2]

Arguably, another reason for the relative ease in finding an

---

1. From prologue, specially written, to theatrical entertainment in St Jarlath's College, 28 November 1889.
2. John Coolahan, *Irish Education: its history and structure*, 1981, pp.61-62.

agreement between the parties involved in the discussions on post-primary education was the position of the archbishop of Tuam. He was always wary of the intentions behind government proposals on education, but MacHale was old, isolated and preoccupied with matters within his own diocese during the 1870s. Consequently, he could not play the same obstructive role that he had in discussions on both primary and university education, when he had been the key figure in mobilising Catholic opposition to government measures. In relation to the national schools system, he remained silent for a few years following its introduction in 1831, but was wary of the opportunities for the proselytism of poor Catholics offered by its non-denominational character. A few years after becoming archbishop of Tuam, he declared his outright opposition to the system. Within the Catholic hierarchy, he fought supporters of the system — notably Dr Daniel Murray of Dublin — lobbying the Church authorities in Rome in support of his own views. And within his own diocese, he prohibited Catholic involvement in national schools, inviting various religious orders, notably the Franciscans, to fill the resulting gap. Then, making a virtue of necessity, he presented the improvised system in his diocese as a suitable model for Irish education, contending that it emulated key aspects of the pre-colonial monastic system, and that its widespread adoption might once again make Ireland a nation of saints and scholars. Later, circumstances in his diocese forced MacHale to make an accommodation with the national system as the lesser of two evils, but he remained critical and suspicious of it. As far as university education was concerned, MacHale was pivotal in sustaining Catholic opposition to the allegedly 'Godless' Queen's Colleges in Belfast, Cork and Galway established by legislation of 1845. Again, he made representations to Propaganda Fide in Rome to undermine the position of those inclined to accept the principle of religiously-mixed education at third-level. These included Drs Crolly of Armagh, Murray of Dublin and O'Donnell of Galway, who secretly encouraged a parish priest of his diocese, Dr Joseph W. Kirwan, to accept the presidency of Queen's College Galway.[1]

Until the passage of the Intermediate Education (Ireland) Bill of 1878, post-primary education was largely unregulated.

---

1. ibid., p.14-24; Costello's *MacHale*, pp.61-77; Mitchell's 'J.W. Kirwan'. Incidentally, Paul Cullen's views on both primary and university questions were close to those of MacHale.

Because they benefited from a species of public funding, Protestant endowed schools were subject to inspection, although, by and large, they determined their own curricula and managed their own affairs. Catholic schools received no public monies and were completely independent of the state. Circumstances in the sector reflected the prevailing attitude to post-primary education, which was regarded as a middle- and upper-class concern, a service to be purchased privately and one, therefore, which would be adequately regulated by the market. If a school was substandard, parents would not purchase education there. And encouraging the social advancement of the the poor through education was not a priority of public policy.[1]

Before 1879, examinations were a matter for individual schools and they were conducted with at least one eye on their public relations impact. In this respect, St Jarlath's exams, held on the final three or four days of the Summer term, were not untypical. They were attended by the archbishop, by distinguished diocesan priests, and by certain local dignitaries, the prestige of these visitors serving to guarantee academic standards. Parents and other guests — including local newspaper editors and 'a large assemblage of ladies and gentlemen from the town and vicinity'[2] — were invited for the the annual prize-giving which brought the examinations to a close. This elaborate ceremony was a showcase for the academic and social accomplishments of those students selected to render public performances of their prize-winning work. A journalist described the 1868 ceremony at St Jarlath's:

> Master E. O'Fay read a splendid piece of Latin composition on the life of Julius Caesar. It was written in the style of Tacitus, and not unworthy a child of Rome. The Greek, by Master O'Connell of Ballinasloe was exceedingly good, natural, idiomatic and simple. Master Leyden of Clifden obtained the solus premium in French composition. He read some pages on the life of Elias and the prophets of the old law. Master Joyce's knowledge of the Irish, as displayed in his splendid essay on the Machabees and their noble mother excited the admiration of those present... The essay in the English language composed by Master Costello of Tuam was not unworthy of some our best modern writers. In declamation, Mr Ansbro was, in French, entitled to the palm

---

1. Coolahan's *Education*, pp.52-56.
2. *Tuam Herald*, 23 June 1866.

of superiority. But the best and most attractive of all in the art of delivery was Master Crampton, who repeatedly received the approbation of the audience and of his youthful associates.[1]

After the students departed for their long vacation, advertisements were taken in local newspapers within the College's catchment area, detailing the prize-winners in the various parts of the curriculum. These advertisements sought to communicate the range and depth of the studies offered. And it was understood that the appearance in such a context of a student's name would reassure his close relatives and, at the same time, stimulate discussion about the College among his family's neighbours and friends. Consequently, the number of examination 'topics' or subjects was large and the number of 'premiums and distinctions' awarded in each was considerable. In 1862, for example, at a time when there was less than sixty students on the roll, prizes were awarded under twenty-nine different headings in St Jarlath's, with several students sharing a first, a second and a third premium under each heading. These headings were not quite 'subjects' in the modern sense, more outlines of a syllabus. Among them, the classics were prominent, with Greek and Latin accounting for two-thirds of the total number of prizes awarded, and authors like Livy, Horace, Homer and Xenophon each meriting separate examinations. However, it is difficult to avoid concluding that the choice of examination topics was made with at least one eye on the effect on the not-so-learned among the local newspaper readership. Why otherwise have a 'subject' entitled 'Natural Philosophy, Electricity, Magnetism, The Magnetic Telegraph & Astronomy' rather than one entitled 'Science' or even 'Natural Science?'[2]

1. *Connaught Patriot*, 4 July 1868.
2. ibid., 5 July 1862. Prizes were awarded under the following headings: (i) Tacitus and Advanced Class of Cicero; (ii) Livy; (iii) Christian Classics — Latin; (iv) Homer; (v) Christian Classics — Greek ; (vi) Anabasis of Xenophon; (vii) Cyropaedia of Xenophon; (viii) Cicero, Second Class; (ix) Horace (Odes Satires & Epistles); (x) Latin Prosody; (xi) Greek Composition, First Class; (xii) Greek Composition, Second Class; (xiii) Latin Composition, First Class; (xiv) Latin Composition, Second Class; (xv) Lucian's Dialogues; (xvi) Greek Testament; (xvii) Greek Grammar, First Class; (xviii) Greek Grammar, Second Class; (xix) Virgil — Ecologue & Æneid; (xx) Sallust (xxi) Caesar's Commentaries and Sallust, Second Class; (xxii) Latin Grammar with Caesar's Commentaries, Syntax, &c.; (xxiii) French, First Class; (xxiv) French, Second Class; (xxv) Algebra; (xxvi) Geometry — Darre's Elements of, with Plane and Spherical Trigonometry; (xxvii) Geometry — Euclid's Elements Of; (xxviii) Natural Philosophy, Electricity, Magnetism, The Magnetic Telegraph & Astronomy; (xxix) Histories of Rome and Ireland.

If the prizeday 'exhibitions' gave the gregarious and the dynamic an opportunity to sharpen their skills before an audience, the tests which preceded them gave the student body as a whole considerable examination practice, something which became important in the increasingly meritocratic second half of the nineteenth century, during which time competitive examinations were introduced for the civil service and army, and the new Queen's Colleges began to hold entrance examinations. For its part, the Catholic University was trying to raise standards in the Catholic intermediate sector by means of performance-based prizes.[1] So, since up to a third of St Jarlath's students went on to 'the professions or the Civil Service,'[2] the introduction of state examinations was less than a leap in the dark as far as the College was concerned.

The Intermediate Education Act did not bring an immediate end to prize-day ceremonies, nor to the ostentatious publication of examination results in the local newspapers. It did, however, have a profound effect on education in Irish colleges, and it went some way towards meeting Catholic objectives in the sector, which were defined as follows by one interested party:

> As to Intermediate education, we demand that the large public endowments now monopolised by schools... which are directly hostile to the Catholic religion, should be taken up by a Commission in which the Catholics of Ireland would have full confidence... for the benefit of the whole nation, of all the Intermediate schools in Ireland without religious distinction, and for the general advancement of middle-class education...[3]

The problem of post-primary education had long been discussed among Irish educationalists. They were variously motivated: some by a desire to define a common standard; some by an aspiration to broaden access; some by the pressing need of their schools for financial support. However, a centralised system seemed to provide part of the solution, regardless of perspective. But, given the convictions and prejudices of the principal parties involved, the type of model which might attract the necessary amount of agreement was not that apparent.

---

1. Coolahan's *Education*, p.61.
2. Educational Endowments (Ireland) Commission: minutes of evidence, 1889, xxx, pars.1953-54.
3. Cited by Thomas J. McElligot in *Secondary education in Ireland, 1870-1921*, 1981, p. 18.

Proposals promoted during the early 1870s by the French Holy Ghost Fathers who ran Blackrock College drew heavily on the recently-introduced post-primary system in Trinidad, not least because staff in the order's sister house on the Caribbean island colony were quite enthusiastic about it. The central feature of the Trinidad scheme was open competition through state examination. As a predominantly Catholic colony of Britain, Trinidad had certain similarities with Ireland, so the model which worked in one case might well work in the other. One feature which recommended the system was that the state subsidy payable was based on examination results and did not involve inspection of Catholic schools by the agents of the Protestant state.[1]

Patrick Keenan, the civil servant who had overseen the implementation of the Trinidad scheme, was appointed Resident Commissioner of Education in Ireland in 1871. Keenan, a noted educationalist and a Catholic, was well-qualified to devise a workable scheme for Ireland, and he was asked to undertake the task by the Chief Secretary, Sir Michael Hicks-Beach. Not unexpectedly, given his background, Keenan's proposals were along the same lines as the Trinidad system.[2]

Despite the wary attitude of some Catholic bishops and notwithstanding personnel changes in the Irish administration, the Intermediate Education (Ireland) Bill reached parliament in June 1878, the signal for two months of relatively constructive debate before the measures passed into law. Because the Bill was the product of a consultative process involving the government and the Catholic bishops, Irish nationalist members — led by Isaac Butt — were broadly supportive. There was some concern that the so-called obstructionists in Butt's party — notably Biggar and Parnell — might delay its passage. They did not. And while some ultra-Protestant reservations were raised, the potential for opposition from the backbenches was reduced by the fact that the Bill was introduced by a Conservative administration. English Liberals, for their part, were guided by the attitude of the Irish nationalist members to the Bill, although they also found some intrinsic merits in its proposals. These were summarised by Gladstone, when he welcomed the fact that the Bill asked students 'no questions as to the place in which they were educated, as to the persons by whom they were educated,

---

1. Larkin, *Emergence*, pp.261-63.
2. ibid.; Seán Farragher's *Pere Leman: educator and missionary, founder of Blackrock College*, 1988, pp.388-416; James H. Murphy, *Castleknock College and its contribution*, 1996, pp.69-70.

or as to the religious principles in connection with which that secular education was obtained.'[1]

The Bill provided for the establishment of an Intermediate Education Board for Ireland; its role was to promote 'intermediate' education by means of public examinations. The standard of these examinations was to be such that certification was a realistic goal for a majority of candidates. Financial inducements for brighter students, in the form of prizes, were intended to support the individual's ongoing education; payments — on the basis of their students' results — to school managers, were designed to provide funding for participating schools. Incidentally, most of the Board's finances came from funds freed by the disestablishment of the Church of Ireland, whose status had changed from state church to voluntary body on 1 January 1871.[2]

The North Galway M.P., Colonel Nolan, was among those concerned about the balance of rewards in the proposed system. He queried whether it would be 'an efficient stimulus to teaching if the money were given to the parent or the pupil, and not to the teacher.' There was a precedent for rewarding teachers, he pointed out, as primary teachers received payments on the basis of results. This defect was not corrected in the legislation, and it had become a substantial grievance before it was addressed several decades later. More successful was the intervention of two other West of Ireland M.Ps — the O'Conor Don of Roscommon and the ex-Jarlath's pupil and teacher, John O'Connor Power of Mayo. They introduced an amendment which would make 'Irish language, literature and archaeology' an examination subject. The instinct of the Irish Chief Secretary, James Lowther, was to oppose the amendment on the grounds that Irish was not 'a sufficiently useful branch of education' and that it 'ceased to be other than a dead language'. He was persuaded to reconsider his attitude, however. The amendment was withdrawn and 'Celtic' was an optional subject in the first examinations.[3]

Another late change, albeit one which little affected St Jarlath's, was the decision to permit girls to sit the examinations. This was contrary to the expressed view of the Catholic bishops. Other features of the new system, however, corresponded with episcopal wishes. In particular, there was satisfaction with the

---

1. Larkin's *Emergence*, pp.268-69, 278, 304-08; McElligott's *Secondary education*, p.37.
2. Coolahan's *Education*, pp.61-65.
3. Larkin's *Emergence*, pp.304, 308, *Freeman's Journal*, 2 July 1878.

important place given to Greek and Latin, which — along with English — were allocated a disproportionate amount of marks and prize-money. The remaining four subject areas were modern languages; music and drawing; mathematics; and natural sciences. Initially, there were three levels of examination — junior, middle and senior — but a preparatory grade was introduced in 1892.[1] With students having to face an annual state examination, with scholarship holders competing with one another and with hungry newcomers to retain their prizes, with schools seeking to attract students on the basis of their performance, it is little wonder that enlightened contemporaries began to see the system as a 'murder machine.'

The Intermediate system was inaugurated on Tuesday 24 June 1879 with an examination in Greek. Thirty-five candidates — from St Jarlath's, from the Protestant Diocesan School and from the Christian Brothers School — presented themselves on that morning at the Tuam Town Hall, one of fifty-six examination centres in forty cities and towns throughout the island. Of the thirty-five, however, only twelve were successful, six of these, including the future historian of the archdiocese, Edward D'Alton, being from St Jarlath's. The overall performance reflected poorly on the schools in the town of Tuam, if its pass rate of 34% was compared with the national figure of almost 60%. However, there was a significant improvement in the following year when the number of passes in Tuam increased to twenty-four, fourteen of them from St Jarlath's.[2]

Within a few years, the College had become the venue for the examinations, probably because the Town Hall could not accommodate the increased numbers sitting the examinations.

The introduction of the new system, as one might expect, did not occur without a few teething problems and some of these are indicated in correspondence between President Kilkenny and the Assistant Commissioners for Intermediate Education. Expectations that injustice should be investigated — and exceptions made if appropriate — could be easily fulfilled in a small institution like the College; such, obviously, could never be the case with a large bureaucracy. This did not prevent the president from trying, however, as can be seen in the series of letters concerning the 1882 Trigonometry exam, which evidently contained

---

1. Coolahan's *Education*, p.63.
2. Claffey, 'The Intermediate Examinations of 1879-'80' in his *Glimpses of Tuam*, pp.98-106.

a few surprises for St Jarlath's candidates. Fr Kilkenny complained as follows on their behalf:

> In connexion with your letter of the 1st inst., I have to say that the programme for 1882 in specifying the matter for Trigonometry examination, senior grade, uses these words, page 30: "plane trigonometry with solution of plane triangles." In the ordinary interpretation of this language, the solution of plane trigonometry is not included. It is possible, even easy, to compose the matter by directing the examiner to divide the number of marks, "600", assigned to Trigonometry between the questions within the programme. If this is not done, a grevious wrong shall be inflicted on some of our boys.[1]

The assistant commissioners, apparently, did not consider it possible to implement Fr Kilkenny's solution, and further letters followed. In one, the president again insisted that the trigonometry question was 'altogether beyond the required range.' Subsequently, he moderated his demand asking only that 'as our boys were all victims of this mistake they be permitted to have passes in the subject…'[2]

It would appear, notwithstanding some protestations to the contrary, that the College's performance during the first decade or so of the new state-run system was disappointing to itself.[3] A possible reason for this is suggested in a comment from Dr MacEvilly to the staff and students in 1887 regarding his satisfaction that the College had 'carefully avoided that pernicious system of cramming, which more or less enters into the training of boys that are being prepared for public examinations.'[4] Given such influential opposition to cramming in the College, it was natural that there also be concern at suggestions that the standards of the examinations be raised. President Kilkenny wrote in strong terms to a fellow Catholic headmaster on this issue, insisting that:

> the Catholic schools of the West are opposed to any alteration of the Rules tending to make the examinations any

---

1. SJC, Kilkenny letter-book, p.93.
2. ibid., pp.99, 101.
3. *Tuam News,* 17 June 1887; *Tuam Herald,* 4 October 1884; Educational Endowments Commission evidence, 1889, pars.1916, 1972-76.
4. *Tuam News,* 17 June 1887.

more severe than they are at present. I believe the result shall be, if these proposed alterations be inserted in a future programme, that our schools shall cease having anything to do with the Intermediate Exams. The patent effect of these rules will be to produce an unhealthy centralisation of education and this will be opposed to the sentiments of the Act.[1]

Once the examinations became established, however, there was pressure on the Board to raise standards, not least because its budget was not raised in line with the increase in the number of candidates taking the examination. 72% of those taking the examinations in 1880 passed, this fell towards 60% a decade later and below 50% on a few occasions after the turn of the century.[2]

Both Patrick Kilkenny, president until February 1888, and his successor Michael O'Connell were witnesses before the Educational Endowments Commission in October 1888. Their answers to the commissioners' questions give good insight into educational life in the College at that time, less than a decade after the introduction of Intermediate examination. Their evidence did not agree in some details, but this merely reflected some changes in policy. Student numbers had fallen acutely in the previous few years, from eighty-six in 1884, according to Kilkenny, to seventy-six in 1885, to seventy-five in 1886, to sixty-seven in 1887 and fifty-six in 1888. When asked to what he attributed the decline, Kilkenny replied: 'To the depression in the country — no other reason.'[3]

Kilkenny's figures, evidently, did not include day students, and when asked about this, he stated that the College did not encourage day-boys because it was thought that 'they were introducing matters that seriously interfered with discipline... contraband of war'. He thought, however, that there were 'two or three' day-boys in the College. President O'Connell's information on this issue was more up-to-date. There were nine day-boys, he said, with 'any amount of accommodation' for others. The relatively low numbers of day attenders, he attributed, not to his predecessor's negative attitude, but to the fact that the pension for living-in was so low that parents were as pleased to send their sons as boarders.[4]

1. SJC, Kilkenny letter-book, p.127.
2. Coolahan's *Education*, p.64-65.
3. Educational Endowments Commission evidence, 1889, pars.1909, 1933.
4. ibid., pars.1913-14, 1945-46.

One of the difficulties the College faced in relation to the Intermediate examinations was that students generally did not arrive in the College until they were well advanced in years, and were therefore not eligible to compete at their own educational standard. The reasons for this were explored by the commissioners:

Commissioner: Is it an ecclesiastical college?

Kilkenny: It is generally ecclesiastical, but there are opportunities for a very good secular education

Commissioner: You send boys to the Intermediate examinations?

Kilkenny: Yes, but we are very much debarred from presenting the best students owing to the age limits. In this part of the country, the people are very poor; and they think that the few years spent by their sons in preparing for the priesthood would be better spent for themselves, and that they can achieve the same results at a later age. Therefore they don't send them in until the last moment, until they are sixteen or seventeen year of age. It takes a year or two then to prepare them for the Intermediate Examinations, and the consequence is that they are excluded.

Commissioner: How are they occupied between the time when they finish their primary education and the time they come to St Jarlath's?

Kilkenny: I could not say. They finish their primary education up to that time. They are going along in the country schools — moving along quietly.

Commissioner: Do they continue on in the country schools until they come to St Jarlath's?

Kilkenny: Yes; they have not very good opportunities for primary education...

Commissioner: And they continue reading the National school course up to seventeen?

Kilkenny: Yes

Commissioner: Do they not enter the National schools at the ordinary age, or is there a bad attendance?

Kilkenny: They are kept at labour.

Commissioner: I suppose they began at from five to eight years old, what are they doing from then until they are seventeen?

Kilkenny: I can only state the fact for you. Their parents keep them at home and on their farms very often.

Commissioner: We were told the same thing in Galway, that the attendance is bad, even at a good school, because the children are kept at work or at home by their parents on market and fair days, and the school-teaching is interrupted and takes a long time in consequence?

Kilkenny: That is quite the fact; and in addition, most of the country boys are taken to help their parents in farm work during the spring time.[1]

Notwithstanding the negative attitude of some to cramming or to professors becoming mere 'professional grinders', Intermediate performance — in the words of one President — increasingly became 'the standard by which the efficiency of schools is judged.'[2] Students protested meekly at this development during their annual pageants:

> We find our night of tribulation
> In Intermediate education.[3]

and

> In these Intermediate times,
> When children pipe in Latin rhymes
> And little time is left for plays,
> Except for those of Sophocles.[4]

Competitive pressure intensified. And as well as the competition within schools and between schools, there was competition between types of schools. Given the broader context in Ireland, this often had a sectarian edge. In the claims of schools regarding their performance, consequently, there was as great an inclination to undermine the pretensions of rivals as to extol their own results. Under the heading 'Brilliant success of St Jarlath's students' the *Tuam News* published the following in 1892:

1. ibid., pars.1915-1923.
2. SJC, Presidents' Report Book, 1907-08 report.
3. *Tuam News*, 6 December 1889
4. ibid., 9 November 1888

Nowadays it is no easy matter to capture an exhibition at the Intermediate Examinations owing to the fierce competition that exists among the various colleges in Ireland for such exhibitions and the bold efforts made by some colleges with their high-salaried professional grinders to carry off all the exhibitions... and to shut out all other colleges from any share in them.[1]

As the Intermediate examination became established, it came to occupy an ever more central role in the life of the College. This was especially the case following the appointment as archbishop of Dr John Healy in 1904. Healy had a strongly academic background, he was not as opposed to cramming as his predecessor, and he placed great emphasis on examination performance, leading him to decree that candidates for Maynooth from the College would henceforth have to fulfil university matriculation criteria. He also altered the daily timetable of the College to allow for more classes.[2] A significant change too was the transferring of the annual College prize-day ceremony to autumn. Since the establishment of the College, the ceremony had been held on the day of the summer vacation. Its new position on the calendar allowed achievements in the Intermediate examinations to be promptly and publicly rewarded.

The change in date brought with it changes in the nature of the occasion itself. For one thing, it became more bureaucratic and less distinctively colourful. The standardisation effected by state examination was enforcing its own bleak functionalism: it was no longer necessary that Johnny read his prize-winning essay, especially as everyone already knew that he had recently won an 'exhibition' in English; Intermediate examiners had been impressed and that fact alone was sufficient to impress everybody else. In any case, the low-key character of the new

---

1. ibid., 2 September 1892.
2. Joyce's *Healy*, pp.259, 284. John Healy (1841-1918) was born in Ballinfad, Co. Sligo, the son of primary schoolteachers. He was ordained at Maynooth in 1867, was briefly on the staff of the diocesan college, Summerhill (Athlone), before serving as curate in Ballygar and Grange. From 1879, he was a professor at Maynooth and, in 1884, he was appointed coadjutor to the Bishop of Clonfert. Before succeeding John MacEvilly as archbishop of Tuam, he had earned distinction as an historian, with *Ireland's Ancient Schools and Scholars* (1890) and the *Maynooth Centenary History* (1895).

arrangements was probably more consistent with the spirit of a more pragmatic and business-like age.

The centre-piece of new-style Prize Day was the reading by the President of his annual report to the archbishop. And, if these reports are any indication, the yard-stick used to evaluate his own performance by Michael Higgins — the new president appointed by Dr Healy in 1903 — was the Intermediate examination. Student numbers, health and welfare, discipline, were all dealt with in a perfunctory sentence or two. But each year of his presidency, Dr Higgins went into tedious detail about the latest examination results, drawing attention to achievements or offering exculpatory justification for shortcomings. The following extracts are from the report for the academic year 1905-06:

> We presented at these examinations 68 boys, and may I add... we made no selections by keeping back boys whom we knew to have no chance of passing in order to obtain a high per cent of passes. Fifty-six passed generally. On looking over the Pass Lists of this year I find that for Ireland the proportion per cent of those examined who passed is 62.8 per cent, for this College the proportion per cent is almost 82.4. In the Senior, Junior and Middle Grades 16 of our boys passed with honours. In these grades the proportion per cent who got Honours is for Ireland, 27... In the total number of distinctions obtained, St Jarlath's hold again 8th place amongst all the Intermediate schools of Ireland — Catholic and Protestant. Amongst the Diocesan Colleges there is none before it... In the Classical Course, both as regards the number and the quality of its distinctions, this College holds the first place in Ireland this year.[1]

Dr Higgins also took this annual opportunity to outline his grievances against the Intermediate Board. Some of these were substantial enough. Bureaucratic regulation, he argued, prohibited those who 'went in' for the classical course from competing for prizes in any course other than the classics, while the reduction in the number and value of exhibitions' was hard on those students from less-than-privileged backgrounds who depended on prize-money to complete their education.

For such students, the introduction of county council scholar-

---

1. SJC, President's Report Book, 1903-1936, report for 1905-06.

ships under the aegis of the Department of Agriculture and Technical Instruction was a boon, but it caused some difficulties in the College. The purpose of these scholarships was to increase the technical skills of the coming generation, an area in which St Jarlath's, with its traditionally academic emphasis, had no particular competence. Indeed, it had not been envisaged that beneficiaries would attend boarding schools, but for many bright West of Ireland boys there were no convenient day schools. On the introduction of the scholarships, the College did its best and employed a part-time woodwork teacher to provide recipients with the required minimum of forty hours a year manual instruction. Such efforts by Colleges were regarded by the Department as insufficient and regulations were tightened in 1907 to the extent that they constituted 'downright tyranny' in the opinion of Dr Higgins. The minimum requirement for manual instruction was raised to 1.5 hours per week for scholarship boys, instruction which should be carried out in an adequate workshop. Dr Higgins arranged that the boys, fifteen in number, attend at the recognised workshop in the Christian Brothers' School, but this was not acceptable to the Department which insisted that if the College accepted County scholars, it had to provide its own workshop. The result, according to Dr Higgins, was that 'many of our county scholars must now leave — some have already left — and they will probably lose their scholarships.'[1]

Difficulties notwithstanding, the Healy era was one of rising academic standards in St Jarlath's. In paying tribute to his predecessor, Dr Higgins, in 1910, President Conroy stated the position bluntly:

> During his term of office, the College gained a position amongst the other Catholic residential Colleges of Ireland that it never achieved before — not a mere temporary position, the result of occasional success, but a position that it has steadily maintained all through up to the present. In former years, St Jarlath's College might be found in the annual lists of Intermediate schools somewhere near the end; for the past five or six years it has been a competitor for the first place among the diocesan colleges of Ireland, and has always been in the first rank.[2]

---

1. ibid, report for 1907-08.
2. *Connaught Telegraph*, 15 October 1910.

Contrary to the wishes of the Catholic church in Ireland which feared state interference in the running its schools, a decision to introduce state inspection of intermediate schools was taken in 1909. As it turned out, St Jarlath's had little to fear from inspectors, and the annual reports of J.J. O'Neill and R.C.B. Kerins were uniformly positive. The first report — for the academic year 1910-'11 — began with the impressions of the visitors which were of a 'fine building, well situated in extensive grounds' with classrooms that were 'lofty and well-lighted and corridors which afforded 'ample means of recreation in wet weather.' Two years later, an exceptionally comprehensive report must have provided enjoyable reading for President Conroy and his staff:

> Excellent work continues to be done in this school. We have nothing to alter in what we said in our previous reports concerning the excellence of the staff, the earnestness, energy and soundness of the teaching, and the good organisation.
>
> It is again a pleasure to refer to the high quality of the classical teaching and to the average high standard of the students in Latin and Greek. We would suggest that, as in some of the classes the boys do not always enter corrections carefully in their exercise books, it would be advisable to revise the exercises orally as this method will serve as a check and will also impress on the boys the avoidance of similar errors. The pronunciation is, as a rule good, though in some cases the distinction between short e and o and long e an o is not observed. More repetition of passages from Classical authors would be useful in raising the standard.
>
> In the Senior Grade English classes the treatment has been very broad and interesting. Both the matter and the form of the prescribed works have been thoroughly discussed, essay writing receives most careful attention and nothing is left undone to ensure a high standard. In the Junior, Middle and Preparatory Grades, the treatment of History was stimulating, and the answering was intelligent throughout. In the treatment of Literature the matter was well known, and larger questions of form received a fair amount of attention. In all classes, however, the teaching of English is exceedingly hampered by the poverty of

vocabulary of the majority of the pupils and by their weakness in expression. It would, therefore, be advisable to devote a larger part of the time assigned to English in the Preparatory Grade to giving pupils a thorough grounding in sentence formation, paragraph arrangement and above all in oral composition. This latter might be made a valuable instrument in raising the standard in pronunciation as well as in fluency in oral expression. the interest taken in history in the Preparatory Grade and the intelligent answering of the majority of the pupils spoke volumes for the interesting nature of the treatment.

In the Irish classes the work is of a very painstaking type, both translation and composition are done with extreme care, the treatment is scholarly and a very fair amount of oral work is done as a result of this the standard reached is high throughout and the pupils are decidedly interested in their work.

In Mathematics the methods continue to be progressive and the work done is thorough. A fair average standard had been reached in the different classes, though the middle grade seemed to be somewhat weak in Arithmetic.[1]

While the report was overwhelmingly positive in tone, the few criticisms and quibbles are of some interest. The observation regarding the 'poverty of vocabulary' and 'weakness of expression' in English, in particular, must have set off alarm bells in the College. But if such was indeed the case, it should not have been a cause of wonder in a district where the language of the majority had changed within a generation or two from Irish to English. No doubt, the shift had left its mark, and the formulations and pronunciations of some owed as much to the Gaelic as to standard English. Moreover, a significant minority of students came from households where Irish was still the principal language. And it is conceivable, given the fact that there was criticism of pronunciation in Latin and Greek as well as in English, that it was the accents rather than the pronunciations of the boys which grated on the metropolitan ears of the inspectors. Nor were the recommendations that exercises be 'revised orally' or that there be more 'repetition of passages from Classical authors', if implemented, going to do much to enliven classes.

---

1. SJC, Inspector's Reports on teaching in the College file, Report for head of school, 1912-13.

Inspectors' reports in the decade following 1913 were similarly phrased. In particular, the 'spirit of the school', the 'high quality of the work done in Classics' and 'high standard' of both students and teachers in Irish was noted. Evidently, the problems identified in English were addressed, for in the report for 1913-14 it was stated that 'the oral side of the English work is being developed in a very satisfactory manner.' Subsequent reports — from the same inspectors — did not return to this matter.

As far as other subjects were concerned, the boys were given a 'good grounding' in French composition, but their pronunciation was poor.[1] And the teaching of mathematics was acknowledged to be 'efficient' but the second-class status of the subject in the College was obvious enough: 'As the boys specialise in languages, the teachers have as a rule to be satisfied with securing a fair average pass standard.'[2] Incidentally, the extremely large size of some classes also engaged the inspectors' attention, and was criticised on a number of occasions during these years. And there was something of the spirit of the times in J.J. O'Neill's suggestion in the report for 1921-22, that the teaching of subjects like history and geography through the medium of Irish was 'quite feasible', given the high standard in the language. If such a course was pursued then the College, in the opinion of the inspector, was 'excellently situated to become one of the best bilingual secondary schools in the whole country.'

Following independence, the Irish Free State set about introducing reforms to the system. The new rulers, by and large, were happy enough with the system of state-funded, denominationally-run secondary education as it had evolved, but they wished to introduce changes in the curriculum and to address some of the long-standing complaints of educators and educationalists. First of all, the old board was abolished and its functions taken over by two commissioners. One of the two, Seosamh Ó Néill, in a previous incarnation had been a familiar enough figure around the halls of St Jarlath's.

A fundamental educational objective of the new administration was to restore the Irish language. To this end, bilingual examination papers were introduced, then Irish was given equal status with English in state examinations, and eventually made compulsory for the awarding of certificates. The rapid pace of change in

---

1. ibid., reports for 1913-14, 1914-15, 1915-16, 1916-17.
2. ibid., report for 1914-15.

this regard caused difficulties in many schools, but not in St Jarlath's. In the first departmental report in Irish, following an inspection by Labhrás Ó Muireadhaigh in May 1925, the improving standard of Irish was noted, as was the capacity of the students to learn other subjects through the medium of Irish.

Other changes quickly followed the establishment of the state. Significantly, the system of funding schools based on examination results was replaced by a system based on capitation grants, payable for those who passed an entrance test and attended for a minimum number of days a year. And the Intermediate Education (Amendment) Act of 1924 reduced the number of examinations from three to two — Intermediate and Leaving — with Certificates awarded to those who achieved passes in five subjects. Despite this change, however, for several decades the exam period continued to be known as 'Inter Week' in St Jarlath's.[1]

---

1. Coolahan's *Education*, pp.73-76; Williams interview.

8. "...an exemplary boy, but he cannot live on air."

For faithful, oh, always so faithful to the
lines of the Master divine
He sought to instruct and enlighten —
he sought from their dross to refine —
The noblest and gentlest, the meekest —
the father, indulgent and kind,
The sagest, the simplest, the wisest in heart,
brain and bosom and mind.[1]

From the earliest period of the College's history, the fees — referred to as pensions — paid by the parents or guardians of students were kept at the lowest levels possible. Advertisements in the *Catholic Directory* during the 1830s indicate that the St Jarlath's annual pension of twenty-six guineas a year was at at the cheaper end of the range for Irish Catholic colleges. Low as this figure was, it was enough to exclude the overwhelming majority of Irish adolescent boys in the pre-Famine period. To give an example, neither the cook employed by the College who was paid £18 a year, nor the parlour maid who got £6, could possibly have contemplated enrolling their own sons.[2]

Reflecting the primary purpose of the College, reduced pensions were paid by 'ecclesiastical students', those who declared their aspiration to enter the priesthood. In 1843, they paid twenty guineas, six guineas less than the regular rate. Apparently however, there was a reminder each dinner-time to those who claimed the reduction. Writing in 1821, Archbishop Oliver Kelly advised that the guardian of an applying student enrol him as a 'parlour boarder' rather than as an 'ecclesiastical boarder' because 'there is a vast difference in the fare, respectability, &c'.[3] In 1862 the terms were £26 a year for lay boarders; £20 for ecclesiastical students and £4 for day students, marginally lower than those obtaining two decades earlier. In those years, parents

---

1. From 'Lines to the memory of the late U.J. Canon Bourke' by Medora, cited by Ó Maolmhuaidh.
2. *Catholic Directory*, Vol.1, 1836 (Elsewhere terms ranged from £24 in the Navan Diocesan Seminary to 45 guineas in Clongowes). Wage levels are for 1843, SJC, Expenditure Book 1837-1856.
3. SJC, Feeney Papers, p.47.

were again advised that individuals who paid the full amount received 'extra attention and higher treatment.'[1] This leads to the conclusion that whether a boy was enrolled as an ecclesiastical or a lay student may have been more a guide to his family's financial position than to his career intentions. There is no indication from his biography, for example, that 1860s ecclesiastical student, Mark Ryan, ever felt that he had a religious vocation; there is, however, ample evidence of his straitened means.[2]

In order to minimise the level of pensions, the running costs of the College were subsidised to an extent by the diocesan clergy. The subsidy was in the form of a levy that may pre-date the earliest record of its collection, which was in 1817. In that year, to finance the move from the Mall to the 'Old College' in the former Ffrench's Bank premises, five guineas was paid to the College by each priest in the diocese.[3] Subsequently, one guinea was levied on each priest annually, and collected by a nominated individual in each of the diocesan deaneries. This was no easy task for the collector. Indeed, the practice of paying the sum in several instalments indicates that many priests did not often have a full guinea to hand. The parish priest of Hollymount, ex-President James McKeal, described the difficulty he encountered in collecting the levy in a letter to Archbishop Kelly in the early 1820s:

> All my applications for College subscriptions have as yet been fruitless with the exception of one half year's subscription from Rev. Mr Green, viz 11s 4d, and the same from Mr Joyce of Partry, which I send per bearer and for which I hope Mr Feeney will send me an acknowledgement... I am to make another effort to procure subscriptions from the dignitaries of our deanery from whom I profess I don't expect much in the way of liberality.[4]

If 'liberality' was in short supply among the clergy during the 1820s, it is little wonder. Thomas Feeney, College president at that time, in expressing gratitude for the amount he received annually from priests, noted the several other demands on their

---

1. *Catholic Directory*, 1862 and 1875.
2. Ryan's *Memories*, pp.20-30.
3. SJC, Accounts 1817-1835, pp.25-28.
4. SJC, Feeney Papers, p.50. A guinea is usually understood to be the equivalent of £1.1.0 but, until the post-Act of Union amalgamation of the currencies in 1826, a guinea in Ireland was valued at £1.2.9. While an Irish guinea was equal to an English guinea, the formal Irish currency traditionally was valued at twelve-thirteenths of the English.

generosity — many were erecting schools and churches in their own parishes, they were expected to contribute towards the building of 'all other new churches in the diocese' and they were responding with 'magnificent donations towards the erection of the Cathedral'. Evidently, pressure had eased sixty years later, when the annual 'traditional subscription' of £1 for curates and £2 for parish priests, would appear to have been relatively easy to collect.[1]

If the clergy of the diocese collectively sponsored St Jarlath's as an institution, individual priests subsidised the education of their nephews and other relatives at the College from the earliest period.[2] In some cases, they were seeking to maintain a family tradition of providing candidates for the priesthood. In other instances, priests were merely acknowledging the sacrifices of their siblings, who had forgone luxuries and opportunities in order that a brother might be put through college and seminary. It was natural, when the opportunity arose and the absence of domestic responsibility allowed, that such a debt be repaid to the next generation. Whatever the motivation, the practice contributed towards some important family connections within the archdiocese.

Of course, not all family connections were sustained by such financial encouragement. In many instances, it was admiration for a clerical uncle which attracted the nephew towards the priesthood. In the case of the MacHales, the most prominent clerical family in the nineteenth century archdiocese, it is likely that the eminence of the archbishop played a part in inspiring nephews, grand-nephews and cousins to join what became, for a time, almost a family business.

Significant numbers of clergy also came from other families. One might refer, for example, to the obituary of Moylough-born and St Jarlath's-educated Canon Geraghty, parish priest of Bekan until his death at the age of 83 in 1894, which pointed out that his family had 'for generations given priests and nuns' to the archdiocese.[3] Biographies of past-pupils like Bishops Duggan and MacEvilly, likewise, show that that there were clergymen in their families in generations before and after their

---

1. ibid., p.285, see also p.133; Kilkenny, p.86.
2. SJC, Feeney, p.15, 83; Kilkenny, p.73.
3. *Tuam News*, 12 January 1894. Incidentally, a few months after Canon Geraghty's death, his grand-nephew, John Moylan, was ordained and appointed professor in St Jarlath's (ibid., 15 June 1894).

own.¹ And a remarkable set of connections is revealed in the obituary of Mrs Cunningham of Ballytrasna, who died in 1904. Attending her funeral were her Jarlath's-educated son, Father Patrick Cunningham of St Paul, Minnesota; her brothers, Canon Ronayne and Rev. James Ronayne; her nephews, Rev. Dominick Ronayne and Rev. Michael Ronayne.² Among Mrs Cunningham's uncles were at least two other priests, one of whom, Rev. James Ronan, had briefly served as president of St. Jarlath's during the 1830s. President Ronan and his brother, in turn, were nephews of 'the sainted Dr Waldron', Bishop of Killala.³ So, four generations of one extended family provided at least eight priests for three different dioceses and a religious order.

Because priests did not leave direct descendants and because less than a third of nephews were likely to bear the same surnames as their clerical uncles, such relationships are not always easy to trace, but there are strong indications, at the very least, that particular families provided clergymen over more than a few generations. A student of the late 1930s (who himself spent a period in Maynooth) was able to trace a family connection with St Jarlath's through a clerical uncle, grand-uncles, and so on, for four generations previous to his own, back to the early decades of the College.⁴

Such a tradition could be supported to some extent by the contributions towards pensions provided by priests for their nephews. Without detailed genealogies it is impossible to be more than tentative, but the few examples given above may represent the continuation of a variant of the *erenagh* tradition of Gaelic Ireland, whereby certain families provided priests just as others had provided brehons and bards.⁵ The pattern of succession in a number of parishes as late as the mid-nineteenth century adds weight to this conjecture. Certainly, the operation of

1. Bane's *MacEvilly*, pp.5 and *Tuam News*, 31 January 1890; Brett's *Duggan*, p.5-7 and *Tuam News*, 8 January 1892;
2. *Tuam Herald*, 12 March 1904.
3. ibid., 3 May 1902; Feeney Papers, p.147.
4. McMyler interview.
5. See Kevin Whelan 'The Regional Impact of Irish Catholicism 1700-1850' in Smith & Whelan, *Common Ground*, p.270, and 'The Catholic Community in Eighteenth Century County Wexford' in Power & Whelan, *Endurance and Emergence*, p.159-64; Keenan, *The Catholic Church in 19th Century Ireland*, pp.61-66. For clerical families in other west of Ireland dioceses, see Liam Swords *The Hidden Church: the dioceses of Achonry, 1689-1818*, Dublin 1998, p.192-93, and Patrick Egan, *The Parish of Ballinasloe*, 1960.

Staff group, c.1943. *Front row*: Fr Charlie Gibbons, Fr James Fergus, Fr Tim Gunnigan (President), Fr Tom Cummins, Fr Charlie Mulrennan, Jack O'Sullivan. *Back row*: Fr Paddy Costello, Fr Pat Prendergast, Fr Louis Hennelly, Fr Jimmy Gibbons, Fr Con Heaney, Sammy Doyle, Fr Charlie Scahill, Fr Joe Cunnane, Fr Tom Molloy.

Studying for the exams?

Playing croquet in 1945: R to L: B. Kavanagh, K. Fahy, M. Walsh and P. Williams. The game was played during 'Inter week' the state examinations period.

The College Céilí Band, St Patrick's Day 1964. *Photo courtesy of Fr Colm Canavan.* Including M. Kitt, J. Donoghue, J.Brennan, A.Corcoran.

Fr Michael Malone, Dean and first College football trainer, 1929-1936.

Senior football trainers, 1947-2000: Fr Brendan Kavanagh, Fr Dermot Moloney, Joe Long, Fr Oliver Hughes, Monsignor Michael Mooney. Inset, Tod Nolan.

Senior Connacht Colleges Champions 1935 with team members listed on blackboard (below).

what one writer has called an 'uncle-nephew nexus' is clear in the case of the parish of Belclare/Cummer, adjoining Tuam. Patrick Duggan, later bishop of Clonfert, came directly from Maynooth to the parish as curate to his uncle, Canon Patrick Canavan, and on the latter's death in 1856, succeeded him.[1] Patrick Duggan's early career, however, was rather anachronistic by the mid-nineteenth century. Although nephews continued to follow their uncles into the priesthood, the era of family parishes had been brought to an end, by and large, by Archbishop Oliver Kelly's reforms of 1817.

If certain families within the archdiocese maintained a connection with the College over generations, others were inclined to look further afield for their sons' education. For decades, pensions had been deliberately kept at the lowest possible level lest those of middling means be deterred, but, somewhat paradoxically, this policy served to deter the better-off who were increasingly attracted by a more exclusive educational ambience. The strength of feeling provoked by this phenomenon was well conveyed in a *Herald* report detailing the strong performance in the Intermediate examinations of St Jarlath's students which concluded with a strong attack on those well-to-do members of the community who sent their sons away to school for reasons of snobbery:

> ...our local college can well hold its own with the boasted, bombastic, loudly advertised educational work of other institutions. We compare its young men and what they have done with those turned out of other schools possessing greater advantages... All this should teach such of our townspeople as imagine that nothing good can come out of the Nazareth of Tuam that if they kept their boys at home under their own eye and direction and at our excellent college, they would have them better reared and better trained... For our part we are convinced that if there was less of that exporting trade in boys carried on, there would be among parents more satisfaction with the consequences. They complain of local schools being backward in professional staff. We deny that impeachment... They

---

1. Brett's *Duggan*, pp.4-7; 'The Careys [Keighreys, Keaghreys] of Tuam' in *Tuam Herald*, 14 July 1917; 'The Canavans and Tuam', ibid., 26 November 1921. Two Canavan brothers of the same extended family were parish priest of Carnacon and curate of Kilmeena in 1921.

pay readily to some high-sounding and self-trumpeting school in England or in Dublin, £70 or £80 a year. If asked to pay £20 at our local college they grumble and growl as if it were a tax and not a duty. For stupid frivolity and fashion's sake they elect to be extravagant.[1]

The polemic ended with a resounding condemnation of the foibles of members of 'the rising generation of an aping and an apish middle class' in Tuam, who acted as if they thought that their children were 'better than the men who are now in the chief walks of professional and mercantile life in the town and elsewhere.'

A short few years later, however, the same 'apish middle-class' would receive encouragement from the same newspaper to 'export' its adolescent sons to Dublin. Richard J. Kelly, barrister and the paper's proprietor, was an old boy of Blackrock College and when he was elected president of the Blackrock Union its affairs received considerable notice in the *Herald*.[2] Moreover, advertisements such as that reminding parents of the beginning of a new academic year in Rockwell College suggest that Blackrock's County Tipperary sister college also was attended by boys from North Galway.[3]

Evidently, the leakage of the sons of the prosperous to more upmarket establishments in Dublin and elsewhere continued to rankle in St Jarlath's. What else could have provoked frequent oblique references to such places in prize day speeches? Typical of these were the 1906 remarks of President Higgins, that 'in a fair field, notwithstanding all the disadvantages we labour under here in the West in the matter of education, we can hold our own with the foremost and most pampered schools in Ireland.'[4]

Impressionistic evidence notwithstanding, there are indications that not all that much changed in the course of the nineteenth century as far as the social background of the student body was concerned. While there is little solid evidence in this regard for the earlier period, the information that we have about a small number of individuals tends to demonstrate that students' families were in reasonably comfortable circumstances. And the remarks of a Maynooth president about the origins of

1. *Tuam Herald*, 4 October 1884.
2. ibid., 3 June 1899, 10 June 1911.
3. ibid., 1 August 1903.
4. SJC, President's Report Book, 1905-06 report. See also...

his students during the 1820s gives a general indication about the contemporary situation in St Jarlath's, since the 'expenses' incurred by students in either institution were broadly similar.

> Our students are generally the sons of farmers, who must be comfortable to meet the expenses I have already mentioned; of tradesmen, shopkeepers; and not a very small proportion of them are the children of opulent merchants and rich farmers and graziers.[1]

The earliest reliable evidence of this nature on the students of St Jarlath's is contained in a register of those who studied science between 1887 and 1891 — 138 boys in total — which was kept to satisfy the educational authorities. This register listed the occupation of each individual's father, his age, the date he entered the College and his home address. The address list shows a major change in the decade or so since the heyday of Canon Ulick Bourke and the death of Archbishop MacHale. Students were no longer sought in — and no longer came from — exotic locations around the globe. Only four were from outside the archdiocese, and a Gibraltar address represented the only student from abroad. Of the Tuam natives, seventy came from County Mayo, fifty-nine from County Galway and five from the parishes of Moore and Ballinlough in County Roscommon.

As the accompanying table shows, the occupational profile presents an almost equally homogeneous picture.

At a glance, there is not much which amends Dr Crotty's earlier delineation. Manifestly, the sons of 'comfortable' farmers and shopkeepers were well represented in the late 1880s, whatever about those of 'opulent merchants and rich farmers'. And if professional and official backgrounds did not merit a mention in the 1820s, their substantial presence six decades later merely reflected the social changes of the intervening decades. National schools, workhouses, the Royal Irish Constabulary, institutions whose officials accounted for the majority in this category, were all innovations of the post-1830 period.

The table's most salient feature, however, is the extent to which farmers' sons predominated. And although the designation 'farmer' does not tell very much about the means of a family — since farms came in all sizes, were variously managed, and

---

1. Cited by S.J. Connolly in *Priests and People*, p.37.

Table 7.1 Occupational background of 138 St Jarlath's students, 1887-91

Agricultural		Artisanal	
Farmer	90	Painter	1
Landed proprietor	2	Tailor	1
Landlord	1		
Land steward	1		
Total	**94**	**Total**	**2**

Professional & Official		Commercial	
National Teacher	5	Licensed Grocer	9
Head Constable	2	Merchant	7
RIC Inspector	2	Grocer	3
Bank Manager	2	Provisions dealer	2
Medical doctor	1	Mill-owner	2
Chemist	1	Pawnbroker	1
Workhouse master	1	Hotel Keeper	1
Lighthouse Keeper	1	Broker	1
Engineer	1		
Total	**16**	**Total**	**26**

Source: SJC, General Register of science students, 1887-1923.

contained soil of differing qualities — the range of other occupations represented does indicate that, predominantly, the home circumstances of late nineteenth century students were comfortable. For one thing, the working class — admittedly a relatively small part of the population of the archdiocese of Tuam — was scarcely represented at all among the students of the College, and the only two boys of such background were sons of tradesmen, generally far better off than the semi-skilled or unskilled. It is revealing also that the ordinary ranks of the constabulary were not represented, while middle and upper ranks were.

As far as the agricultural sector was concerned, the fact that 'landed proprietors', as well as a landlord and a land steward chose to send their sons to the College must be regarded as significant. It may well be that they were relatively impoverished specimens of their class but, nonetheless, they must have expected that their sons would find compatible companionship among the children of merchants, bank managers and police inspectors. Moreover, it is possible to make a tentative judgement about the social status of the ninety farmers' sons on the register. Because (usually partial) home addresses appear on the science register, it was possible to trace — with a fair degree of certainty — the family circumstances of eleven of the farm families in the household returns for the 1901 census.[1] Almost two-thirds (7 of 11) occupied first class houses while the remainder lived in second class accommodation; by comparison, only 5% of the population of County Galway and 2.5% of that of Mayo lived in first class houses at that time.[2] Admittedly the sample is rather small, but this pattern would tend to establish that the majority of students came from relatively prosperous backgrounds, with a substantial enough minority coming from poorer families.

Evidence given by two presidents before the Educational Endowments Commission in 1888 indicates also that the student body was socially mixed. Seven students — more than 10% of the student body of the time — came from families which were 'considered' to have an income of over £200 a year, and were consequently prohibited from competing for prizes in the Intermediate examinations. In the circumstances, it is likely that these were clear-cut cases and that borderline cases from strong farming families where income was not easily assessed were not excluded from the examination. Regarding the other end of the social scale, it was stated that some boys were kept at home for a few years to assist on their families farms, before being sent to the College, while those 'whose parents are pretty well off' generally arrived at a younger age. The severe fall in enrolment in the previous few years, President Kilkenny was certain, was attributable 'to the depression in the country'.[3] If this was the case, then some less-well-off families who might, in other circumstances have sent a son to St Jarlath's were unable to do so in those years. Consequently, the sample from 1887-91 used in the above table may not have been typical of the late nineteenth century as a whole.

---

1. It should be pointed out that it is somewhat easier to trace the better off. Sometimes, their houses had names and, almost always, the farm attached to a first class house occupied a large proportion of a townland. The occupants of second and third class houses were more likely to share a surname with other families in the townland, as a result of earlier sub-division.
2. 1901 Census, Province of Connaught.
3. Educational Endowments Commission evidence, par.1933.

Any expansion in student numbers had to take account of the fact that only a limited number of families within the archdiocese could afford, from their own resources, to send a son to St Jarlath's. During the 1860s and 1870s, President Bourke's solution to this fundamental problem had been to seek recruits among emigrants and Fenians. The result of that policy was distasteful to Bourke's successors and, anyway, the same successors had less appeal for the diaspora and for alienated nationalism. So, if numbers were to be maintained in the post-Bourke and post-MacHale era, incentives would have to be put in place to attract additional students from the College's hinterland. Archbishop MacEvilly acknowledged this reality by establishing eight scholarships to the College, which he paid from his personal resources.

The context in which these scholarships were established was one of some difficulty as far as the collection of pensions due to the College was concerned. This difficulty, it seems likely, was not entirely attributable to an inability to pay. There may for instance have been laxity in this, as in other financial matters, during the long Bourke presidency, prompting parents to procrastinate in paying. The letter-book of President Kilkenny, covering the years 1882-86, reveals a man pre-occupied with this issue above all others. In much of the correspondence, the President's tone was brusque and indignant. He emphasised repeatedly that he was responsible to the archbishop as far as pensions were concerned, implying but not quite stating that he was personally liable to make good any shortfall. In several instances, it is clear that he thought that the pension-shy were quite capable of paying:

> I have written to you several times about your son's pension for the past academical year — you have not condescended to reply. I beg to say this is not fair towards me;
>
> ... Forward five pounds please, unless I have the money by the 10th inst, it will be necessary for Richard to retire from the College until the sum is paid. This I regret as Richard is a good and exemplary boy, but he cannot live on air;
>
> ...I regret that you disregard courtesy as far as to ignore my general letters to you asking for the balance due by you to the College;
>
> ... Just a word before I put you to the expense and

shame of being brought before the law courts for a debt that is the first paid by every honest man — the pension of your son in this College... Do not blame me for further proceedings, it is yourself that has brought them on.[1]

In other cases, Fr Kilkenny was more circumspect, even apologetic. For example, when writing to an impoverished widow gently reminding her of her promise to pay 'after the May fair', he prefaced his request with his regrets that he had 'to annoy you with letters of this nature.' Another parent was assured that because of 'the difficulties of your present position, I would not trouble you in a money matter if I could avoid it, but I am personally accountable for the pensions of scholars'.[2]

It is probable that Dr MacEvilly's scholarships were designed to meet such cases. The Kilkenny letters would further indicate that the archbishop occasionally used his discretion to 'excuse' parents who were unable to pay pensions.[3]

After the introduction of the Intermediate examination in 1879, some students were enabled to pay for their own education by winning prizes. However, the prospect was open only to a small minority of the very brightest and, in order to compete for these prizes, candidates had to have already spent a (fee-paying) period in Intermediate education. In any case, most of the prizes offered were for a relatively small amount — welcome as a bonus but unequal to the task of supporting a young man in full-time education.

The physical capacity of the College was increased at the beginning of the twentieth century, early in the episcopacy of John Healy. At the same time, the new archbishop inaugurated a scheme of scholarships, supplementing the 'secret sacrifices' of parents and 'helping to give a number of boys a secondary education who could never otherwise hope to get it.'[4] The Department of Agriculture and Technical Instruction was similarly motivated in establishing so-called 'county scholarships',

1. SJC, Kilkenny letters, pp.73, 110, 159. Patrick Kilkenny was born in Annagh and educated at St Jarlath's and Maynooth. After ordination, he served as curate to his uncle, Canon Lyons, in Spiddal (1869-72) A professor in St Jarlath's from 1872, he succeeded Ulick Bourke as president of the debt-ridden College in 1878. In 1888, he again succeeded Bourke as P.P. of Kilcoleman. He remained in Claremorris until he died, an archdeacon, in 1921 at the age of 74.
2. ibid., pp.85, 137.
3. ibid., p.91.
4. SJC, President's Report Book, 1905-06 report.

paid through the county councils and coming with the condition that beneficiaries be given a technical training. It was stated that most of the sixteen 'county scholars' who attended the College during the 1907-08 academic year would have been unable to afford Intermediate education without their scholarships.[1]

The lowering of financial barriers by the actions of the archbishop and of the government department undoubtedly contributed to a change in the class composition of the student body in the early decades of the twentieth century. Rising living standards during the same period would have reinforced this development. Meanwhile, further encouragement to attend St Jarlath's was given to poorer families by the establishment of a number of 'burses' or bequests. Most of these were created by legacies left by priests of the diocese. And while the wills which brought some of them into being were made many years earlier, a large number of these burses came into affect in the first decade or so of the new century.

By the academic year 1926-27, a total of fifty-four boys were supported to a greater or lesser degree by twenty different agencies or foundations. Nine of these students were fully funded by two local authorities, the Mayo and Galway County Councils which offered grants of £40 to senior students and £35 to juniors — the College fees at the time were £35 a year. Twelve 'College Scholars' enjoyed a 50% reduction in fees, the loss of which was borne by the institution itself. Then there were fourteen burses which fully or partially covered the annual commitments of one or two boys each. All of them operated independently of each other, were governed by their own particular conditions and were known by the names of their donors: Cunningham (James) and Cunningham (Thomas); Flatley; Gallagher; Higgins; Lavelle; Lynskey; Dr. MacHale (Achill) and Dr. MacHale (Milltown); McLaughlin; McHugh (Carna) and McHugh (Claremorris); Waldron (Canon W.) and Waldron (Rev. Peter). Two further burses — the Gibbons and the Old Blake — were left vacant during 1926-27.[2] Finally, there were the more substantial 'New Blake' scholarships which fully met the fees of two students and partially met those of fourteen others.

The New Blake Scholarships were established by the will of Lieutenant Colonel Llewellyn Blake, D.L., J.P., of Clough, Ballymore, Co. Galway. The founder was a papal count who

---

1. ibid., 1907-08 report.
2. SJC, Notes on scholarship holders, 1921-28.

had earlier set up the-called 'Old Blake' scholarship in the College to support candidates for the foreign missions. Count Blake died in September 1916, leaving income from a range of stocks to a number of Catholic colleges to enable the 'founding of as many burses as possible… for the purpose of enabling poor students for the Roman Catholic priesthood who cannot afford to pay for their College course to receive their education free or to be assisted.' The bequest was divided in the following proportions: two-fifteenths to St Jarlath's College; two-fifteenths to All Hallows, Dublin; two-fifteenths to Mungret, Limerick; two-fifteenths to the African Mission College, Wilton, Cork; six-fifteenths to Ballinfad College, Mayo; one-fifteenth for the Propagation of the Faith. The income from St Jarlath's share was £178.16.2 in 1917. However, the bequest was challenged by two close relatives, Count Blake's niece and his nephew — Colonel Maurice Moore of Moore Hall — who petitioned the Pope to 'grant them some concession from the estate of their uncle to remedy pressing needs'. The matter was referred to the executor, the Bishop of Cork, who recommended that £1000 be given to the niece and £500 to the nephew for 'the education of his son.' Not satisfied with this, the two appealed to Rome, whereupon their award was doubled. The effect on St Jarlath's portion of the bequest was to reduce its value by about twenty pounds a year.[1]

The other burses were modest enough, most being established by clergymen of no great means. But it is remarkable how many of them specified that preference be given to relatives. Some were doing no more than continuing into later generations their habit of contributing to the education of nephews and grand-nephews. Others were attempting to sustain (or inaugurate?) a family tradition of providing candidates for the priesthood. The Lavelle Burse was for 'the education of a relative in St Jarlath's College'; the Lynskey Burse was for the education 'of one who is recognised by the Archbishop and the president of the College as a relative of mine and a fit and proper subject for the sacred ministry… for the term of 500 years after my death'; the McHugh (Carna) Burse was for 'the education of relatives and friends, and next in order anyone bearing the name McHugh'; the Roche Burse left the income from the rent of a house and land for the 'education to the priesthood of a person named Roche; the Kilkenny Burse — initiated by a former

---

1. SJC, Count Blake Charity, 1917-75.

College president who was well aware of the difficulties encountered by the College authorities in collecting fees — was for the 'education of a relative, if no relative any student named Kilkenny or Lyons from Bekan or Annagh.' The McHugh (Claremorris), Ryder and Greally scholarships expressed similar preferences. A few, however, had broader social objectives. The James Daly bequest was 'for the maintenance and education of two poor boys from the town of Tuam' while the Ryan Bequest went to 'the boy who is most proficient in the writing and speaking of Irish.'[1]

Inevitably, such bequests sometimes caused disappointment among those who had counted on being more substantially remembered in a relative's will. But only rarely did such disappointment reach the courts. One challenge in 1916, however, forced the College to considerably tighten its financial administration. And in the same case, the late Fr Lavelle's stipulation that the benefits of the burse should go to his relatives came under scrutiny. If the intention of the dead man was to make provision for the education of his relatives rather than to benefit the College then, the challenger argued, a valid charitable bequest had not been established.[2] The court decided, however, that the intention was, in the first instance, to benefit the College, so the challenge failed.

Most of the priests who created burses were serving in their native diocese but one of them, Rev Owen Gallagher of Pennsylvania, had spent a lifetime on the American mission. This in no way diminished his desire to assist the descendants of his fellow Gallaghers who had stayed behind in the old country. But before proceeding to the principal provisions, he first got some personal business out of the way:

> that the execution of the [headstone] lettering be at least equal to that already on it for my mother; ...I bequeath to my faithful housekeeper, Ann M, a picture of myself now hanging in the second floor front room [and] the sum of $1000 provided she continues to live with me until my death; ...I direct that 50 low masses be said each year for a period of thirty consecutive years, beginning as soon as possible after my death...[3]

---

1. SJC, Notes on some of the College burses.
2. *Tuam Herald*, 31 January 1914.
3. SJC, Will of Owen P. Gallagher, printed document, 12pp.

Fr Gallagher then made several philanthropic bequests, the most important of which was the establishment of the 'Gallagher Scholarship' for St Jarlath's and Maynooth. The name of this burse announced his instruction that 'those bearing my own surname be given preference whenever prudent and possible':

> It is my desire and intention to establish a perpetual scholarship bearing my own name for the preparation and education of the hereinafter described class of poor deserving Roman Catholic young men for the calling of the Roman Catholic priesthood. These young men shall be chosen perpetually and as often as necessary by the Roman Catholic Archbishop of the See of Tuam, Ireland, and his lawful successors in said office forever, from such poor deserving Roman Catholic young men residing in and native born to the parish of Achill, County of Mayo, Ireland... If the said parish of Achill shall at any time choice is to be made, prove after due enquiry not to contain a fit person or persons as aforesaid, then I direct the scholarship shall be filled by students chosen in like manner... from the same class of young men... in that portion of the See of Tuam... contained in the present boundaries of the County of Mayo.[1]

If none suitable were to be found in the Mayo part of the archdiocese, then they were to be sought in other parts of Mayo and, that failing, 'in any part of the County of Donegal, Ireland.' Fr. Gallagher further directed that on the 'ordination, forfeiture, death or otherwise' of a burse-holder, a replacement be chosen immediately, 'it being my desire, will and intention that there shall be perpetually and at all times students being prepared and educated as above described.' As for the education of the young men it was to be 'done thoroughly in every branch, particularly in their classical studies.' And after beneficiaries were educated — but before they were ordained — the serving Catholic Bishop of Pittsburgh, who had 'first right to them', was to be notified. After ordination, Gallagher scholars were required to remember their benefactor by celebrating 'for the repose of my soul every year during their respective lives a high mass of requiem, except when they may be prevented by

---

1. ibid.

absolute impossibility.¹ In order that people be 'perpetually reminded of their duty', a printed copy of the will was to be sent to relevant parties every fifth year.

The restrictive conditions, however, made it difficult to fill this scholarship. Soon the search for 'poor deserving' Gallaghers with a vocation to the priesthood was abandoned. Instead, a competitive examination was held in Westport which was open to boys, Gallagher or not, from Achill and surrounding areas.² In the case of other scholarships, occasional vacancies were advertised in the local papers'.³

The various burses administered by the College were intended to benefit, in the first instance, those with a vocation to the priesthood. But such an aspiration, however strongly held at the age of thirteen or fourteen, often weakened in the course of a decade and many of those with early vocations failed to make it as far as ordination. Gallagher scholarship holders can be taken as a sample group in this regard. Eleven years after the first scholarship was awarded in 1903, a total of nineteen beneficiaries had concluded their second-level education. Of these, two were ordained by 1914 and ten were still attending the major seminaries of Maynooth and All Hallows. Of the seven who had opted for a secular career, three — including the lad 'expelled from All Hallows for drink' — had spent a period at a major seminary.⁴ Incidentally, just three of the nineteen were surnamed Gallagher, and they were all among the group of seven in the *ad vota secularia* category.

The Gallagher figures would indicate a rate of attrition of something more than a third among scholarship holders. Apparently this was acceptable enough as far as the College was concerned, but what about an instance where a vocation was never sincerely held by a claimant to a scholarship? Suspicion of such a scenario led the authorities to seek legal advice on one occasion. The question arose when the executor of the burse's founder (also a close relative) sought to claim it for his second son, the first son having already benefited. Since the burse had clearly been established for 'deserving aspirants for the priesthood,' and the executor's first son had not pursued this career, the College authorities wondered whether the trustees of the fund might be entitled to recover the College fees

1. ibid.
2. SJC, Register of scholarships in St Jarlath's College.
3. *Tuam Herald*, 10 July 1915, 27 July 1917.
4. SJC, Register of scholarships in St Jarlath's College.

from the individual concerned or from his father. The legal view was that they could not, since 'it could not be contemplated that every aspirant would necessarily attain the priesthood.' Then, on the basis that the executor concerned was prosperous, the trustees wondered whether his second son might be excluded on the grounds that he was not 'deserving'. On that point, the lawyer advised that '"deserving" does not merely mean "in poor circumstances"' and that regard must should also be paid 'to the fact that the object of the burse is education with a view to the priesthood.' Where there was 'more than one contender', however, he advised that preference should be given to the individual in worst circumstances.[1]

This executor was not the only individual in comfortable circumstances who sought to avail of a burse. It would appear that the extended families of the creators of these bequests regarded the enjoyment of their benefits as a legacy rather than as a charity. The following extracts from correspondence relating to one burse show that applications came from people with a range of social backgrounds and educational attainments:

> My Mother's Father having the Rev Simon X First Cousin of my Mother once removed, So now I Clame Burse for my son Michael left by Rev Simon X now vacant.
>
> ...In the matter of the estate of the Late Father Simon X, P.P deceased, I Mary X of BunA, Co Mayo, wife of Dr Patrick Y and aged 30 years and upwards do make oath and say as follows: 1) I am a lawful daughter of Michael X, late of BallyA deceased, and the said Michael X was a lawful son of Thomas X; 2) The above named Thomas X was the lawful paternal uncle of Reverend Simon X; 3) I am the lawful mother of James, 14, at present at St Jarlath's College
>
> ...Dear Father Eaton, Your letter came to hand some time ago asking the relationship of my boy re the Father Simon X Burse. My father was second cousin of Fr Simon X and brother of William J. X of BallyA, Co. Mayo. If the young boy you spoke about is John A. X's son of CaherA, he is the same relation as my boy and I understand he has got a good turn of the burses. I hope you will kindly let me know if I get it so that I can have the boy ready.[2]

---

1. Tuam diocesan archive, documents regarding College burses
2. SJC, Notes on some of the College burses.

As well as the twenty-two burses already mentioned, a number of others were created in the decade or so after 1926-27. These included the Lynch, the Morrin and the Kitt-Sheehy scholarships. Incidentally, one of these was established during his own life-time by a successful past-pupil, a layman who had been a burse-holder during his own College days. The proliferation of burses was such that, several decades before the introduction of free education, Archbishop Walsh was able to announce that many families who were 'not blessed with great means' could 'have their boys educated along the best possible lines' in the College.[1]

Events would show, however, that those benefactors who instructed that eligible students should benefit 'for ever', 'in perpetuity' or 'for the term of 500 years after my death' had been somewhat optimistic. Inflation, brokerage fees and a conservative investment policy all contributed to a significant loss in the value of bequests within a generation or two of their establishment. Remedial measures were taken to maintain the value of investments during the 1960s after President Mooney was advised by a stockbroker that funds in several of the burses were reaching 'a level where they are unable to fulfil the original object of the bequest'.[2] By then, the state had begun to take measures providing for the second-level education of the majority of 'poor deserving' boys and girls, so future generations would not be as dependent upon the benevolence of individuals.

1. Tuam diocesan archives, Pastoral letter, 13 October 1946.
2. Notes on College burses.

9. "... uniform observance of rule."

When a Professor from his chair
Gives us a counsel that looks fair,
Without a word we do obey.[1]

In common with other diocesan colleges, and reflecting the ecclesiastical seminary tradition, there was a strong emphasis on discipline in St Jarlath's from the very beginning. Indeed, the twin virtues of discipline and order were prized above all others for it was believed that, without them, teaching was impossible. In this respect, the forceful language used by the first superior of the College, Archbishop Oliver Kelly, in outlining the duties of the College staff, was as telling as the order in which he prioritised them. The principal tasks of professors and president, he instructed, were to 'enforce the observance of discipline, to forward the literary improvement of their pupils, and strictly to adhere to the rules and regulations of the seminary.' Nor were these objectives merely aspirational, for on the same occasion, Dr Kelly paid tribute to the 'zeal' of the staff, 'in promoting order, discipline, and study.'[2]

On paper, at least, little had changed two generations later when President Ulick Bourke insisted that 'without discipline and the exact observance of rule in the College, there can be no piety.' Moreover, during Bourke's presidency prizes were awarded for the 'uniform observance of rule.'[3]

Parents and guardians, evidently, did not disagree with the prevailing emphasis. One letter introducing a new student to President Thomas Feeney gave permission to 'dispose of him as you please'; another advised that a boy was 'wild and foolish and will require to be closely watched'; a third requested that the president ensure that his James's time was 'not thrown away.'[4] Students too accepted that the enforcement of rule was vital to the running of the institution and, while their tributes to departing staff members customarily included a reference to the individual's benign disposition, this was always balanced with an acknowledgement of his rigour as regards the rules.[5]

---

1. From specially written prologue to dramatic entertainment in St Jarlath's, *Tuam News*, 9 November 1888.
2. SJC, Feeney Papers, letter from +Oliver, 8 February 1821.
3. *Tuam Herald*, 11 November 1865, 3 July 1869.
4. Feeney Papers, pp.75, 77.
5. For example, see *Tuam Herald*, 8 July 1837, *Tuam News*, 24 February 1888.

If there was to be 'uniform observance of rule', a range of sanctions was required to punish transgressors. That there was also a system of rewards for good behaviour in the College's early years is indicated by the instruction from President Feeney: 'it is required that any Act of Grace as well as of Punishment do come exclusively from the President.' Feeney, however, was remembered more for the physical punishments he bestowed than for the 'acts of grace.' But just a 'slender rod' was available to him. This, as we have seen, was designated by Archbishop Oliver Kelly in 1819 as 'the only instrument to be used in inflicting punishment.'[1] Kelly's rules did not mention expulsion but other evidence in the Feeney correspondence indicates that it was the punishment of last resort during the 1820s. Exceptionally, an even severer penalty was imposed on the brothers Egan, who were briefly excommunicated from the Church for attending a duel.[2]

President Bourke's College timetable of 1867 listed several grounds for expulsion, including 'reading, or study, or lighting of candles during the night'; leaving the College grounds without permission; the consumption of 'illicit drinks'; possession of 'novels, or any other thing calculated to vitiate the mind, or bring on bad habits, or opposed to discipline, morals, or piety.'

Otherwise, the 1867 document described a very severe regime. The day began at 6 a.m., when students were exhorted to rise 'at first toll of bell.' Between then and 9.15 a.m. — during prayer, study and breakfast — strict silence was to be observed. At 8.25 a.m. all were to 'proceed to the Cathedral in the most orderly manner, if possible in a line or a row,' and without 'conversing or unseemly conduct'. Absolute silence was demanded also during mid-day and evening study periods and from the beginning of night prayer at 9 p.m to the following morning. To facilitate supervision, the students had to stay together during leisure periods and were not allowed to visit their own (or others') rooms except for a few minutes on Mondays, Wednesdays, or Saturdays to organise clothes for laundering. So that all of this could be enforced, it was required that the prefect of studies be 'never absent from the students.'[3]

As has been shown in previous chapters, however, Bourke's St Jarlath's was not quite as austere and monastic in practice as

---

1. Feeney Papers, pp.38-9; Brett's *Life of Duggan*, p.11.
2. Feeney Papers, pp.38-9, 49, 81-2.
3. SJC, Order of Studies and Classes, 1867. See Appendix A below.

in print. Nevertheless, the rules do offer a glimpse into the College regime of the period, although there is little concrete contemporary evidence on how strictly these rules were enforced or, for that matter, on how severely breaches were actually punished.

One might expect that an examination of the letter-book of Patrick Kilkenny, Bourke's successor as President, would help to complete the picture as regards discipline in the late nineteenth century College. Unfortunately, it is not that helpful. In fact, Kilkenny's correspondence is peopled largely by 'good and exemplary' boys and 'attentive industrious' children who were 'making great efforts to learn' or who, at least, appeared 'anxious to apply (themselves) seriously' to their studies. Only the student who was advised to 'endeavour to curtail his unnecessary expenses' seems to have given any cause for concern.[1]

One series of letters in 1882, however, dealt with a matter that had disciplinary implications. This was the case of the two senior students who had been entrusted with the task of dealing with Messrs Gill & Son, publishers, regarding the supply of textbooks. It would appear that they were paid a commission by the company and that they were expected to process orders from their comrades without reference to the College. In this instance, the publishers were not paid for the books forwarded to Tuam and they complained to the archbishop. He referred the matter to President Kilkenny, who promptly wrote to Gill's. In his letter, the president disclaimed legal responsibility, insisting that it was entirely a matter between the company and its agents. He did promise, however, that he would seek to persuade the two to pay their debt — amounting to the then substantial sum of forty pounds.

If the College authorities did not feel legally responsible for debts incurred in such a fashion by their students, they clearly felt morally responsible. Strong pressure was applied on the two students/agents and they were threatened with one of the strongest sanctions available to the president: 'the Archbishop will not give you a letter of appointment to Maynooth until Messrs Gill give you a discharge of this debt.'[2]

For more than impressionistic evidence of disciplinary routine, one has to wait until the early years of the twentieth century. The minute-book of the College's Discipline Council,

---

1. SJC, Kilkenny letter-book, 1882-1886, pp.72, 73, 83, 159.
2. ibid., pp.100-103

beginning in 1909, provides information in systematic form on the range of disciplinary problems experienced at particular times, the range of sanctions employed, and the disciplinary structures of the institution.

Discipline in those years, it would appear, was a particular responsibility of the prefect of studies, there being no dean of discipline. But some responsibility, the minutes make clear, was devolved to the students themselves, specifically to monitors appointed at the beginning of the academic year by the college authorities. Such an arrangement was commonplace, although the equivalent functionaries in some colleges held the title of prefect. The designation 'monitor' followed the practice in Maynooth and indeed, continues to the present day in St Jarlath's. This term probably derived from one of the tasks carried out by selected students in the early years of the College. A monitor, in early nineteenth century education, was a senior student — usually an aspiring teacher — who assisted the teacher by taking a section of a class for routine exercises, especially for rote learning. It is likely that individuals like Martin A. O'Brennan and Michael J. McCann became teachers for a time as a result of such experience.

In the years around 1910, four monitors supervised a student body of approximately one hundred. The head monitor was then — and still is — known as the procurator, a designation, incidentally, which was originally applied to an imperial representative of ancient Rome. Two of the other monitors had specific responsibilities, one for the study hall, the other for the sacristy. All were expected to keep order in their respective dormitories at night and to keep the college authorities informed, in broad terms, about areas of difficulty. Such responsibility was regarded as part of a general training in leadership for future clergymen, and monitors were accordingly chosen from among those aspiring towards the priesthood.

The records of Discipline Council meetings are worth examining in some detail. Its rules and laws reveal a lot about an institution, but the transgression of laws, and mechanisms for the detection and punishment of the transgressors tell even more. For one thing, the pattern of behaviour — and misbehaviour — will tend to show the extent to which there was an 'us and them' mentality in the relationship between staff and students at various times. The rare gestures of collective defiance were the starkest manifestations of a clash of outlooks, but persistent collusion in the breaking of some rules was a more typical student expression of disagreement with appointed authority.

The Discipline Council, composed of the President, the dean of studies and the Professors, was inaugurated in June 1909.[1] The innovation was probably attributable to one or more of the following: a belief that a more formal approach to discipline was required to deal with the growing student population of the period; a conviction, heightened by widespread rule-breaking, that order was breaking down; a perception that structures needed to reflect the democratic spirit of the age. Or, it may simply have been a whim of either Archbishop Healy or President Higgins. In any case, the experiment was short-lived in its first incarnation. Probably because it failed to avert one of the most serious break-downs in authority in the College's history, the Council was discontinued after less than three years. However, it was revived a decade later.

The first offence considered by the Council in 1909 was that hardy perennial, the consumption of 'illicit drink'. While on his nightly patrol, President Higgins had encountered an empty whiskey bottle and an intoxicated student in the dormitories. The student denied that he had taken alcohol, but was contradicted by the smell from his breath. The Council decided that he should be 'immediately removed from the other students of the College,' but advised the culprit to take lodgings in the town, from where he could attend daily until the end of the Intermediate examinations.

More persistent problems included disorder in the study hall, theft by students from students, and fighting. Penalties for such breaches normally fell short of expulsion. Indeed the penalties for fighting, unless there were aggravating circumstances, were so mild as to almost condone it.

One case in 1909 involved the beating of a junior by a senior student while they were on a public walk. The victim — whose spectacles were smashed in the fracas — admitted that he had jostled the older boy's brother when he 'stepped forward to claim his place of seniority.' Having examined the monitors, the council found that the accused had acted 'deliberately and maliciously, without any provocation' and ordered that he be reprimanded by the president before the student body. Another fight, which broke out in the ball-court in May 1910, was

---

1. SJC, Discipline Council Minutes, 1909-1962. Unless otherwise indicated, all following references derive from this volume.

deemed to have been 'the result of a sudden fit of passion' and, accordingly, it was considered sufficient to 'warn both solemnly.' Yet another incident involved two classmates. The aggressor in this instance claimed that he had acted in order to protect a junior from bullying. Evidence from the prefect of studies confirmed that the recipient of the blows was a known bully, so it was decided that the matter should only be 'taken into account when deciding good conduct marks at the end of the year.'

The most serious encounter of those years resulted in one student being 'badly beaten, his nose broken, and slightly deformed.' This fight, evidently, was a fair one but it was expected that the injured party's father would take an action for damages. Some time later, the fathers of the combatants were advised that 'the usual course in this College where one student injures another has been that the injured man is compensated for any medical expenses he incurs.' This gentlemanly course proved acceptable to both parties.

If the ball-court was the venue for occasional fights, it also provided sufficient privacy for smoking. This breach of discipline was known to occur 'after luncheon' when sentries were posted to warn of professorial approach, so it was difficult to detect. Suspects were sometimes searched. When cigarettes were discovered during one such search, their owner claimed that he had them in his pockets since the Christmas vacation. But because the cigarettes were in good condition and because four months had passed since Christmas, his protestations were not believed. His punishment was the loss of his burse for the half year and the threat that he would not be received back in September if his conduct during the remainder of term was not 'satisfactory in every respect.' The misconduct of another smoker was reported to his father, after the suggestion that he be publicly flogged was over-ruled on the grounds that the boy's conduct was otherwise satisfactory.

Two boys appeared before the committee for 'absenting themselves' from Vespers on a Sunday evening. One told a 'deliberate lie' to excuse himself and asked others to corroborate his story. For this, it was ordered that he be publicly flogged and that his father be informed. The other gave an unacceptable excuse, which if true would 'only make his case worse.' He also was flogged before all the students. In the same month two others were 'caned in the presence of all the students' (was there a distinction between caning and flogging?) for stealing nitric acid from the science hall and for throwing it over a colleague's coat. The thief was barred from the science hall for the remainder of the year and asked not to return after the summer; the destroyer of the coat was ordered to pay ten shillings in compensation.

Hunger, evidently, was the cause of some lapses. A student who was discovered in another's cell at midnight pleaded that:

> he had occasion to get up to the closet and having heard as he thought this student some short time before eating cakes when passing by his cell he was tempted to turn in and searched for some of the cake under the students pillow.

Because it was accepted that his crime was not premeditated, this student was let off with the warning that 'his conduct in future must be more satisfactory.' A more persistent thief who was 'constantly remarked to be knocking about the corridors and dormitories' and who admitted removing 'parcels of sweets and cakes' from another's trunk was punished more severely. His father was advised to remove him from the College if he wished to avoid the disgrace of expulsion.

Such lapses by individuals were dealt with easily enough. And if punishments were not always consistent, this was because a student's general disposition and attitude was necessarily subjected to scrutiny when his name came before the Discipline Council. Altogether, about 20% of the students attracted the notice of the Council in the first eighteen months of its existence. If this seems high, it may be because of an early burst of enthusiasm on the part of the new body. However, it is more likely that serious rule-breaking of this order reflected general difficulties in the administration of the institution. These difficulties came, dramatically, before the readers of the national newspapers in November 1911:

> 'Strike' of College boys: A remarkable "strike" of the students of St Jarlath's College took place yesterday morning, our Tuam correspondent wires, about eighty of the boys leaving the institution. Four boys, it is stated, were expelled the previous evening and about eighty of the remainder decided on leaving the College "in sympathy." About forty remained in and on the call of the roll yesterday morning the President announced that the students

who left would not be allowed back. The majority of them are from county Mayo, a small proportion being from Connemara for which they left by the morning train. The others walked the railway line to Castlegrove to catch the morning train for their homes in Mayo and places north of Tuam.[1]

Evidently, 'Tuam correspondent' had second thoughts about the accuracy of his account — no doubt its errors were brought very forcefully to his attention — and he sent a second wire. And although he was unable to 'spike' the story, some editions rounded off their version with an important qualification: 'A later telegram from Tuam considerably discounts the earlier report and adds: — The matter is not worth mentioning.' The following day, all the papers published the text of a telegram from President Conroy: 'I content myself for the present with saying that it is absolutely inaccurate, every line — President, College, Tuam.'[2] The story was indeed inaccurate, but the key detail was absolutely correct — the students of St Jarlath's had gone on strike.'

The complete break-down of order was the result of the mishandling by the College authorities of a minor disciplinary matter. In other circumstances the resulting sense of grievance might have simmered for a while before cooling off during the following vacation. The atmosphere during the second half of 1911, however, made it likely that some protest would be attempted. It was an era of widespread social militancy, of agrarian agitation and women's suffrage activism. It was also the era of 'Larkinism' when the 'labour question' forced itself into the consciousness of parliamentarians, ecclesiastics and editors. During September, a national railway strike had brought trade unionism from the metropolis into towns and villages — including Tuam.[3] Large labour meetings and picket lines were a novelty which, in commanding press attention, acquired a certain glamour. Labourers and shop assistants in the provinces emulated the railwaymen, but the action had an impact outside of working class circles. In schools and colleges throughout the country, students aired their grievances in uncharacteristically militant fashion.

---
1. *Irish Independent*, 22 November 1911.
2. *Evening Telegraph*, 21 November 1911; *Evening Herald*, 21, 22 November 1911.
3. Emmet O'Connor, *A Labour History of Ireland*,1992, pp.70-80; Cunningham, *Labour in the West of Ireland*, pp.147-48.

Although cloistered in Bishop St., St Jarlath's students were not immune to the prevailing mood. Indeed, it would appear that they were aware of a specific episode in the Franciscan College, Mountbellew, during which a student protest had succeeded in overturning an expulsion.[1]

The event which led to the 'remarkable strike' was the discovery one night by Professor Eaton of cayenne pepper smouldering in the new dormitory. When the monitor of the Limbo dormitory was asked about the matter, he insisted that he was asleep and that he knew nothing. Suspicion then fell on the senior student previously reprimanded for nose-breaking. Under questioning, he admitted the cayenne pepper offence and it was decided that he would have to leave the College. A short time later however, another student approached the president to claim responsibility for the prank. Furthermore, he insisted that he had got the permission of the monitor in Limbo dormitory before lighting the pepper. The monitor was duly reprimanded. He was also reminded that such a dereliction was almost inexcusable in a candidate for Maynooth. The monitor insisted that he had no clear memory of the incident and, anyway, that he had changed his mind about Maynooth.

Another prank involving a holy water font convinced the College authorities that the 'taste for practical joking' was getting out of hand. The monitors, it was decided, had become too lax. Because he was considered to have neglected his duty, and because he had opted out of Maynooth, it was decided to make an example of the Limbo dormitory monitor, so he was removed from his position. It was expected that 'this proceeding would make the monitors more alert.' But it had a rather different effect.

The opinion among students was that the monitor had been shoddily treated and, the evening of his dismissal, there was 'a slight demonstration' in the study hall. Later there was much 'pounding and hammering' in the top dormitory and, in the morning, there was 'considerable disorder' at breakfast. Afterwards, all of the students marched around the walks headed by two seniors carrying a large pole and chanting in a 'terrible' manner. They refused to go to morning study, instead sending for the president. He addressed them, as did the sacked monitor who said he had no grievance against the College.

---

1. For Mountbellew, see Discipline Council minutes; for another local 'schoolboy strike' of the period, see *Connacht Tribune*, 30 September 1911.

President Conroy asked for a promise that there would be no further demonstrations. After a signal from the senior student regarded by the authorities as the leader of the disturbances, the promise was given and things returned to normal for a time.

At his point, Archbishop Healy intervened personally, imposing the ecclesiastical equivalent of martial law. His Grace convened a special meeting of the discipline council and, afterwards, he berated the students in the study hall.

Following an incident-free night, the boys congregated around the toilets after breakfast. Professor Eaton tried to disperse them but encountered resistance. According to one member of the staff an 'idea seemed to have taken possession of the boys' minds that if they went out in a body, the professors would be begging them to come back again.' At nine o'clock, forty-eight students left the college, some of them, it was later stated, only because they had been threatened by senior boys. After a short time, all returned. The archbishop intervened again to insist that no senior student was to be accepted back without his express permission. Furthermore, all of those receiving burses or other 'pecuniary privileges' from the College were to forfeit them for a half-year. Eleven boys were expelled. Thirty-eight others were required to sign a declaration apologising to Dr Healy, to the professors, and to their fellow-students, expressing their regret for their 'disgraceful conduct' and promising 'solemnly' never to do it again. Incidentally, one of the latter group would later achieve great prominence as bishop of a neighbouring diocese.

As far as the expelled group was concerned, Dr Healy decreed that they were liable to pay full fees for the half-year. Evidently acting collectively, they refused, offering to pay half of the amount demanded. President Conroy would not accept this, but eventually agreed that 'they were to be charged per month'. Those who did not pay were to be sent 'an attorney's letter'.[1]

After the strike, a dean of discipline was appointed and the discipline council fell into abeyance for a time. Meetings were not resumed until 1923 on the appointment of President Ryder. The records during the remainder of the 1920s and the early 1930s reveal priorities and preoccupations that are somewhat different to the 1909-11 period. There were also changes in the type of punishment meted out, insofar as the 'public flogging'

---

1. SJC, Various Reports of Presidents, report of 11 January 1912.

of miscreants would appear to have ceased in the interim. Change, however, was not always reflected in the formal regulations of the institution and the printed set of rules formulated by Archbishop Gilmartin in the late 1920s was strongly reminiscent of the document which appeared over the name of Ulick Bourke more than half a century before. There were echoes, even, of the 1819 rules of Archbishop Kelly:

> Any student who goes without permission outside the College boundary, or who takes or introduces drink, tobacco or bad books, or who is guilty of dishonest or dishonourable conduct, or who is guilty of insubordination towards any member of the College staff incurs the penalty of expulsion. It shall be considered a grave violation of discipline to hold familiar intercourse with servants or to hold communication with externs save in the recognised way.
>
> Any student who is generally unruly and not amenable to College discipline shall be considered unfit to associate with other students and shall incur the penalty of expulsion.
>
> The authorities of the College reserve to themselves (1) the control of all the correspondence of the boys and all communication with interns; (2) the liberty of at once resigning the charge of any student whose conduct or progress is in their opinion unsatisfactory.[1]

Fighting, a regular occurrence around 1910, did not once trouble the disciplinary council during the 1920s and 1930s. It is possible that football, which grew enormously in status in the intervening years, offered an alternative and more acceptable outlet for adolescent aggression. While it is unlikely that fighting was eliminated completely, it was not pervasive enough to be perceived as a problem.

Smoking, however, had become much more pervasive. As in other Colleges, much effort was expended in trying to eliminate it, but to little apparent avail. The authorities in Maynooth had eventually given up the struggle against tobacco in 1918, but it was not possible to contemplate such a step in a second-level College at this time.[2] The essential problem was that the

---

1. SJC, Horarium issued by +Thomas, January 1929.
2. Corish, *Maynooth*, pp.297-300.

legitimacy of the no-smoking rule was not accepted by students — if the widespread violation is any indication. Even 'good' boys and impeccably behaved candidates for Maynooth enjoyed an occasional cigarette. There was also a half-heartedness and inconsistency about the attempts to stamp out the habit. The usual penalty during the 1920s for those caught smoking was draconian, a £5 fine. However, it was rarely collected, being 'remitted' at the discretion of the president, if the culprit's behaviour was considered to have improved. In some instances, the penalty was not even imposed, as in the case of the candidate for Maynooth who was found smoking during a visit from his brother in June 1926. Because he was not believed to be 'in the habit', it was decided to overlook the incident. And although the College careers of some terminated prematurely as a result of being caught smoking, it was never the sole factor in an expulsion. Rather a lighted cigarette might spotlight otherwise 'unsatisfactory conduct' or focus attention on the fact that an individual was 'wasting his time' academically.

Exceptionally, one student was asked to leave in 1926 for smoking. He had previously been given a warning for having 'a box of cigarettes and a box of matches', marking him as a confirmed smoker. On the second occasion, he was caught smoking in the dormitory and, more seriously, encouraging others to light up, so it was felt that there was no alternative to his removal.

When pressed during the academic year 1924-25, the monitors advised the College authorities that 'some students, and amongst them juniors, sometimes smoked in the lavatories after dinner.' No doubt, the staff were already aware of this and, later on in the year, the dean of discipline acted on the information and discovered four surreptitious smokers in the lavatory. Among them was the procurator.

In this instance, the usual remittable fines were levied on three of the offenders, but the head-monitor was to be 'excluded from Maynooth.' He would not be denied, however, a letter of recommendation for any other ecclesiastical college.

After Joseph Walsh took over as president in 1928, there was an attempt to introduce more consistency in the penalties for rule-breaking. The fine for a first smoking offence was reduced to a more realistic — and non-remittable — £1 fine, with £2 for a second offence. But the new approach, clearly, was no more successful than the old. During May 1932, the College's sports day committee was discovered smoking while having a 'meeting' in a locked store-room. Four of the five-man-committee were monitors.

During the academic year 1935-36, President Walsh considered it necessary to stiffen the penalties for smoking and, at the same time, involve the student body in policing the ban. Following consultations with his professors, he decreed:

1) If any student is found smoking, he must pay a fine of £1 and he will be deprived of privileges of every kind. His parents are to be informed;
2) If any student is known to be repeatedly violating the the rule against smoking, he will be expelled without notice;
3) The general body of the students will be deprived of all privileges such as football matches, pictures &c. until ... the abuse has ceased.

A few months later, on Shrove Tuesday 1936, two students were placed under a 'solemn caution' for smoking. And because of a promise extracted from them in the previous October 'to stop all smoking in the College' the senior students were deprived of all privileges — starting with the customary Shrove outing to the cinema. Later in the year, however, when another incident again raised the question of the withdrawal of privileges, it was decided after lengthy discussion by the staff that the students in general would not be penalised, 'since they had not in any way condoned this breach.' Clearly, a generalised loss of privileges was considered too draconian an instrument to invoke against a practice students regarded as a minor breach of the rules.

After smoking, the most frequent offences during the 1920s and 1930s were theft and the breaking of bounds. Both were usually punished severely although, in the case of theft, it would appear that a distinction was made between the stealing of food and the stealing of less perishable property.

The behaviour of some thieves appears obsessive or attention-seeking, suggesting that it was sparked off by separation from family and friends. Was this the problem of the lad who was discovered with 'an accumulation of pencils taken from other students'? The relatively lenient response of the College authorities on some occasions may indicate that such a possibility was recognised. Most thieves had more utilitarian motives, but rarely to the same extent as the enterprising young man accused of stealing colleagues' textbooks in September 1934. It was established that he had taken a large number of books and that he had made 'a trade of stealing books and selling them.'

Stealing, unlike most other breaches of discipline, very directly affected the thief's fellow students. So, unlike the situation with smoking, the boys did not need to be encouraged to police one another. Evidently, a strict code of conduct obtained in this respect. For example, two boys accused by the Disciplinary Council of 'raiding dormitories' in 1923 had already faced a 'private meeting' of the senior students, where they had been convicted of stealing money, fined a half-crown each, and ordered to make restitution.

In cases of bounds breaking, distinctions were also made. It would appear that 'running away,' probably because it was often a reaction to separation, was treated less severely than 'going out town,' which merited an automatic and immediate expulsion. 'Going out town', of course, was often attempted in order to meet members of the opposite sex, something which also might have implications for discipline among Mercy and Presentation boarders. Such was the situation with the chivalrous fellows who were charged in 1924 with 'leaving the College grounds on more than one occasion without permission, and holding communication with Mercy Convent boarders.' They readily admitted the first charge, but denied that they met the Mercy students by arrangement, thereby protecting the young women from disciplinary procedures of their own. A 'Mayo footballer' was among those reported by a vigilant citizen — perhaps a jilted lover! — in 1937 for leaving the College to attend a Sunday night dance in Moylough. The footballer was not successfully identified, but two brothers from the Moylough area were, and they were promptly sent to pack their bags.

Apparently, there was a minor rebellion in the College in 1935. Details are scant — there are no clues as to the grievance involved — but it would appear that there was a half-organised attempt to boycott the College sports in that year. The incident was nowhere as serious as the 1911 outbreak; punishment, accordingly, was milder. Three students, all candidates for Maynooth, were questioned about their involvement. One of them was barred from entering the national seminary, while the significant blot on the records of the other two was brought to the attention of the Maynooth authorities.

One striking feature of the transactions of the disciplinary committee was the consistently feeble and far-fetched nature of the excuses, half-truths and blatant untruths offered by students who got into trouble. Among the least credible were the three who were discovered in the grounds by the Dean at 2.30 a.m on the morning of the summer vacation of 1923. When questioned, they admitted that they left the dormitory with the intention of going to the cinema. However, they insisted that they had changed their minds and had not left the College grounds. Their dirty boots they explained by claiming to have crossed the vegetable garden on their way to the refectory in search of food. Almost as unlikely was the tale spun by a boy discovered in his classroom with a lighted cigarette. He insisted that he did not smoke, but that he had been experimenting with a magnifying glass and had eventually succeeded in lighting a cigarette by directing sunlight through the instrument.

As was evident in his attempts to address the smoking issue, President Walsh was a disciplinarian who believed in consistently enforcing clearly defined rules. And from the beginning of his presidency, he set about raising academic standards by means of the disciplinary code. The Gilmartin rules of 1929 specified that students could be removed if their 'conduct or progress' was considered unsatisfactory. Even prior to that, parents were occasionally asked not to send back students who were 'wasting their time' in full-time education. Walsh transformed this vaguely accepted practice into a firm rule in 1930 when he decided that 'students who had been really unsatisfactory during the year should not be allowed back.' Six boys were immediately excluded under the new provision. On the same occasion, it was 'strongly recommended' to the parents of three others that they not be sent back, two were the subjects of 'special letters', one was given a 'special warning' and it was ordered that a thirteenth should be 'specially watched' during the following year. Similar, albeit usually smaller, culls were carried out in subsequent years.

Another incentive available to a rigorous presidency was a financial one. A large proportion of students were in receipt of burses and scholarships, and it was not unknown for students to lose these for a half-term or longer as a penalty for misbehaviour. In 1929, a student who handed up only a blank sheet of paper after his Latin exam had his scholarship suspended. The incident provoked discussion among the staff, resulting in a decision that all scholarship holders were required, on pain of losing same, to perform well in house exams and to achieve honours in the Intermediate exam. Four years later, another decision, described as a 'law' in the minute-book, ordained that scholarship holders were required to get honours grades in house exams.

Such developments served to increase the academic pressure on the students. This may have been one cause for the perception in 1932 that 'the tendency to copy at examinations had been on the increase for some years.' In the same year, an example was made of three who were caught copying during the Religious Knowledge test in the Easter house examinations. As punishment they were forbidden to sit the summer exams. They were also advised that they would not be accepted back after the summer, but this part of the penalty was later remitted. A fresh regulation resulted from the affair: 'any student found in possession of a book or notes at any examination will be left at home immediately.'

Several years passed before another incident of copying came before the Discipline Council. Again, the examination copied was in religious knowledge but this time, embarrassingly enough, the offence was discovered during the Concursus examination for Maynooth. Moreover, it was the culprit's comrades who spotted what was happening and later formally reported it. But, if the episode discredited the individual concerned, it reflected positively on the seventeen- and eighteen-year-olds who brought the complaint. Rather than following adolescent instinct and colluding or covering up for their colleague, they acted to protect the integrity of the examination. Arguably, the incident showed that they were well on the way to making the transition from school-fellows and to becoming disciplinarians themselves.

10. "...four was normal, six was considered a bit much..."

> *Recherche dishes deck the board,*
> *And Lar in shining livery bold*
> *Struts up and down with beaming smile*
> *Much like the Greeks of old*
>
> *"Pie Lar" ringing through the ref,*
> *"O, bring me pie not cold,"*
> *The College butler nods his head,*
> *Not like the Greeks of old*
>
> *O, Lares, Lares, have a heart,*
> *Dish out more pie not cold*
> *Since you fought at Oliphant*
> *Be like the Greeks of Old.*[1]

This chapter presents, under several headings, the direct testimony about their experience in the College of students who attended St Jarlath's between the early 1920s and the late 1950s. Interviews were conducted by the author with ten past pupils of that period: John Fitzgerald (1938-44), Padraic Folan (1952-57), Liam Kitt (1931-36), Conor Heaney (1922-26), Tommy Heraty (1935-40), Jim Kearns (1944-49), Patrick McMyler (1940-45), Jack Mahon (1945-50), Tommy Shannon (1945-50), and Paddy Williams (1940-45).[2] Additional material was found in the memoirs of Monsignor Horan and in articles of reminiscence in the Past Pupils' Union journal, *Iarlaith*.

"...a strong connection with the College."

...My only reason for going to St Jarlath's was that the parish priest at home in Westport called to tell my parents that, since I had won a Mayo county scholarship, the president of St Jarlath's would advise me to come to his College, where I would have a

---

1. From 'Lares and Penates' in a students' publication, *The Charioteer*, March 1946. Larry Kennedy was the College butler.
2. Unless otherwise indicated, the quotations which follow are from interviews with these ten men. Because several of the interviewees asked that some of what they said should not be attributed, I have not given more precise citation. Most of the extracts, of course, will be easily attributed by those who know the individuals concerned.

completely free education. That did not wash with me, because I felt that the school at home in Westport was equally good. But my father said to me: "If you're not happy there, you can come back home."...

...I was from Ballinlough, Co.Roscommon. There were no secondary schools for boys around my area, the nearest was Roscommon CBS. Cousins of mine had attended St Jarlath's, and my granduncle, a former P.P. of Castlebar, must have gone there too, but there was no great consciousness about it. So, there was that family connection and, anyway, Tuam was the obvious place to go to, being the diocesan school. I came from a small farm, and the opportunity came my way when an aunt offered to pay for me. She was a teacher and she wasn't married. I had another aunt too, in business, and she was very helpful. That's why I got to secondary school. My brother attended at the same time...

...I had a great desire to go to St. Jarlath's, simply and solely because they were just making a name for themselves in football, and we had football here from the cradle in Mountbellew. In other ways too, Jarlath's was cut out for us — having a grand-uncle who was president, having uncles, the Sheehys, who were all there. The girls went to the Presentation and I followed a brother into the College. There was never any doubt that I was going to St Jarlath's...

...I grew up in Westport but my people came from Louisburgh, and Louisburgh at that time was synonymous with St Jarlath's. There was more than twenty students from the area when I arrived. And there was a family tradition: we had a strong connection with the College. I had cousins who attended, and I had two uncles who were priests of the diocese who went there. They also had an uncle, Fr James Prendergast, who became parish priest of Athenry. And it even stretched back further, to his uncle Fr Richard Prendergast who died in the early 1900s as PP of Roundfort. Then there was his uncle, Fr Richard Prendergast also, who died around 1870, who must have been in the College very early on, probably in the 1820s. These Prendergasts were connected with John MacHale. Incidentally, my own sons attended later...

...Is it a paradox or a truism to say that my first memories of Tuam came from Louisburgh? But this was natural in a town where as mere schoolboys we were kept very much in our places by a migrant scholarly band. In our society, a new verb

Bishop Michael Browne throws in the ball for Connacht final versus St Mary's, 1940s.

Training in the snow for the 1947 All-Ireland final.

Goalmouth action from 1947 All-Ireland final.

All-Ireland Colleges champions, 1947. *Front row:* W. Flynn, S Morrison, P. Solan, V. MacHale (capt.) M. Flanagan, T. Lyons, S. Purcell. *Back row:* J. Flanagan, S. Shiel, M. O'Malley, Colm Canavan, C. MacHale, T.J. MacHale, T. Joyce, S. Jordan. M. Mooney (trainer).

Patsy Sheridan accepts the Hogan Cup, 1960.

Action from 1961 All-Ireland final versus St Mel's, Longford, at Athlone. Left to right (wearing white), Larry O'Brien (capt.), Paddy Gibbons and Jimmy Saunderson.

Action from 1982 All-Ireland semi-final versus St Mel's, Longford, at Athlone. Left to right (wearing white), Michael Molloy scoring a goal, and Martin Gallagher.

All eleven Hogan Cup winning captains pictured at function in Corrib Great Southern, Galway 1997, to mark the golden anniversary of first Hogan Cup success. *Front row:* Larry O'Brien (1961), Padraig Nolan (1958), Vincent MacHale ((1947), Pat Sheridan (1960), Senan Downes (1964). *Back row:* Padraig Joyce (1994), Rory O'Dwyer (1982), Henry gavin (1974), Jimmy Duggan (1966), Martin Joyce (1978), Mark Butler (1984). *Courtesy of Connacht Tribune.*

had crystallised — to "go to Jarlath's" — a verb strong, transitive and very indicative... It was as inevitable in our growth as to "wear the long ones", with which indeed it was associated — often, as cause with effect. To go-to-Jarlath's was distinction: by this a young man arrived... Sand ran on, and a time came when we joined the "college-lads" and henceforth ceased to notice. For the Tuam we got to know lived up accurately to the Tuam we had already known. The lay Baptism in the font in the recreation shed was a cold reality in our first new-suited days. There was the wet-day banter and horse-play at the seats inside the side-door; the reckoning of the "horse-power" of each other's chestnuts; the incessant kicking of a football at the junior goal; the accurate materialisation in the flesh of characters who were mere names or photographs at home; the notes passing to these names in study; the list of past monitors on a back page of the Dudley-Stamp with the present Professors' names underlined in red; the slant-eared deputation of Job's comforters moving abreast to hear you after your interview with the dean...[1]

...I grew up in Glenamaddy, a small village in North Galway and when I entered sixth class, all my classmates were going to some secondary school: one to Cavan, another to Garbally, a third to Castleknock. My parents — my mother in particular — having a certain amount of pride, felt that maybe we should have the opportunity too. It was quite difficult because a few years earlier, my nine-year-old brother had died of cancer, after a long illness; this meant that we were in debt. It took several years to clear the debt, and only for my mother's use of the gift that God gave her — which was to knit, and to knit awfully well — we'd never have made it. She used to go to shows all over the province, and she won lots and lots of prizes which swelled the income and enabled her, first to send my two sisters to the Mercy, and then to send me to St Jarlath's College. As it turned out, I did have an uncle — my mother's brother — who attended the College before 1920, but he wasn't a good student and I think he had to go to St Mary's to complete his studies. I wasn't aware of this, although my mother obviously was...

...I was the third of my family to go to St Jarlath's. My oldest brother did a lot of talking about the College, but it was my other brother who went in just a year before me who was probably the greater influence. He came home talking about the

---

1. Leon Ó Mórcháin, 'Grafted' in *Iarlaith*, 1959, pp.14-15.

things they did. I remember him describing an opera he was in and he came home singing these strange songs at Christmas...

...I had no family connection with St Jarlath's. Indeed, I had started to attend the Bish in Galway, when the curate in the parish, Fr Tommy Heraty, got to hear about it. He knew me as a mass-server, and he insisted that I go back to primary school and take the Gaeltacht scholarship exam. That scholarship led me to St Jarlath's. In the normal course of events, if I'd gone to a boarding school at all, it should have been to St Mary's in Galway, but our parish of Spiddal was in the archdiocese of Tuam, and it was unheard of at the time for anyone in the archdiocese to go to a boarding school other than St Jarlath's...

...My father came from farming stock, he joined the guards soon after the force was established — as a mounted policeman at first. And my mother was a nurse. She was the daughter of an RIC man and a distant connection of Canon Gunnigan, the president before Canon Heaney. My parents recognised that education was the most desirable thing as far as improving oneself was concerned. There's no doubt but that they made a great sacrifice in sending me — and my two brothers — to St Jarlath's. I would say, it was because St Jarlath's had a great reputation, and rightly so, at the time. Now when you think of Athenry, even though it was part of the Tuam diocese, not many went to the College. They tended to go to Galway schools, to the Bish and so on. They'd take the train in the morning at eight or nine o'clock, and that was that. So, it was primarily because they thought that they couldn't do anything better for me educationally that my parents sent me to Tuam. I should say that we had a tremendous teacher here in Athenry by the name of Walsh. When I went, at thirteen, to Jarlath's, we had three books of Shakespeare done and up the Theorem 21 in Geometry. I had no problem therefore, in fact, I hardly needed to learn another thing before Inter Cert. Dunmore would have been a close runner up but it didn't have a reputation anything like as good as that...

...My father was a primary teacher. He didn't get to attend St Jarlath's himself, although he had great regard for it. His ambition was for all five of us to attend the College and every single one of us won a scholarship. The day of the scholarship exam was the big day in our household, because of my father's interest and ambition. At this stage, he had got to know the president, Tim Gunnigan, and subsequent presidents, and he was able to anticipate the minds of the people who set the papers. He kept the papers from year to year and they were part of the teaching system in Dunmore school. But it wasn't purely a selfish thing of 'my family and no-one else', for a large number of other Dunmore students won scholarships to St Jarlath's. My own year was the best ever, for one of my class-mates took first place, and myself and another lad tied for second. So that was the way it went, and it was a big day. I remember the Saturday evening — the exam was always on a Saturday — my father and mother used to cycle into Tuam to get the results. I remember waiting with trepidation to see did I get the scholarship. I raced up the garden to run away, but I had to face the music anyway, and I found that I'd got second. I'd had no great belief, but he'd always have given you a trial run with previous years' papers.

"...overawed by the size of the seniors."
...And, of all times, I entered Jarlath's when there was a retreat among the students. That gave me a tremendous opportunity to get a good look at everybody. You weren't supposed to talk during the retreat but the boys used copious notes to communicate their needs. It was a strange thing for me, as an only son, to be away from home, but I didn't find the College to be very lonely. You see, there was a wonderful spirit among the boys; they all seemed to have a common purpose, that they were condemned to being in St. Jarlath's — that's the way they looked at it — and consequently there was an attitude of survival of the fittest...

...My uncle Patrick, who was home on holidays from the United States, hired a Model T Ford to take us to Tuam for the scholarship examination. We arrived there on the day before because the examination was due to begin at ten o'clock on the following morning and we didn't want to be late for it. On my first night my father and uncle brought me to a circus. It was a wonderful treat for me as I always enjoyed circuses. One of the compositions on the examination was 'My Journey to Tuam' which of course suited me down to the ground. I not only described my journey in the Model T motor-car, but I wrote on my visit to the circus as well. I do not know what marks I got for the composition but I could not have done too badly as I got my scholarship. My father wanted to bring me home after the examination so that he could buy me a suitcase, but the President of St Jarlath's, Fr Denis Ryder said I had to do with what I had and that I must stay the night. That night I slept in a big room called a dormitory. One of the other lads there was feeling very sorry for himself and he cried all night... On my second day in St Jarlath's I stood back watching the older students, and I was envious of them because they looked so confident, big and strong, and here was I just starting off...[1]

...At home, the College was referred to as 'Tuam': "I'm going to Tuam," was the colloquial way of saying you were off to St Jarlath's. I don't think we dwelt too much on what to expect when we got there. Of course, we were busy preparing for a few weeks, but we definitely regarded it as something to look forward to...

...You'd be overawed by the size of the seniors, in particular, because they looked to be monsters. When you came in, you were a 'Connor' and, although it didn't happen much in my time, you might be given a 'baptism'. You were immersed, your head put under a tap or whatever — a sort of initiation rite, I suppose...

...The loneliness was beaten away by the strangeness of it all, going into all these different rooms. And coming from a two or three teacher school you were overwhelmed by the size of the place. Even Tuam itself seemed big to us lads from Dunmore. I don't think I'd ever gone beyond Galway at that stage. You were meeting strange lads, then meeting the different teachers and different professors; it was all so new. Of course, we were in short pants at that stage, maybe for the first two years...

...I travelled to Tuam with a local taxi-man called Lar Curley. We drove down in the late evening, perhaps around five or six o'clock. There's very little about the first day that I recall, but I do remember that I'd got a new sportscoat and a long pants for the first time. Shortly after I got to the College, I slid down the bannisters from the very top, but waiting down at the bottom was the dean, Christy Langan. It was a case of six of the best soon afterwards. I also remember that the bell made a great impression on me...

...I certainly was overawed when I arrived in Tuam, there was no question about that. First of all travelling by train, it was my first time travelling by train — going from Galway to Athenry, change there, then on to Tuam. And arriving in Tuam late, because the results of the scholarship exam came out in mid- or

---

1. Micheál Mac Gréil (ed.) *Memoirs of Monsignor James Horan, 1911-1986*, Dingle 1992, p. 28..

late September. Therefore, I lost a very valuable opportunity to bond with the first years. That affected me, and indeed others, for our duration in the school. So I arrived late, with two others and it was certainly a traumatic experience. I remember arriving at about two o'clock, being met by the dean, Fr Christy Langan, and being bundled straight into a class. Because I was late, I didn't even get a bed by the wall in the dormitory, but in the middle row, where I felt rather vulnerable. I can't remember how I made friends in the first weeks, but when I did they were from small rural areas. Big numbers came from places like Dunmore, Milltown and Ballyhaunis, and they tended to stick together.

"...all shapes and forms of suitcases."
...I believe I am right in saying that no vacation, and no homecoming, can ever again equal the morning of that very first vacation. A hurried breakfast (not that the tempo of eating was ever too slow); a mad dash to collect all shapes and forms of suitcases; a long line of heavily-laden boys panting their way through slush and snow to the station. There had to be a break on the way of course, these shops had teased us long enough! And then that wonderful journey home. We were young boys again — young brothers and sons eager to be with their families...[1]

"...occasionally you might get an egg."
...The food was plain, good plain, honest food, Breakfast was after mass — usually porridge, tea and bread. It wasn't that different from home, sometimes you might get jam or whatever. Lunch and dinner were soup and potatoes. The tea again in the evening was like the breakfast, bread and jam, and that was about it, but occasionally you might get an egg. I used to go around the walks with my late friend, Paddy Kavanagh from Annaghdown and a group of others but I never heard them complaining: "I'm starved in this lousy place". Maybe some of the unfavourable comparisons arose after people went home for their first Christmas vacation when, naturally, they would have been spoiled a bit with turkey and so on. But I do think that generally the food was comparable with what people had in their own houses...

...I've often wondered since just why it was necessary for the professors to dine in the students' refectory. Or why, above all,

---

1. Thomas McCann, *Iarlaith*, 1959, p.58.

their table should be placed at the far end of the room, making it necessary for Larry, laden down with a tray of bacon and eggs, to walk the full length of the refectory under the eyes and highly-sensitive noses of ravenous teenagers. Nothing could be more calculated to foster self-denial. Small wonder that not a few failed the test. How well I recall the odd fearless student during meals gliding to the professor's table, and returning in triumph with his spoils. What matter if the booty, at times, consisted of no more than a few lumps of sugar and a few slices of golden pan-loaf...[1]

...We had dinner at about half past three or quarter to four. It could be something good or a total disaster, depending on where you were at the table, whether the thing was conducted in a civilised way or whether there was what we called a 'grab'. If there was a a 'grab' and you didn't get anything, you spent a hungry afternoon. So it was most unsatisfactory from that point of view. I can't remember the food particularly, but there were potatoes and there was meat. There was a monitor at each table. It seems to me that if you were at the bottom of the table, you got less than the person at the top. There was a certain amount of favouritism obtaining, I would say...

...The monitors cut the bread, while the proc handed out the butter. The proc also carved the meat at the table, and went around with the post at lunchtime...

...It was during the war years and conditions weren't the best — the food certainly wasn't the best. We used to get butter that you couldn't eat, it was rancid. At one point, they ran short of tea, so they gave us coffee. But when we got it first, we weren't used to coffee, and we couldn't drink it. But all we got was bread and butter and you needed something to wash it down, so you started with one or two sips of coffee, then you found you were taking one third of the cup, and finally you got to like the coffee. It was very good coffee, I would say. If you were well in with the monitor, you could get an extra bit of bread, and if you could collar an extra piece, it was customary that you got a knife and stuck it through the bread, and stuck it under the table and it would be there when you came back for the next meal. It was known as a 'feck'...

(...Travelling home at Christmas was a great adventure... Down in the cabin, the students from the three islands gathered and talked earnestly about school. Most of the talk concerned

---

1. Thomas McCann, *Iarlaith*, 1961, p.101.

food, or the lack of it, and it seemed to me that in comparison with some of the other colleges we were living in luxury in Coláiste Einde. Tales of hunger pangs from St Jarlath's College were particularly memorable.)[1]

...Our parents used to send parcels then because they realised that we weren't very well fed. St Jarlath's didn't have a good name for food. The parcel would contain things like fruit, fruitcake and various things like that. They were kept in a suitcase under the bed. So, quite often, if you didn't get anything to eat, you made for the dormitory, although you weren't allowed to. I remember that this friend of mine got a parcel from home, and on the same day we got a bad dinner. So we decided to go up afterwards to get something to eat. He went to the top of the stairs, and he beckoned to me that all was clear. But when we got to the top, there was the dean. We got six apiece, so we were both hungry and sore...

...During the winter of 1946-47, snow stayed on the ground for months and there was a bad outbreak of flu. There was a terrible air of depression everywhere. But you'd have to raise your hat to St Jarlath's for the way they tried to lift our spirits. On three days a week — Tuesday, Thursday and Saturday — they served us up a fry. I can still almost get the smell as it wafted through the corridors. Rashers, sausages, black pudding especially.

"...a certain combustible and habit-forming commodity."
...It was always an important day when you had a visitor who brought a 'mag' with him. A 'mag' could be anything from a sweet cake to apple and oranges. If a student was a smoker, a visitor might have cigarettes hidden in the 'mag'. Cigarettes were forbidden in the College and the dean often raided the toilets where the boys smoked...[2]

...But the Tuam town lads were the quietest of all; due, probably, to the fact that they were mostly day-boys, and to some degree, cut off from the social life of the College. And they were unlike dogs in this at least; they did not seem to feel stiffer near their own doors. Occasionally, too, it would happen in those wicked old days that certain burly boarders, whose wishes were

---

1. Breandáin Ó hEithir, *Over the Bar: a personal relationship with the GAA*, Dublin 1984, pp.43-44. The author did not attend St Jarlath's but met students from the Aran islands on their vacation journeys.
2. Horan Memoirs, p.32.

not lightly to be disregarded, would put a day-boy under bonds to smuggle into them, a certain combustible and habit-forming commodity which was strictly contraband. So, whenever we saw a day-boy returning from his dinner and the town, and looking as scared as if he had just burned down the town, sweet-shops and all, we knew that this was due to one or other of two things. He was carrying contraband, and he feared the authorities, or he was not carrying contraband and feared the disappointment of his patrons...[1]

...Jim Diskin in the pantry, and Larry Kennedy were important because they sold sweets — unofficially. People would order from them — there was no sweetshop in the College and if you went out to the pictures you weren't supposed to go into a shop — so they used to supply people on the quiet. And the day-boys, but there were only a few of them, they would bring in stuff too. You'd give the men the order when they were going out, and then afterwards the stuff would be handed out discreetly around the pantry area. They made a small amount of money, but never very much, a penny or two. I think it was mainly that they took pity on us. The practice was frowned upon, but a blind eye was turned as well. They were good workers, good at their jobs, so the sensible thing was to leave well enough alone. Then there were enterprising students who might get out town for some reason and get supplies — say the big toffee bars. Then they'd break them up and sell them at so much a square...

...One feature of study was that after an hour, people would start going out to the toilet. Only one was allowed at a time, and you'd see the smokers going out, in turn, for their little smoke. This, of course, was illegal, but there was quite a bit of smoking, among the seniors especially. The seniors, by and large, disapproved of juniors smoking. The Senior 'jacks' was the place for smoking; that or the old 'jacks' behind the alley. The 'jacks' was also the place for fighting, and there were a few notable fights where reputations were won and lost. There were gangs, I suppose, from the different areas and there might be no love lost between them. So the two fighting would be supported on by their own supporters. There was a very strongly identifiable group from Louisburgh, they went around in big heavy shoes, eight or nine together around the walks. They were called the 'Hoplites' [after the foot-soldiers of ancient Greece]. Ballyhaunis

---

1. M.J. Molloy, *Iarlaith*, 1955, p.30

would have had a big group as well, and Dunmore. The main friction, in my time, was between Louisburgh and Ballyhaunis...

...One night some of the boys were going out on the town but I refused to go and went to bed. They did not like this so when they came back and found me asleep they put a string around my big toe and tied it to the bed. Then they shook me awake; of course I woke with a start and nearly cut the toe off myself. That is the kind of thing that goes on where boys are concerned. You had to take it and offer it up. In St Jarlath's, and I suppose, all colleges, there was a kind of spirit that, no matter what happened to you, you did not report it. If you tried to get your own back by reporting it to the dean, then it was too bad because something else would happen to you...[1]

... It was almost accepted that on days that the seniors were playing a match — or maybe if the juniors were playing in Tuam — even first years and second years went into the Senior toilet, and they were given a cigarette. I can remember in my very first year, on the days of matches, Mick Flanagan, the Lord have mercy on him, giving me as many cigarettes as I wanted down in that area. I was never caught, but there were times when the dean came close to catching me — and he could be fairly severe, to put it mildly. But generally, a blind eye was turned to it and unless other factors put him in bad form, we got away with it.

"...it was rather easy to amuse us."
...But of all the old institutions that have gone, and not before their time, the one of whose going we would most approve was the long country walks. This was, perhaps, the most unpopular aspect of the whole college scene with the great majority of students. We had a walk every Sunday except when the weather was too bad or when influential seniors managed to arrange a match with the town. In either case, it was only a postponement, for we had to take to the country on a subsequent Wednesday, which was then the half-day. For all walks, we assembled in the ambulatory in ranks of threes or fours; and each student had to wear the regulation monogrammed cap, which sat I remember, most unsuitably on the heads of the seniors. Each rank took its place in the procession according to the seniority of its most senior member. During the walk every student was conscious of his seniority. At one end of the procession, there were opportunities to nip into a shop, purchase instant contraband and rejoin

---
1. Horan Memoirs, p.32.

the ranks unspotted... Like the captain of a wartime ship they alone [monitors] knew whither we were heading, but their lips were sealed. So while the dean was reviewing us and seeing to it that some measure of dressage was achieved, we prayed for rain and indulged in a guessing-and-betting game as to whether we would be gracing the Dunmore road, the Bermingham road, the Dublin road, the Ballygaddy road or the Tullinadaly road. As the mystery tour reached the Cathedral gates at Bishop Street, speculation was reduced by a third...[1]

...We got to the pictures about four times a year. I remember the first picture I got to was 'The Twenty-Six Martyrs of Japan'; the next was 'The Girl of the Golden West'. One picture we didn't get out to, a very good film I believe, was 'A Hundred Men and a Girl'. The dean, Tom Cummins, said it was "hopelessly masculine". We very much looked forward to these outings. These were special showings, the whole school would go out to the cinema, and there might be a chance to get a bit of chocolate or whatever...

...It was the day before we departed the College, known as the day of 'vak'. Now, extraordinary things were done in Jarlath's before the day of 'vak', as lads tried to leave their imprint on the place, so far as they could. That took the form of ripping up mattresses and pillows and other vandalism of that order...

...At the end of the year, there might be something we called a 'raid', when one dormitory attacked another, maybe during exams. It would end up with pillows broken, feathers everywhere, and the dean would arrive. Then there would be the sound of the cane down the corridor. That was enough to silence the whole place...

...The fourth years would make up a sketch and do it in the study hall the night before Christmas 'vak'. It was all simple and innocent; it was rather easy to amuse us. I remember one in particular was a take-off of a Marx Brothers film that we'd all seen. When it came to our own year, I remember a sketch which was probably based on another film we'd seen, but it had easily recognisable characters: Sammy Doyle, the science teacher who wore a bowler hat; Dr Tom Costello, the College doctor — he'd always get to you to stick out your tongue and say "Ah!", regardless of your complaint; another was a man who worked in the College, Jack Ridge. Anyway, this play was supposed to go

---

1. Kirrane, *Iarlaith*, 1966, pp.41-42

on for all of second study, but it was over in a quarter of an hour. We were stuck, but we were rescued by Leo Morahan, a senior who was accustomed to performing in Feiseanna. He took the Sammy character's top hat and the doctor's stick and kept the study hall in stitches for the next hour...

...On wet days we went to the rec. — the recreation hall — and walked up and down there, because we were discouraged from hanging around inside. It was a lot shorter than going around the walks, but as least you remained dry. The odd time we would have had a 'hooley' in the boot-room. There'd be Irish dancing, 'Siege of Ennis', 'Walls of Limerick' and so on, and sometimes a few songs. The chief musician was a very good accordion player, Purty Conneely from the Carraroe area...

...On a wet day, we'd put up the boxing ring in the boot-room — we had a proper ring. There were lots of good boxers. In fact, we did two things in the boot-room on wet days: we boxed and we recited poetry. We used to invite in competition from the town, people like Frankie Stockwell, who was the Irish lightweight champion for a number of years. He loved boxing in St Jarlath's, but few of us could match him...

...St Jarlath's College was, and no doubt still is, a very good place for observing parochial differences. There were recreation periods immediately after dinner and tea during which games were little played, and instead students walked around the great circular walk in groups of four, five, six, or even eight: walking rapidly, but unhopefully, like all prisoners... Except that in St Jarlath's silence was not required, and we gabbled like geese. Students from the same parish generally went around the great walk together, and this made it all the easier to study local characteristics. The Hollymount men were giants in those days, mighty men, and men of renown. Seven or eight strong they advanced in compact single line, swinging around the great walk with military precision and mighty strides. As the familiar thunder of their concerted size tens grew louder and nearer, the lesser groups from inferior parishes retreated into the grass margins and let them pass, basely preferring dishonour to death untimely. Not that these Hollymount lads were quarrelsome; on the contrary they were just big simple fellows to whom it had never occurred to go around a man or to go through him, or over him... At the opposite pole from the big simple Hollymount men were the Castlebar group. Not even in New

York or London subsequently was I to meet such metropolitan slickness and sophistication as I can remember in those youths from the Mayo metropolis. At a time when radio sets were rare, they had all the very latest in jazz tunes and gags and cinema slang and neckties and haircuts. Whereas we bog-trotters tended to think there was something effeminate in paying any attention to one's hair at all, and went around with hair like bandits, these Castlebar lads had their hairs cut according to plan, brushed and parted according to plan, and sleeked with hair-oils which smelt of all the perfumes of Arabia for their first hour, and thereafter of dead men's bones and all uncleanness...[1]

...Wednesday was the half-day for games, but I remember a particular afternoon when it must have been too frosty to play football. Instead, we were taken a few miles out the Dunmore road to Garrauns. It was a place which was subject to flooding and which had frozen over. We spent the afternoon sliding on the ice. It was one of the most enjoyable days that we had...

...I remember going out to chase hares one time. Fr Loftus used to go coursing in Castlebar and he wanted some hares. We went to some commons somewhere or other, and we had a great day out, ...

...Nicknames were widespread, nearly everyone had a nickname, and some of them were quite cruel. There were particular names, like 'Mad-eye' held by somebody in nearly every year and, I think that names like that affected the way that you thought about the person. A tall thin fellow might be called 'Hat-pin'...

...There were some mighty scraps, maybe between lads in Leaving Cert. Now sometimes these might be about rivalries on the football field, or rivalries about something else... Some of these scraps were quite serious. Many of these rivalries were let go until the Inter or Leaving Cert when discipline was looser, so scores might be settled then. I think that these fights went on entirely unknown to the authorities...

...We had many visiting shows. If there were any good artistes around, Jarlath's always made a point of engaging them. They were keen to expose the students to everything possible. We had Anew McMaster, vaudeville, the circus and so on. They would have been brought in to do a piece from what ever performance was going on in the town...

...I do remember us getting up at a desperately early hour —

---

1. Molloy, p.29.

were doing the Leaving Cert course with the lads who were doing the Leaving. You stayed in Senior One the next year...

...Honours maths, you did in the library, which removed it from the regular run of things. It was very much a minority interest and there was a certain mystique attached to it. Science wasn't really a serious subject at that time. If you wanted to do it after Inter Cert, you went out during night study once a week to the Science Hall, but you still mightn't take the Leaving Cert science exam...

...Fr Joe Cunnane was our teacher of Irish and he had a novel approach to teaching the subject. He would spend some time on grammar, and then he'd read an extract from a book. I've never been able to trace the book, but it had a character called Páidín Ó Ceallaigh and it was situated, I think, around Castlehackett. He read a paragraph every day and made us write it out that evening for presentation the following day. It was a beautiful book, but I've never been able to trace it. That was the way he did first year. He was very severe on grammar. He would mark an 'X' on the side of your exercise for major grammatical errors, and for that 'X' you were later rewarded, as it were. Being from the Gaeltacht, I was fairly good at Irish, so every week, I'd have four or five Irish essays to correct before they'd reach him. So I became popular in that way, by providing this service...

...The arrangement of benches and apparatus in the Science Hall was especially favourable to the successful (i.e. with impunity) carrying out of schoolboy pranks. Each generation will recall its own quota of diverting incidents. Most will recall that press on the far corner on the right which contained a large collection of chemicals. It did not take the inventive genius of some students very long to discover what particular combination of them produced the most odious smell. In our time we had an explosion which sent three students to the Infirmary for a week with burns. We were engaged in an experiment to show that when hydrogen burns, water is formed... However, we applied the match too soon and the three students in the front took the brunt of the explosion. However, they were eventually none the worse for wear and were the objects of much sympathy and interest in both students and staff. Through all such escapades, Mr Doyle showed considerable patience and forbearance...[1]

...And I would go so far as to say that pedagogy, the art of

---

1. P.Prendergast, 'Thomas F. Doyle', obituary, *Iarlaith*, 1961.

teaching as such, was not considered worthwhile — compared, for instance to the study of theology. Some of them were frustrated, they didn't like their job... However, a number of people there impressed me with their learning. But I cannot forget the two laymen, Mr Doyle and Mr Sullivan, who worked in very difficult conditions. They didn't have the back-up of strap or cane that the others had, so they taught by sheer dint of personality. They were interested in what they did and they didn't regard it as a purgatory: it was their life. But I don't think that they got the support that they deserved. For one thing, they rarely went into the priests' dining room. They were regarded as second-class teachers. I can't recall them ever sending anyone to a dean or a president, or having access to anyone higher to correct somebody. They never carried a strap, nor did they use any form of physical violence, something which could not be said of the others. I suppose there was another aspect to it. Some of the priests tried to be humane — I'm thinking in particular of Fr Mick Walsh in my time — but they had to change tack because the classes took advantage. So, perhaps, a certain amount of the harshness that was there had to be there.

"...trying to make gentlemen of us."
...Discipline was strict, but the regime was relatively humane. You'd get 'batters' if you were caught smoking, for playing cards, for prompting at study and, in instances, for missing something in class. But when you got 'battered', you didn't mind, you accepted it. Mostly you acted the hard man, and pretended that it didn't hurt you. Four was normal, six was considered a bit much, eight was unusual, anything more meant that the person had lost it...

...There was one thing lacking in my day. The priests were very much removed from the boys, and very formal in their dealings with them. Rarely would a boy be called by his Christian name, sometimes both Christian name and surname would be called out, but more often, the boy's Christian name would be unknown to the priest...

...At St Jarlath's one always had the reassuring feeling that life was stage-managed. The "parental supervision" so touchingly advertised in the College prospectus was indeed a reality and comforting, if occasionally uncomfortable. The scenes and movements, if not quite the lines, of the five-year drama were carefully prescribed and mostly adhered to. The days went by in a steady succession of study, recreation and sleep, punctuated by films and football matches, and given individuality by distance to or from 'vak'...[1]

...I have one example of how rigorously fair Doc Mooney was. It was while I was procurator and he was games master, and there must have been some little theft going on of football gear. Anyway, the Doc announced that in three or four weeks there would be an inspection of all property — shoes, socks, sports gear, football gear. You had to have a distinguishable mark, and they had to be in reasonable condition, they couldn't be rags. He made this announcement once a week until the fatal day, and said that he would give six to a man in senior grade, and four to a a man in junior grade who didn't have everything tip-top. Then the day came. Now my gear was pretty well marked, but my socks were not. I remember I dodged Irish class to darn my socks. Then we went into senior boot-room for the inspection and the first person for six batters was Brian M, the junior captain, with a brother on the staff, and from the same parish as Doc Mooney himself. Then he came to me, saying "I hope you have yours marked," which meant that if I hadn't, I would have got six too and my pride would have been hurt to the core. I realised that position would not have excused me. That sticks out to this day...

...A 'lob' was a winning shot in handball, but it was also the name given to a clout that you might get from a teacher. And some teachers were known to have a ferocious lob...

...He put us all out on the floor for not knowing our Greek and gave us all a 'lob' across the face. Now the man had pair of hands as strong as Christy Ring's. When it came to my turn, I screwed my face up some way, and he made me feel smaller by not hitting me at all. He said: "Musha, will you be a man". I ended up feeling disappointed that I didn't get the clatter...

...One of the things that Christy Langan taught us was table manners — during Sunday homilies, I seem to remember. It left an impression: the business of eating soup, and holding the spoon away from you; approaching cutlery from the the right, moving in; not using your knife like a *peann luaidhe*. He had a difficult task trying to make gentlemen of us, but he persisted...

...Our teachers were all tremendously talented men, very learned and extremely well qualified, yet they never made

---

1. John Higgins, *Iarlaith*, 1966, p.57.

much of it. The biggest virtue, we were always told we could have, was humility. And by and large, humility was practised. Archbishop Walsh used to give these sermons, around Latin phrases like *virtus in medio stat*, emphasising this point. And you very seldom heard a Jarlath's lad boasting.

"...leanings towards the priesthood."
...Tuam, you could say, was a religious town. You had the convents, you had the cathedral, you had the archbishop's house, you had the College. So you were always surrounded by men in black and you saw them reading their breviaries, saw that they were leading special lives. You had daily mass, you had certain special religious ceremonies in the Cathedral, you had religious exercises on a daily basis. It was pervasive, and you had little contact with the world outside. And when you went out to football matches, it was invariably to play another seminary — St Mary's, St Nathy's. There were two very solemn occasions in the year when the archbishop came in to present prizes, one for academic performance, one for sporting achievement. It was like the arrival of royalty. There was colour and pomp and ceremony attached…

…We were all brought out to the Cathedral every year for the anniversary of the death of John MacHale. There was a solemn mass of requiem celebrated with great solemnity, with Gregorian chant, with the archbishop in all his finery, with a catafalque built in the centre. For a young fellow coming from the country, this was an extraordinary sight and one that left a lasting impression — the solemnity with which it was done. Really, a lot of that as been lost since, the whole ceremonial aspect of things. Of course, the archbishop lived beside us, and as we went around the walks in first year we used to see him on his way to the cathedral in his red soutane. We were in awe, because it was something very new to us to see an archbishop…

…Even as a young lad at home in Glenamaddy, I would have thought of the priesthood. I used to go down from school every day to serve mass for the old PP — a lovely man — but my father was furious at my missing so much school. Then, there was a house across the road, where three of the lads became priests. Later, during College vacations I became friendly with the young curate in the parish. I had a lot of clerical company as a young man, so the possibility was always there in front of me. Of course, there weren't many other opportunities at the time, unless you decided to become a teacher or maybe go to university. At that time, therefore, I think everybody considered the priesthood — maybe as much in career terms, as in terms of a vocation, because our notion of what the priesthood involved was very hazy. Then in St Jarlath's a few times a year, men came around from Dalgan and sometimes from Kiltegan looking for vocations. It seemed the most natural thing in the world. You wouldn't be regarded as a 'holy joe' if you said you were going up to see the man from Navan or wherever. Of course the lads knew that if you did go up you got a cigarette. Monitors, above all, were expected to consider the priesthood. Early in Leaving Cert, you had to declare your hand as it were, when you sat the Christian Doctrine exam. At that point you had to decide if you were going to sit the Concursus, and if you sat out in the middle row during that Christian Doctrine exam, that said you were interested in Maynooth. And there would be no surprise if six, eight or ten lads in the Leaving Cert class sat out in the middle row...

...The monitors were held in awe. There were five of them, and a procurator. Generally they were remote people, with authority, and you didn't cross them. To be appointed a monitor was considered a great honour. Quite a few of them went to Maynooth. The whole place, anyway, was focused on Maynooth at that time, probably too much so. If you had any talent at all, you were expected to go to Maynooth, to give it a try anyway. It was very much a minor seminary, even in the subjects you studied. There was a strong emphasis on the classics, but no place for commerce, for example...

...Almost everybody would have grown up in a strongly Catholic home. People would have done the stations themselves as a matter of course during Lent. Then there was the Rosary every evening as well as mass in the morning. Of course, there would always be a few 'hobos', or whatever, who might be less devout, but they couldn't get away with much, because the rest of the lads wouldn't tolerate it. I remember one fellow appearing in a black suit in the last term. I suppose he intended going on for the priesthood, and his parents mightn't have been too well-off, so there was no point wasting money on a suit that wasn't going to get much wear. That wouldn't have been too exceptional. The majority — maybe twenty-five out of a class of forty — would have gone on to Maynooth, All Hallows, Carlow, or another seminary. Neverthless, nobody would ever say that they were thinking of becoming a priest. In fact, most fellows would pretend that it was the last thing on their minds until the very last minute. Everyone wanted to appear to be a hard man...

...It was never clear who might have leanings towards the priesthood. It was never obvious. There was an expectation that the high achievers would go on to the priesthood. And they did, so the expectation was not groundless. But I never discerned any real difference between the guys who became priests and the rest of us...

...There were thirteen boys anxious to go to Maynooth in my time. We sat a special exam called the Concursus and, of the thirteen, only four were allowed to go the Maynooth. The others went to All Hallows, Clonliffe and other Colleges. One class fellow of mine who wasn't considered good enough to go to Maynooth, but went to All Hallows, later became one of the youngest bishops in Australia...

...Twenty-six boys did the examination for Maynooth. there were only seven places and the boys who failed to get into Maynooth went to other Colleges to study for the priesthood. There was great activity among the missionary societies who sent speakers to St Jarlath's quite often. I remember Fr Whitney of the Kiltegan fathers and Bishop Shanahan from the African missions coming to speak to us. There were great efforts made to recruit students for the mission, and there were many vocations...[1]

---

15. Horan Memoirs, p.34.

11. "...Football is life."

It's May the fifth in '84,
And Jarlath's seek one Hogan more
We crushed the might of Cork's Chríost Rí,
And savour still that victory
So out ye boys, with captain Mark,
And give your best up in Croke Park
Bravo, well done, you'll hear us sing,
As home to Tuam the cup we'll bring[1]

In one sense, the St Jarlath's connection with the GAA is as old as the organisation itself. When Michael Cusack and his associates sought a suitable patron for their proposed new sporting organisation in 1884, it was Patrick Duggan, the Cummer-born and Jarlath's-educated bishop of Clonfert, that they first approached. Duggan declined on health grounds, but he nominated Dr Croke of Cashel in his stead.[2]

In approaching Duggan, the Fenians and fellow-travellers who founded the GAA had been seeking a figure-head rather than an active promoter of 'Gaelic pastimes'. The bishop of Clonfert's agrarian record made him acceptable to 'advanced' nationalists; his age meant that his involvement would be minimal; his office, it was calculated, would secure the support of a portion of the clergy for the enterprise. The much younger Croke fulfilled two of these criteria, and he was joined as patron by Davitt and Parnell who bestowed political credibility of their own. But, the machiavellian calculation of the founders notwithstanding, the GAA divided into Fenian and clerical wings in November 1887. Coincidentally, a meeting to establish a football club in Tuam was held in the same month.

In the circumstances, the meeting attracted the attention of

---

1. Lines composed by T. Shannon to encourage the 1984 Hogan Cup team and their supporters. Following the one point victory, another stanza was added by Fr Shannon and his passengers on the journey home: 'And now to you my gallant men, / Who've made this Hogan number ten, / Be sure your names we will recall / Fore'er within St Jarlath's walls / For now our dreams have all come true, / The greatest day for royal blue, / Bravo, well done, let's raise a cheer, / We won it in Centenary Year.'
2. P. Ó Laoi, *The annals of the GAA in Galway*, vol.i, 1983, pp.8-9; W.F. Mandle, *The GAA and Irish nationalist politics,* 1987, pp.8-9. A somewhat different perspective is offered by Marcus de Búrca in *The GAA: a history of the Gaelic Athletic Association*, 1980.

the clergy, not least because of a provocative episode in Dunmore a few weeks previously. Fenians in the village named their just-established football club in honour of Dr MacHale — a calculated insult both to their anti-Fenian parish priest, Jeremiah MacEvilly, and to his brother the archbishop. The administrator of Tuam, Fr Michael O'Connell, acted quickly to avert like developments in the cathedral town, persuading the new club to adopt association (soccer) rather than GAA rules. But his efforts only delayed by a few months the introduction of Gaelic football to Tuam. In April 1888, the Tuam Shamrocks began to organise in the rural part of the parish; in January 1889, the Tuam Star club was founded. By then, Fr O'Connell was president of St Jarlath's — and still hostile to the GAA.[1]

The Parnell split of 1890-91 deepened sporting tensions. Generally, the GAA supported Parnell while the clergy opposed him. In Parnellite Tuam, President O'Connell led the clerical rearguard, just as he had led opposition to the GAA. As we have seen, anti-Parnellites found shelter in the College when driven from the streets of Tuam. Meanwhile, soccer became a casualty of the crisis when members of Tuam F.C. abandoned their club to join the firmly-Parnellite Stars. Thus reinforced, Tuam Star proceeded to win five county titles in a row.[2]

The Gaelic code won the battle for hearts and minds, but clerical antipathy towards Tuam Star lingered on. In 1900, the College assisted the consolidation of a rival club, Tuam Krugers — despite its pseudo-paramilitary strip and Boer general's title — by allowing it the use of a field. Incidentally, the two town clubs merged in 1904 and, as Tuam St Jarlath's, took the county title in the following year.[3]

As Gaelic football became rooted in the College's hinterland, it was inevitably going to be adopted by students. This, evidently, had not happened by 1896 since Richard Kelly's account, which comprehensively described the 'ample accommodation for healthy sport' in the College, did not mention a football field.[4] Surviving team photographs, however, indicate that the

1. Noel O'Donoghue, *Proud and upright men*, n.d., pp.35, 43, 51-52, 72, Michael Leyden, *Dunmore MacHales*, 1983, pp.8-14.
2. *O'Donoghue's Men*, pp.122-9, 170-75.
3. ibid., pp.183-95. Incidentally, the Athenry De Wets was another club which identified with England's enemy by taking the name of a Boer general.
4. *Tuam Herald*, 24 October 1896.

game was played in the College early in the first decade of the new century.

The first game involving a St Jarlath's team of which we have an account was played in the College on Sunday 18 March 1906. The *Herald* report indicates that the students facing the 'hitherto unbeaten' Young Irelands, a Tuam under-age side, were not novices at the game. Playing with the wind, the town side scored the only point before the interval against a 'stubborn' College defence. The tables were turned in the second half, the students taking four points without reply, thanks to 'the good play of Messrs O'Donnell, Mongan, Kelly and Walsh.'[1]

Tim Gunnigan, who later became president of St Jarlath's, played football with the College during those years but, half-a-century later, he recalled that handball was far more popular among his contemporaries. Describing what they played on the field, he said it was 'very much a he-man's game', in which 'brawn was much more valuable than skill or science'. It was unrestrained, played mostly on the ground, and there was little combination play. And because they could expect little protection from partisan referees, players wore both ankle shields and shin-guards. Gunnigan remembered three regular matches a year, one against the town team, and a home and away fixture with the Franciscan Agricultural College in Mountbellew.[2] St Jarlath's usually won these encounters, but on one occasion — 'mainly by the efforts of the referee, Brother Dominic' — according to Gunnigan, Mountbellew were the victors. His recollections continued:

> While the College team were licking their wounds and preparing the return game, they looked around for a Tuam referee who could come up to Mountbellew standards. Finally, they selected Frank Guy — Dr Healy's nephew — who was then on the College staff. Frank knew nothing about the rules of the game, but he was willing to do his best for the home side. On the day of the game, he

---

1. ibid., 31 March 1906.
2. Mooney, 'Fifty years' football' in *Iarlaith*, 1955, pp.92-93. Timothy Gunnigan, a native of Aughamore, was ordained at Maynooth in 1915. After a year of post-graduate studies in the Dunboyne establishment, he was appointed a professor at St Jarlath's, where he remained until transferred to the parish of Westport in 1933. Between 1940 and 1947 he was president of the College. Thereafter, he was parish priest of Ballinrobe, and he was vicar general of the diocese on his death in 1966.

was as good as his word and really excelled himself when he disallowed the only Mountbellew score — a point — because it was too high! His reason had at least the merit of originality.[1]

Although there is no record, it is possible that there were encounters in those years between St Jarlath's and the Christian Brothers' school. Certainly, the latter trounced the second team of the town-based St Jarlath's club in 1908 by nine points to two.[2] The student teams would have been convenient opponents for each other.

If there was to be regular involvement in inter-collegiate competition, the attitude of the College authorities was critical. Away games, at least, could not have been played without both permission and active support. A new attitude is indicated by the expenditure in 1909 of 17/6d (82.5p) on 'goalposts for the students' — the earliest football-related spending noted in the account books.[3] And the appointment of Irish professor, Fr Michael Conroy, as president in July 1910 was extremely important as far as football was concerned. Conroy was a strong supporter of Gaelic games and, significantly, the annual report covering the first year of his stewardship was the first to refer to sport:

> I should like to mention also that games — Irish games — are not neglected here, and that in those healthy contests of physical energy, strength and skill, not less than in intellectual competition, our boys are well able to hold their own against the students of any other college. Last year both our seniors and juniors had a unique record — they never lost a match. And this is a matter of which we are very proud. We attach a good deal of importance to manly games, for we recognise their great value as educational factors in the fullest and best sense of the term.[4]

1. ibid.
2. *Tuam Herald*, 18 April 1908.
3. SJC, Expenditure Book, 1903-70, 23 October 1909.
4. *Tuam Herald*, 7 October 1911. Michael Conroy, a native of Omey, Clifden, came from a strongly nationalist family. He was ordained in 1883 and served in Castlebar for some years. From 1890 to 1892, he was a professor at St Jarlath's. After 1892 he served in Omey, Clare Island, Bekan and Ballinakill. He returned as a professor to the College in 1905 and succeeded Michael Higgins as president in 1910. In 1915, he was transferred to the parish of Kilmeena and in 1929 to Athenry. He died there, a canon, in 1938 at the age of 79.

Fr Conroy's remarks show that participation in inter-college games was regular enough by 1911. But if he recognised the 'educational factors' associated with sport, it was a belated recognition, coming half a century after such observations became commonplace throughout the Anglophone world. In order to appreciate why this was so, it is necessary to consider the broader context.

Boarding schools, specifically public schools, played a seminal role in the codification and popularisation of sport in nineteenth century Britain. Games were consciously integrated into the curriculum of many such schools since the 1850s. And the need to justify what was a radical departure led to the emergence of an ideology of athleticism, which in the process of devising an educationally-justifiable philosophy, linked sport to Britain's imperialist project. This development was linked to change in society at large. Traditionally, public schoolboys had run free in the countryside, hunting, fishing and stealing chickens as fancy took them. Population growth, industrialisation, the commercialisation of agriculture, made such behaviour impractical as well as undesirable. In these circumstances, organised games — with rules which confined them to school grounds — were introduced as instruments of social control. To two such sets of rules, both rugby and association football can trace their gestation.[1]

Catholic boarding schools, even English Catholic public schools, had rather different traditions. Their regimes were based on the continental seminary model, which had always stressed discipline and took definite school boundaries for granted. Fresh air was consumed in formal walks rather than in the course of poaching expeditions, so there was no particular need for their authorities to encourage games. In time, however, Catholic college students fell under the influence of the prevailing athleticism.[2] And when such students grew into the next generation of educationalists, many of them became active promoters of sport.

But such enthusiasts in Ireland, even those who were otherwise irreproachably nationalist, were not necessarily promoting Gaelic games. For one thing the GAA was a relatively late arrival: both soccer and rugby were played in Ireland during the

---

1. J.A. Mangan, *Athleticism in the Victorian and Edwardian public school*, 1981, pp.13-28; Richard Holt, *Sport and the British: a modern history*, 1989, pp. 74-86.
2. Mangan's *Athleticism*, pp.58-66.

1870s. And in its early years, the GAA was too easily distracted from the task of codifying and popularising its games. To the uncertainty in diocesan colleges about whether it was quite proper for seminarians to participate in the rough-and-tumble of team sport, was added the suspicion that the GAA was no more than an elaborate recruiting arena for Fenianism.[1]

The early GAA embraced athleticism, adapting the ideology to its own needs.[2] In the minds of the radicals who founded the organisation, the priority was not the moulding of a colonial elite, but the creation of a great mass movement at home. From the beginning, therefore, the GAA was self-consciously democratic and, at the same time, critical of elitism in other sports' organisations. It was more concerned to recruit the mass of tenant farmers' sons and artisans, than to cultivate the small upper- and middle-classes. Consequently, by the time the partisans of the GAA began to pay any attention to the matter, 'foreign' games, especially rugby, had sunk substantial roots in Irish second-level schools. In 1911, it was considered necessary to inaugurate an 'Irish games in Irish schools' campaign in order to win back lost ground.[3] By then, Gaelic football was becoming securely established in St Jarlath's, if not in certain other schools in Connacht.

As if to emphasise the enhanced status of football, President Conroy took the train to Ballina with the seventeen-member college squad for a game with St Muredach's in March 1911. The game was the second leg of a competition against the Killala diocesan college. Both games were mentioned in the *Herald* and were, as far as has been established, the earliest inter-college Gaelic football matches involving St Jarlath's to receive newspaper coverage. Unfortunately, the report of the first round, played at Tuam's Parkmore, was rather perfunctory. The encounter, refereed by a Muredach's student and described as 'very exciting' with 'much give and take', was won by St Jarlath's on a score of 1-1 to 0-1.[4]

1. Mandle's *GAA*, pp.1-17; Corish, *Maynooth*, p.229.
2. In the words of one writer: '...the GAA, in expressing a range of unblemished Irish nationalist traits that involved the outward rejection of all things British, adopted wholesale the British model of codified sport and sporting organisation, and an intensely British ethos towards sport'(Mike Cronin, *Sport and Nationalism in Ireland*, 1999, p.80).
3. *The Leader*, 2 December 1911. A Munster Colleges Hurling and Football League, —which was independent of the GAA— was formed in December 1907. The GAA Congress of 1909 approved the playing of College championships; in 1910 a Leinster Colleges Committee was formed.
4. *Tuam Herald*, 11 March 1911.

A much longer account of the away game told a lot about the train journey, about the town of Ballina, about the dinner and post-prandial speeches but, except for the information that St Jarlath's were the victors, revealed little of events on the field. The writer, probably a member of the College staff, was no connoisseur of sporting skill, given his observation that 'the game was like all good games, with just the names of the players changed'. However, he was clearly entranced by the spectacle, finding it 'wondrous and awe-inspiring to see the ball whisked from the feet, or perhaps from the hands, of the young contestants, and whirled over the field'.

But if our source lacked expertise as a sports commentator, he became an instant devotee of athleticism:

> Football is life: apart from the health value of the games, much inter-collegiate foregatherings are the pulling down of barriers, the making and binding in warm young hearts, just on the threshold of the maze-fraught world, of life-long friendships. The young fellows who play these senior matches will be thrown together in great seats of learning, in professions, ...either in the kindly motherland or in exile, and they will befriend, encourage, counsel, and if weak nature needs it, uplift one another for the memory of the good old days.[1]

After welcoming his guests to the post-match dinner in St Muredach's, the president, Fr Naughton, expressed the hope that contests like the one just ended 'might become general in Connaught, perhaps in Ireland'. And President Conroy in his reply was less than orthodox in suggesting as a suitable motto for such a departure Oisín's legendary riposte to St Patrick: 'Strength in our arms; truth on our lips; purity in our hearts'. The team captains next spoke and they advanced the discussion by suggesting further matches. Before dinner ended, firm plans had been made for a provincial colleges championship, with one guest, Dr Keane, going so far as to promise to provide the cup for such a competition.[2]

Years passed before the plans made in this genial atmosphere came to fruition, but informal inter-college competition continued. One has to wait until November 1913 for the first adequate

---

1. ibid., 1 April 1911.
2. ibid.

report of a game involving St Jarlath's. It was a second leg of a fixture with St Flannan's of Ennis, whose team travelled by train to Tuam. Clearly, the writer was not one of those who regarded one game as being like all others:

> The home team pressed, but a sound defence kept the Jarlaths at bay. Fast exchanges followed... neither side had much advantage and the pace was terrific. A quarter of an hour elapsed when the superior speed and stamina of the Jarlaths broke through a vigorous defence and notched a point... The advantage was followed up and a goal was soon afterwards registered. The boys of St Flannan's, while not losing heart, seemed unable to cope with the strategic passing of the St Jarlath's, although they manfully strove to break through several times. The second half witnessed a wonderful improvement in Clare's brigade... They possessed plenty of doggedness and grit but were unable to handle the ball with the knacky facility of their opponents.[1]

The final score was 2-3 to 1-2 in favour of the home side, with the winning tally being contributed by Doyle and Clancy. Speed and skill triumphed over 'doggedness and grit'. This 'splendid exhibition' the writer insisted was a powerful argument in favour of the introduction by the Connacht Council of the GAA of a 'provincial Gaelic championship for our High Schools'. Such an initiative, he argued, was especially urgent since 'in certain schools in Sligo' boys were 'being coerced into playing foreign games'. St Jarlath's, by contrast, was managed by a president who was 'an enthusiastic supporter of Gaelic pastimes' and staffed by professors who were equally committed to the cause. In these circumstances, the writer predicted that the College team — an 'unbeaten combination' whose scalps included those of junior county finalists, Tuam Fianna Éireann — could be relied upon to make a bold bid for the Connacht title when it was inaugurated.[2]

Notwithstanding the increased interest in football of the College authorities, team selection remained in the hands of the

---

1. ibid. 29 November 1913.
2. ibid. Incidentally, when the GAA did begin to seriously attend to the position in the colleges a decade later, it was in order to enforce a ban on 'foreign games' in Gaelic-playing Colleges (see Fleming & O'Grady, *St Munchin's College, Limerick, 1796-1996*, 1996, pp.203-04).

students. And team strategy, insofar as it was considered at all, was entirely a matter for the captain. Gabriel Murphy, who represented St Jarlath's on the football field between 1915 and 1917, later described how the team was constructed. Evidently, it was a rather convoluted process, and not one that was guaranteed to produce the best possible team. Captains were selected at the beginning of the year by popular vote; then the remaining members of the previous year's team got together to select a few more. The expanded group selected the last two full members of the team. Three substitutes were then chosen, two on merit and one by popular election. The first sub, because he might be expected to get a game, had no additional duties, but the second and third were responsible, respectively, for the team strip and for the boots.

Murphy's memory was that just one game a year was played involving Collegiate opposition against, alternately, St Nathy's, St Flannan's and St Mary's. For this highlight, the team 'hardened up' by playing games against the Tuam Star club. A limited amount of gymnastic training was undertaken, there was fielding and target practice, but for general fitness, players depended on regular, hard-fought games of handball.[1]

Expenditure on travel to matches by the College would indicate that games were rather more frequent than Murphy remembered. In this context, it should be borne in mind that home games, which amounted to at least half of those played, left no trace in the accounts. Between 1915 and 1920, train fares were paid for away games as follows: Ennis, 2 November 1915; Ballina, 15 April 1916; Ennis, 18 November 1916; Ennis, 2 November 1917; Galway, 1 December 1917; Ennis, 6 November 1919; Athenry, 26 March 1920. At that point, according to a contemporary, the Black and Tans 'brought an end' to the annual fixture with St Flannan's. But, by 23 March 1922, it was considered safe to travel to Athenry again. For the game held on that date, if the venue is an indication, the College's opponents were either St Mary's or St Flannan's.[2]

This was an important match, probably the first to be held following a meeting in Galway's Railway Hotel during February, at which it was decided to inaugurate a Western Colleges championship under GAA auspices. St Jarlath's was

1. Gabriel Murphy, 'Football in Jarlath's fifty years ago' in *Iarlaith*, 1966, pp.50-55.
2. SJC, Expenditure Book, 1903-70.

represented at that meeting by the dean, Father Killeen; other delegates came from Garbally, from St Mary's and from St Flannan's.[1] The timing of the meeting was not auspicious, however, and the Western Colleges competition was not the only sporting casualty of the Civil War which broke out later in the year.

Fr Killeen recalled that during the years that followed, the College 'had once more to rely on friendly matches.' The expenditure records would indicate that these were few and far between during the remainder of the 1920s, and only for a match in Ennis on 30 April 1928 was the destination noted. Because of its location on the railway line, Athenry was the favoured location for games during the period. And since it was a neutral venue, there was no need to play home and away rounds in each challenge. But if Athenry had advantages as a venue, it also had disadvantages. Dr Michael Mooney spoke to veterans who recounted that on the occasions of games in Athenry, the players on getting off the train had to look for a field, obtain goal posts, mark the ground, obtain a referee and then have the match finished in time to catch the evening train to Tuam.[2]

Some of this pressure might have been relieved by the new mode of transport adopted towards the end of the decade. During December 1929, £4.10.0 was paid to the Connemara Bus Co. with the explanation: 'for football match'.[3]

'Friendly' games during the 1920s retained several of the conventions of the previous decade, as described by Gabriel Murphy. Although it was usual that teams field one member of the professorial staff, games were still under the control of the students with captains, for instance, still being chosen in an annual election by the boys.[4] Such traditions, however, were an early casualty of the decision of new president, Canon Joseph Walsh, to enter the College in the just-established Connacht Colleges competition in 1929. Things would never be the same again. The first indication of a completely new approach, was the appearance in a coaching capacity on the senior pitch of one of the professors — a phenomenon which provoked 'amazed surprise' among the rest of the students. But it was soon commonplace to see Fr Malone 'teaching the "big fellows" how to

1. Mooney, 'Fifty years', p.93.
2. ibid., p.94-95.
3. SJC, Expenditure Book, 1903-70.
4. Murphy, pp.54-55; Mooney, 'Fifty years' p.94.

field and kick a ball properly and explaining to them a few points of match-winning technique.'[1]

A quarter of a century later, the then games master and future president, Dr Michael Mooney, took the trouble to trace the story of football in the College. He collected reminiscences from four aficionados of the game, fleshed them out with the fruits of more casual conversations, added his own memories and opinions and, under the title 'Fifty Years' Football', published a substantial account in the first issue of the Past Pupils Union journal *Iarlaith*. The result was an extremely valuable resource, which the compiler modestly insisted was not a history, but merely 'some impressions.' A few of these impressions — Gunnigan's and Killeen's — we have already encountered, but of especial interest is the account provided by Fr Malone, the College's first games master.[2] Given Malone's seminal contribution, it is noteworthy that he considered that it was his work with the previously neglected 'Connors' which provided the foundation for the College's success during the 1930s:

> It all began from the Sunday walk. Everybody (including the Dean) hated the dreary procession through the town to Gardenfield, or Birmingham, or around by Ballymote every Sunday and Wednesday, but there was nothing else to do, or more correctly no other way to keep us out of mischief. So, to kill the walk, we started to reorganise the games. Three sections were already in existence but the Connors or minors were hardly receiving their due rights. They were confined to a narrow strip of ground below the lower walk and did not dare to appear on the other fields except perhaps to stand behind the goals and fag the ball for their lordly betters. We moved the juniors across the wall and now the Connors had goalposts in their own proper pitch and a ball strictly their own — and a league for themselves. They took themselves very seriously. I remember the solemn conclaves that were held to draw up the Minor League... [The] foundation of our prowess was laid in the minor field. Progress from minor to junior and

---

1. Mooney, 'Fifty years', p.95.
2. A native of Westport, Michael Malone was ordained in 1922. He served in Kilkerrin, Cashel and Clonberne before being appointed dean at St Jarlath's in 1929. After leaving the College in 1936, he served in Claremorris and Glenamaddy. He was administrator of Knock (1947-56) and parish priest of Kiltullagh from 1956 until his death in 1966.

to senior field was made under the most critical and searching scrutiny from the whole house. Many a night, after lights out, as I strolled quietly along the corridors, I could hear the heated discussions on the merits of the candidates for the Senior team going on in the rooms. Often I heard myself quoted in support of one or other of the candidates — and my judgement rejected with scant respect. But I had the satisfaction of knowing that they had two absorbing interests — healthy sport and a pride in their College.[1]

So, after a two-decades-long flirtation, St Jarlath's firmly embraced athleticism in 1929. But it was the allocation of responsibility for sport to a member of the staff, rather than the participation in formal competition, that should be considered the important departure. In this regard, it is significant that there were echoes of the nineteenth century public schoolmaster's language of social control in Fr Malone's subsequent justification of his efforts — inculcating 'pride in their College'; keeping boys away from mischief; an emphasis on the 'healthy' consequences of participation in games. And the development was as sudden as it was unequivocal. If young Michael Mooney was shocked to witness a 'Pro' taking charge of senior pitch, one of his contemporaries later recalled that during a specific term in his first year, football definitively replaced the 'famous walks' in the country on the College's weekly schedule.[2]

Success was not immediate: St Jarlath's was defeated by St Nathy's of Ballaghadereen in its very first Connacht Colleges match; in the following year, the team fell to Sligo's Summerhill in the Connacht final. The support for junior and minor players had begun to pay dividends by 1932, however, and the College took its first Connacht title in that year, without a single score being registered against its team. It was the first in a remarkable run of successes and the Connacht Senior cup remained on the sideboard of the 'Pro's Ref' in St Jarlath's for the rest of the 1930s. Fr Malone believed that his teams of those years were the best ever produced by the College, and with score-lines like 9-8 to 0-0 and 3-15 to 0-0 to support his argument, it would be foolish to disagree. Imitation, the only worthwhile form of flattery, was one product of success, and Fr Malone was satisfied that

---

1. Mooney, 'Fifty years', p.95.
2. McCann, *Iarlaith*, 1959, p.58.

his teams' example in the early 1930s changed the style of football played in Connacht. It is not entirely clear what aspects of the College's game he saw adopted by county teams, because Malone was critical of the persistence of individualism at that level, something he contrasted with the team-work of College teams. On his sides, he insisted, there were 'no solo runs to catch the gallery but disorganise your own team', nor was there any 'running around the field to take all the frees and pile up a tally of scores for yourself.' Rather:

> We had the stars in each team, but they never tried to shine at the expense of their fellows. They played to the plan arranged before-hand and at the post-mortem, anyone who tried to steal the lime-light at the expense of victory was severely dealt with by his fellows.[1]

Preparation for games in the 1930s was a laborious, but fascinating process which included something called 'Swedish drill' on wet evenings in the bootroom, 'physical jerks' carried out on an old mattress and 'a little bit of boxing' which was discontinued when the students began to take it too seriously. Strategy came from a rather eclectic scrap-book nick-named 'the Koran' which contained everything from action photos of leading players to cuttings about such rugby and soccer tactics as might be adapted to the Gaelic football field. Innovation was the Holy Grail, and, apparently, at least a degree of individualism was permissible:

> Every year we tried something new. Someone always discovered some new plan to pull out of the bag when the other Colleges had caught on to our old trick. There was always the incentive to be as good or better than the hero of last year's win.[2]

One of the football 'stars' of the period, Fr Liam Kitt, describes Malone as being a 'genius' who was 'at least a generation ahead of his time,' in believing that every player should be able to utilise 'both hands and both feet'. This belief extended to his having players' dominant foot 'tied up' in some way, thereby forced them to develop the other. He was single-minded, almost obsessive, in pursuit of excellence and if a player had a

---
1. Mooney, 'Fifty years'
2. ibid.

Rory O'Dwyer (wearing white), senior captain, 1982.

Going to the match.

Senior 'B' team, 1989. *Front row*: A. Coyne, R. Dolly, A. Glynn, P. O'Reilly, R. Slevins, D. Byrne, G. O'Neill, G. Gannon, D. Parsons, B. Fallon. *Back row*: A. Grimes, F Moffit, A. O'Toole, E. Flynn, F. Moran, M. Rooney, L. Reddington, S. McGee, P. Gallagher, J. O'Hagan, M. Burke, A. O'Grady, C. Murphy, Terry O'Regan.

The agony… …the ecstasy…

…and the picnic. Supporters on the road to Dublin for the 1999 All-Ireland final.

Padraic Joyce accepts the Hogan Cup from Michael Fahy, following 1994 Colleges final.

Hogan Cup final versus St Pat's, Maghera, 1994. Left to right (in dark shirts), Derek Reilly, Michael Cloherty, Mark Waldron.

The Master looks on. Seán Purcell at the 1994 All-Ireland Colleges final.

All-Ireland 'B' hurling champions 1972. *Front row*: John Carroll, Paul O'Shea, Michael Hogan, John Hehir, John Power, Tom earley, Fred Power, Paddy Mullery, Peter Walsh. *Back row*: Niall Barrett, Dermot O'Loughlin, Morgan Hughes, Breandán Walsh, John Flaherty, Padriic Walsh, Liam Whyte, Frank Daly, Eddie O'Shea.

Past pupils from the Galway senior footballer team visited the College with the Sam Maguire, September 1999. *Front row:* K. Fallon, R. Silke, B. Silke. *Back row:* P. Griffiths, J. Long, M. Cloherty, M.Donnellan, T. Joyce, O.Hughes, J. Fallon, S. de Paor, T. Davin.

Training for the 1999 Colleges football championship.

Pictured at the premiére of *Archie Dean,* December 1997: Noel Kirrane, musical director; Peter Kennedy, composer; and Joe Donoghue, producer.

My Fair Lady, 1996. Neil Carney as Prof. Higgins, Clare Waldron as Eliza Doolittle.

College of Science Cup winners for All-Ireland senior athletics, pictured with All-Ireland finalists at intermediate and junior level, Santry stadium, Dublin, June 1972. Front row: J. Power, E. Murphy, B. Walsh, F. Harty, T. Earley, D. Nee, E. Comer. Back row: F. Power, C. Dunning, H. Campbell, T. Vaughan, H. Gavin, E. Diveney, P. Walsh, G. King, P. Bracken, P. Durkan, P. Jordan, A. Hennelly, G. Hennigan, Unidentified, E. Campbell, J. Flaherty.

Padraic Jordan in the house sports, 1974.

Clearing a hurdle in Tullamore.

Tony Waldron and Michael Leyden in *The Arcadians*, 1961

Tom Casby with members of the chorus in *Pirates of Penzance*, 1965.

College Cooks. Chef Pat Cleary and Rita O'Rourke.

John Kilgarriff with potatoes.

President Michael Mooney with College employees, Jack Ridge and Máirtín Harte, 1960s.

Sisters Barnabas, Justine and Rosalie of the Sisters of Christian Retreat Order, pictured at a reception to mark their departure from the College, 22 December 1986.

Presidents, 1947-1994: Michael Walsh, Michael Mooney, Conor Heaney, Tommy Waldron, Dermot Moloney.

Members of the Leaving Cert class of 1965 reunited on P.P.U day, 1990. Front row: Eamonn Waldron, Seán McGarry, Pat Finnegan, John Joe Brady. Second row: Dennis Hannon, Joe Donoghue, Tom Crowe, Jack Morris. Third row: Martin Flatley, Frank gaynor, Frank Reynolds, John Mooney, Donal Igoe. Back row: Seán Mannion, Mattie Gannon, Martin Shannon, Pat Halvey.

particular skill or talent, such as the remarkable 'shift' or feint possessed by Mike Heaney, other team members were required to spend hours in attempting to emulate it. And when he ran out of ideas, Malone wrote to past masters like John Joe Sheehy, Paul Doyle or Larry Stanley seeking tips and advice. Tactics were carefully worked out around the talents and other attributes of team members — if there were tall players he adopted a direct approach utilising what he called the 'backbone of a fish' formation; if the team was small, he had them play the wings. Training sessions used the field and the bootroom, but also the classroom blackboard.[1]

Fr Tom Cummins[2] took over as games master in 1937, and steered the team to Connacht titles in 1938 and 1939. For a generation of students — even for some members of staff — the notion that the seniors could be defeated was becoming inconceivable. But defeated they were by Roscommon CBS in 1940, after winning eight titles in a row.

On Sunday 18 February, the St Jarlath's squad had travelled confidently to Roscommon; indeed Fr Cummins regarded his charges as among the best combinations ever fielded by the College. But, in a game characterised by close marking, the visitors did not succeed in registering the extent of their early superiority on the scoreboard. During the first half, four or five easy points were missed, a goal was disallowed and, at the other end, a penalty kick was saved. This left the home team ahead at the interval by 1-1 to 1-0. A goal immediately after the restart augured well for St Jarlath's, but it proved to be their last score. Roscommon, meanwhile, managed to add three points to their tally and were leading by a point in the closing minutes. A Tuam free from inside the fifty yard line threatened to equalise matters, but the scoreline remained: Roscommon CBS, 1-4; St Jarlath's, 2-0.[3]

On the following morning, still in mild shock, the monitors approached President Joseph Walsh to request what had become the customary free day following the Connacht final.

---

1. Kitt interview.
2. Moylough-born Tom Cummins was appointed prefect of studies at St Jarlath's following his ordination in 1935. From 1936 to 1944, he was dean of the College. Between 1944 and 1971, he served in Westport, first as curate and then as administrator. He was P.P. of Lackagh from 1971 to 1981, when he retired to Castlemagarrett. He died in 1990, having been a Canon since 1967.
3. *Connacht Tribune*, 24 February 1940.

According to a member of the deputation, they were refused the privilege, then scolded for 'being no better than a crowd of old women' and for 'letting down the College very badly'.[1]

There was consolation for eight members of the 1940 team, who were selected — along with two from Summerhill of Sligo, two from Coláiste Einde of Galway, and one each from St Joseph's of Galway, Tuam CBS and Roscommon CBS — to represent Connacht in the All-Ireland Colleges inter-Provincial competition. They played an Ulster selection in the semi-final in Tuam's Parkmore and went on to meet Munster at Tralee in the final. By all accounts, the St Jarlath's midfield pairing of Liam Hastings and Tom Byrne was crucial to the victory which brought the inter-provincial title to Connacht for only the second time.[2] In the absence of a national inter-Colleges championship, this competition enjoyed a very high status during these years.

A Connacht Colleges junior championship was introduced in 1939 but, at first, fixtures were not always easy to fulfil because of travel difficulties during the war years. Roscommon CBS, meanwhile held on to the Senior cup for three years, but it was won back by St Jarlath's in 1943, the last year of Cummins's reign as games master.

While victory in competition was almost insisted upon in St Jarlath's, by everybody from the lowliest 'Connor' to the president, such competition was still only the tip of the footballing iceberg in the College. Senior and junior teams were supported by a vibrant footballing culture — of Leagues, of 'stumps', of incessant kickabouts. One indication of the pervasiveness of football in the institution was the coining of a disparaging word to describe the minority who did not play, whether because they were bookish, lazy or just plain awkward — they were the 'bowjers'.[3] But even bowjers, according to one who belonged to that select band, were knowledgeable enough about football and were as fiercely loyal as anybody else to College teams. For non-bowjers during the 1940s, every spare moment was spent kicking football. Even for the five or ten snatched minutes of morning break, one former student remembers, the majority ran on to the pitch in their ordinary clothes. Longer intervals provided enough time to play a

---

1. Heraty interview.
2. *Tuam Herald*, 9 March, 13 April 1940.
3. Fitzgerald interview.

match, and it was not unknown for an enthusiast to play up to four matches on a Sunday.[1]

Dr Michael Mooney, a member of the 1933 team, was appointed to the College staff in 1943, and became games master in the following year. His approach was 'to inculcate the lessons, particularly in forward play, which I had picked up from Father Malone.' His methods also owed something to those of his mentor: 'We used the blackboard, the copybook, newspaper cuttings, quotations from Caesar and photographs, and then tried out our skill with the town team.'[2] One stalwart of the Mooney era, Jack Mahon, later recalled his trainer's style:

> From mid-October on, he never missed a training session. By training, I mean a game among ourselves, a game with the town team..., or some kind of game. We never used any kind of physical training other than ball play. Dr Mooney watched from the sideline. He did not shout insults at any game but quietly took you aside afterwards and told you to combine more or to move after you passed the ball so as to be available for the return pass. He was the complete team manager, sole selector and he kept us informed with his notices on the College notice-board meticulously written in his familiar turquoise blue Quink ink. As class ended you ran to the board to see what was on next, where you were selected.[3]

Victory was no less Mooney's objective than of his predecessors, but not victory at any price. Mahon recalled:

---

1. McMyler interview, Shannon interview; Folan interview. An annual 'bowjers' match' has been played intermittently in the College, with teams togged out in the College strips but selected from among those least talented at, and least interested in, football. One student remembers the mock presentation of a trophy, constructed with silver foil collected from cigarette boxes and labelled 'Corn Sinsir na mBowjers'.
2. Mooney, pp.97-98. Michael Mooney, a native of Dunmore, was educated in St Jarlath's and Maynooth, where he was ordained in 1940. He undertook post-graduate work at Dunboyne House and was appointed to Annaghdown in 1942. In 1943, he became Professor of Classics in St Jarlath's and, in 1961, he succeeded Conor Heaney as President. Later, he was parish priest of Clifden (1971-77), of Abbeyknockmoy (1977-82), and of Athenry (1982-93). He was Dean of the Cathedral Chapter from 1990 and he died in 1994.
3. Mahon, 'The Spirit of St Jarlath's College, Tuam' in Action Replay, pp.22-23.

Rough uncouth play he never allowed and I remember him once putting a bully off the field and leaving him without a game for some time... For as long as I can remember there has always been a code of good behaviour associated with Jarlath's royal blue... You play the ball at all times. Never retaliate no matter how often or how much you are provoked... The code of behaviour or conduct is equally true of Tuam supporters. Never will you hear the Jarlath's supporters barracking opponents as they take near-in frees...[1]

After winning Connacht titles in 1945 and 1946, Mooney led the College into a new era. As champions in the province, St Jarlath's represented Connacht in the first Colleges All-Ireland competition in 1946. Having easily disposed of Munster champions, St Brendan's Killarney, in their own home ground, St Jarlath's took on St Patrick's of Armagh in the final, only to lose narrowly in a hard-fought and high-scoring game, by 3-11 to 4-7.

The 1947 championship was run off during the worst and the longest winter of the century, with training sessions being held on a senior pitch that was snow-covered until the month of May. Moreover, a flu epidemic played havoc with preparations. Nevertheless, the senior squad, which was powered by the likes of Sean Purcell, Mick Flanagan, Peter Solan and captain, Vincent McHale, left little doubt about their intentions, hammering Roscommon CBS in the Connacht final by 7-6 to 0-3, and, uncannily, matching that scoreline with 5-12 to 1-0 in the semi-final in Tuam against St Brendan's of Killarney. Armagh were again the opponents in the final played at Croke Park on Sunday 11 May. After a 'shaky start', a disallowed goal and, in the words of the *Herald* reporter, 'a Western scoring machine [that] did not run as smoothly as usual' the Tuam boys were trailing by two points at half-time. To the dressing room, Mooney invited Dr Seán Lavin and Bill Carlos, asking

---

1. ibid., pp.23-28. Incidentally, one of the first tasks undertaken by Mooney was to re-direct the competitive urges of his charges. He prohibited the previously-tolerated matches between Mayo and Galway students, which had been very bitterly fought and had resulted in long-lasting acrimony. These matches were replaced —possibly on the initiative of Fr Kavanagh— by less divisive 'Greeks v Barbarians' encounters pitting classicists against those studying science (Shannon interview, Williams interview).

them 'to give some advice and encouragement to the boys from the West'.[1] The 'encouragement' had the desired effect:

> Right from the start of the second half it was evident that a great change had come over the St Jarlath's team during the interval. The uncertainty and doubt were gone and the whole side played with confidence and determination. The first headlong rush by the forwards was checked at the goal line, but they returned almost from the kick-out and Flanagan had a great goal and a point to leave Jarlath's two points in the lead. St Patrick's tried vainly to transfer play to the other end, but Purcell and Joyce had, by this time, erected that famous "iron curtain" and refused to budge an inch.[2]

The final score was 4-10 to 3-8 in favour of St Jarlath's. In those years, only a few senior students were permitted to travel to away games. The majority supported with their prayers and good wishes, while waiting anxiously in Tuam for news. The results of the semi-finals of 1946 and 1947 were conveyed to the boys in the study hall. One student recalls the theatrical announcement of the 1946 semi-final result by Fr Christy Langan who, adopting a dead-pan manner, had convinced his audience that he was the bearer of bad tidings, before revealing the extent of the victory in Killarney. The All-Ireland finals were broadcast live on radio, and listened to with rapt attention by the assembled students. But the tension proved too much for some, and there were those who waited nervously outside for the final result.[3]

On the Monday evening following the 1947 final, the team members arrived back to a tremendous welcome in Tuam. They were greeted at the outskirts of the town by their fellow students and by the townspeople. A Boy Scouts band led a procession of footballers and supporters to the Square, where Town Commissioners and local GAA dignitaries awaited them. When the crackling bonfire and the al fresco speakers had exhausted themselves, celebrations continued in the Imperial Hotel. Then on to the College itself — which was decorated with bunting borrowed from the Mercy Convent — where the team was met by the archbishop (and former College president), Joseph Walsh.[4]

---

1. Mooney, p.99.
2. *Tuam Herald*, 17 May 1947.
3. Shannon interview.
4. ibid., *Tuam Herald*, 17 May 1947.

Being 'somewhat exhausted', according to trainer Mooney, the senior team lost the Connacht title in 1948 to Roscommon CBS, while the Hogan Cup in that year was taken by St Mel's of Longford. Then the All-Ireland tournament was abandoned because of pressure from the Catholic hierarchy, who felt that Leaving Certificate students in diocesan Colleges were being distracted from their studies during the final term because of the intensity of the competition.

Provincial competition continued, with successes being registered in 1950, 1951 and 1953 — not a particularly good run by the standards of the College, which only took three Connacht titles in the eight years following the Hogan Cup success. But impact is not measured in titles alone. Reviewing his decade in charge of the St Jarlath's senior team in 1955, Michael Mooney noted that twenty-six of his players had since played at senior inter-county level; twelve for Galway; nine for Mayo; two for Roscommon and three for London-Irish. And of six county teams in Connacht — senior, junior and minor — that had won all-Irelands since 1950, five had been captained by products of St Jarlath's. Moreover, since the inauguration of the Connacht Colleges Senior championship, sixteen of the twenty-six titles had been taken by the College. And at junior level, St Jarlath's held thirteen of the sixteen titles.[1]

By any criteria the College's performance in the quarter century after it embraced football was outstanding. However, development was frustrated by the restricted arena in its which teams played. During only three of the twenty-five years was there a full national competition. Otherwise, opposition had come from a relatively small number of colleges in Connacht. And the glamour of the inter-provincial competition was, if anything, antithetical to the fullest development of team spirit at individual College level. However, the inter-provincial series was abandoned in 1956-57 and replaced by a revived Hogan Cup competition. It was the task of another former College player, Fr Brendan Kavanagh, the Annaghdown-born science teacher who succeeded Dr Mooney as games master, to put the St Jarlath's stamp on the footballing decade that followed.[2]

---

1. Mooney, 'Fifty years', p.100.
2. Brendan Kavanagh was born in Annaghdown and educated in St Jarlath's College and Maynooth, where he was ordained in 1952. From 1952 to 1974, he was Professor of Science in St Jarlath's. For the remaining twenty years of his life he served in the parish of Cong, first as curate (1974-85), then as parish priest (1985-94).

Kavanagh's stewardship began inauspiciously — the sideboard of 'Pro's Ref' was completely bare in 1954-'55 — but both senior and junior Connnacht titles were won in the following year. Hopes that the Hogan Cup might be brought back to St Jarlath's were dashed in a one point defeat by St Nathy's in the 1957 Connacht final, with St Nathy's going on to become the first winners of the revived All-Ireland championship.

This only sharpened appetites in St Jarlath's. Fr Kavanagh and Fr Paddy Williams attended a coaching course for College athletics trainers in Dublin during the summer vacation of 1957 and grafted some of the expertise thus gained onto the Jarlath's tradition. Mondays evenings, thereafter, were reserved for 'physical training and athletic exercise', a session which attracted a large number of participants. Eager to learn more, Kavanagh and Williams attended an intensive course for coaches at Loughborough, England, during the following summer.[1] This willingness to learn, to adapt, to innovate, on the part of their coaches gave College teams the edge against any opposition and quickly made them, indisputably, the Hogan Cup specialists. And the introduction of a Connacht championship at juvenile level in 1959-60 further boosted the College's football culture, providing the opportunity for identifying and nurturing talent at an even earlier age.

Meanwhile, Tuam's town fathers were becoming well-practiced in the organisation of civic receptions, as they welcomed home All-Ireland winning St Jarlath's senior teams in 1958, 1960, 1961, 1964 and 1966, and had to make preparations for the reception of finalists in 1962 and 1967. On these occasions, a link with the past, specifically with the 1947 Hogan Cup team, was provided by Seán Purcell — who had gone on to achieve fame with Galway as one of Tuam's 'Terrible Twins'. He was on the welcoming platform as captain of the Tuam Star club in 1958, but his prowess on the field gave him the status of dignitary regardless of the formal office he held.

The journey to the 1958 civic reception had been a difficult one. The distinguished display against Gormanston College at Croke Park that afternoon, which ended with a score of 1-7 to 2-3, had been somewhat exceptional. Up to then, the College team had disappointed itself and its supporters in struggling through by narrow margins against poor opposition, but that was forgotten in the celebrations.

---

1. Michael Mooney 'College highlights: 1957-58' in *Iarlaith*, 1959; Williams interview.

College players continued to go on to greater things. The 1959 issue of the Past Pupils' Union journal *Iarlaith* reported that ten past-pupils had played at senior inter-county level in the previous two years. They were: J. Biesty (Mayo), J.O. Moran (Roscommon), J. Donnellan, S. Colleran, E. Sharkey, M. Walsh, S. Concannon, J. Kennedy, M.J. Hawkshaw (Galway football), I. Gavin (Galway hurling). Of that group, John Donnellan would lead Galway to the Sam Maguire in 1964. But he was only one of the graduates of the Brendan Kavanagh regime, who featured in Galway's greatest ever team which took three All-Irelands in a row in the mid-1960s. The others included Enda Colleran (captain in 1965 and 1966), Pat Donnellan, Johnny Geraghty, Colie McDonagh and Jimmy Duggan. While St Jarlath's continued to supply Mayo teams with players of the calibre of John Morley, Galway were very much the glamour team of the period. And much of the glamour was provided by these products of Kavanagh's imperious, rigorous and sharp training style.

A future college team trainer, Oliver Hughes, who played in All-Ireland Colleges finals in 1961 and 1962, provided the following assessment of Fr Kavanagh as trainer:

> Brendan was a great coach in three respects. In the first place, he worked very hard all through the year to develop physical fitness, using physical training, various exercises, running, and so on. In this much, at least, he was way ahead of anyone else in the country. He also had a great football brain, in that he taught us that we were playing a team game, that we were playing with fourteen other guys. And when you got the ball, you delivered it to someone better placed, if there was someone. Most of all, he was a wonderful motivator: he made you want to give your best. You believed that the cause was important and that to give less than your all was unacceptable. He was a guy we respected and we feared — both. You did it or you got into trouble with him; there were no half measures with Brendan. Even if you were injured and unavailable for training or for a game, you felt that you had to justify yourself.[1]

Under Brendan Kavanagh, the decade 1957 to 1966 was very much the golden age of St Jarlath's football. While his predeces-

---
1. Hughes interview.

sors did not have equal access to a national platform, and his successors faced stiffer competition in the free education era, Kavanagh's achievement of five All-Ireland victories in ten years has to be considered remarkable. And if, in the words of one chronicler, the period was one of 'endeavour, disappointment. achievement', expectations in the College were very high indeed. So high that uneasiness was generated in some quarters. Probably for this reason, the sporting review in the 1966 issue of *Iarlaith* concluded on a rather defensive note, stressing the need to keep games 'within their proper perspective' and reminding those who might have forgotten that success was 'not to be measured by the honours won but by the degree to which the games have helped the boys to become men.' Reassuring those who had reservations about the planned addition to the College's sporting amenities, the writer concluded: 'We will have a college with a gymnasium attached, not a gymnasium with a College attached.'[1]

*

Since Fr Brendan Kavanagh surrendered the position there have been four coaches of senior teams. With the exception of the most recent appointee, all have taken the Hogan Cup to Tuam. Fr Dermot Moloney, a former swimming champion, took over in 1966-67. He served until the end of the 1973-74 season and was succeeded by Fr Oliver Hughes, who had played in two College All-Ireland finals in 1961 and 1962. Joe Long was the first lay teacher to take responsibility for the seniors, working with Oliver Hughes from 1984 and taking sole charge from 1986. Oliver Hughes made a comeback in 1998 and, at the time of writing, assists Fr Tod Nolan in managing the team.

The period since Fr Moloney took over the team has seen considerable change in the College, much of it traceable to the introduction of free education and free school transport at around the same time. Although change was scarcely perceptible at first, these reforms marked the beginning of a process which diluted the boarding school character of the institution. And the 'rise of the day-boy' would eventually see St Jarlath's becoming more representative of North Galway and less so of the archdiocese of Tuam as a whole. The altered circumstances, in the opinion of one senior trainer of the period, made it more

---

1. P. Williams, 'Sports Chronicle 1961-66', p.90.

difficult to win All-Irelands during the 1970s, 80s and 90s. Until the introduction of free education, the 'cream of the football crop' from counties Galway and Mayo, and even to an extent from Roscommon, came each year to Tuam. But from the late sixties, with the establishment and development of secondary schools in towns throughout Connacht, promising footballers remained in their native areas, and the supply to which St Jarlath's had become accustomed was reduced.[1]

But some characteristics of the College were resistant to change. If Fr Malone had eavesdropped on dormitory conversation in the mid-1970s as he had done forty years earlier, some things would have been familiar:

> Football was a consuming passion in St Jarlath's. During our first weeks it soothed the pangs of this great adjustment away from our families. Almost everybody played football. When we didn't play we watched. When we didn't watch we talked, discussed, and argued football. When we slept we dreamt. Our discussions covered every imaginable topic in football; from the merits of Pat Spillane and Kevin Moran to whether the Neale could beat Ballinrobe in the South Mayo Under-16 League. Michael Kelly from Roscommon was the cleverest boy in our class. Though he lived just across the river from Galway he was a Roscommon man to the tips of his toes. He rarely or never played anything. But he was a football aficionado and his sharp observation and cultured articulation made him a most formidable opponent in football arguments. He was the dormitory barrister championing the causes and merits of Roscommon teams, players, and clubs.[2]

But not all young lads arrived in the College as ready-made football fanatics. Some were more gradually seduced by the enthusiasm of their peers and by the atmosphere surrounding games:

> In my first year, I liked to go home on Sunday and my father would come to collect me. But when the inter-col-

---

1. Hughes interview.
2. Tom McHugh, 'Contrasting Connacht football styles', *Sunday Independent*, 26 July 1998.

lege games started, you couldn't get an exit out of the College on a Sunday, because the Leaving Certs would have them all blocked. You'd be ushered down to the Senior bootroom, the recreation room under the oratory, for the 'spiff'. There, senior students gave rabble-rousing speeches to the supporters, to work them up for the match. It all seemed very strange at first, but gradually you got into it. As you went to matches, you got caught up in the whole atmosphere. Then we won the All-Ireland — it would have been my second year — and when you experience victory and the taste of heading off on buses on a Sunday morning, it gets to you. All the time, after first year, you got more and more involved, more het up, more excited. Soon, you longed for the football; it broke the year for you.[1]

Fr Dermot Moloney led the seniors to a Connacht title in 1972 and to All-Ireland final appearances in 1973 and 1974. Unfortunately, the high-point of the 1973 campaign was a 'classic' semi-final victory against St Brendan's, Killarney, and the Morgan Hughes-captained College team was defeated by Gormanston in the final.

Expectations were high in 1974 — not just inside the College, but among those concerned for Connacht football in general One hopeful sportswriter remarked that 'the strength of this team lies in its unity and cohesion rather than in individual brilliance — although there is an amount of this in evidence as well.' Trainer Moloney would not be drawn into extravagant praise of his charges but he did acknowledge that the team was 'a better balanced one' than the previous year's. Some were not so reticent, however, and another thrilling victory at the semi-final stage over Killarney stimulated an anonymous 'ex-Galway star' to telephone noted commentator 'JBD' to advise him that the 1974 thirteen were 'the greatest ever to represent the famed Tuam school'. He insisted, moreover, that 'even Seán Purcell, Jimmy Duggan and Morgan Hughes in their schooldays were nothing superior to Brian Talty, Cyril Moran or Henry Gavin of the current Jarlath's All-Star outfit.'[2] Gormanston again provid-

---

1. Nolan interview.
2. *Connacht Tribune*, 22, 29 March 1974. Jack Mahon wrote that in terms of 'sheer entertainment', the best games of College football that he had ever seen were the semi-finals of 1973 and 1974('Spirit', p.42).

ed the opposition on All-Ireland final day in Athlone but this time the result of 1973 was reversed: sweet revenge for Brian Talty, Henry Gavin (1974 captain) and Gerard Hennigan who featured on both teams; double disappointment for Tom Vaughan who, having changed schools, played for the losing finalists in both years.

In his second year as coach, in 1975-76, Oliver Hughes took the team to an All-Ireland final against Moate, which they lost narrowly. Two years later in 1977-78, Hughes was conscious from the beginning of the year that he was dealing with a 'group of exceptional players'. They did not disappoint and concluded a run of comfortable victories by overcoming St Colman's of Newry in Croke Park in the All-Ireland final.

In sporting reminiscence, the might-have-beens sometimes loom larger than the successes. In this regard, the replayed 1979 All-Ireland final against Árdscoil Rís when St Jarlath's were 'clearly the better team' but missed two penalties before losing narrowly, forces Fr Hughes to acknowledge the role that luck plays in competition:

> People will say that you make your own luck, that fortune favours the best prepared, but there's an element beyond all that. There are days when the ball will hit the crossbar or come back off the upright, when frees won't go over, that you can't account for in any other way except luck.[1]

1980 and 1981 were lean years — years when Connacht senior titles are not won are considered lean in St Jarlath's — but three All-Ireland appearances in a row between 1982 and 1984 atoned for the lapse. Again, the might-have-been, the unexpected defeat of 1983, is more vividly remembered than the victories of 1982 or 1984. The centenary year title was taken courtesy of a last minute point by team captain Mark Butler who is rated by Oliver Hughes as probably the best of the three-hundred-odd college players that he has trained. And in his experience, it is almost impossible to win an All-Ireland title without one or two exceptional players — like Butler, like Padraig Brogan or Jimmy Lyons — footballers with the capacity to inspire their teammates in adverse circumstances. But whether an 'exceptional' player is available or not, great care is taken each year in choosing the senior captain:

---

1. Hughes interview.

> The role of the captain is important for a number of reasons. It would be important, in the first instance, that he would get on well with the trainer, that it would be someone that the trainer could trust, because they would have a lot of dealings with each other. The second thing is that it would be important that the captain would get on well both with the team and within the general community of St Jarlath's College: that he be respected; that he be well-liked. Obviously, thirdly, it would be important that he be a good footballer, that he enthuse guys and inspire guys. And that he inspire them by the way he did things, that he trained hard and played good football. So the role of the captain was very important and would always have been treated as such. At the beginning of the school year, when the selection of monitors and other positions took place, the senior trainer was given the first choice from among the senior students. The Proc would have been the second choice. That remains the way until this day. So in a sense, the senior captain is the first student in the house.[1]

More generally, Fr Hughes summed up his own approach to coaching:

> I tried to be very respectful of the young fellows. At the same time, I tried to have a 'professional' approach to the whole thing: that if training was scheduled for half past four, it didn't mean twenty-five to five; that practice matches started on time; that there would be a referee; that the showers were working; that there would be jerseys; that everything was as professional as possible, out of respect for the young guys that you were dealing with. I would have put great emphasis on physical fitness; we would have worked hard on that during the winter months. And I would have tried to reduce the game to its essentials. For example, if you're playing a game you need to get the football, so how do you actually get the football? It seems almost stupidly simple, but I would spend a lot of time teaching fellows how to get the football: how to catch it in different ways; how to pick it off the ground, and so on.[2]

---

1. ibid.
2. ibid.

Joe Long joined Oliver Hughes in coaching the senior team for the 1983-84 season and took sole charge two years later. According to his predecessor, Long was an 'extraordinarily dedicated' trainer who gave more time and commitment to the role than anybody else had done and who, because of this, succeeded in keeping the Jarlath's tradition to the fore, 'even in years when the College had few good footballers'. Long's most successful period was in the early 1990s, when he led senior teams to All-Ireland finals in four out of five years. A run of bad luck saw defeats in 1990, 1992 and 1993, but success was achieved in the 'thoroughly inspirational' final of 1994.[1] A national newspaper described the encounter:

> A whirlwind start... provided the platform for the Galway college's first win in the competition for ten years. Their 3-11 to 0-9 win over St Patrick's, Maghera, included three high quality goals... A tactical switch which brought man of the match, Michael Donnellan, to mid-field, produced long periods of St Jarlath's dominance in the second half. He controlled the game from that position and set up a series of Tuam attacks, culminating in his side's third goal, scored by Derek Reilly, in the final quarter.[2]

As well as maintaining the national profile of College teams, the Moloney, Hughes and Long eras also saw other developments in football. In particular, there was growth in the number of competitions. The Connacht championship for first years began in 1983, while the College also began to field 'B' and 'C' teams at senior level. More recently, Connacht leagues at the various levels during first term have served warm-up teams for championships. The objective of giving the opportunity to every student who wished to avail of it of wearing the St Jarlath's jersey came closer to realisation.

*

Amidst the excitement of victory, it was not always easy to sustain the 'proper perspective', the sense of 'humility' (or at least modesty), which St Jarlath's, by all accounts, has tried to inculcate in its team members and their supporters. Success sometimes bred smugness, which was interpreted as arrogance by some outside the walls, particularly by followers of St Patrick's,

---

1. Hughes interview.
2. *Irish Times*, 2 May 1994.

the College's nearest neighbour. Such smugness rarely found its way into print, but local sensibilities were not at the forefront of the mind of the Hogan Cup winning player who wrote:

> So onward we marched to face a somewhat over-rated [Tuam] CBS team. As usual they shrank at the sight of the royal blue, and before they knew it they were telling their hard-luck stories. On the day the scoreboard read 3-11 to 1-4, although this could have been much greater.[1]

Insensitive attitudes and language are inevitable features of local derbys everywhere, but occasionally the boot was on the other foot, and triumphalism was something which had to be endured rather than indulged in. On such occasions, St Patrick's supporters seemed to derive rather more satisfaction from the discomfiture of their neighbours than from their own victory. This was especially apparent following the Connacht Senior final of 1995 when St Jarlath's were the reigning All-Ireland champions. On that evening a St Patrick's teacher asked a past-pupil of his school, songwriter Padraic Stevens, to be laureate for the occasion. And Stevens's composition reflected the sentiments of his audience, when he performed 'We Got the Blues' at a celebratory gathering of hundreds of St Patrick's students on the following morning:

> Five years at school, on a bike or on a bus;
> Them College boys seemed to look down on us,
> But down in the pitch on Sunday, have you heard the news?
> We won the Connacht final; what's more, we got the Blues.[2]

Later in the week, writing in the *Herald*, a 'neutral' Declan Varley was slightly more ponderous but no less wounding:

> For the neutral observer, this was the dream result: the power of St Jarlath's with their substantial resources on and off the pitch against the down to earth honesty of St Patrick's... On the terraces last Sunday stood the St Jarlath's past pupils, their expensive raincoats testimony

---

1. 'Hogan Cup 78' in *Torch* 1978, pp.6-8.
2. I am grateful to Padraic Stevens for providing the above lyrics and information. Incidentally, he was anxious to point out that he has written in positive terms about St Jarlath's football in another context.

to how life has treated them since since they came out the gates of the College, and year after year, they come back to support the team as it traditionally shows the way to the rest of the province. St Patrick's had no such support. Their supporters came in anoraks and hope. The expensive raincoats came in expectation. And although many of the Jarlath's players hail from rural parishes, when the chips were down on Sunday, they played like townies, just when it was most important for them to play like country lads.[1]

But the keen rivalry which accompanies Tuam derbys is a fragile flower, which comes and goes with the daffodils. Partisans of either College are happy to see the other do well in later stages of competition. And nobody is bothered about where a player learned his skills when he goes on to represent his county. Three years after the 1995 Connacht final, four of the thirty players were heroes to everybody in the vicinity of Tuam, regardless of their allegiance on 12 March 1995. Derek Savage who contributed two points of St Patrick's total on that day was joined on Galway's 1998 Sam Maguire-winning team by Michael Donnellan, by John Divilly, and by Padraig Joyce of the Jarlath's team. In all, eight of Galway's fifteen in that remarkable final, and five of her substitutes, were past students of the College. Such a level of representation, which had not been achieved even in the three-in-row era of the 1960s, focused attention on St Jarlath's role as a nursery of football. One national newspaper commentator speculated on how the College could supply 50% of the county team when it accounted for, at most, 5% of the male attendance at post-primary schools in the county. He then provided the answer to his own question:

> Its location in the heartland of Galway football allows it draw from Galway's richest vein of talent, but it is the way it nurtures, encourages and develops this talent that sets it apart. The great love affair between St Jarlath's and Gaelic football dates from the turn of the century and, over time, football has been woven into the very fabric of College life. The football fields have always been special. Sport mirrors life and life mirrors sport. All part of a good education. The numerous coaches and team trainers that

---

1. *Tuam Herald*, 18 March 1995.

have nurtured fledgling talent have always sought to be innovative and pioneering.[1]

Over the years, and especially since the 1930s, football has indeed been 'woven into the very fabric of College life.' It has provided a common interest for successive generations of St Jarlath's students and teachers and has helped to forge a strong sense of community in the College. Moreover, football has given former pupils an annual opportunity to maintain a connection with their old school by supporting her teams. And whenever two or more past students meet, the footballing exploits of their contemporaries invariably find their way into the conversation. It seems apt to leave the final words to Fr Tod Nolan, the current senior team manager, interviewed just after completing his first year in charge of sport in St Jarlath's — a year, incidentally, during which all of the Connacht 'A' colleges football titles were won by the College and in which the Senior team appeared in an All-Ireland for the first time in five years. Clearly, Fr Nolan regards himself as a custodian of the St Jarlath's footballing tradition and is conscious of following in the footsteps of a long line of distinguished coaches:

> We would never play a short hand-passing game, like the northern teams play. We play a particular brand of football: it's more direct, a bit more traditional in that there's high fielding with the backs out in front — a quick ball to the forwards, that type of thing. It doesn't always work, but when it does, it's beautiful to watch. It's our brand of football, which Joe Long would have learned from Oliver Hughes, which Oliver would got from Dermot Moloney, which he would have got from Father Kavanagh and so on, all the way back. We would all have had different emphases and preferences in training the lads, on the amount of weight training for example, but it's essentially the same type of game that we try to produce. It's not so much that we are attached to a particular style, but that we believe that this is Gaelic football in its purest form — that this is the way that Gaelic football should be played. And even if is unfashionable at the moment, it has been successful, and continues to be successful.[2]

---

1. Tom McHugh, 'Aspiration and perspiration in the fields of Tuam' in *Sunday Independent*, 4 October 1998.
2. Nolan interview.

12. "...a tendency to make the best of our life here."

The students they are rioting
On almost every day,
They are not a crowd of thugs
As many people say.

They are out now for civil rights
It's time they made a try,
There is so much injustice
They have to rectify.

Do not blame the students
If they break some window panes
They're out to equal black and white
They have justice in their veins...[1]

On 16 September 1961, Hurricane Debbie ripped across Ireland, leaving uprooted trees and roofless houses in its wake. Fifteen people were killed and hundreds were injured by collapsing walls, by falling branches, and by capsizing boats. There were no deaths in Tuam but, according to a report, the gales left the town with 'the appearance of having been bombed from the air.'[2] In St Jarlath's, considerable damage was done to the Old College, but the newest part of the establishment, the Heaney wing completed only a decade earlier, proved least resistant to the 100 mile-an-hour winds. And if the loss of its copper roofing was not bad enough, the lack of insurance on the new wing gave further cause for regret.[3] Unquestionably the worst storm in Ireland this century, Debbie will not be forgotten by any of those who sought shelter from her.

As Debbie's impact faded from the landscape over the following decade, Ireland was being more fundamentally changed by metaphorical 'winds of change', blowing from the United States, from Britain, from Northern Europe and, in the aftermath of the second Vatican Council, from Rome. The society

---

1. Thomas Hayes, 'Student riots' in *Torch*, 1968-69, p.16.
2. *Irish Times*, 18 September 1961; *Connacht Tribune*, 23 September 1961.
3. Pat Hoyne, 'Past Presidents', reminiscences of Presidents Heaney and Mooney in *Torch* 1990, pp.33-34.

was being transformed in almost every aspect: economic, educational, cultural and religious.

Of course, no society is immune to change. Even the allegedly stagnant Ireland of the 1930s, 40s and 50s embraced certain technologies, and sought fresh solutions to underlying economic and social problems. During those decades, cinema and radio became part of the cultural landscape, rural electrification was completed, the population became slowly more urbanised, while new political formations — Clann na Talmhan and Clann na Poblachta — were adopted and then discarded. What was different, therefore, about the period following 1960, was not the fact of change, but the pace of change.

In 1979, a leading sociologist described an Ireland that had experienced 'social, economic, cultural and political change on an unprecedented scale'.[1] And, twenty years later, it is clear that the tempo of change has, if anything, quickened since then. But it is not just in comparison with her own recent past that Ireland's transformation has been dramatic. Referring to southern Ireland over the past four decades, one economist maintains that 'economic change has occurred faster than in any other country in western Europe.'[2]

And change in economic policy and circumstance has been at the root of more general change. In particular, the policy U-turn of the late 1950s and early 1960s exposed Ireland to a world that was itself changing rapidly. An international economic upswing, facilitated by the interaction of two major factors — the widespread lowering of barriers to international trade and technical innovation on an unprecedented scale — brought about an upbeat and optimistic social environment. Ireland shared in both the boom and the optimism. In the circumstances, it was possible for government to abandon crusty frugality, and to adopt a more expansionist approach.[3]

Arguably, the policy area where this was most evident was in education. And again, this was in line with the prevailing social policy thinking in the economically-advanced world at that time: a technological age would mean a rapidly changing world; an educated workforce would be required to handle the

---

1. Liam Ryan, 'Church and Politics: the last twenty five years' in *The Furrow*, vol.l, 1, 1979.
2. Jonathan Haughton 'The dynamics of economic change' in Crotty & Schmitt, *Ireland and the politics of change*' 1998, pp.27-28.
3. J.J. Lee, *Ireland, 1912-1985*, 1989, pp.341-58.

technology and to manage the change; buoyant economies and Keynesian policies would free up the capital necessary for the expansion in educational provision. But there was another underlying concern, one increasingly shared by philanthropically-minded and by pragmatically-inclined policy-makers: the need for greater social inclusion. For the latter, education was a route into the mainstream for talented members of marginalised groups. It was therefore a safety-valve, lessening a sense of grievance which, if allowed to fester, might push the marginalised into embracing alternative world-views — communism, for example.

The 'revolution' in Irish education of the late 1960s was not, as it has often been presented, the result of a whim of Donagh O'Malley. Rather, it was the culmination of a strategy pursued by that minister and by his predecessors in the Department of Education, Patrick Hillery and George Colley. The OECD report of 1966, *Investment in Education*, confirmed what everybody knew — and what some were already trying to address: that there was a low level of participation in second-level education in Ireland; that there were strong links between social and economic status and educational attainment; that educational attainment was lowest among those whose parents were unskilled, semi-skilled, or skilled manual workers. The OECD report, therefore, was itself part of the attempt to solve the problems which it highlighted. What O'Malley did, in his own audacious way, was to speed up the pace of reform. At the time, he was criticised for seriously — and perhaps deliberately — underestimating the level of resources necessary to fulfil his plans, in order that he might be allowed to proceed with them.[1]

A by-product of the post-war economic up-turn was a flourishing youth culture. Greater educational provision meant that more people remained in a 'youth' environment for longer; reduced working hours gave young workers more leisure time; rising standards of living gave the generality of young people more disposable income. For its part, the same disposable income resulted in young people being identified as a 'niche market' to be exploited by leisure and fashion industries. And by exploiting youth identity, advertisers consolidated the phenomenon. Elements of the nascent youth culture were quickly

---

1. Sister Eileen Randles, *Post primary education in Ireland*, 1975, passim; Patrick Clancy, 'Education in the Republic of Ireland: The project of Modernity?' in Clancy et al, *Irish society: Sociological perspectives*, 1995, pp.467-494.

and widely communicated by established media — radio, cinema and magazines — but increasingly by television. And if Ireland's young people did not yet have the disposable income of their English or American peers in the early 1960s, Radio Luxembourg and — from New Year's Eve, 1961 — RTE television made them aware of the latest fads and trends. But it was not all hedonistic. As the 1960s went on, and continuing prosperity provided young people with the space and the confidence to challenge established practices and institutions, idealists gave a radical political edge to the youth culture. Not only were many semi-moribund egalitarian movements — socialist, feminist, anti-racist — given new life as a result, but some of their values were incorporated into the broader youth culture, not least their anti-authoritarianism.[1] If the verses quoted at the beginning of this chapter are an indication, this process was followed with interest by St Jarlath's students.

For established organisations too, the 1960s was a time of reappraisal and re-evaluation. The radically changed circumstances of the period forced many institutions to examine themselves and to consider their role and their place in a changing world. The Second Vatican Council was precisely such an undertaking on the part of the Roman Catholic Church. In the intensely Catholic Ireland of the time, its progress was followed with great interest, and not a little excitement. Parallel to the ferment in worldly affairs, religious certainties were being challenged and the traditional Catholic world-view was being turned upside down. Fr Seán Freyne, then a young theologian, attended the Council. He summed up the debate for his fellow past-pupils of St Jarlath's in *Iarlaith*:

> In the pre-conciliar writing and thinking, two clearly defined schools were already emerging. The liberal or modern approach was not content with the traditional presentation of the Gospel message, a presentation which, they maintained, was no longer suited to the needs of modern man. They insisted on a return to original and fundamental well-springs of the Christian life, the Scriptures and the Liturgy. The defensive argumentative approach which had coloured all Catholic thinking since the Reformation no longer corresponded to an actual

---

1. See Arthur Marwick, *The Sixties: Cultural Revolution in Britain, France, Italy and the United States, c.1958-c.1974*, 1998, passim

situation where non-Catholics of all denominations were earnestly seeking for the truth of Christ... The conservatives adopted a more negative approach. They regarded any such ideas as a danger to the truth of the Gospel. The 'ecumenical dialogue', as the attitude of the liberals was currently styled, could only bring harm to the Church. The articulate representatives of either view were, at the opening of the Council in the minority among the bishops... The liberal view found its most convinced adherents in the Northern European countries, while Roman-based or Roman-trained theologians were the most outspoken conservatives.[1]

Notwithstanding his efforts to present a balanced picture, Freyne's sympathy evidently lay with the 'modern approach'. And the indications are that this too was the response of St Jarlath's students and of the younger priests in the College.

New attitudes and adjustment to change

The presidency of Conor Heaney came to an end in 1961. Heaney had succeeded Tim Gunnigan in 1947, and had presided over a number of developments in the College. Most notable, probably, was the new wing, built to commemorate the College's 150th anniversary. This project was initiated by Archbishop Joseph Walsh, however, and there was less input from the president than he himself would have wished. Walsh, it would appear, was anxious to complete the work carried out during his own presidency twenty years earlier and, consequently, paid insufficient attention to the needs of the establishment as they were in 1950.[2] Later in the 1950s, as a result of alterations to the Cathedral entrance, the College too acquired a new entrance and, at the same time, obtained additional dormitory space in the former archbishop's palace, which had previously been used by the Presentation boarding school.

Heaney is remembered as a progressive president, who sought to ease the rigours of institutional life for the students. In particular, he took measures to make the diet more palatable and more varied. This, he found, could largely be achieved without additional spending. Contributing to the diet was the College farm, still an important part of the institution during

---

1. Seán Freyne, 'Rome and the Council' in *Iarlaith* 1966, p.36.
2. Heaney interview.

the 1950s. And its management was one of Heaney's particular pleasures as president. Students remember that he also participated in the physical work of the farm, and that the president was often to be found, in his wellingtons, in the farmyard.[1] Many students also vividly recall their own brief involvement in the physical work of the College farm — the few days, in their fourth year, that some of them spent picking potatoes.[2]

Heaney's departure for Athenry coincided with the retirement of lay teacher and A.S.T.I. stalwart, Jack O'Sullivan. Consequently, when Dr Michael Mooney took over the presidency, at the beginning of the 1961-62 academic year, the teaching staff was entirely composed of priests. Such would remain the case until the appointments of Joe Donaghue and Pat Griffiths in 1968.

If the 1960s was one of the few extended periods in the College's history when there was no lay member of the academic staff, this did not mean that the College was closed to outside influences. Indeed, the opposite was the case. From the beginning of the decade, students were affected by the prevailing youth culture. In the era of so-called 'skiffle' music, for instance, with its 'do-it yourself' emphasis, the president noted 'a spontaneous growth of interest in instrumental music'. Almost every class, he went on, could 'boast of its own band', some playing rock and roll, but others specialising in classical or traditional genres.[3] And if the teaching staff was completely clerical, it was not static, being regularly replenished by newly-ordained recent graduates of Maynooth, itself a place beginning to engage with the outside world from the mid-1960s on. Indeed that College would soon give birth to a radical Western Students Movement in which St Jarlath's past pupils were active.[4]

Within St Jarlath's, to go to Maynooth remained the ambition of many. The number of vocations to the priesthood had fallen — up to the 1950s there was competition for places in Maynooth, and candidates also for the Chinese mission at Dalgan Park, which had maintained strong connections with St Jarlath's — but there was still an average of three or four ordi-

---

1. ibid., Hughes interview.
2. Mahon interview; Michael Marren, personal communication.
3. Mooney 'College Chronicle, 1959-61' in *Iarlaith* 1961, p.120.
4. Corish's *Maynooth*, p.370-78; Pat Staunton, 'Maynooth Viewpoint' in *Western People*, 13 January 1971. The WSM was 'concerned about underdevelopment in the West and its effects socially, economically and spiritually on the lives of our western people'.

nations a year for the Tuam diocese during the 1960s and early 1970s.[1] These priests, at that time, were almost all products of St Jarlath's and, obviously, many more students than that considered the priesthood, something which contributed to the high level of interest among students in religious affairs through the 1960s. Moreover, much of the Vatican Council discussion seemed quite relevant to life in the College. In particular, the Decree on Priestly Formation of 28 September 1965 must have attracted the attention of staff and students alike. It recommended that seminarians should be subjected to far less rigorous discipline than formerly, so that could 'gradually learn to discipline themselves'.[2] Incidentally, Vatican Two was directly responsible for one significant improvement in the lives of St Jarlath's boarders. While Archbishop Walsh was in Rome attending the Council, President Mooney took it on himself to introduce a break at Hallowe'en, thus dividing up the sixteen-week-long first term.[3]

More than skiffle groups or record clubs, the advent of the student magazine in the mid-1960s reflected the active interest of students in the world around them. The titles of ephemeral publications like *Newsview* and *Perspective* are suggestive of an earnest purpose, but the annual *Torch* — founded with the encouragement of Fr Enda Lyons during the academic year 1964-65 — proved more durable than either. That magazine has increasingly filled the role of 'newspaper of record' for the College with all significant events — sport, the opera, educational tours, the arrival and departure of staff — given faithful coverage each year.[4] Interestingly, the archive copy of the first issue contains the following item of marginalia: 'Remember when No.1 of TORCH came out on Sun. 7th March 1965. Also first day of New Liturgy. Eas.VAK=5+2'.

One's impression of an alert and questioning attitude among the students of the mid-1960s is heightened by the inclusion in early issues of *Torch* of articles with titles like 'Is a student capable of forming an opinion of his own?', 'Economic crisis — the

---

1. I am grateful to Fr Brendan Kilcoyne for compiling 'Ordination statistics, 1960-1999'.
2. Corish's *Maynooth*, pp.370-78.
3. Hoyne, 'Past presidents', p.34.
4. Thirty-five years later —now supported by staff members Padraic Nolan and Christopher Kelly— *Torch* remains a forum for student opinion, an outlet for reflective lyricism and a vehicle for adolescent humour intelligible only to members of the generation which produces it.

answer?' and 'My idea of education'. The impression is confirmed by the vibrant activity of recently established student-run clubs. In 1966 — as well as established activities like football, handball, athletics, hurling, the opera and the fourth year concert — there was a debating society, a student-run lending library, a swimming club, a non-smoking association with 150 members, a dramatic society, a branch of the Pioneer Total Abstinence Association, a camera club, a céilí band, a table tennis club, a modern history society, a stamp club and a carpentry club. In the same year, a chronicler regretted the recent demise of a gardening club and of the College's F.C.A. unit which had, for more than a decade, 'practised and marched on the terrace' and attended Sunday mass 'dressed in their uniforms and ready to go for their field-day.'[1]

Not alone was there activity on all fronts, but contemporaries were aware that they were living through a period of fresh possibilities. A few years earlier, it would have been 'not alone unthinkable, but also impossible', President Mooney told an interviewer in 1966, for students to have published 'their own views on questions concerning the College'.[2] In the same year, a senior student noted that 'lack of enthusiasm has disappeared, and a completely new spirit of progress and understanding has grown up here, together with a tendency to make the best of our life here in the College, and to get every possible advantage from it'.[3] Meanwhile, past pupils marvelled: one that the College now tolerated 'a céilí band, an operatic troupe, a college magazine and fraternising professors'; another — a veteran of the late 1950s, 'when the only activity outside of football was to walk around the walks in yawning F.C.A. boots discussing it' — that the students could be bothered producing a magazine. As far as his own contemporaries were concerned, he wrote, it would have been surprising to discover that they had even read a magazine.[4]

The very existence of a College magazine enabled certain students to carry out interviews with their teachers, to ask questions that might otherwise be considered cheeky, and to receive answers to them. An interview was conducted with the

1. Gerard McCarthy, 'Student Activities' in *Torch* 1966, pp.82-87.
2. Corcoran & Colleary, 'Interview', p.5. In fact, it had been possible to publish a student magazine, *The Charioteer*, during the 1940s.
3. Charles Kelly & Seamus O'Beirne, 'This is our College' in *Torch* 1966.
4. Tom Kirrane, 'The Walk' in *Iarlaith* 1966, p.41; John Higgins 'Foreword, by a past pupil', in *Torch* 1965, p.ii-iii.

just-retired football coach, Fr Brendan Kavanagh, in 1967, while President Mooney also endured a grilling. But, in both instances, as far as the issues of the day in St Jarlath's College were concerned, the questions asked by the students were more revealing than the answers given. Mooney was asked: What are your views on compulsory morning mass?; Do you think that students from this College make sufficient impact on the world after they leave here?; Do you think the students get enough career guidance here?; How many students have to emigrate to find work after they leave?; Have vocations to the priesthood fallen in the College in the last few years and why?; How will the comprehensive school plan affect the College?

President Mooney was at his most expansive in outlining his plans for a major extension. There was an acute shortage of classroom space throughout the 1960s, something the president had been unable to rectify because of the financial position. 'As soon as the credit squeeze finishes', he promised students, he would make the necessary provision:

> It is planned to build a completely new teaching unit on the site occupied at present by the cloister, the garden and the farm buildings. It will, I hope, have about fifteen class-halls, as well as two science laboratories, a language laboratory, a geography room, a library, an assembly hall and an art room. It may possibly also have a woodwork room and a commercial room. It will be a very big — probably about two hundred feet long and three storeys high.[1]

In fact, the project was not completed until 1970, and the plans were altered considerably. The development occurred on the opposite side of the College to that envisaged in 1966, and it had two storeys rather than three. However, almost all of the amenities promised were provided, with the assembly hall being equipped for use as a gymnasium or theatre.

Sociology — the vogue discipline of the 1960s — had its adherents in the student body and opinion surveys were a regular feature of the early *Torch*. Thus we learn that in the autumn of 1966 Fianna Fáil, with 137 supporters, was the most popular political party among the students, followed by Fine Gael with

---

1. John Corcoran and Gearóid Colleary, an interview with the President, *Torch*, 1966, pp.5-8.

98, Labour with 12 and the Communist Party with 2.[1] The Beatles were the most popular pop group, followed by the Rolling Stones and the Beach Boys; Brendan Bowyer was the most popular solo singer, followed by Elvis Presley, Dickie Rock and Larry Cunningham; Manchester United had 92 'fans' while their nearest rivals, Shamrock Rovers, could muster only 30. Gay Byrne was the favourite T.V. personality.[2]

In a more serious vein, 'Priests and their role in the community' was the topic of a remarkable survey undertaken by Walter Waldron and Séamus O'Dwyer of the Leaving Cert class of 1968-69. Intended as a contribution to the Vatican Council's 'work of total Christian renewal', the survey sought the opinions of the Senior Grade students and their professors on five topics: 'Priests and the missions', 'Priests in colleges', 'Priests and confessions', 'Priests and local organisations', 'Priests and celibacy'. As such, it is an invaluable insight into attitudes in the College during a period of social, religious and political uncertainty. The authors described their methodology:

> ...a cross section of the Senior Grade students wrote brief articles on the priestly life as they saw it. From these articles, questions were devised which were then put to the Senior Grade in general. Then it was decided to give the same questionnaire to the College professors in order to compare the different answers.[3]

Evidently, staff members had reservations about 'the validity of such a survey', but they co-operated nonetheless, supplying a collective answer to the questions put. As far as the budding

---

1. A similar survey carried out exactly ten years later, near the end of the 1973-77 Fine Gael-Labour coalition's term , produced the following result: Fianna Fáil, 50%; Sinn Féin, 30%; Coalition parties, 20%. (*Newsview*, Xmas 1976 issue).
2. Charles Mulchrone and James Mongey 'Survey' in *Torch* 1967, pp.4-7. Gay Byrne, it would seem, was informed of his popularity among the students and wrote to the compilers of the survey: "You ask me what St Jarlath's means to me. Well, of course, I have never been there, but I have a mental picture of a fine Georgian country house, with a drive-way of at least five miles long, set in 2.000 acres of roaming pasture and surrounded by stately elms and beeches. The sun shines continually, the teachers are clever and kind, and amidst the drone of contented bees, the happy, courteous, well-mannered and smartly-dressed students pursue learning with steady dedication'.
3. Waldron & O'Dwyer, 'Survey', in *Torch* 1969.

sociologists who undertook the survey were concerned, their work was a rebuke to those who would dismiss student opinion as immature since it showed 'a remarkable similarity between the views expressed by the students and those of the priests'. Indeed, on some issues, the Woodstock generation in St Jarlath's seems to have been less radical than its elders. On the question of priestly celibacy, for example, the priests were unsure but allowed that there was 'a place for married [clergy] in certain areas,' while the boys voted 'No' by a margin of 35 to 15 to the question 'Should the clergy be free to marry?' On other topical issues, the students voted 45 to to 5 against the abolition of confession boxes, 39 to 8 in favour of permitting priests to run football clubs and drama societies, and 38 to 11 in favour of making service on the foreign missions compulsory for priests.

Because it was the subject with which the participants were most familiar, and because changes in staffing were happening anyway, the most meaningful part of the survey was the section dealing with 'Priests in Colleges'. It was the section also where bias was most evident in the phrasing of the questions, but the generally clear-cut response from the students indicates that they were eager for change. The following were the six questions on this topic, together with the collective response of the Senior students:

> Should there be just a president, a dean and two spiritual advisers in a diocesan boarding school? Yes, 39; No 8.
> Can a priest devote himself as fully to the job of teaching as:
>   a) a married layman? Yes, 36; No, 17.
>   b) a single layman? Yes, 23; No, 21.
> Would priests be better employed on the missions than teaching here at home? Yes, 36; No 10.
> Would vocations to the priesthood drop if there were only four priests on the staff? Yes, 4; No, 44.
> Does seeing priests with their human weaknesses, and the familiarity of living with them for five years, lessen the image of the priestly vocation? Yes, 19, No 29.
> Has the time come for the Catholic Church to hand over its educational activities to Catholic laymen? Yes, 24; No 17.[1]

---

1. ibid. The view that 'the Church should hand over its educational activities' in boarding schools, so that priests might engage in more socially useful work was shared by young priests at around this time (see Padraig Standún, *Súil le breith* pp. 34-36, and Máirtín Ó Fathaigh, 'Agallamh leis an Athair Padraic Standún' in *Torch* 1993, p.58.

To the last question, the priests responded that 'the Church should hand over jobs to qualified laymen as these become available' but in the meantime should 'trust its own members[?] to do these jobs which will be gradually handed over'. On other points, they argued that four priests would not be sufficient to manage diocesan colleges 'as they are constituted at present' and argued that a married layman could not be expected 'to devote himself to extra-curricular work to the same extent as a priest'. And, reflecting a new policy, the priests allowed that 'a 50/50 representation [of priests and lay teachers] would be desirable'.

Two qualified laymen, in fact, were already on the staff, having joined in September 1968. Free secondary education, with free school transport to enable young people to avail of it, was introduced a year earlier, but some teething problems remained to be resolved. Among those were disagreements between the teachers' union, the A.S.T.I., and the Department of Education. These were brought dramatically to the attention of the students of the College in February 1969. One student wag noted: 'Our lay teachers are on strike; we knew there would be trouble when they arrived.'[1]

In the following two years, more lay teachers were appointed. Charles Kelly, Christopher Kelly, John McLoughlin, Padraic Nolan and John Silke joined the staff in 1969; Tommy Davin, Pat Finnegan Michael Leyden and Martin McDonnell in 1970. The 'desirable' 50/50 balance between lay and clerical staff was achieved in just over two years. The new arrivals were young men, most of them just graduated. All but two were past students of the College. And the shortage of teachers meant that they did not have to spend much time looking for employment. Indeed, several were sought out by President Mooney on graduation, and completed their education diplomas during their first year as teachers.[2]

Already, curricular changes had begun. Greek — no longer a requirement for Maynooth — was phased out between 1962 and 1965. Its place was taken by French. Later in the decade, Music and Art were added to the curriculum for Junior grade students. In 1969, with the appointment of John Silke, Commerce and Economics became available.[3] And Physical Education became a formal part of the curriculum in 1971 with the employment of the College's first P.E. teacher.

---

1. 'Diary' in *Torch* 1969.
2. Charlie Kelly, personal communication.
3. Tommy Davin, John Silke, personal communication.

Changes in the curriculum and in the staffing reflected the broader changes in the Irish educational system, but they were also symptomatic of changes in the character of St Jarlath's. The College always had twin objectives which, as was seen in Chapter Two, were defined as follows by the resolution of the 'Roman Catholic inhabitants of Tuam' in 1817: 'the education of the community at large and particularly the education of zealous, enlightened missionaries'. The objectives might have remained the same over a century and a half later, but the secular element was incontrovertibly foremost by 1970. This development, together with changing perspectives on priestly formation in the wake of Vatican Two, prompted the realisation that students need not be insulated from female company to the extent that they had been. Indeed, female company might even be a civilising influence.

During most of the College's history, adolescence was regarded as something that boys needed to be distracted from. A full weekly programme, close supervision, minimal holidays, plenty of vigorous exercise, an emphasis on masculine qualities, segregation from his opposite numbers in the Convent schools, would guide the student through the sexual minefield of his teenage years, and on to chaste adult-hood.

It became clear to many survivors of the traditional regime, that this was an inadequate preparation for the modern world, and the post-Vatican Two opening up of Irish society made it possible to approach matters differently. One area where this was evident was in sex education. Parents of many prospective students of the late 1960s were surprised to receive in the post, in the same envelope as the College prospectus and news of their son's performance in the entrance exam, a slim volume outlining the 'Facts of Life' and a request that their boy be apprised of its contents before he arrived in the College in September.

At around the same time, there was also a change in the traditional policy of the local boarding schools, defined by one past student in the following terms: 'the student teenagers of Tuam were not supposed to be either seen or heard: by each other that is.'[1] During the academic year 1969-70, Fr Padraic O'Connor was permitted to organise so-called 'hops' for the Leaving Cert students of St Jarlath's and of, alternately, the Mercy and Presentation schools. These dances were immediately popular,

---

1. Tom Kirrane, 'The Walk' in *Iarlaith* 1966, pp.41-43.

and the novelty had not worn off by the end of following school year, if one is guided by a student's description of the atmosphere surrounding the last hop of the year 'with both Convents present, with some of our own fourth years to make up the numbers':

> Senior dormitory at 7.30 that night looked more like the Dandelion Market than a 'dor'. Shoes, after-shave lotion and Brylcreem all changed owners, either temporarily or permanently. Everyone kept assuring everyone else that he looked 'alright'... The first spot prizes caused absolute chaos and soon pandemonium broke loose... Old favourites like 'Twenty-one years' and 'I'll forgive and I'll try to forget' showed the students' craze for old time waltzes, while the quickstep and the slow foxtrot were given a new lease of life by others.[1]

Even a venerable institution like the annual opera which had run successfully since 1944, with pre-pubescent boys playing female roles, was not immune to the winds of change. Fr Séamus Cunnane, who had appeared in operas under the musical direction of Fr Charles Scahill, and who had trained choruses under Fr Gabriel Charles, took over as musical director in the late 1960s. Cunnane, who had lived through the days when Tuam boarding schools had 'led very separate and segregated lives' when 'even to visit one's own sister was a privilege not to be taken for granted', felt that the opera needed shaking up. 'Somewhat nervously', he approached President Mooney with the suggestion that the College should join with one of the girl's schools for the 1969 production. Then, surprised at how positively his suggestion was received, he contacted both Convents. Plans were already well advanced for another production in the Presentation, but Sr Magdalen of the Mercy was encouraging, and her girls were available.[2] Thirty years later, the resulting partnership is still thriving. In 1969, for 'The Quaker Girl' only lead roles were taken by the Mercy students, with girls' parts on the chorus line continuing to be filled by 'boys in female costume and make-up', but in 1970, for 'Oliver', there was a full participation by the Mercy. Incidentally, the role of Mr Bumble

---

1. Padhraic Ó Ciardha, 'The Last Hop' in *Torch* 1970-71.
2. Séamus Cunnane, 'The Second twenty-five' in 'The Mikado', 1993 commemorative programme.

in 'Oliver' was taken by Noel Kirrane, who is the present musical director.[1]

The 1970 production of 'Oliver' marked another departure for the opera. Since the 1944 presentation of 'The Mikado' in the Mall cinema, all other operas had been held in the Odeon, with dress rehearsals in the Mercy and Presentation. The extension of the College completed in 1970, however, included a large gymnasium-cum-theatre, so the St Jarlath's Operatic Society was able for the first time to put on a show in St Jarlath's College. There were some mixed feelings about this:

> The Odeon Cinema era was over, enjoyable as that had been. No more walking down the town in full costume and wigs, to the amusement of the locals. No more frantic last minute fit-ups and wiring. No more scenery painting in the emptied swimming-pool. Much of the old atmosphere was probably lost, but the convenience of one's own hall and stage probably compensated.[2]

Achievements and diversions

The Mooney decade ended in 1971. A student paid tribute to the departing president's service to the College in various capacities — as a teacher, as a sports trainer, as an administrator. Mooney, it was acknowledged, had never courted popularity, but he had 'gained respect'. The tribute went on (unconsciously echoing earlier tributes to Presidents Browne and Kilkenny): 'True, he enforced rules, some harsh, but with a manner that they seemed rather the counsel of a loving father, than the dominion of an exacting overlord'.[3]

Fr Michael Walsh, who had been secretary to Archbishop Walsh, succeeded Mooney as President, and served until 1977. In personality, he was quite different to his predecessor. Befitting the times, he placed far less emphasis on discipline and made

---

1. Kirrane provided the following biographical snippet for the 1993 programme: 'As this year it has happened that I am the new M.D. / I've to make a little list, I've to make a little list. / From my twenty-five year's training, yes a musical C.V. / I did modestly desist, but the ed. he did insist: / In 'The Gondoliers' in sixty sev'n a little girl was I, / In 'White Horse Inn' in sixty-eight as alto sang 'Goodbye', / Old Bumble I in 'Oliver', the first show in our hall, / The part of Sky in 'Guys and Dolls' made me feel ten feet tall; / Then eight years later here I was —orchestral pianist, / And just to keep well in with God, Cathedral Organist.
2. Cunnane, in 'Mikado' programme.
3. Noel Kirrane, 'An appreciation of Canon Mooney' in *Torch* 1972, pp.13-15.

Current and former teaching staff, February 1972. *Front row*: Christopher Kelly, Charles Kelly, P. Griffiths, J. Donoghue, J. Gibbons, J. O'Sullivan, J. Cunnane, M. Walsh, J. Walsh, M. Mooney, J. G. McGarry, J. Costello, P. Prendergast. *Middle row*: B. Kavanagh, P. Ó Tuairisg, F. Ryan, M. Laing, M. O'Grady, C. Canavan, G. Charles, J. Fitzgerald, C. Langan, A. King, M. Moran, T. Cummins, C. Scahill, T. Treacy, T. Shannon, L. Durkin, T. Dooley, S. Cunnane, P. Williams, J. Silke. *Back row*: J.J. Cribben, M. Leyden, D. Maloney, P. O'Connor, P. Nolan, T. Davin, J. McLoughlin, P. Finnegan, M. McDonnell, M. O'Malley, G. Ferguson, J. Maloney.

Teaching staff, 1996-97. *Front row*: Fr Fintan Monahan, David McDonagh, Cammy Gallagher, Michael Cannon, Gabrielle Gallagher, Fr Oliver Hughes, Christopher Kelly, Seán Stanley, Terry O'Regan, Michael Leyden: *Middle row*: Éamonn Ó Loinsigh, Pat Griffiths, Therese Curley, Geraldine Dineen, Charles Kelly, Eilín Nic Dhonnacha, Donal Blake, Tommy Davin, Kieran Day, Daithí Quinn, Sandra McGreal, Peadar Conroy. Back row: Tom Craddock, Kevin Keady, Padraic Nolan, George Moran, John McLoughlin, Fr Tod Nolan, Martin McDonnell, John Silke.

THE NAME IS COOL

THE HAIR STYLES ARE COOL

Valentine Dolan
Dublin Road

What the 'cool' mid-1970s student looked like. Advertisement in College magazine, *Torch* 1975.

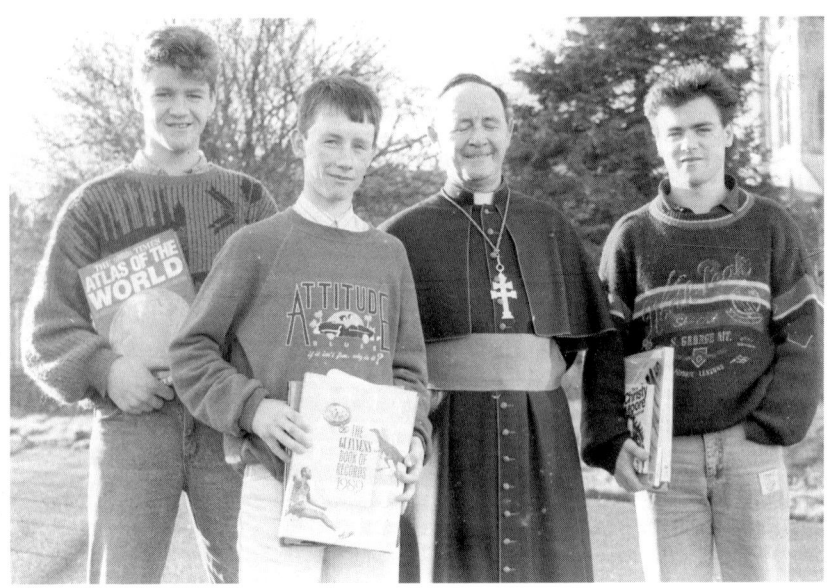

Academic prize-giving, 1989, with Archbishop Cassidy.

School tour to Russia, c.1990, with Fr Ciarán Blake.

Climbing the Reek.

The College Astronomy Club, 1990, pictured with the Birmingham telescope. The telescope was the property of the astronomer John Birmingham (1816-1884) of Millbrook House, Milltown, who had associations with the College. The telescope was purchased for the College by President Patrick Kilkenny in July 1886.

Máistir Éamonn Ó Loinsigh with winners of All-Ireland Irish Schools' Drama Competition, 1989.

Today's students at work in the language laboratory and in the computer suite.

Members of the the College's Legion of Mary band. They provide regular entertainment for senior citizens.

'The Legend of Jarlath' by the renowned stained glass artist, Evie Hone (1894-1955). The piece was purchased by the bi-centenary committee and is now displayed in the College.

The Bi-Centenary Past Pupils' Union Committee 1999/2000.
Front Row: Fr. Tod Nolan, Michael Marren (President), Fr. Oliver Hughes (College President), Proinsias Kitt (Treasurer). Back Row: Charles Kelly, Fr. Michael Molloy (Secretary), Padraic Rhatigan and Gerry Burke.

efforts to eliminate the drabness in students' surroundings. The removal of the wall around the sportsfield, and its replacement by trees, reduced the institutional atmosphere, while vivid hues of paint and the provision of cubicles had the same effect in the dormitories. The extension of the refectory — incorporating the old science hall and the old 'Pro's Ref' — also added to the students' comfort.[1] Staff comforts were not forgotten either, and a larger 'Pro's Ref' was fashioned from two surplus classrooms. Walsh was popular among the students, having been, according to the recollection of staff, always eager to accede to requests for half-days from the monitors. The only stern act of his presidency which is still remembered was the suppression of *Torch* for a year, when the 1977 issue was considered to have included an excessive proportion of 'slagging' and *double entendre*.

More than a decade after he left the College, Walsh fondly remembered the 'wonderful spirit of co-operation which existed between teachers and students at that time':

> While the teachers supplied bright ideas, hard work and dedication in a most impressive manner, students, for their part, responded with great goodwill and enthusiasm to all that was being done for them. The picture of the scenes here on a half-day remains vivid. Every pitch was occupied by football and hurling teams soon after dinner. Even after afternoon tea, students were to be seen playing. Inside, there was basketball, badminton, table-tennis and volleyball, while the swimming pool used to be so full that championship swimmers were allowed out to the town pool to practice.[2]

It was appropriate that Walsh's reminiscences gave prominence to sporting activity, because his presidency was one of considerable sporting achievement. As has been shown in Chapter Eleven, the period 1972-74, with three Connacht titles in-a-row and one All-Ireland, was one of several high-points as far as football in the College was concerned. It was also a time of achievement in other sports, when St Jarlath's won its highest ever honours in both athletics and hurling. In athletics, the Science Cup, the highest award in Irish Colleges athletics, was won on three successive years, 1972, 1973 and 1974 — a feat

---

1. Hoyne, 'Past presidents', pp.37-38.
2. ibid.

which has not yet been matched in football — while in hurling, the 'B' All-Ireland was won in 1972.

Athletic competition, as we have seen in Chapter Five, has a long history in the College, with the annual sports day dating from the late nineteenth century. It was not until the 1940s, however, when Fr Christy Langan took the initiative, that there was any serious effort made to improve on the natural talents that many individuals possessed. Sportsmen had their outlet on the football field, went the prevailing attitude; track and field events could be left to schools like Garbally.[1] Langan's efforts resulted in the winning of 'a considerable number of medals in sprints, jumps, pole-vaulting, weight-throwing and javelin throwing' at both Connacht and All-Ireland level during the late 1940s and 1950s. It was Langan's 'contagious enthusiasm', however, rather than methodical coaching which brought about this limited success.[2]

The formal training in coaching technique received by Fr Brendan Kavanagh and Fr Paddy Williams, and later by Fr Colm Canavan, transformed the situation and was rewarded when the College's first all-Ireland senior athletics gold medal was taken by Máirtín Clancy in 1960, for the long jump. Three years later, St Jarlath's won the Senior Connacht Shield, in the process breaking a Garbally stranglehold of thirteen years. Other milestones followed: in 1964, Seamus O'Beirn became the first St Jarlath's athlete to win two all-Ireland gold medals; in 1965 the College team took home the President's Shield for runners-up, its first ever all-Ireland athletics trophy.[3] And when the Dr Walsh Cup for the combined best performance of all age-groups in Connacht Colleges athletics was first presented in 1971, it was won by St Jarlath's. Remarkably, it was not relinquished until 1997. As far as the singular success of the 1972-74 period was concerned, it was achieved principally because of the presence in the College at the time of several remarkable athletes, of whom the most outstanding were Padraic Jordan and Eddie Campbell.[4]

The Science Cup has not been won since 1974, although as the twenty-six successive Walsh Cup successes prove, the

---

1. Williams interview.
2. Mooney's 'Football', p.100.
3. Williams, '1961-66' pp.81, 84, 87.
4. Michael Leyden, personal communication. Both Jordan and Campbell, incidentally, broke Irish Senior Colleges records, something which was achieved at junior level by Justin Durkin for the pole vault.

College had, until recently, maintained a leading position in Connacht in boys' athletics. There were also regular successes in cross country competition. Impressive individual performances notwithstanding, College teams have not challenged for national trophies in several decades. In one opinion, the intensification of academic competition since the early 1980s has been detrimental to athletics. National championships take place at a time when even the doughtiest athletes are preoccupied with the state exams.[1]

Hurling has been played in the College since early in the century, but at a relatively low-key level. The College's catchment area — whether the Archdiocese as a whole or the Tuam district — has never been a hurling stronghold and only in a few southern parishes such as Athenry, Turloughmore and Abbeyknockmoy, has the game been strong. Students from that area have ensured that hurling was kept alive, with the assistance of interested and practiced individuals from other parts of the country. Generally, however, it has been the role of College teams to fill the part of valiant loser rather than that of victor.

Senior and junior teams began to take part in senior and junior colleges competition in 1944, but had to wait until 1954 for their first success, which was at junior level. Eighteen years went by before that achievement was surpassed, when a senior team trained by Joe Donaghue qualified for the 'B' All-Ireland final in 1972, beating the holders, St Mary's, Belfast, in the semi-final. The memorable final finished with one of the most remarkable turn-arounds ever seen in sporting competition; as the *Torch* annalist put it, the story of the game was 'the story of the final three minutes'. At that point, Offaly hurling nursery, Presentation College, Birr, was coasting to victory with a lead of 4-8 to 3-2. What happened next was described by Leaving Cert student, Gerard McHugh:

> And then the miracle happened: a long ball from Niall Barrett landed just outside the square, and big Dermot Loughlin was there to score one of the most important goals of the championship. For many, it was still too late, and for Birr supporters, it seemed the consolation goal that often comes at this time. But for the St Jarlath's senior hurling team and the faithful supporters who still believed amid all the unbelieving, of the glorious possibility, it was

---

1. Nolan interview.

merely the start of a display of the talent and spirit that only the best possess. Within seconds the mighty Flaherty pointed to leave five points between the sides. A glorious long ball from Hughes came off the cross-bar, and in the goalmouth struggle, where only the fittest and hardest survive, Paul O'Shea found the net. Now things could not go wrong for Jarlath's and from the puck-out, the brilliant left-half back, Michael Hogan, from way out on the wing, with the force and tremendous determination that Hogan is capable of, lofted the sliotar over backs, forwards, midfielders and goalkeeper, all the way to the net. And make no mistake about it, it was no fluke, for within seconds a point followed from the cool and shrewd Morgan Hughes. It was only fitting that the last puck and score of the championship should come from a 65 yard free from that hurler of hurlers, John Flaherty.[1]

Having scored 3-3 in the last three minutes, St Jarlaths won the game by a margin of three points, 6-5 to 4-8.

Since then, there has been occasional success at provincial level for College teams. Most recently, Connacht Senior 'B' titles were taken in 1993 and 1994. The consequent promotion to the 'A' championship, however, left St Jarlath's somewhat out of its depth. Since then, College hurlers have had to gain their satisfaction from participation rather than from victory.

Sporting achievement was one tradition of the College which survived the transition of the late 1960s. Other more mundane traditions also lived on into the 1970s. For one thing, the slang words of the 1920s and 1930s remained in everyday use: a slice of bread was still a 'feck'; sweets and such treats were 'mag'; day students were 'shams'; the unit of corporal punishment was a 'batter'; those next in line to use handball alley or tennis court were said to have had 'stone'. And every student had at least one nickname, generally derived from their native place, from a personal attribute, or from an embarrassing episode, but sometimes inherited from a brother or an uncle. Many of the given names were wounding to their bearers, but they seemed merely exotic to those on the outside. One student of another Connacht College contrasted the conventions in his own school with those in St Jarlath's:

> They even had cool nicknames, wonderfully creative even in their mischief-making. With us, every Murphy was a

---

1. Gerard McHugh 'Sport' in *Torch*, 1972.

Spud and every Burke was a Burkie; Fitzgerald was always Fitzy. a brain box was Brain Box; in St Jarlath's he could become Homer.[1]

Initiation rites, of the type found in all-male societies everywhere, also persisted. Students of the 1930s, the 1940s, and much later, described the mock 'baptism' of first-year students. A student of the 1970s remembered another annual ritual:

> When I entered St Jarlath's College..., we were introduced to the real curriculum on the evening of the first day. Before second study the lads would gather out the front for some fresh air. Here we first years, known as 'Connors', were filled in by some seniors on the traditional first night 'Connors' Races': first prize a Gold Watch. A good body of 'Connors' was organised into a pell-mell dash around the walks. The bell for second study went at the first furlong point (roughly half-way). The finishing athletes found no audience, no sporting impresarios and no gold watch.[2]

Evidently, however, the time-honoured rituals and the particular language of the St Jarlath's student community have been in decline since the 1980s. This is attributable to the fall in boarding numbers and to the provision of more individualised sleeping accommodation.[3]

Other traditional aspects of the College's culture still persist. In this context, one notes that the school tour has been revived in recent decades after a lapse of half a century. There is a difference, however, for the destination nowadays is more likely to be Moscow or Venice than Castlehackett or Killaloe. Another link with the nineteenth century is the continuing interest in handball among students. The game has been played, sometimes fanatically, since the College's earliest years but, recently, the improved facilities for other activities has lessened demand for the alleys. Although many students have represented St Jarlath's with distinction — notably, Colm Canavan in the 1940s, Damien Warde and Aidan Kelly in the 1960s — handball has

---

1. Liam Horan, 'Schools' GAA has taught us all a lesson' in *Irish Independent*, 8 April 1998.
2. Michael Kelly 'Seeking intelligent answers to a Roscommon problem' in *Sunday Independent*, 26 July 1998.
3. Nolan interview.

generally been regarded more as a pastime than as a sport.¹ The same could be said of swimming. The pool has been a popular amenity for seventy years, but occasional competitive success has been usually the result of involvement in a swimming club outside of the College.

The continuing vitality of Irish language activity is a significant link with the College's past, and interest is by no means confined to students from Gaeltacht areas. The work of John MacHale, of Presidents Ronan and Bourke, of past pupils like Seán Mag Fhlainn, Dr Thomas Bodkin Costello and Rev. Malachy Eaton, has been continued in recent decades by An Cumann Gaelach in the late 1970s, by Feachtas in the late 1980s and by An Cumann Drámaíochta and An Cumann Díospóireachta in the 1990s. The impressive range of activity in Irish during the Seachtain na Gaeilge of March 1999 was recognised by Conradh na Gaeilge with the presentation of a computer to the College.²

If football, the opera, handball, and other traditional pastimes like tennis and table tennis, continue to engage St Jarlath's students, the modern emphasis on leisure activity provides plenty of competition for their attention. The unprecedented flourishing of clubs and societies during the mid-1960s has already been described and, in the period since then, many recreational pursuits have thrived for a time. Among the formally organised was a Hobbies Club, established in 1969 and a Student Debating Society in 1972. Fr O'Connor revived the Gardening Society in 1979, and a group with the name Crann took an interest in planting trees in the late 1980s. During the late 1980s also, an active branch of Young Ireland exhorted everybody, from the President Moloney down, to buy Irish goods. A Photo Club has existed at various times, as has an Astronomy Club, and a Video Club. In addition, depending on the level of interest, extra-curricular classes have been provided in woodwork, in electronics, in computing, in life-saving and in first aid. Music remains the passion of many, with the success of local band, the Sawdoctors, having motivated student bands like Róisín Dubh, the Ceoláns and Draíocht Dubh. Sports like basketball, badminton and golf, have become popular with some, while soccer continues to be played non-competitively. Noteworthy too is the *Saol Plus* programme which was intro-

---

1. Tommy Davin, personal communication.
2. See *Torch*, 1980, 1989, 1994, 1999

duced in selected secondary schools in the mid-1980s. Participants are monitored as they progress 'through a year of training specifically designed to improve flexibility, muscle tone, endurance and co-ordination'. Certificates are awarded to those who complete the programme at the end of the year. Evidently, for the past number of years, St Jarlath's has been the only school still taking part in *Saol Plus*.[1]

Students with a developed sense of social concern have had various outlets over the years. In the late 1960s, the Carissime society was active, raising awareness and seeking to 'collect funds for the underprivileged people of the world'. More recently, the idealistic and philanthropic urges of students have found an outlet through the activity of the Legion of Mary branch. Founded in 1976, and sustained since then through the commitment of John MacLoughlin, the Legion enrols students in their fourth and fifth years. A varied programme includes a weekly meeting and pilgrimages to Knock Shrine, as well as regular visits to entertain senior citizens and residents at the Toghermore Rehabilitation Centre. Recently, Legion members have travelled to London and Glasgow during their Easter holidays to do social work with marginalised inhabitants of those cities.[2]

Day-boys and boarders
Since November 1977, there have been three presidents of the College: Fr Tommy Waldron, a teacher of French and an active supporter of athletics and of the opera, who had joined the College staff in 1958, was president from 1977 to 1986. Mathematics teacher, Fr Dermot Moloney, took over from then until 1994, when he was succeeded by another former football coach, French teacher, Fr Oliver Hughes.

Waldron was considered to be an extremely cultured individual. He was an exceptional public speaker, both as preacher and teacher, who took great pains to communicate ideas to his listeners. And, considering it his responsibility to 'civilise' his charges, he had copies of art masterpieces placed on walls around the College.[3] Something of his spirit is captured in the reflective nature of the compliment he paid to the contributors to *Torch* 1983:

> They carry a torch that is passed down the generations,

1. 'Saol Plus' in *Torch* 1993, p.96, and 1999, p.70.
2. Hubert Curran, 'Carissime' in *Torch* 1969; Cathal Carty, 'The Legion of Mary' and Vinny Browne, 'Legion work in Scotland' in *Torch* 1999.
3. Hughes interview.

and their function and value is that of their own ancestors — chroniclers, historians and penmen. They preserve in writing a time, a people, a picture, that would otherwise fade from human memory. In these pages are recorded not just the events of one year, but something much more subtle — the flavour of the time. In the little bits of poetry, of story, of comment are glimpses of the present, of the way we are now, of the way students think and feel in A.D.1983.[1]

Fr Moloney had spent twenty-five years on the teaching staff before his appointment as president. Appropriately, given developments during his presidency, he was a day-boy during four of his five years as a student in the 1950s. At that time, day students were a tiny minority, and those who wished to enter Maynooth were required to have spent at least a year boarding in a recognised diocesan college.

The context was changed by free education and free school transport and, although there was no immediate surge of day students into the College, there was a gradual increase in their numbers. By the mid-1970s, day students had a significant presence in the College. In the enrolment of first years in 1974-75, for example, they numbered twenty-five — 30% of the total intake of that year.[2] There was no strategy at that time, however, of attracting day students, nor was there a clear conception of how they fitted into what was still, predominantly, a boarding school. Historically, the few day-boys in the College had been town-based, and they participated in the life of the institution to a greater or lesser degree, according to personal inclination. But the 'bus day-boys', of the free school transport era who arrived at 9 am and departed at 4 pm were excluded, unless they made a conscious effort, from many of the extra-curricular activities which gave St Jarlath's College its character.

Occasional concern was expressed by staff members about the lack of recreational facilities for those day-boys who did not

---

1. Canon Thomas Waldron, 'Foreword', in *Torch* 1983, p.3. Castlebar-born Tommy Waldron was ordained at Maynooth in 1954 and spent the following year in the Dunboyne establishment. He served in Headford from 1955 and joined the staff of St Jarlath's in 1958. From 1977 to 1986, he was College president. In 1986, he was appointed administrator of Tuam and, in 1989, parish priest of Claremorris. Already a Monsignor, he became Diocesan Chancellor in 1993. He died in 1995.
2. Minutes of staff meetings, 10 October 1974.

play football, but there was wariness that any attempt to address the issue — through the provision of a billiard table for example — should not 'segregate the day boys entirely from the boarders'. In 1976, a staff member was allocated specific responsibility for day-boys and the issues and problems specific to them. At that time these were perceived to be: 'transport forms, Saturday absenteeism, Wednesday match, and meetings with boys and their parents when and where possible'.[1]

By the late 1970s, there was a recognition of the need to attract more day students and a discussion took place on how this might be achieved. It was suggested that there be a 'planned method' of approaching potential students but, in the meantime, the benefits of 'newspaper publicity' and of 'actively cultivating the students who are already with us' were not to be overlooked. In 1981, a proposal that the parents of day students should be enabled to 'know more about the school' was acted upon, resulting in a series of 'information evenings'. Meanwhile, the need to more fully integrate day students, in the first instance by increasing their involvement after 4 pm, was addressed by giving individual teachers particular responsibility for seven day-students each. If the growth in numbers is any indication, the efforts made were successful: in 1984, the intake of first years included 49 day students.[2] Problems persisted, however and, in 1986, a 'Day-Boy Committee' of the staff offered solutions for some of these: 'occasional spot-checks' would reduce Saturday morning absenteeism; more 'manpower' would stop the tendency to gather 'downtown' during the Wednesday afternoon half-day for games; better lunch facilities might keep students within bounds during lunchtime; supervised study in the College for more of those who lived nearby would improve academic performances. The members of the Committee did not assume that they had all the answers, or indeed that they had identified all of the problems, so they suggested that the establishment of one or more committees from among the day students should be considered, 'so as to to enable them to share their ideas.'[3]

In fact, one Leaving Cert day-student had already shared his ideas with the general body of students and staff in the 1985 issue of *Torch*. In an effort to increase 'mutual understanding'

---

1. ibid., 13 September, 5 October 1976.
2. ibid., 23 May 1979, 2 December 1981, 30 April 1984.
3. ibid., 7 April 1986.

between his fellows and the boarders, according to himself, he presented a description of the 'life and vitality' introduced into the College by the day students. And, in his own sardonic way, he addressed many of the preoccupations of staff meetings at the time:

> If not for us, there would be the undesirable phenomenon of silence in the library at all times. If not for us, Mr Kelly would not have to patrol the school on Monday mornings, tapping rhythmically on doors, to seek out and interrogate the 'Saturday people' or the 'five-day-weekers'... If not for us, Mr Griffiths would not have the challenge of maintaining law and order as we queue up riotously for Mrs Coen's irresistible tea. If there were not day-boys, the College would be looked upon by locals as a school only for 'aristocratic foreigners'. But because of the favourable reports transmitted by day-boys already here, more and more of the local people have abandoned their unwillingness to send their sons here...
>
> Our routine is often more strenuous and demanding than [boarders] imagine. We rise at the break of day and dress, wash in a rush, hurry breakfast and run for the bus. The buses themselves lack comfort; most are old and inadequate.
>
> One feature of the day which is patiently awaited, and without which the day doesn't feel the same, is going down town. Many feel this is wrong and say that it must be stopped but our light-hearted spirit prevails, and out town we go...
>
> It is all too easy for a day-boy to neglect study, and here he has to be more self-dependent than a boarder. The temptation to watch T.V., to ramble off, or go out at night is all too easy. The addition of Saturday school practically rules out the chance of going out over the weekend. Of all aspects of College life it is probably the most challenging...[1]

---

1. Michael O'Connor, 'Day Boys' in Torch 1985, p,81. An earlier perspective on life as a day-boy was offered by Peter Hughes, Murt Dunleavy and Pat Dunleavy in the *2C Times*, (1979), p.2: '...The number of day-boys is rising so fast that now a third of students are day-boys, whereas there were only a few. The reason for this is that boys from the country used to leave school after they finished national school. Another reason is that there are buses now whereas in the years gone by there was no transport. Day-boys are becoming more interested in sport. This is because there is transport

The Saturday morning classes were challenging also for other reasons. Ever since the other boarding schools in Tuam discontinued Saturday classes in the early 1970s, the College had hired mini-buses to collect and deliver its own students for the half-day. Many day students, however, preferred to lie on in bed, a preference which became very noticeable in class as the number of day-boys increased. Most lay teachers too, would have preferred to spend Saturday mornings with their families and the question of a five-day-week was broached regularly by A.S.T.I. members during the 1970s and 1980s. From the perspective of the College authorities, however, this was difficult to concede. It would have resulted in 350 boarders having almost two-and-a-half unstructured days at the week-end. This, it was felt, would almost inevitably lead to discipline problems. The other alternative — five day boarding — would have made the College unattractive for many parents of prospective boarders. It proved possible, however, when the constraints of timetabling allowed, to give individual teachers another morning in the week without classes, or to allow a rotating few each year to take the full week-end off. And flexibility was also shown with regard to the wishes of day students when, following representations from parents, the Saturday starting-time was put back to 9.45 am. This latter experiment, however, was short-lived.[1]

It was not just existing students who were affected by the Saturday morning classes. Many potential day students, it was felt, were discouraged from attending the College because of this element of the timetable. While some town-based parents were happy to see their sons usefully occupied for part of the week-end, it was argued, the majority regarded it as disruptive of family life. But if they did, more of them than ever were sending their sons to St Jarlath's. In 1987-88, for the first time, there were more day students than boarders in the new intake of first years, heralding the day when boarders would become a minority in the College as a whole.

Eventually, following discussion and in respose to 'the

---

    for day-boys who have to travel a long way. Some day-boys come to St Jarlath's because of the sporting facilities. The half-day on Wednesday makes them more interested in sport, but they don't like coming to school on Saturdays. The town day-boys have more advantages than the country day-boys...'

1. Minutes of staff minutes, 3 June 1974, 3 October 1976 1 June 1976, 6 May 1980, 12 February 1981, 25 October 1985.

changing face of the school population', President Maloney announced that Saturday morning classes would cease from September 1990. The boarding school would continue to operate over seven days and parents of boarders were informed that the development sub-committee was 'planning an intensive programme of activity to aid their son's development.' A preliminary list of suggestions from the teachers included the following:

> The development of various skills in the area of sport, drama, debating and question time, day-trips, project work, extra study, type-writing, computer studies, local history, social studies, grinds, first-aid, technological studies, technical drawing, woodwork, do-it-yourself projects, communications library work, gardening and other outdoor activities.[1]

Lay teachers could continue to be involved, on a voluntary basis, in the new Saturday morning programme, which would comprise two one-hour sessions — from 10.00 to 11.00 and from 11.15 to 12.15. That the students felt that the change was overdue was indicated by the tone of a humorous article in the following issue of *Torch*, giving credit for the new dispensation to the 'Popular Peoples Liberation of Saturday Morning Front'. Interestingly, the writer presented his saga as a struggle between lay and clerical staff which, arguably, was not too wide of the mark. The piece concluded with an afterword: 'It's a change for the better, with an improved timetable which is appreciated by all day-boys, especially on Saturday mornings. Sincere thanks to all concerned for changing tradition'.[2]

The rise in the numbers of day students was accompanied by a decline in the number of boarders. This was not a phenomenon which was confined to St Jarlath's nor, for that matter, to Ireland. In the past decade or so, many renowned boarding schools have become day schools due to falling demand for their residential facilities. In Tuam, both Presentation and Mercy secondary schools have ceased to take boarders while there is no remaining Catholic boarding school for boys north of Tuam in the western half of the country. The reasons for the decline of boarding are complex, with the easier access to day schools of

---

1. ibid., 28 May 1990.
2. Shane Grennan, 'Top Secret: How Saturday morning was won' in *Torch* 1991, pp.76-78.

recent decades providing only part of the explanation. Smaller family sizes and a greater emphasis on the individuality of the child have made many parents reluctant to be separated from their children during their formative years. And negative portrayals and perceptions of institutional life have discouraged many from considering boarding.

Like many other long-established institutions, St Jarlath's has faced difficulty and disappointment in the past decade. Particularly distressing was the discovery that a student had been the victim of sexual abuse. The abuser was later convicted in the courts.[1] This episode prompted a review of procedures to ensure that such a thing could never happen again. The greater sense of alertness in the College reflects the situation in the larger society.

The experience of boarding has changed considerably since the 1970s. About half of the 150 boarders go home each week-end, and the College closes completely during one week-end every month. Most of the arrangements made a decade ago are still in place. For those who remain in the College, day-trips, woodwork and gardening occupy Saturday mornings for non-exam classes; exam classes spend extra time at study. There is time for games during the remainder of the week-end, and permission to go 'downtown' at designated times. Evidently, students appreciate the ambiance of Supermacs during these periods.[2] But, despite the apparent variety, students find the week-ends spent in the College, to be 'the worst aspect of boarding'. Peadar King and Eamonn Day Lavelle, both from Inishbofin, told the *Irish Times* that Saturdays and Sundays were 'boring' and that inactivity allowed 'more time to get homesick'. Teenagers from Inishbofin — if they wished to go to secondary school — have always had to board away from home and, because these islands are in the archdiocese, many have come to Tuam. Island students of previous decades only got home three or four times a year — at most. If the weather was bad, Inishbofin lads might spend most of a vacation on the mainland at Cleggan, looking out to sea and waiting for the winds to calm. By contrast, King and Lavelle now go home 'almost every weekend'. On 'home Fridays' they get a lift from a teacher to Galway, where they take the bus to Cleggan, and the 7.30 pm ferry from there. The journey back is as long and as arduous, but they consider 'it's worth it to get home'.[3]

---

1. *Tuam Herald*, 30 March 1996.
2. Charlie Kelly, Tommy Davin, personal communication
3. *Irish Times*, 10 November 1998; Chris Day, personal communication.

The balance between day students and boarders might have altered radically in the past decade or more, but the presence of boarders is valued by the College management:

> Boarding has been important, insofar as the maintenance of the character of the school is concerned — in passing on tradition. In a boarding school, there is life and activity seven days a week, morning, afternoon and evening. The boys are together a lot more, and they discuss and analyse the events of the day, whether on the football field or in class. The day students, meanwhile, would have scattered to different places and wouldn't have the same opportunity for discussion. Boarders, for this reason, form the core of the support for College teams in football matches. The same is true with regard to the annual opera and to the activities of the Legion.[1]

Staff and students

If the influx of day students and the increasingly humane nature of the regime for boarders are the two most salient developments in the recent history of St Jarlath's College, the past two decades have also brought other changes. The staff has grown in line with student numbers, but it has also altered in other ways. There are now only four priests on the staff, and they are outnumbered, eight-to-one, by lay teachers. The first permanent female lay teacher, Mary Murphy, joined the staff in 1978, and there is now a total of ten women teachers, full-time and part-time.

In 1986, Sister Justine, Sister Barnabas and Sister Rosalie retired from working in the College. Their Christian Retreat Order had provided the nursing service and supervised catering services in the establishment during four decades.[2] Growing student numbers again put pressure on space and a further extension was completed during 1985 and 1986. A 'Super-draw', in the jargon of that decade, was organised to pay for the building. Curricular development continued apace. Reflecting this was a decision to include 'Computer Studies' on students' report sheets in 1984. Already 'Relationships Courses' were being provided for senior boys. And there were some innovations which would have been unthinkable even a short time earlier. In this

---

1. Hughes interview.
2. Tom Kelly, 'Farewell' in *Torch* 1987, pp.67-68. The Sisters of Christian Retreat had replaced the Bon Secours sisters in 1959.

category was a decision to provide a Home Economics room with cooking facilities for the Social & Scientific option being taken by some of the boys.[1]

Boys might be taught how to cook and how to better conduct their relationships with others, but the possession of such knowledge, it would seem, did not significantly improve their behaviour. If the minutes of staff meetings since the 1970s are an indication, disciplinary issues have been an ever-present preoccupation of teachers. Indeed, the view that each intake of students was more difficult to manage than its predecessors has found frequent expression: the 'increasingly noticeable' appearance of obscene graffiti was remarked upon in 1979; four years later 'the business of writing on desks' was considered to have 'got out of hand'; in 1987, it was the 'new problem' of disruptive pupils which was attracting attention, while in 1991, there was concern about local manifestations of the 'new lawless attitude which seems to be creeping into society'. Over the years 'long' or 'wide-ranging' discussions on disciplinary issues were noted in the minute book, with particular alarm being evident in the report of a meeting in the late 1980s:

> A number of teachers felt that standards of discipline and general good manners were slipping, and that something needed to be done about this. The areas of greatest concern were litter, smoking, side-line support, language, dress, punctuality, Saturday absenteeism, and attitudes towards teachers and authority. Some teachers felt that the litter problem was getting out of hand; that smoking, and the spitting which accompanied it, were disgusting habits; that the recent side-line chants were an insult to those involved and no help to any team. Language was at an all time low as was particularly evident when one sat in the staff-room between studies... Students would knock one another down in the corridor without a word.[2]

At the same time, however, others pointed to the need for a sense of proportion, arguing that 'disciplinary problems were no greater than in the past', and that apparent changes in student behaviour were attributable to the fact that 'corridors for

---

1. Minutes of staff meetings, 22 November 1979, 26 October 1984, 7 April, 1 Sept 1986,
2. ibid, 3 April 1989.

350 were now being used by 650'.[1] That the additional 300 in the corridors were day-students and, therefore, not subject to the boarding school discipline traditionally exercised by deans, must have contributed to an impression that things were 'getting out of hand'.

The management of more students presented its own challenge, but new pedagogical approaches, which saw the student as an active rather than as a passive partner in the educational process, were raising questions about established strategies for managing misbehaviour, even altering conceptions of what constituted misbehaviour. Ultimately, the new thinking would find legislative expression — in the abolition of corporal punishment in 1982. But long before then, practices were changing anyway. In 1977, staff were instructed by President Walsh that 'to hit on the head is completely out' and that 'a slap on the hand must be for misconduct only, and never for failure to answer a question'. A year later President Waldron advised that corporal punishment, 'other than by a slap on the hand could not be stood over, and even slapping on the hand should be avoided where possible'. In 1981, the same president stated that he would prefer if corporal punishment was not employed by any teacher in the school. Another traditional sanction — putting disruptive students out of class — was discontinued in 1984.

Goals and perspectives

Oliver Hughes became president in 1994, his twenty-third year on the staff of the College. Having spent such a long period teaching, he welcomed the change to an administrative position. The role — as Hughes expected, having observed his predecessors — is a challenging one which combines a number of functions: president of the boarding school; principal of the secondary school; school manager; manager of the College's property. Among others, the president has to work with Department of Education officials, with third-level institutions, with suppliers, with parents and, on a daily basis, with staff and with students.

Their president finds present day students altogether more pleasant than their counterparts of two or three decades ago. They are instinctively co-operative, and are not as angry or as hostile toward authority as the generation he faced as a young teacher in the early 1970s. Nevertheless, students nowadays are

---

1. ibid.

more difficult to motivate and more difficult to entertain. This, he attributes to ever-increasing competition for their attention from the entertainment media and elements of the youth culture.[1] As president, Hughes has a number of guiding objectives:

> I am conscious of St Jarlath's long tradition as a diocesan college. I am conscious that it is a Catholic college and, perhaps more importantly, that it is a Christian college. We must, therefore, ensure that the establishment is flavoured by the Christian ethos. By this I mean that we show — and teach — respect for people; that we try to give the young people a sense of their own dignity; that we develop in them an awareness of their importance to this God of ours.
>
> Students, nowadays, need a lot of direction. They don't have fixed values, so they need guidance — from their parents in the first instance, but also from their school. We owe them clear guidance, and not just in relation to education, but with regard to what to eat, to their entertainment, to the company they keep, to drinking and so on. We try to provide that guidance in as humane a way as possible.
>
> More generally, we try to ensure that every fellow sees himself as successful. The staff try to give them all some experiences of success — whether academically, on the sportsfield, in debating, or in the Legion of Mary. A little taste of success, we believe, is helpful in the development of self esteem. And we try to provide a pleasant environment for our students, by maintaining their surroundings to the highest standard possible.[2]

And these are more than mere aspirations. Academic and sporting achievement are hallmarks of the College, but high standards are evident in everything from the carefully-tended gardens to the conspicuous commitment of the teaching staff.

Approaching the third millennium, and its own third century, St Jarlath's College is faced with opportunities and challenges. These are being actively anticipated. In the light of falling numbers, the future of boarding is one topic that has

---

1. Hughes interview.
2. ibid.

been examined. Clearly, there is a level below which boarding simply would not be viable, but there are also other considerations. Will there be, for example, sufficient priests available in future years to run a boarding school? Viability now seems assured. The long-term decline in boarding numbers has been reversed in the academic year 1999-2000, and there are indications of increasing demand for the service, particularly from the parents of post-Junior Certificate students. And although there are only four priests on the staff at present, members of the lay staff have been taking on some of the responsibilities previously undertaken by priests. Most recently, the role of a dean is being filled on a rotating basis by three lay teachers.[1] Other recent discussions have considered the future of secondary education in Tuam. Can a small town — albeit one with more than 1500 post-primary students in its catchment area — continue to support five second-level schools? Some change is inevitable but, equally, it is certain that St Jarlath's College will continue to play an important part in the educational life of the west of Ireland.

Almost two centuries ago, Henry J. Prendergast, *Freeman's Journal* journalist and past pupil of the College, described St Jarlath's as 'a place admirably adapted to the wants and circumstances of the youth of the present time', which provided 'excellent boarding and a liberal and able instruction'. The language might seem archaic, but the sentiments are clear. And those sentiments are not very different to those expressed by a Leaving Certificate student of 1999 — a young man who repeated that exam after spending a year in the the 'outside world' — :

> I firmly believe that we here at Saint Jarlath's College are given something extra, something special. My short experience of the outside world has truly shown me what makes St Jarlath's the envy of so many others... That is not to say that we are more elitist than any other school in Tuam or elsewhere... The atmosphere within the College is one of hard work and dedication. The amount of goodwill and commitment shown by both staff and students is phenomenal. The inter-actions and rapport that develop between teacher and student are, I feel, unique to St Jarlath's College.[2]

---

1. Hughes interview; Charlie Kelly and Tommy Davin, personal communication.
2. Paul Carroll, "Where to?' in *Torch* 1999, p.30.

Appendix A:
Weekly Timetable, 1867
✠
AD MAJOREM DEI GLORIAM

ORDER OF STUDIES & CLASSES

Morning 6 — Rising — Up at first toll of bell. Strict silence to be observed until after breakfast (at 9 o'clock).

Morning 6.30 — Morning prayer from DR. MACHALE'S Catechism. Meditation or Spiritual Lecture.

Morning 7 to 25m. past 8, Study. Strict silence to be observed. 8.25 All students to proceed to the Cathedral in the most orderly manner, if possible in a line or in a row, one after the other. No conversing or unseemly conduct. Each student should remember he is going to assist at the Holy Sacrifice — the offering of the Son of God himself to His Eternal Father.

Morning 9.15 to 10, Free Time —*ad libitum*— recreation should be taken in the parks or ball-court, if the day be fine; if raining, on the corridors, but no going to Rooms. On Mondays and Saturdays permission is given to go to Rooms at this hour, for, or with, one's "Washing".

CLASSES

10 to 11 —REV. TIMOTHY KEVILLE —

— *Latin*, Cicero or Livy {Monday & Thursday}

— *Greek*, Xenephon, Plato or Demosthenes {Tuesday & Friday}

The History and Literature of the Latin Language in Lectures occasionally.

English parsing, orthography, and writing for beginners, and for English students, by a Lecturer.

10.30 to 11 — REV. RICHARD MACHALE —

— Latin Grammar Class, Syntax. Swaine's Sentences, Greek Grammar for beginners {Each of the four days, Monday, Tuesday, Thursday & Friday}

11 to 12 — Horace and Prosody, Virgil, (sometimes) Juvenal or Tacitus, particularly at the end of the academic year. {Monday & Thursday}

Homer or Euripides, with Greek Parsing and Grammar. Advanced Lucian classes. {Tuesday & Friday}

Lectures occasionally on the History and Literature of the Greek language.

11 to 12 o'clock — REV. U.J. BOURKE — Logic, Metaphysics.

12 to 12.30 " — French, Italian.

Electricity, Galvanism, Hydrostatics, Pneumatics, Astronomy, Globes, Mensuration — taught by means of lectures delivered at opportune occasions during the Academical year.

12.30 to 1 — Recreation, outside doors in the College fields, when the day is fine; on the corridors of New College whenever it rains at this time.

1 to 2 — Study in the Large Hall, strict silence to be observed; each student to be in his proper place, namely that which has been marked out for him.

From 1 to 1.30, while the advanced Students are at Study, the younger boys, or those who are learning only English, are taught Arithmetic or Mensuration, or at the end of season, Book-keeping in their own Class-hall.

1.30 to 2 — Irish and History of Irish Literature — on Tuesday & Friday — by REV T. KEVILLE.

1.45 to 2.15 — Sallust and Latin Grammar, on Monday & Thursday.

2 to 2.15 — Ditto on Tuesday & Friday.

2.15 to 10m. to 3 — REV T. KEVILLE — {On Mondays and Thursdays — Greek Composition, Arnold} {On Tuesdays and Friday, Latin Composition, Do.}

From 10m. to 3 to 20m. after 3 o'clock, Algebra — Darre — FATHER KEVILLE.

From 2.30 to 2.45. REV R. MACHALE. Henry's First Book Latin Composition, Syntax — on Mondays and Thursdays. Greek Testament and Greek Grammar — Tuesdays and Fridays.

2.45 to 20m. past 3. Euclid, Mondays and Thursdays; Algebra, Tuesdays and Fridays.

ON WEDNESDAYS AND SATURDAYS

10 to 11. Rev T. KEVILLE History (Roman or English); 2, English Grammar; 3, Belles Lettres;4 History of English Literature.

11 TO 11.30. Free Time

11.30 to 12.30 REV. U.J. BOURKE — Elocution, Bible, or Church History, Catechism.

12.30 to 1. Free Time

1 to 2. REV RICHARD MACHALE — Grecian History and Geography; (Saturday) Irish History and Geography.

On Sundays Catechism in Irish and English from 11 to 11.30; ceremonies are taught for half an hour (11.30 to 12 o'clock). The Students get a walk for an hour and a half (from 1.45 to 3.15)

Music on Wednesdays from 2.30 to 3.15

20 minutes after 3, visit to Our Lord in the Blessed Sacrament 3.30, Dinner

From 4 to 5.30, Free Time: all at play if the day be fine, in the College parks; if raining on the corridors.

Study to 8 o'clock — at 8 supper; at 9 night prayer; at 9.15 candles quenched. All in bed.

No reading, or study, or lighting of candles during the night. One, if found by the Superiors, is liable to expulsion. Observe — While at recreation all should be together in the play-grounds, or all on the corridors, but not separate or in different places at the same time.

No Student to be absent from Prayer without special leave.

STRICT SILENCE IS TO BE OBSERVED

Firstly —From night prayer to 9.15 the following morning; Secondly —During study hours, namely: in the morning, mid-day, and evening; Thirdly — Going to Mass or coming from Mass — to Visitation, or coming back.

The prefect of studies, the Rev. J. Corbett, or one of the Superiors, is never absent from the Students

No Student should, during study hours, or class hours, go to his room without first getting leave. No one is to go into the room of any other Student without leave.

Leave is given to go to one's own room between 9 o'clock and 10 o'clock on Saturdays and Mondays for washing —say for 5 or 10 minutes; Leave is given also on Wednesdays and Saturdays from 2 to 3 o'clock.

(1) No one under pain of expulsion is to go, without obtaining leave, out to town, or any way outside the prescribed boundaries of the College and playgrounds. (2) Any illicit drinks expose one to be expelled the College. (3) Also novels, or any other thing calculated to vitiate the mind, or bring on bad habits, or opposed to discipline, morals, or piety, if found, expose a Student to be be expelled.

Ulick J. Bourke,

President. Feast of the Holy Name of MARY, 1867.

Appendix B: Senior Football

Hogan Cup winners

1947 (St Patrick's Armagh), V. McHale capt.

1958 (Gormanston), S. Nolan capt.

1960 (St Finian's), P. Sheridan capt.

1961 (St Mel's Longford) L.O'Brien capt.

1964 (St. Mel's Longford), S Downes capt.

1966 (St Finian's), J.Duggan capt.

1974 (Gormanston), H. Gavin capt.

1978 (St Colman's, Newry) M. Joyce capt

1982 (Skibereen), R. O'Dwyer capt

1984 (St Patrick's, Maghera), M. Butler capt.

1994 (St Patrick's Maghera), P. Joyce capt.

Defeated All-Ireland finalists

1946, P. Solan capt,

1962, M.O'Malley capt.

1967, E. Rooney capt

1973, M. Hughes capt.

1976, G. Hassett capt.

1979, S. McCormack capt.

1983, J. Fallon capt

1990, E. Feeney capt.

1992, P. Devane capt.

1993, R. O'Toole capt.

1999, J. O'Hara

Other Connacht Senior titles

1932 (J.Tuohy), 1933 (M.Hannon), 1934 (J.Higgins), 1935 (J.Higgins), 1936 (J. Salmon), 1937 (G. Carey), 1938 (P. Fitzgerald), 1939 (S. Moran), 1943 (F. Moran), 1944 (J. Kilroy), 1945 (F. Purcell), 1946 (P. Solan), 1950 (W. McMenamon), 1951 (B. Mahon), 1953 (S. Freyne), 1956 (F. Neelis), 1963 (F. McDonnell), 1965 (M. Shannon), 1972 (A. Durkan).

Appendix c: Procurators, 1937-2000

1937-38, Gerry Moran
1938-39, James O'Malley
1939-40, J. Conneely
1940-41, Mick Turner
1941-42, Séamus Downey
1942-43, Liam Downey
1943-44, Bernard Lee
1944-45, Brendan Kavanagh
1945-46, Frank Mannion
1946-47, Peter Solan
1947-48, Brendan Ryan
1948-49, Martin Gleeson
1949-50, Tom Shannon
1950-51, Michael Horan
1951-52, Michael Hastings
1952-53, Colm Burke
1953-54, Michael Cunningham
1954-55, Paddy Coady
1955-56, Padraic Concannon
1956-57, Tom Glennon
1957-58, Kevin McMorrow
1958-59, Martin Newell
1959-60, Vincent McGagh
1960-61, Jimmy Saunderson
1961-62, Paddy Gibbons
1962-63, John Higgins
1963-64, Con Heaney
1964-65, John Coughlan
1965-66, Séamus O'Beirne
1966-67, Brendan Day
1967-68, Michael Delaney
1968-69, Joe Waldron
1969-70, Tommy Feeney
1970-71, Frank Fitzgerald
1971-72, Frank Harty,
1972-73, Cyril Moran
1973-74, Liam Whyte
1974-75, Barry O'Sullivan
1975-76, Barry Brennan
1976-77, Donal Blake
1977-78, Stephen Farragher
1978-79, John Noel Gallagher
1979-80, Kenneth O'Sullivan
1980-81, Ezra McMenamon
1981-82, Seán Dunleavy
1982-83, Frank Coleman
1983-84, Ray Tully
1984-85, Séamus Kelly
1985-86, Pat Boland
1986-87, John Fallon
1987-88, Ciaran Moran
1988-89, Séamus Meehan
1989-90, Tommy Geraghty
1990-91, Enda Meehan
1991-92, Kevin McMurrow
1992-93, Paul Byrne
1993-94, Frank Chambers
1994-95, David Lally
1995-96, Noel Meehan
1996-97, Padraic Maher
1997-98, Ronan Loftus
1998-99, Michael Webb
1999-2000,Tommie Monahan

Appendix d: The College Opera

	Opera	Producer	Musical Director
1944	The Mikado	Fr Christy Langan & Fr Joe Cunnane	Fr Charlie Scahill
1945	H.M.S. Pinafore	"	"
1946	The Gondoliers	"	"
1947	The Quaker Girl	"	"
1948	The Country Girl	"	"
1949	The Pirates of Penzance	Fr Joe Cunnane & Fr P.V. O'Brien	"
1950	The Maid of the Mountain	Fr Christy Langan & Fr P.V. O'Brien	"
1951	The Arcadians	"	"
1952	The Geisha Girl	"	"
1953	Lilac Time	"	"
1954	The Vagabond King	"	"
1955	Iolanthe	"	"
1956	Patience	"	"
1957	The Student Prince	"	Fr Gabriel Charles
1958	The New Moon	"	"
1959	The Yeoman of the Guard	Fr P.V. O'Brien	"
1960	The White Horse Inn	"	"
1961	The Arcadians	"	"
1962	The Country Girl	"	"
1963	H.M.S. Pinafore	"	"
1964	Brigadoon	Fr P.V. O'Brien & Fr T. Waldron	"
1965	The Pirates of Penzance	"	"
1966	Iolanthe	"	"
1967	The Gondoliers	"	"
1968	The White Horse Inn	Fr T. Waldron	"

Year	Show		
1969	The Quaker Girl	Fr T. Waldron	Fr S. Cunnane
1970	Oliver!	"	"
1971	Guys and Dolls	"	"
1972	Annie Get Your Gun	"	"
1973	Oklahoma!	"	"
1974	H.M.S. Pinafore	"	"
1975	My Fair Lady	"	"
1976	Oliver!	"	"
1977	Kiss Me Kate!	"	"
1978	South Pacific	"	"
1979	Fiddler on the Roof	"	"
1980	The Pirates of Penzance	"	"
1981	The Gondoliers	"	"
1982	The Arcadians	"	"
1983	Iolanthe	"	"
1984	The Quaker Girl	"	"
1985	Oklahoma!	"	"
1986	Fiddler on the Roof	Fr P. O'Connor	"
1987	H.M.S. Pinafore	Mr J. Donoghue	"
1988	How to Succeed in Business	"	"
1989	Oliver!	"	"
1990	Brigadoon	"	"
1991	The Pirates of Penzance	"	"
1992	Carousel	"	"
1993	The Mikado	"	Mr N. Kirrane
1994	Chess	"	"
1995	Finian's Rainbow	"	"
1996	My Fair Lady	"	"
1997	God Bless Archie Dean	"	"
1998	Guys and Dolls	"	"
1999	Jesus Christ Superstar	"	"

Appendix E: P.P.U. Presidents

The St Jarlath's College Past Pupils' Union was formed in 1952 after a deputation of 'eminent lay past students' approached Archbishop Joseph Walsh to seek his blessing for such a step. He agreed to become patron of the Union. According to its constitution, the objectives of the Union were:

> to strengthen the affection of its members for the Alma Mater and for each other, by bringing them together and thus affording opportunities of renewing old friendships and forming new ones; to render mutual aid; to undertake such charitable or benevolent work as the members at a general meeting may decide.

The sociable objectives are fulfilled through the organisation of annual 'Union Days' and dinner dances, while the benevolent work has improved facilities in the College.

The College's bicentenary commemorations are being overseen by a sub-committee of the P.P.U.

Presidents

Dr Tom Walsh, 1953-55
T.P. Flanagan, 1955-57
J.P. Griffith, 1957-59
Dr L.A. Macken, 1959-60
Dr J.F. McHugh, 1960-61
J.N. Malone, 1961-62
Joe Hanley, 1962-63
Michael F. Kitt, 1963-64
Fabian Walsh, 1964-65
John Silke, 1965-66
Dr M.B. Farrell, 1966-67
L.J. McGuire, 1967-68
M. Gilligan, 1968-69
Dr P. Fitzgerald, 1969-70
P.J. Finnegan, 1970-71
Billy Flynn, 1971-72
Shane Mooney, 1972-73

John O'Malley, 1973-74
Jim Nestor, 1974-75
Brian Mahon, 1975-76
Jim Kearns, 1976-77
P.J. Gilmore, 1977-78
P.J. Finnegan, 1978-79
Séamus Colleran, 1979-80
Micheál Kitt, 1980-81
Patrick McMyler, 1981-82
Jack Mahon, 1982-83
Pat Holian, 1983-84
E.M.D. Kearns, 1984-85
John McDonagh, 1985-86
Padraic Rhatigan, 1986-87
Padraig Ó Durcáin, 1987-88
Tom Connolly, 1988-89
Christopher Kelly, 1989-90

Fr Padraic O'Connor, 1990-91
Chris Glancy, 1991-92
Tom Donoghue, 1992-93
Charles Kelly, 1993-94
John Waldron, 1994-95

Proinsias Kitt, 1995-96
Dr Mattie Gannon, 1996-97
James Saunderson, 1997-98
Gerry Burke, 1998-99
Michael Marren, 1999-2000

Bibliography

(i) Archival sources

a. St Jarlath's College
Most of the archival material used in this study was found in St Jarlath's College itself. The College archive is housed in a large steel cabinet in the administrative area. This cabinet has three shelves, and the material on the top shelf, forty-two items dated between 1817 and 1943, has been listed. Material on the middle and bottom shelves, generally of more recent origin, has not been listed. A 'Report on the archives of St Jarlath's College, Tuam' prepared by the present author for the College's Past Pupil's Union in January 1997 describes, in broad outline, the contents of the archive.

For the nineteenth century, the archive is of mixed quality. A large proportion of its contents are financial records: accounts; expenditure books; receipt books. Notable exceptions to the generally mundane nature of the early record, however, are the 'Subscriptions and Accounts' volume from 1817-35; the Feeney Papers, a collection of miscellaneous material relating to the life of College president and Bishop of Killala, Thomas Feeney, assembled for an uncompleted biography; and the Letter-Book of President Patrick Kilkenny (1882-86). Interesting for marginalia and for unusual detail are the financial records kept by President Ulick Bourke (1865-78).

Towards the twentieth century, the record becomes quite diverse. Lists of students are available from 1881 (it is possible to compile lists for earlier periods from the financial records), while there is information on the social backgrounds of students in a 'Register of Students Studying Science' 1887-1922'. There is a considerable amount of information on the various burses and scholarships open to students dating from the early part of the twentieth century. Valuable too were the minutes of the College's Discipline Council (1909-62); the reports of Presidents, beginning in 1912 and the reports of Intermediate Board and Departmental inspectors.

Supplementing the College archive is a 'History File' which contains recently-collected miscellanea of historical interest. For recent developments, the staff meetings minute book (1974-94) was enlightening and useful.

b. Tuam Diocesan archives

A distinct body of material relating to the diocesan College is held in the Archbishop's residence. Most of the documents relate, in one way or another, to the College property, and their location reflects the traditional role of Archbishops as patrons and trustees of St Jarlath's. Predictably, there are deeds, covenants and leases, but also correspondence and plans relating to twentieth century infrastructural development in the College. Miscellaneous items of interest include an envelope of newspaper cuttings concerning St Jarlath's, details of the response to a 1946 appeal for funds for the College, and an unpublished letter to the *Connacht Tribune* from 'Justitia', an anonymous, but disgruntled past pupil of St Jarlath's.

Valuable for biographical detail on the diocesan clergy was the manuscript 'Sacerdotes Tuamensis', compiled by Rev. M.A. Heaney.

c. Dublin Diocesan archive

The papers of John Thomas Troy (Archbishop of Dublin, 1786-1823) were consulted for detail on the background to the establishment of St Jarlath's and other diocesan seminaries.

d. National Archives

The Fenian papers were consulted for detail on the careers of Mark Ryan and of John O'Connor Power.

e. Galway Diocesan archive

A letter from Dr John Keaghry, priest of the Tuam diocese, dated 17 March 1791 and located in the Wardenship papers, was examined.

(ii) Newspapers and Periodicals

To complement the archival record, a local newspaper was read for each week of the years 1830-1922. The *Herald* (Tuam), a newspaper with a vigorously independent tradition since its establishment in 1837, was available for most of the period. For the years 1830-37, the *Telegraph* (Castlebar) was used. And, because of their close connections with St Jarlath's College and with the Tuam archdiocese, two less-than-independent local newspapers, *The Connacht Patriot* (1859-69) and the *Tuam News* (1870-1904) were read in preference to the *Herald*, for the short periods for which they were available. Other national and local newspapers were consulted for specific information.

A search of the *Catholic Directory* (Dublin) for relevant material was carried out with the assistance of an index prepared by Padraig Ó Tuairisg.

(iii) Official publications:
British Parliamentary Papers, *Irish Education Inquiry: First report of the Commissioners*, [400], 1825, vol.xii.
British Parliamentary Papers, *Irish Education Inquiry: Second Report of the Commissioners*, 1826-7, vol.xii.
British Parliamentary Papers, *The Census of Ireland for the year 1851, part vi, General report*, [2134], 1856, vol.xxxi
British Parliamentary Papers, *Educational Endowments (Ireland) Commission: minutes of evidence*, [c.5838], 1889, vol.xxx.
British Parliamentary Papers, Census of Ireland, 1911, Province of Connaught [Cd.6052], 1912.

(iv) Oral Sources
Formal taped interviews were conducted by the author with twelve former students of the College. Two were serving members of the College staff, while five had previously served on the staff. Information was also obtained and facts confirmed in informal conversations with many others. Those formally interviewed —with their years as students and the date of interview— were the following:

John Fitzgerald (1938-44)	13 March 1998.
Padraig Folan (1952-57)	29 May 1998.
Conor Heaney (1922-26)	29 July 1997.
Tommy Heraty (1935-40)	13 March 1998
Oliver Hughes (1957-1962)	28 June 1999.
Jim Kearns (1944-49)	26 March 1998.
Liam Kitt (1931-36)	20 May 1998
Paddy McMyler (1940-45)	2 March 1998.
Jack Mahon (1945-50)	11 March 1998.
Tod Nolan (1976-1981)	2 July 1999.
Tommy Shannon (1945-50)	31 March 1998.
Paddy Williams (1940-45)	4 March 1998.

(v) Material published from St Jarlath's College
Five issues of the Past Pupil's Union journal, *Iarlaith*, were published between 1955 and 1966. The student magazine, *Torch*, commenced publication in 1965 and still appears annually. Other occasional student publications have included *The*

Charioteer (1940s), *Newsview* (1960s and 1970s), *Perspective* (1960s) and *Grapevine* (1980s). The following articles are cited above:

Anon., 'Lares & Penates' in *the Charioteer*, March 1946.

Vinny Browne, 'Legion work in Scotland' in *Torch* 1999.

Paul Carroll, "Where to?' in *Torch* 1999.

Cathal Carty, 'The Legion of Mary' in *Torch* 1999.

John Corcoran and Gearóid Colleary, 'An interview with the President', *Torch*, 1966.

Séamus Cunnane, 'The Second twenty-five' in 'The Mikado', Opera commerative programme, 1993.

Hubert Curran, 'Carissime' in *Torch* 1969.

Patrick Diskin, 'Irish scholars and language workers in the West, 1800-1900' in *Iarlaith*, 1961.

Seán Freyne, 'Rome and the Council' in *Iarlaith* 1966.

Shane Grennan, 'Top Secret: How Saturday morning was won' in *Torch* 1991.

Thomas Hayes, 'Student riots' in *Torch*, 1969.

Pat Hoyne, 'Past Presidents', in *Torch* 1990.

John Higgins, 'Poor Scholar of the Sixties' in *Iarlaith*, 1966.

— 'Foreword, by a past pupil', in *Torch* 1965.

Peter Hughes, Murt Dunleavy and Pat Dunleavy 'The Day Boys' in *2C Times* 1979.

Gabriel Keane et al, 'Survey' in *Newsview* 1976.

Charles Kelly & Séamus O'Beirne, 'This is our College' in *Torch* 1966.

Tom Kelly, 'Farewell' in *Torch* 1987.

Noel Kirrane, 'An appreciation of Canon Mooney' in *Torch* 1972.

Tom Kirrane, 'The Walk' in *Iarlaith*, 1966.

Thomas McCann, 'Third thoughts' in *Iarlaith*, 1959.

— 'No bird in last year's nest' in *Iarlaith*, 1961.

Gerard McCarthy, 'Student Activities' in *Torch* 1966..

Gerard McHugh 'Sport' in *Torch*, 1972.

Michael J. Molloy, 'Some odious comparisons' in *Iarlaith*, 1955.

Rev Michael Mooney, 'Fifty years' football' in *Iarlaith*, 1955.

— 'College highlights: 1957-58' in *Iarlaith*, 1959.

Charles Mulchrone and James Mongey 'Survey' in *Torch* 1967.

Gabriel Murphy, 'Football in Jarlath's fifty years ago' in *Iarlaith*, 1966.

Rev. Patrick V. O'Brien, 'Pages from the history of St Jarlath's College' in *Iarlaith*, 1955.

Padhraic Ó Ciardha, 'The Last Hop' in *Torch* 1971.

Michael O'Connor, 'Day Boys' in *Torch* 1985.

Máirtín Ó Fathaigh, 'Agallamh leis an Athair Padraic Standún' in *Torch* 1993.

Leon Ó Mórcháin, 'Grafted' in *Iarlaith*, 1959.

P. Prendergast, 'Thomas F. Doyle', obituary, *Iarlaith*, 1961.

Canon Thomas Waldron, 'Foreword', in *Torch* 1983.

Walter Waldron & Séamus O'Dwyer, 'Survey', in *Torch* 1969.

Rev. Patrick Williams, 'Sports Chronicle 1961-66' in *Iarlaith* 1966.

(vi) Books, articles, and unpublished academic theses

A.P.N. 'Notes on the School of St Jarlath' in *Connacht Tribune*, 18 February 1933.

Liam Bane, *The Bishop in Politics: Life and Career of John MacEvilly*, Westport, 1993.

Thomas Bartlett, *The Fall and Rise of the Irish Nation: The Catholic Question, 1690-1830*, Dublin 1992.

Paul Bew, *Land and the National Question in Ireland, 1858-82*. Dublin 1978.

Peter Birch, *St Kieran's College, Kilkenny*, Dublin 1951.

T.P. Boland, *Thomas Carr: Archbishop of Melbourne*, Queensland 1997.

Ulick Bourke, *The Life and Times of the Most Rev. Dr MacHale, Archbishop of Tuam*, Dublin 1882.

Desmond Bowen, *The Protestant Crusade in Ireland, 1800-1870: a study of Protestant-Catholic relations between the Act of Union and Disestablishment*, Dublin 1978.

John Brady, *Catholics and Catholicism in the Eighteenth Century Press*, Maynooth 1965.

— and Patrick Corish 'The Church under the Penal Code' in vol.iv of Corish (ed.) *History of Irish Catholicism*, Dublin 1971.

Rev. Thomas Brett, *Life of Dr Duggan*, Kilmaine 1921.

Terence Brown, *Ireland: a Social and Cultural History, 1922-1979*, Glasgow, 1981.

Oliver J. Burke, *History of the Catholic Archbishops of Tuam*, Dublin 1882.

Éibhlín Bean Mhic Choistealbha, *Amhráin Mhuighe Seóla: Traditional Folk-songs from Galway and Mayo*, Dublin 1923.

John A. Claffey, 'The Intermediate Examinations of 1879-80' in Claffey (ed.) *Glimpses of Tuam since the Famine*, Tuam 1997, pp.98-106.

Patrick Clancy, 'Education in the Republic of Ireland: The Project of Modernity?' in Clancy et al, *Irish Society: Sociological perspectives*, Dublin 1995, pp.467-94.

Samuel Clark, *Social Origins of the Irish Land War*, Princeton 1979.

Martin Coen, 'The Choosing of Oliver Kelly for the See of Tuam,' in *Journal of the Galway Archaeologiocal & Historical Society*, vol.xxxvi, 1977-78, pp.14-29.

— *The Wardenship of Galway*, Galway 1984

Nick Coleman & Nick Hornby, *The Picador Book of Sportswriting*, London 1996.

W.J.V. Comerford's 'Recollections of Tuam, 1912-16' in Claffey (ed) *Glimpses of Tuam since the Famine*, Tuam 1997, pp.178-91.

S.J. Connolly, *Priests and People in pre-Famine Ireland,1780-1845*, New York 1982.

John Coolahan, *Irish Education: its History and Structure*, Dublin 1981.

Nuala Costello *John MacHale, Archbishop of Tuam*, Dublin 1939.

Patrick Corish, *Maynooth College, 1795-1995*, Dublin 1995.

Henry Coulter, *The West of Ireland: its Existing Conditions and Prospects*, London 1862.

Mike Cronin, *Sport and Nationalism in Ireland: Gaelic Games, Soccer, and Irish Identity since 1884*, Dublin, 1999.

John Cunningham, *Labour in the West of Ireland: Working Life and Struggle 1890-1914*, Belfast 1995.

— 'Bobby Burke: Christian Socialist' in Claffey (ed) *Glimpses of Tuam since the Famine*, Tuam 1997, pp.239-54.

— 'Report on the Archives of St Jarlath's College, Tuam' prepared for Past Pupils's Union, 1997.

Terence P. Cunningham & Daniel Gallogly, *St Patrick's College, [Cavan]: a Centenary History*, Cavan 1974.

Monsignor E.A. D'Alton *History of the Archdiocese of Tuam*, 2 vols, Dublin 1928.

Mary E. Daly, 'Language and Literacy Change in the Late Nineteenth and Early Twentieth Centuries' in Daly & Dickson (eds) *'The Origins of Popular Literacy in Ireland,* Dublin, 1990.

Marcus de Búrca in *The GAA: a History of the Gaelic Athletic Association,* Dublin 1980.

Mairín Doddy, 'Tuam Architectural Survey Report,' Tuam n.d.

Hely Dutton, *A Statistical and Agricultural Survey of the county of Galway,* Dublin 1824.

Patrick Egan, *The Parish of Ballinasloe,* Dublin 1960.

J.A. Fahey, *The History and Antiquities of the Diocese of Kilmacduagh,* Dublin 1893.

Seán Farragher, *Pere Leman (1826-1880): Educator and Missionary, Founder of Blackrock College,* Dublin 1988.

Hugh Fenning, 'Clerical Recruitment, 1753-1783', in *Archivium Hibernicum,* vol.xxx, 1972, pp.1-20.

John Fleming & Seán O'Grady, *St Munchin's College, Limerick, 1796-1996,* Limerick 1996.

Padraic Flynn, 'A Study of Local Government in Galway in the early Nineteenth Century, unpublished M.A. thesis, University College Galway, 1981.

Cathuldus Giblin, 'Irish exiles in Catholic Europe' in vol.iv, of Patrick Corish (ed.) *History of Irish Catholicism,* Dublin 1971.

R. Gillespie & G. Moran, *'A various country': Essays in Mayo History,* Westport 1987.

The Knight of Glin, 'Castle Hackett' in Christie's Castlehackett catalogue, 2 vols, London 1986.F

Francis Guy, 'St Jarlath's College, Tuam: its Life Story' (in eight parts) reprinted from the *Irish Catholic* in the *Tuam Herald,* 24 November, 1, 8, 22 December 1906; 9, 16, 23 February, 2 March 1907.

K.P Hackett, 'Phases of Education in Galway City during the early part of the Nineteenth Century' unpublished M.A. thesis, University College Galway, 1935.

Mr & Mrs Samuel Carter Hall, *Hall's Ireland,* 2 vols, London (1984 edn).

James Hardiman. *The History of the Town and County of the Town of Galway,* Dublin 1820.

Karen J. Harvey, *The Bellews of Mountbellew: A Catholic gentry family in Eighteenth Century Ireland*, Dublin 1998.

Jonathan Haughton 'The Dynamics of Economic Change' in Crotty & Schmitt, *Ireland and the Politics of Change*' London 1998.

Richard Holt. *Sport and the British: a Modern History*, Oxford 1989.

Theodore Hoppen, *Ireland since 1800: Conflict and Conformity*, Harlow 1989.

Monsignor James Horan, see Micheál Mac Gréil

Liam Horan, 'Schools' GAA has taught us all a lesson' in *Irish Independent*, 8 April 1998.

Michael J. Hughes, *History & Folklore of the Barony of Clare (Co. Galway)*, Galway n.d.

Tom Inglis, *Moral Monopoly, The Catholic Church in Modern Irish Society*, Dublin 1987.

D.S. Johnson, 'The Belfast Boycott, 1920-1922' in Goldstrom & Clarkson (eds), *Irish population, Economy, and Society: Essays in honour of the late K.H. Connell*, Oxford 1981.

Donald Jordan, 'John O'Connor Power, Charles Stewart Parnell and the Centralisation of Popular Politics in Ireland' in *Irish Historical Studies*, vol.xxx, 1986, pp.46-66.

— *Land and Popular Politics in Ireland: Co. Mayo from the Plantation to the Land War*, Cambridge 1994.

Rev. P.J. Joyce, *John Healy: Archbishop of Tuam*, Dublin 1931.

Desmond Keenan, *The Catholic Church in Nineteenth Century Ireland: a Sociological Study*, Dublin 1983.

Michael Kelly 'Seeking intelligent answers to a Roscommon problem' in *Sunday Independent*, 26 July 1998.

Richard J. Kelly, 'St Jarlath's College, Tuam' in *Tuam Herald*, 24 October 1896.

Kieran A. Kennedy (ed.) *From Feast to Famine: Economic and Social Change in Ireland, 1847-1997*, Dublin, 1998.

Dermot Keogh, *Twentieth Century Ireland: Nation and State*, Dublin 1994.

Donal A. Kerr, *Peel, Priests and Politics: Sir Robert Peel's Administration and the Roman Catholic Church in Ireland, 1841-1846*, Oxford 1982.

Emmet Larkin's *The Making of the Roman Catholic Church in Ireland, 1850-1860*, Chapel Hill 1980.

— *The Consolidation of the Roman Catholic Church in Ireland, 1860-1870*, Dublin 1987.

— *The Roman Catholic Church and the Home Rule Movement in Ireland, 1870-1874*, Chapel Hill 1990.

— *The Roman Catholic Church and the Emergence of the Modern Irish political system, 1874-1878*, Dublin 1996.

— *The Historical Dimensions of Irish Catholicism*, Dublin 1997 edn.

— *Alexis de Tocqueville's Journey in Ireland, July-August 1835*, Dublin 1990.

J.J. Lee, *Ireland, 1912-1985, politics & Society*. Cambridge 1989.

Marie Louise Legg, 'Martin A. O'Brennan and the Connaught Patriot' in Claffey (ed) *Glimpses of Tuam since the Famine*, Tuam 1997, pp.67-72.

— *Newspapers and Nationalism: the Irish Provincial Press, 1850-1892*, Dublin 1999.

Samuel Lewis, *A Topographical Dictionary of Ireland*, 2 vols, London 1837.

Michael Leyden, *Dunmore MacHales*, Dublin 1983.

Thomas J. McElligot in *Secondary Education in Ireland, 1870-1921*, Dublin 1981.

— *The story of handball: the Game, the Players, the History*, Dublin 1984.

Tom McHugh, 'Contrasting Connacht football styles', in *Sunday Independent*, 19 July 1998.

— 'Aspiration and perspiration in the fields of Tuam' in *Sunday Independent*, 4 October 1998.

Joseph McGlade, 'The Missions: Africa & the Orient', vol.vi of P. Corish *A History of Irish Catholicism*, Dublin 1967.

Micheál Mac Gréil (ed.), *Monsignor James Horan: Memoirs, 1911-1986*, Dingle 1992.

— *Quo vadimus: Report on the Pastoral Needs and Resources of the Archdiocese of Tuam*, Tuam 1998.

Demot McGuinne, *Irish Type design: a History of Printing Types in the Irish Character*, Dublin 1992.

Jack Mahon, 'The Spirit of St Jarlath's College, Tuam' in Mahon, *Action Replay*, Galway, 1984, pp.17-42.

William J. Mahon, ed., *Doctor Kirwan's Irish Catechism by Thomas Hughes*, Cambridge, Mass, n.d.

W.F. Mandle, *The Gaelic Athletic Association & and Irish Nationalist Politics*, London, 1987.

J.A. Mangan, *Athleticism in the Victorian and Edwardian Public School: the Emergence and Consolidation of an educational Ideology*, Cambridge 1981.

Arthur Marwick, *The Sixties: Cultural Revolution in Britain, France, Italy and the United States, c.1958-c.1974*, 1998.

Mairín Ní Mhuiríosa, 'Seán Mag Fhlainn agus *An Tuam News*, in Claffey (ed) *Glimpses of Tuam since the Famine*, Tuam 1997, pp.154-61.

David W. Miller, 'Irish Catholicism and the Great Famine' In *Journal of Social History* (1975) vol.ix, pt.i, pp.81-98.

James Mitchell, 'The appointment of Revd J.W. Kirwan' in *Journal of the Galway Archaeological and Historical Society*, vol.li, 1999, pp.1-23.

T.W. Moody, *Davitt and the Irish Revolution, 1846-82*, Oxford 1981.

— & W.E. Vaughan, *A New History of Ireland,vol.iv: Eighteenth Century Ireland, 1691-1800*, Oxford 1986.

Gerard Moran, *A radical priest in Mayo: Fr Patrick Lavelle, the Rise and Fall of an Irish Nationalist*, Dublin 1994.

James H. Murphy, *Nos Autem: Castleknock College and its Contribution*, Dublin 1996.

Thomas Murtagh, 'Power and Politics in Galway, 1770-1830', unpublished M.A. thesis, University College Galway, 1982.

Willian Nolan, 'Introduction' to Gerard Moran, ed., *Galway: History & Society*, Galway, 1996.

Séamus Ó Buachalla, *Education Policy in Twentieth Century Ireland*, Dublin 1988.

Emmet O'Connor, *A Labour History of Ireland: 1824-1960*, Dublin 1992.

Noel O'Donoghue, *Proud and Upright Men*, Tuam, n.d.,

Tomás Ó Fiach, '"The Patriot Priest of Partry": Patrick Lavelle, 1825-1866' in *Journal of the Galway Archaeological and Historical Society* vol.xxxv, 1976, pp.129-48.

Breandáin Ó hEithir, *Over the Bar: a Personal Relationship with the GAA*, Dublin 1984.

Pat O'Kelly, *The Eudoxologist or an Ethnographical Study of the Western Parts of Ireland.*, Dublin 1812.

P. Ó Laoi, *The Annals of the GAA in Galway*, vol.i, Galway, 1983.

Prionsias Ó Maolmhuaidh, *Uilleog de Búrca: Athair na hAthbheochana*, Dublin 1991.

Daithí Ó Murchú, *Tuam*, Tuam 1971.

Bernard O'Reilly, *John MacHale, Archbishop of Tuam*, 2 vols, New York 1890.

Fintan O'Toole *The Traitor's Kiss: The life of R.B. Sheridan*, London 1997.

Padraic Ó Tuairisg, 'Faisnéis faoi Oilibhéar Ó Ceallaigh,' *Galvia: Irisleabhar Chumann Seandálaíochta is Staire na Gaillimhe*, xii, 1978, pp.46-55.

— 'Ábhar a bhaineann le Ard-dheoise Thuama sa 19ú aois i gcartlann Choláiste na nGael sa Róimh', unpublished M.A. thesis, University College Galway, 1982.

Gearóid Ó Tuathaigh, *Ireland before the Famine, 1798-1848*, (2nd edn), Dublin 1990.

— 'Religion, Nationality and a Sense of Community in Contemporary Ireland' in Ó Tuathaigh (ed.) *Community, Culture and Conflict: Aspects of the Irish Experience*, Galway 1986, pp.64-81.

— 'Seán Mac hÉil, Ardeaspag agus Conspóidí: Athbhreithniú' in Áine ní Cheannain *Leon an Iarthair*, Dublin 1983, pp.73-87.

Caesar Otway, *A tour in Connaught, Comprising Sketches of Clonmacnoise, Joyce Country, and Achill*, Dublin 1839.

John O'Connor Power, 'The Irish Land Agitation' in *The Nineteenth Century*, no.xxxiv, December 1879, pp.953-67.

T.P. Power & Kevin Whelan (eds) *Endurance and Emergence: Catholics in Ireland in the Eighteenth century*, Dublin 1990.

Sister Eileen Randles, *Post-primary Education in Ireland, 1957-1970*, Dublin 1975.

Paul Rose, *The Manchester Martyrs: a Fenian Tragedy*, London, 1970.

Liam Ryan, 'Church and Politics: the last twenty five years' in *The Furrow*, vol.l, no.1, 1979, pp.3-18.

Dr Mark F. Ryan, *Fenian Memories*, Dublin 1945.

J.G. Simms, 'Connacht in the Eighteenth Century' in *Irish*

Historical Studies, vol.xi, no.42, 1959, pp.116-33.

John Solan, 'Religion and Society in the Ecclesiastical Province of Tuam before the Famine', unpublished M.A. thesis, University College Galway, 1989

Padraig Standún, *Súil le breith,* Indreabháin 1983.

— (Pat Staunton) 'Maynooth Viewpoint' in *Western People,* 13 January 1971.

Liam Swords, *A Hidden Church: The Diocese of Achonry, 1689-1818,* Dublin 1997.

Brian Taylor, *The Life and Writings of James Owen Hannay, (George A. Birmingham) 1865-1950,* Lewiston/Queenston/Lampeter 1991.

Michael Tynan, *Catholic Instruction in Ireland, 1720-1950: the O'Reilly/Donlevy Catechetical Tradition,* Dublin 1985.

Charles Vane (ed.), *Memoirs and Correspondence of Viscount Castlereagh edited by his brother,* vols i, ii, iv, London 1848.

Jarlath Waldron, *Maamtrasna: the Murders and the Mystery,* Dublin 1992.

John J. Waldron, 'Tuam and the Irish Volunteers, 1914-15' in Claffey (ed) *Glimpses of Tuam since the Famine,* Tuam 1997, pp.192-203.

William J. Waldron, 'The Catholic Church in the Archdiocese of Tuam 1770-1817,' unpublished M.A (minor) thesis, University College Dublin, 1993.

Brian D. Walsh, 'Patriot games: the G.A.A. in Galway, 1884-1934' unpublished M.Phil. thesis (minor), University College Galway 1995.

Dr Joseph Walsh, *Pastoral letter to the clergy and laity of the archdiocese of Tuam, to be read Sunday, 13 October 1946,* Tuam 1946.

Kevin Whelan, 'The regional impact of Irish Catholicism, 1700-1850' in W. Smyth & K. Whelan's *Common Ground: essays on the historical geography of Ireland,* 1988, pp..252-277.

Gregory K. White, *A History of St Columba's College, 1843-1974,* Dublin 1980.

Leslie Whiteside, *A History of the King's Hospital,* (2nd edn), Dublin 1985.

J.H. Whyte, *Church and State in Modern Ireland, 1923-1979,* (2nd edn), Dublin 1980.

Tony Varley's 'Farmers against Nationalists: the Rise and Fall of Clann na Talmhan in Galway', in Gerard Moran (ed.) *Galway: History & Society*, Dublin 1996.

Index

Presidents of the College are indicated by an asterisk

A.S.T.I., 237, 243, 257
Abbeyknockmoy, 249
Achill, 161, 162
Achonry, diocese of, 38
Act of Union, 20
adolescence, 244
African Mission College, Cork, 159
Albany, United States, 43
All Hallows College, Dublin, 159, 162, 200, 201
American Civil War, 94
American revolution, 11-12
Ancient Order of Hibernians, 123
Anglican disestablishment, 105
Anglo-Irish Treaty, 125
Annagh, 160
Annaghdown, 43, 49, 60, 187, 220
Ansbro, Mr, 130
Ansbro, Rev. Laurence, 49
anti-conscription campaign, 122
Archbishop's residence, 51, 64, 199
Archbishop's palace (Anglican), 51
Archdeacon, Bishop Nicholas, 22
Ardagh, diocese of, 38
Árdscoil Rís, 226
art, 243, 253
Association football (soccer), 206, 252
Astronomy Club, 252
Athenry, 81, 122, 182, 184, 186, 210
athletics, 83-4, 247-49
Aughagower, 49

badminton, 252
Balla, 43, 72
Ballina, 207, 208, 210

Ballinasloe, 83, 102, 130
Ballinderry, 105
Ballindine, 18
Ballinfad College, 159
Ballinlough, 153, 182
Ballinrobe, 18
   District Council, 123
Ballintubber, 43
Ballyhaunis, 95, 187, 190
Barnabas, Sister, 260
Barrett, Niall, 249
basketball, 252
Beach Boys, 241
Beatles, 241
Bekan, 43, 149, 160
Belclare, 77, 122
Belfast boycott, 123, 124
Bellew, Christopher, 24, 25
Bellew, Bishop Dominic, 21
Belvedere Musical Society, 77
Beresford, Archbishop William, 2, 7, 8n, 10, 24
Bermingham, John, 23
Biesty, J., 221
Biggar, Joseph, 133
Biggins, M.R., 104
billiards, 87
'Bish', St Joseph's College, Galway, 184
Bithery, Mr, 4
Blackrock College, 133, 152
Blake, Charles, 25
Blake, Isodore, 25
Blake, James, 25
Blake, Master John, 33
Blake, John, 25
Blake, Lt. Col. Llewellyn, 158-59
Blake, Master Martin, 33
Blake, Martin J., Ballinafad, 25
Blake, Maurice, Ballinafad, 25

Index   289

Blake, Maurice, Tower Hill, 25
Blowick, Joe, 126
boarding, decline of, 258
boarding, future of, 263
Bodkin, John, 24, 25
Bon Secours sisters, 260n
Boston Pilot, 98
bounds breaking,178
*Bourke, Rev. Ulick 37, 49, 50, 58-60, 71, 73, 76,78, 84, 95-98, 100-08, 113, 153, 156, 165, 175, 252
'bowjers', 216
Bowyer, Brendan, 241
boxing, 193, 214
Brogan, Padraig, 226
Brotherhood of St Patrick, 95
Browne, Edward, 33
Browne, George, 107
Browne, John, 23, 25
*Browne, Rev. Martin, 43, 45, 54, 71, 72, 246
Browne, Vinny, 253n
buildings, 24-27, 39-40, 51-69, 236, 240, 247
Burke, James, 46
Burke, Rev John, 25
Burke, Rev. Bernard, 25, 40, 41
Burke, Rev. Peter, 25
Burke, Rev. Tom, O.P. 112
Burke, Thomas, 61
burses and scholarships, 6, 116, 142, 157-64, 179, 181-2, 184
Butler, Mark, 202, 226
Butt, Isaac, 133
Byrne, Gay, 241
Byrne, Tom, 216

Caherlistrane, 122
camera club, 239
Campbell, Eddie, 248
Canal School, Athlone, 8
Canavan, Rev. Colm, 248, 251
Canavan, Rev. Patrick , 99, 151
Carissime, 253
Carlos, Bill, 218

Carlow, 35, 200
carpentry, 239, 259
Carr, Archbishop Thomas, 73, 110, 115
Carr, Master Thomas, 99
Carroll, Paul, 264n
Carty, Cathal, 253n
Castlebar, 18, 24, 106, 182, 193, 194
Castlehackett, 79-83, 196
  Cnoc Ma, 79
  Kirwan's of, 79-80
Castleknock College, 183
catering staff, 45
Cathedral, 39, 40, 46, 51, 52, 56, 57, 70, 91, 96, 115, 149, 192, 236
Catholic Banner, Glasgow, 98
Catholic Directory, 147
Catholic Emancipation, 88
Catholic University, 101
Catholics in 18th century Connacht, 14-20
céilí band, 239
Ceoláns, 252
Charles, Rev. Gabriel, 245
Charioteer, The, 239n
cigarette smoking, 170, 175-79, 189, 190, 191
civil rights, 232
Civil Service, 132
Civil war, 125, 211
Claddagh, 81
Clancy, Máirtín, 248
Clancy, Master, 209
Clann na Poblachta, 233
Clann na Talmhan, 126, 127, 233
Claran, 78
Claremorris, 76, 86
class background of students, 33, 151-55, 181-85
Classical, or 'latin' schools, 11, 17
Cleggan, 259
Clifden, 130
Clogher, diocese of, 38
Clonliffe College, Dublin, 201

Coen, Mrs, 256
Coláiste Chríost Rí, Cork, 202
Coláiste Einde, Galway, 189, 216
Colgan, Rev. Patrick, 66
Colleary, Gearóid, 239n
College farm, 38, 46, 66, 236
Colleran, Enda, 222
Colleran, Paul, 126
Colleran, Séamus, 221
Colley, George, 234
Collins, Bartley, 46
Commerce and Economics, 243
Commissioners for National Education, 116
Communist Party, 241
Computer Studies, 260
Concannon, S., 221
Concursus examination, 180, 201
Cong, 83
Connacht Colleges football, 208, 209, 211, 213, 216, 220, 228
Connacht Tribune, 5
Connaught Journal, 34
Connaught Patriot, 58, 62, 95, 96
Connaught Telegraph, 72, 98
Connaughton, Michael, 33
Connellan, Thady, 17
Connemara Bus Co., 211
'Connors', 186, 212, 251
Conradh na Gaeilge, 252
*Conroy, Rev. Michael, 142, 143, 174, 205n, 206-08
Conway, Bishop Hugh, 107
Conway, Rev. Peter, 78, 105
Conway, Simon, 74
copying at examinations, 180
Corcoran, John, 239n
Costello, Dr Thomas Bodkin, 54, 130, 192, 252
Costello, tailor, 47
Coulter, Henry, 52
Counter-Reformation, 9
Coyle, Joseph Stirling, 74
Crampton, Master, 131
Crann, 252

cricket, 85
Croagh Patrick, 80
Croke Park, 221, 226
Croke, Archbishop Thomas William, 202
Crolly, Archbishop, 129
croquet, 195
Crossboyne 42
Cullen, Cardinal Paul 92-96, 99, 103, 108, 109, 111, 112
Cullen, Thomas J., architect, 67
Cullinane, Mr 46
*Cullinane, Rev. William, 43
Cullinane, William, 30
Cumann Díospóireachta, An, 252
Cumann Drámaíochta, An, 252
Cumann Gaelach, An, 252
Cumann na nGaedhal, 126
Cummins, Rev. Tom, 192, 215, 216
Cunnane, Archbishop Joseph, 196
Cunnane, Rev. Séamus, 245, 246
Cunningham Rev. Patrick, 150
Cunningham, James, 158
Cunningham, Larry, 241
Cunningham, Mrs, (Ballytrasna), 150
Cunningham, Thomas, 158
Curley, Lar, 186
Curran, Hubert, 253n
curricular change, 243, 244
Cusack, Bryan, T.D. ,123
Cusack, Michael, 202

D'Alton, Edward, 135
Dalgan, 23
Dalgan Park, 200, 237
Daly, James, bequest, 160
dancing, 72, 193, 244
Dandelion Market, 245
Davin, Tommy, 243
Davis, John, 23
Davitt, Michael, 101, 102, 202
day-boys, 189, 190, 223, 253-256, 261

De Valera, Eamon, 122, 126
Department of Agriculture and
   Technical Instruction, 142, 157
Department of Education
   Inspectors, 4
Derham's plot, 23
Derry, Bishop John, 103
diet, 38-39, 187-89
Dillon, Archbishop Edward 2, 7,
   8, 10, 13, 20, 73
diocesan clergy, support of, 149
Diocesan school, Tuam
   (Anglican), 16, 135
diocesan seminary tradition, 89,
   182, 206, 244, 254
discipline, 165-80, 197, 198, 261
Discipline Council, 167-69, 171,
   178-80
Diskin, Jim, 190
Divilly, John, 230
domestic staff, 47, 147
Donaghpatrick, 77
Donegal, 161
Donnellan, John, 221, 222
Donnellan, Michael, 228, 230
Donnellan, Michael, T.D., 126
Donnellan, Pat, 222
Donoghue, Joe, 237, 249
Dorcan, James, 33
Doyle, 'Sammy', 192, 193, 196, 197
Doyle, Master, 209
Doyle, P., 99
Doyle, Paul, 215
Draíocht Dubh, 252
Drama, 71, 194 (see opera)
Drapers Assistants Association,
   123
Dublin, 28, 38, 95
Duggan, Bishop Patrick, 149, 151,
   202
Duggan, Jimmy, 222, 225
Dunleavy, Murt, 256n
Dunleavy, Pat, 256n
Dunmore, 184, 185, 186, 187, 190
   MacHales 203

Dunne, Master E.F., 99
Durkin, Justin, 248n
Dutton, Hely, 51
Dwyer Gray, Edmund, M.P., 115
Dwyer, Séamus, 241

East Clare by-election, 122
Eaton, Rev. Alexander, 125, 173,
   174
Eaton, Rev. Malachy, 252
economic change, 233
education and literacy, 16
education policy, 233
Education Commissioners, 34, 37
Educational Endowments
   Commission, 137-39, 155
Egan, Andrew, 56
Egan, Archbishop Boetius, 9, 11,
   20
Egan, Dean Boetius, 7, 22, 24, 25
Egan, Stationmaster, 82
Egan, Noel and John, 84
Egan, John, 25
electricity, 65
elocution, 72
Elphin, diocese of, 38
endowed schools, 130
Ennis, 209, 210
erenagh tradition, 150
Erris, 29
etiquette, 198
Ewart, William Oliver Anselm, 99
Excursions, 77-83
expulsions, 166, 169, 174, 178

F.C.A., 239
*Fallon, Rev. John, 63
Famine, The Great, 48, 49
farmers' sons, 153-55
Feachtas, 252
'feck', a, 188
*Feeney, Bishop Thomas 18, 28,
   29, 31, 33, 35, 39, 42, 43, 51, 83,
   84, 88, 90, 148, 165, 166
fees and pensions, 147-48, 156-57

Fenians, 94, 96-97, 100-08, 111, 113, 128, 202, 203
ffrench Whitehead, Catherine, 23, 24
ffrench Whitehead, Rev. Robert, 23, 61
Ffrench's Bank, 1, 23, 26, 42, 51, 53, 148
Ffrench, Honourable Thomas 23
Ffrench, Lord, 23, 24, 25, 26, 33, 39
Ffrench, Nicholas, 33
Fianna Fáil, 126, 240
fighting, 169, 170, 175, 194
films, 67, 77, 177, 179, 192, 233
Fine Gael, 240
Finnegan, Pat, 243
fireworks, 86
Fitzpatrick, Rev Bartholemew, 25, 27
Fitzgerald, Rev. John, 181
Flaherty, John, 250
Flanagan, Mick, 191, 218, 219
*Flannelly, Rev. John, 43
Flannelly, William, 18
Flately, Thomas, 66
Flatley bequest, 158
Flatley, Rev. Patrick, 49
flogging, 170, 174
Folan, Padraic, 181
football, 85, 175, 182, 202-231, 269
Foxford, 120
Franchi, Cardinal, 112
Franciscan order, 129
free days, 195, 247
free education, 223, 254
Free State, 145
Freemans Journal, 35, 115,117, 264
French language, 243
French Holy Ghost Fathers, 133
French revolution, 7, 12, 19, 20
Freyne, Rev. Seán, 235, 236
Furlong, Rev., 45

GAA, 123, 202-03, 206, 207, 209, 210
Gaelic football, (see football)
Gaelic League, 120, 121
Gaelic tradition, 15
Gallagher, Owen, bequest, 158, 160, 161, 162
gallicanism, 92
Galway, 81, 186
   'Tribes' of, 14, 18, 19, 24
   Arch. & Hist. Soc., 2
   Blackrock, 81
   Industrial School, 76
   population, 97
   Queen's Coll, 81, 104, 129
   Racquet Ct. Theatre, 77
   Railway Hotel, 81, 210
   Warden of, 19
Garbally, St Joseph's, 183, 211, 248
Gardening Society, 252
Garrauns, 194
Garribaldians, 94, 95
Garry, Michael, 18
Gavin, Henry, 225
Gavin, I., 222
George III, King, 20
Geraghty, Johnny, 222
Geraghty, Rev. Peter, 83, 149
Gibbons bequest, 158
Gibbons, Rev Patrick, 25
Gill & Son, Messrs, 167
Gilmartin, Archbishop Thomas, 68, 82, 124, 125, 175
Gladstone, William Ewart, 133
Glasgow, 99
Glenamaddy, 183, 199
golf, 252
Gormanstown College, 221
Gort, 83
'grab', a, 188
Greally bequest, 160
Greally, Mr, 85
Greek, 131, 135, 144, 195, 243
Green, Rev. Mr, 25, 148
Grennan, Shane, 258n
Griffin, Eugene, 60

Griffin, Rev Peter, 25
Griffiths, Pat, 237, 256
Grocers' Assistants Association, 123
*Gunnigan, Rev. Timothy 184, 204, 212, 236
Guy, Francis, 2, 13, 121, 204
gymnasium, 67, 86, 87, 223, 246

Hall, Mr and Mrs Samuel Carter, 51, 52
handball, 27, 69, 84, 86, 251
Handcock family, 54, 55, 57
Hannay, Rev. James Owen, 120
Hardigan, Rev. Redmond Snr, 25
Hastings, Liam, 216
Hawkshaw, M.J., 221
Hayes, Thomas, 232n
Hazelton, Richard, 121
Headford, 77, 122
Healy, Archbishop John, 63, 65, 121, 140n, 141, 142, 157, 169, 174, 204
Healy, Rev. Martin, 119
*Heaney, Rev. Conor, 119, 181, 184, 195, 236
Heaney, Mike, 215
heating, 63
hedge-schools, 11, 17
Heffernan, Rev. Peter, 25
Heneghan, Mrs, 46
Hennigan, Gerard, 225
Henry, Mitchell, M.P., 61
Heraty, Rev. Tommy, 181, 184
Hicks-Beach, Sir Michael, 133
Higgins bequest, 158
*Higgins, Dr Michael, 64, 120, 141, 142, 152, 169
Higgins, John, 239n
Hillery, Patrick, 234
Hobbies Club, 252
Hogan Cup, 219, 220, 221, 223, 228
Hogan, John, 74
Hogan, Michael, 250
Hollymount, 148, 193

Home Economics, 260
Home Rule conference, 106
'hops' 244, 245
Horan, Rev. James, 181
Hort, Archbishop Josiah, 23
Hort, Sir John, 23, 55
Hosty, Rev. Professor, 51
house examinations, 34
Hoyne, Pat, 232n
Hughes, Morgan, 225, 250
Hughes, Peter, 256n
*Hughes, Rev. Oliver, 222, 223, 226, 227, 231, 253, 262
Hughes, Thomas, 37
hurling, 247, 249
Hurricane Debbie, 232

Iarlaith, 181, 221, 223, 235
Illinois, 99
Inis Meáin, 259
Inishbofin, 259
Innislacken Island, Roundstone, 60
Inquisition, The, 102
'Inter Week', 146
Intermediate Education Amendment (1924), 146
Intermediate education, 120-21, 132-46
investment in education, 234
Irish Catholic, 121
Irish Colleges abroad, 11, 18
  Paris, 95
  Rome, 92
  Salamanca, 7, 18
Irish emigrants, 59, 98
Irish industrial movement, 120
Irish language, 16, 36, 37, 94, 96, 97, 145, 146, 196, 252
Irish Transport & General Workers Union, 123
Irish Volunteers, 121, 122

'jacks', the, 190
JBD, 225
Jordan, Padraic, 248

Joyce, Padraig, 230
Justine, Sister, 260
'Justitia', 5, 6

Kavanagh, Paddy, 187
Kavanagh, Rev. Brendan, 220n, 221-223, 231, 240, 248
Kean, Rev. Thomas, 25
Keane, Dr, 208
Kearns, Jim, 181
Keenan, Patrick, 133
Keighley, Yorks, 99
Keighrey Park, 57, 58
Kelly, Aidan, 251
*Kelly, Archbishop Oliver, 2, 7, 10-13, 18, 21, 24-26, 28, 30-33, 37, 39, 40-46, 54, 55, 84, 147-48, 151, 165-66, 175,
Kelly, Celia, 55
Kelly, Charles, 239n, 243
Kelly, Christopher, 238n, 243
Kelly, Laurence, 18
Kelly, Mary, 47
Kelly, Master, 204
Kelly, Michael, 224, 251n
Kelly, Mr, 85
Kelly, Rev. Professor, 125
Kelly, Richard J., 2, 86, 152, 203
Kelly, Tom, 260n
Kendrick, Bishop, 43
Kennedy, J., 221
Kennedy, Larry, 190
Keogh, Judge William Nicholas, 91, 105
Kerins, R.C.B., 143
Kielty, Rev. Thomas, 13, 14, 27, 29
Kilbride, Mr, 119
Kilcolman, 44
Kilconly, 101
Kilkenny, 35
*Kilkenny, Rev. Patrick, 71, 85, 113, 115, 135, 136, 137, 138, 155, 156, 157n, 167, 246 bequest, 159
Kilkerrin, 66

Killala, diocese of, 38, 41, 45, 88
Killaloe, 81, 82
Killarney, 35
Killeen, Rev. J., 211, 212
Killererin, 119
Kilmacduagh, diocese of, 18, 38
Kilmeena, 13
Kilmore, diocese of, 38
Kilrush, 38
Kiltegan Fathers, 200, 201
Kilthomas, Peterswell, 18
Kiltulla, 42, 43, 44
Kincora, 82
King, Peadar, 259
Kirby, Nicholas, 111n, 113, 114
Kirrane, Noel, 246n
Kirrane, Tom, 239n
Kirwan's catechism, 36
Kirwan, Dr Joseph W., 129
Kirwan, Robert, 25
Kitt, Rev. Liam, 181, 214
Kitt-Sheehy bequest, 164
Knock Shrine, 253
Knowles, Sheridan, 75
Labour Party, 241
Laherdane, 96
Land League, 108, 116, 118
Langan, Rev. Christy, 186, 187, 198, 219, 248

Larkin, Emmet, 114, 117
Larkin, Michael, 'Manchester martyr', 99
Larkin, Patrick, 99, 100
Latin, 131, 135, 144, 195
Lavan, Stephen, 78
Lavelle bequest, 158-160
Lavelle, Eamonn Day, 259
Lavelle, Mr, 35
Lavelle, Rev. Patrick, 95, 103-06, 107, 126
Lavin, Dr Seán, 218
lay teachers, 243, 258
Le Clair, Monsieur, 77
Leamington Spa, 29

Leaving Certificate, 146
Legion of Mary, 253, 260, 263
Leyden, Master, 130
Leyden, Michael, 243
library, 61, 66, 239
Limbo dormitory, 173
Limerick, 82, 83
Liverpool, 99
Liverpool Times, 98
'lob', a, 198
Loftus, Rev. Matt, 194
Loftus, Rev. John, 25
Loftus, Rev. Martin, 37
London-Irish football team, 220
Long, Joe, 223, 227, 228, 231
'Lord Edward Fitzgerald', 73, 74
Lough Corrib, 80
Lough Cutra, 83
Lough Derg, 81, 82, 83
Loughborough, 221
Loughlin, Dermot, 249
Louis XVI , King, 19
Louisburgh, 182, 190
Lowther, James, 134
Lynch bequest, 164
Lynch, Francis, 25
Lynch, Henry E., 25
Lynskey bequest, 158-159
Lyons Rev. Enda, 238
Lyons, Dean, 29
Lyons, Jimmy, 226

Mac Diarmada, Seán, 121
MacCosker, John, 99
*MacEvilly, Archbishop John, 1, 2n, 42, 44, 49, 50, 62, 63, 92, 93, 95, 109-19, 122, 136, 149, 156
MacEvilly, Rev. Jeremiah 203
MacHale Archb. 43, 57
MacHale family, 149
MacHale, Archbishop John, 2, 18, 27, 36, 37, 40, 41, 43, 45, 56, 57, 59, 65, 70, 72, 73, 78, 88, 89-96, 114-15, 129, 153, 156, 158, 182, 199, 252

MacHale, Dr Thomas, 93, 109, 110n, 111-15
MacHale, Rev. John, 116
MacHale, Rev. Richard, 113
Macken, Rev Patrick, 120
MacLaughlin, Joseph, 99
MacMahon, Master, 99
MacManus, Séamus, 64
MacManus, Terence Bellew, 95
MacPhilpin, John, 60, 73, 118
Madden, Dominick, 40
'mag', 189
Mag Fhlainn, Seán, 252
Magdalen, Sister, 245
magic lantern, 77
Mahon, Jack, 181, 217
Mall, The, 2, 13, 14, 51, 148
Malone, Rev. Michael 211, 212n, 213, 214, 217, 224
Manchester martyrs, 99, 103
Manchester United, 241
Manning, Cardinal, 112
Manulla, 86
Marx Brothers, 192
Maynooth, St Patrick's College, 1, 7, 12, 24, 28, 29, 34, 35, 37, 42, 43, 44, 47, 55, 63, 88, 96, 97, 114, 140, 152, 162, 167, 173, 175, 176, 178, 180, 200, 201, 237, 243
Mayo, 153, 155, 161
   election, 1874, 106
   football team, 220, 222
   population, 97
   Earl of, 91
McCabe, Cardinal Edward, 113
McCann, Michael J., 44, 90, 168
McCarthy, Gerard, 239n
McCorry, Patrick, 99
McDonagh, Colie, 222
McDonagh, Fred, T.D., 126
McDonnell, Eneas, 24
McDonnell, Martin, 243
McDonnell, Matthias, 24, 25, 40, 45

McDonnell, Rev. Michael, 120
McEvoy, Rev. Robert, 12
McGettigan, Archbishop Daniel, 115
*McGreal Rev. Paul 13, 25
McHale, Vincent, 218
McHugh bequests, 158-60
McHugh, Gerard, 249
*McHugh, Rev. Michael, 63, 120
McHugh, Tom, 224n, 230n
*McKeal, Rev. James, 27, 42, 148
McLaughlin bequest, 158
McLoughlin, John, 243, 253
McMaster, Anew, 194
McMyler, Patrick, 181
Meath, diocese of, 38
Mellows, Liam, 121, 122
Mercy, school and convent, Tuam, 54, 115, 178, 244, 245, 246, 258
Milltown, 187
Mitchell, John, 50
Moate, Carmelite College, 226
Mobile, Alabama, 99
mock 'Baptism', 183, 186, 251
modern history society, 239
*Moloney, Rev. Dermot, 223, 225, 228, 252-54, 257
Mongan, Master, 204
Mongey, James, 241n
monitorial system, 33, 34
monitors, 168, 173, 188, 195, 200
*Mooney, Rev. Michael 164, 198, 211-13, 217n, 218, 220, 237, 239-46
Moore, Co. Roscommon, 153
Moore, George, of Moore Hall, 104
Moore, Maurice, of Moore Hall, 159
Moran, Cyril, 225
Moran, J.O., 221
Moran, Rev. James, 125
Morley, John, 222
Morrin bequest, 164

Morris, Michael, 55
Mountbellew, 24, 182
    Agricultural College 204
Moylough, 178
    Synod of, 21
Mulchrone, Charles, 241n
Mullally of Mullingar, plumbers, 67
Mullin, Rev Pat, 25
Mulloy, Rev John, 13, 25
Mungret College, Limerick, 159
Murphy, Bridget, 46
Murphy, Gabriel, 210, 211
Murphy, Mary, 260
Murray, Archbishop, Daniel, 129
music, 72, 73, 75, 76, 77, 90, 243, 252

Napoleon, 21
Napoleonic wars, 26
Nation, 44, 73, 90, 97, 115
National education, 129
National Foresters, 123
Naughton, Rev., 208
New College, 55
New Departure, 106, 108
Newport, 116
Newsview, 238, 241n
nicknames, 194, 250-51
Niland, Darby, 46
Nolan Padraic, 238n, 243
Nolan, Rev Patrick, 25
Nolan Rev. Tod, 223, 231
Nolan, Captain John Philip, M.P., 61, 105, 117, 118, 119, 134
non-smoking association, 239

O'Beirn Seamus, 248
O'Brennan, Martin A., 62, 70, 95, 96, 168
O'Brien, Rev. P.V., 3
*O'Brien, Rev. Patrick J., 56, 58, 91, 97
Ó Ciardha, Padhraic, 245n
O'Connell, Daniel, 88, 90

O'Connell, Master, 130
*O'Connell, Rev. Michael, 118n, 119, 137, 203,
O'Connor, Michael, 256n
O'Connor, Rev. Padraic, 244, 252
O'Conor Don, the, 134
O'Donnell Abu, 28, 44
O'Donnell, Master, 204
O'Donnell, Bishop Laurence, 129
O'Donovan Rossa, sons of, 74, 100
Ó Fathaigh, Máirtín, 242n
O'Fay, Master E., 130
O'Flaherty, Anthony, M.P., 91
O'Hagan, Baron, 61
O'Kelly, Rev. Malachy, 25
O'Leary, Professor James, 94
O'Malley, artist, 75
O'Malley, Donagh, 234
Ó Móracháin, Leon, 183, 192
Ó Muireadhaigh, Labhrás, 146
O'Neill, J.J. 143, 145
Ó Néill Seosamh (see J.J. O'Neill)
O'Regan, Hon. Andrew, 33
*O'Regan, Bishop Anthony, 30, 43, 47, 48, 49, 50, 61
oratory, 62, 67
O'Reilly, Dr, Archbishop of Armagh, 22
O'Reilly, Rev. Bernard, 115
O'Shea divorce case, 117
O'Shea, Paul, 250
O'Sullivan, Jack, 197, 237
Odeon Cinema, 246
OECD, 234
'Oliver', 245, 246
opera 183, 245, 246, 271-72,

Parnell, Charles Stewart, 100, 109, 116, 117, 121, 133, 202
Parnellites (and anti-Parnellites) 117, 118, 119, 203
Partry, 103
Past Pupils' Union, 121, 181, 212, 273-74
Peel, Sir Robert, 47
Penal Laws, 11, 14, 15, 88, 92, 93

Pennsylvania, 160
pensions, (see fees)
Perspective, 238
Philadelphia, 60
Philips, Archbishop Philip, 19
Photo Club, 252
Physical Education, 243
Pigott, Richard, 100
Pinkerton, Mr, 119
Pioneer Total Abstinence Association, 3n, 239
Pittsburgh, 161
'Pizarro', 76
Plan of Campaign, 116
Pope Clement XIII, 19
Pope Paul III, 9
Pope Pius VII, 21
Pope Pius IX, 78
Power, John O'Connor, 74, 75, 100-102, 105-07, 108-09, 126, 134
Prendergast, Henry J., 35-36, 264
Prendergast, Rev. James, 182
Prendergast, Rev. Richard, 182
Presentation, school and convent, Tuam, 54, 178, 182. 236, 244, 245, 246, 258
Presentation College, Birr, 249
President's Shield, 248
Presley, Elvis, 241
priests, their role, 241-43
Primary education, 128
prize-giving, 130, 131, 140
procurator 168, 176, 195, 198, 200, 227, 270
pronunciation problems, 143
Propaganda Fide, 15, 109, 114, 129
proselytisers, 111
Proven, John, 23
public schools, 206
Purcell, Seán, 218, 219, 221, 225

Queen's Colleges, 129, 132
Queensbury, Marchioness of, 99
Queenstown, 94

Radio Luxembourg, 235
'raid', a, 192
Railway Cup competition, 216, 220
Rebellion, 1798, 8, 14, 20
  commemoration, 1
Reddington, P., 82
Redmond, John, 121, 122
Reilly, Derek, 228
Relationships Courses, 260
Relief Act, 1782, 7-8
religious practice, 15, 16
Republican courts, 124
retreat, 185
*Reynolds, Rev. Peter 42, 44, 49, 91
Ridge, Jack, 192
'Robert Emmet' 64, 73, 76
Roche bequest, 159
Roche, James, 46
rock and roll, 237
Rock, Dickie, 241
Rockwell College, 152
Róisín Dubh, 252
Rolling Stones, 241
Rome, 93, 109, 110, 112, 159, 232, 238
*Ronan, Rev. James, 37, 43, 45, 54, 252
Ronayne family, 150
Ronayne, Rev. James, 110
Rooney, Mr, 18
Rosalie, Sister, 260
Roscommon, 220, 224
  CBS 182, 215, 216, 219
Ross Errily abbey, 78

Roundfort, 182
Royal Irish Constabulary, 153, 154
RTE television, 235
Ruane, Patrick, 60
rugby, 206-07
Rules of College, 31-33, 175, 179, 265-68

rural electrification, 233
Ryan, Mark, 100-05, 108, 148
Ryder Burse, 160
*Ryder, Rev. Denis, 66, 120, 174, 185

Salamanca, Irish College, 7, 18
Sam Maguire, 222, 230
Saol Plus, 252-53
'Sarsfield', 76
Saturday morning classes, 256, 257, 258
Savage, Derek, 230
Savannah, Georgia, 99
Scahill, Fr Charles, 245
Science, 47, 48, 131
Science Cup, 247, 248
scholarships (see burses)
Seachtain na Gaeilge, 252
Second Reformation, the, 91
sex education, 244
sexual abuse, 259
Shamrock Rovers, 241
Shanahan, Bishop, 201
Shannon, River, 81, 82
Shannon, Rev. Tommy, 181, 202
Sharkey, E. 221
Shaw, George Bernard, 123
Sheehy, John Joe, 215
Sheridan, Richard Brinsley, 76
Shortall, sculptor, 66
Silke, John, 243
Sinn Fein, 121-23
Sisters of Charity, 120
Sisters of Christian Retreat, 260
Skerret, Archbishop Mark, 11
'skiffle' music, 237
slang, 250
Sligo, 83, 121
Smyth, Vincent, 86
Sociology, 240, 242
Solan, Peter, 218
'spiff', the, 224
sports day, 85, 86
St Alphonso Liguori, 59

Index

St Brendan, 2
St Brendan's Killarney, 218, 225
St Colman's College, Fermoy, 94
St Colman's, Newry, 226
St Flannan's, Ennis, 209-11
St Gregory's Day, 77-79
St Jarlath, 2, 66
St Jarlath's Day, 70, 81
St *Jer*lath's College, 89
St Kierans, Kilkenny, 8
St Louis, 43
St Mary's, Belfast, 249
St Mary's, Galway, 183, 184, 199, 210, 211
St Mel's, Longford, 219
St Muredach's, Ballina, 207, 208
St Nathy's, Ballaghadereen 199, 210, 213, 220
St Patrick's, Armagh, 218, 219
St Patrick's, Cavan, 183
St Patrick's, Maghera, 228
St Patrick's (CBS), Tuam, 101, 205, 216, 228-229
St Paul, Minnesota, 150
Stack, Mr, 45, 72
stamp club, 239
Standún, Padraig, 237n, 242n
Stanley, Larry, 215
state inspection, 143
Staunton, Patrick, 18
Staunton, Major, 33
stealing, 170, 171, 177, 178
Stevens, Padraic, 229
Stewart, James & Co., 67
Stockwell, Frankie, 193
Stockwell, Mr, 46
strikes, 171-74, 243
Stuart dynasty, 18, 19
Student Debating Society, 252
Sullivan, A.M., M.P., 115
Summerhill College, Sligo, 213, 216
Supermacs, 259
surveys, 240, 241
swimming, 69, 239, 252

table tennis, 239
Tablet, The, 98
Talty, Brian, 225
Tanner, Charles, 118, 119
Templeboy, 17
tenant right, 105
tennis, 87
'Terrible Twins', 221
'The Mikado', 246
'The Quaker Girl', 245
Thomas & Sealy Bryers, printers 122
Tighe, Thomas, 107
Times, The, 90, 100, 123
Tobin, Terence, 99
Toghermore Rehabilitation Centre, 253
Torch, 238, 239, 240, 247, 253, 255, 258
Trench, William le Poer, 105
Trench, Archbishop Le Poer, 46
Trent, Council of, 9
Trinidad education scheme, 133
Troy, Archbishop John Thomas, 9
Tuam, 51-54, 68
    Boy Scouts, 219
    Cathedral choirboys, (Anglican), 79
    Catholic Temperance Society, 82
    'ecclesiastical quarter', 65
    housing, 52
    population, 52
    Power and Light Company, 65, 66
    railway, 81
    sack of, 124
    Synod of, 22, 26
    Town Commission, 44, 219-21
    Town Hall, 56, 120, 124, 135
Tuam F.C. 203
Tuam Herald, 2, 43, 54, 55, 56, 63, 71, 75, 76, 86, 117, 118, 121, 151, 218

Tuam Krugers, 203
Tuam News, 74, 75, 76, 86, 102, 119, 139
Tuam Shamrocks, 203
Tuam St Jarlath's, 203, 205
Tuam Star, 203, 210, 221
Tuam Young Irelands, 204
Tuffy, Rev. John, 120
Tully, Rev. James, 45
Turloughmore, 249

Ulster Examiner, 98
ultramontanism, 92
United Irish League, 120, 123
United Irishmen, 20, 73
United States, 78, 79
University education, 128

Vahey, James, 86
'vak' (vacation), 187, 188, 192, 198, 238
Varley, Declan, 229
Vatican Council, First, 59, 93
Vatican Council, Second, 232, 235, 236, 238, 244
Vaughan, Tom, 225
Verso Brothers, plumbers, 68
Vespers, 170
Video Club, 252
vocations, 199, 240
Volunteer movement, 11

Waldron bequest, 158
Waldron, Bishop Peter, 43, 150
Waldron, Rev Laurence, 25
Waldron, Rev. Michael, 13
*Waldron, Rev. Tommy, 253, 262
Waldron, Walter, 241
walks, the, 193
*Walsh, Archbishop Joseph, 4-6, 68, 121, 126, 164, 176-79, 211, 215, 219, 236, 238, 246
Walsh Cup, 248
Walsh, M., 221
Walsh, Master, 204
Walsh, Mr. 184
*Walsh, Rev. Michael, 197, 246, 247, 262
Ward, Mrs 28
Warde, Damien, 251
Waterford, 35, 99
Waterford Citizen, 98
Western Students Movement, 237
Westport, 13, 40, 68, 181, 182
Wexford, 35
Whelehan, Professor J.B., 123-25
'William Tell', 72, 75
Williams, Rev. Paddy, 181, 221, 248

Young Ireland, 96, 252
youth culture, 234, 235, 237